CONSTRUCTION MANAGEMENT

CONSTRUCTION MANAGEMENT
A Professional Approach

THOMAS C. KAVANAGH, P. E.

FRANK MULLER, P.E.

JAMES J. O'BRIEN, P.E.

McGRAW-HILL BOOK COMPANY

New York   St. Louis   San Francisco   Auckland   Bogotá
Düsseldorf   Johannesburg   London   Madrid   Mexico
Montreal   New Delhi   Panama   Paris   São Paulo
Singapore   Sydney   Tokyo   Toronto

Library of Congress Cataloging in Publication Data

Kavanagh, Thomas C
Construction management.

(McGraw-Hill series in modern structures)
Includes index.
1. Construction industry—Management. I. Muller,
Frank, joint author. II. O'Brien, James Jerome,
date,   joint author. III. Title.
TH438.K38   658.5   77-12597
ISBN 0-07-033386-6

567890 BPBP 87654321

The editors for this book were Jeremy Robinson and Virginia Fechtmann Blair,
the designer was Elliot Epstein, and the production supervisor
was Teresa F. Leaden. It was set in Baskerville
by University Graphics, Inc.

Printed and bound by The Book Press.

Contents

Preface

To meet the needs of the times, the construction industry has come up with a new marriage contract for owners, contractors, and designers: it is called *Construction Management,* or *CM.* In keeping with the wedding whimsy, CM brought to the industry "something old, something new, something borrowed. . . ."

Everyone involved with CM agrees that it is not a totally new concept, yet it is not just more of the same old thing. The "something borrowed" applies to a number of new techniques that have evolved, including network analysis, systems analysis, fast tracking, value engineering and/or analysis, life-cycle cost studies, the design-build approach, and turn-key organization.

There is no question that CM is more than just a reformation of old procedures and methods. In some cases, it is having its impact as a vehicle to introduce new concepts and new management techniques to an industry that is not only tradition-bound but resistant to change.

CM has established itself as a viable approach to meeting the needs of the industry, and in turn, the needs of the users of the industry. CM may well be the first step for the construction industry to meet the challenge of the last portion of the twentieth century, which will see not only a changing market but a changing economy. The construction industry, representing more than 10% of the GNP, not only will be influenced by these changes but also should have an influence on them.

John F. Kennedy made the statement that "Success has many fathers." The same can certainly be said for construction management, but with more purpose, since its performance takes many forms. The thrust of this book is not to single out any approach as the very best or the only one. It is, rather, to describe construction management, whatever its form, as a professional service.

It is interesting to note that as construction managers become more widely accepted, the differences between the various approaches become more narrow. Contractor-type construction managers are now performing in a manner very similar to that of the professional engineer. Professional engineers and professional construction managers are providing contractor-type services, such as general conditions.

As competent people perform a service and have the opportunity to observe other competent organizations performing similar but different services, the beneficial result has been the adoption of the better techniques of the different approaches. It is the authors' belief that the true key to success in the construction management approach lies in the identification of professional construction managers with their clients, the owners. Adversarial positions and conflicts of interests are set aside. Owners have the advantages of the best advice and information available, while construction managers work on a risk-free basis, able to provide all their insight and experience to their clients.

The authors have emphasized time, cost, and quality—the elements that can be controlled by a construction manager. Because of decreases in construction productivity, there has been a continuing failure to meet budgets and a correlative problem of controlling quality. CM practitioners must direct their efforts and energies to the improvement of productivity, the meeting of schedules, and the establishment of better control. There continues to be a need for innovation in the form of new products and new materials to combat rising costs; CM can encourage these innovational approaches through value engineering and analysis and optimum construction techniques.

Construction management is an evolutionary process. It will encourage the industry itself to evolve to produce the best results for the owner from the combined efforts of architect, engineer, contractor, and project manager. It is this correlation of the professional participants to the owner which will produce success for the construction management approach.

JAMES J. O'BRIEN, P.E.

CONSTRUCTION MANAGEMENT

1
Introduction

Construction management is the composite of all modern project management methodologies having as their objective the control of time, cost, and quality in the design and construction of a new facility.

The construction industry has been for years the major contributor to the national economy, accounting generally for over 10 percent of the gross national product. It provides a comparable employment market, in addition to supporting many manufacturing, development, real estate, and other interests connected with the construction industry.

The industry is large but diffuse, comprising a fragmented agglomeration of small units, and as a result suffers from a high incidence of failures. Its products are essentially one-of-a-kind, site-produced, labor-intensive, highly dependent on local conditions, and have not been subjected to much mass production or standardization. The industry lacks coherence, with facilities constructed by a loose aggregate of independent design professionals, builders, land developers, financiers, skilled craftsmen, manufacturers, suppliers, managers, and others—all of whom disperse on completion of a project. Research and development are relatively nonexistent compared with other manufacturing industries.

Construction management offers a fresh approach to meeting the forthcoming demands of society for new housing; for energy self-sufficiency; for rebuilding our cities; for improved mass transportation; and for continued maintenance, repair, and renewal of existing structures.

The related component programs and methodologies entering into construction management—namely, systems analysis, the systems approach, systems engineering, systems building, comprehensive planning, operations research, value analysis, cost engineering, life-cycle costs, cost-benefit analysis, technology assessment, network analysis, simulation (modeling), phased construction, scheduling, expediting, monitoring/control, and other procedures involved with the application of scientific management and the scientific method—are reviewed and clarified with respect to their interactions with construction management.

CONSTRUCTION MANAGEMENT

Since the first use of the term and up to present time, the term "construction management" has been used in numerous and differing contexts. As a result, the term has sometimes been used as an "umbrella" to encompass all aspects of the construction industry. It has been used (and in many cases unfortunately abused) to describe a field which hopefully will serve as a panacea for all the problems within the construction industry. The purpose of this book is to place the term in its proper perspective and to show, not that it is a new magic wand, but to identify its scope, aims, and objectives when placed into their proper and total concept.

Within the industry the term not only is used in an all-inclusive manner but is utilized by practitioners who serve a limited area within the field. As a consequence a practitioner, professional, contractor, or executive may offer a "construction management" service which may only consist of one integral part of construction management, such as cost estimating or CPM (critical path method) scheduling. The public, therefore, has good cause not only to be confused—or even suspicious—of this service or skill or business, if when seeking such service, it is offered a wide range and differing array of services. It is not sufficient explanation to state that such services may be components of the total field. It is first necessary to define the total concept.

As utilized herein, the terms construction management (CM) and project management (PM) are used synonymously. Although the construction process does not necessarily span the full life or life cycle of a project, the single term construction management is intended to refer to, and encompass, the full scope of management activities of a project. For this reason and for the purposes of this presentation no distinction is made. This does not ignore the field of "project management" which is utilized to address this area as a separate discipline and treats construction management as a component within PM.

Construction management, as the term is used in the United States, is the composite of all modern management methodologies having as their objectives the control of time, cost, and quality in the design and construction of a new facility. *Project management* is the term by which this process is more frequently referred to abroad, in order to emphasize that the conceptual planning, predesign, and design phases may be of equal or greater importance to the control process as compared with the field, or construction, phase. Therefore, again, in this text the acronym CM includes *both* philosophies of management.

In order to comprehend the importance of the modern CM concepts as compared with conventional processes, an understanding of the complexity of the construction industry is necessary as well as the nature of any constraints on the introduction of modern scientific management principles.

THE CONSTRUCTION INDUSTRY

The construction industry itself has been for years the major industry contributor to the national economy, accounting generally for 10 to 15 percent of the gross national product (GNP) in most countries. Since labor accounts for about 72 percent of the construction dollar, it follows as a consequence that the construction industry also employs over 10 percent of the total labor force. In addition, other manufacturing industries (such as cement, steel, aluminum, lumber, stone, clay, and glass products) are largely or partly dependent on construction. For the United States, of the 1975 gross national product of $1,516 billion, a total of $66.5 billion alone is attributable to construction (Ref. 1). In the same year a total of 3.5 million persons were employed in contract construction alone, yet unemployment in the construction industry was about double the average rate in the United States. Although the construction unemployment rate is normally always higher than the manufacturing rate, as well as the national average, the recession years of the 1970s have seen the construction rate increase more rapidly to reach the doubling of the average rate. The industry is comprised of over a million contractors, and 1½ million subcontractors. To handle financial, insurance, and real estate dealings requires another few million employees. The building design professions include some 30,000 registered architects, 100,000 registered engineers, plus a large number of auxiliary specialists and professionals, such as planners and landscape architects.

THE AMERICAN CONSTRUCTION INDUSTRY

In the United States the construction industry is large—but diffuse—and consists of a loose agglomeration of mostly small units. There are relatively few design-construction firms with an annual volume greater than $1 billion, and very few materials and equipment producers rank among the nation's 500 largest industrial firms. This is reflected in the high incidence of failures in construction enterprises. Generally, the construction industry is relatively backward, rooted in the past and held static by tradition.

In terms of organization, facilities are constructed by a loose conglomeration of independent design professionals (planners, architects, and engineers), builders, land developers, financiers, a host of skilled crafts, manufacturers, distributors, managers and lawyers brought together for a single project and then dispersed on completion of the work. A vertically integrated firm performing all these functions is rare, in contrast with Japan and the European countries. Also, as contrasted with manufacturing industries, where legal responsibility rests primarily with the manufacturer, in the construction field responsibility is not centralized but is shared by the contractor, the engineer, the client, and the governmental or licensing authority. Other characteristics of the construction industry which delimit the opportunity for progress are the nature of the product, which restricts the possibility of standardization, or of labor-saving through mass production, mechanization, and automation. Every facility is basically one of a kind, is site-produced, and is dependent on local conditions (such as real estate values, building codes, and the rigorous constraints of seasonality, climate, and the weather). In addition, the life span of most structures (50 to 100 years) is long, leading to relative permanence once built and to lack of turnover by trade-in. The nature of construction labor is such that it is conventionally done by a broad range of independent, highly mobile, skilled trades on a special contract basis which, when unions are involved, frequently results in jurisdictional labor disputes.

In comparison with other industries, research and development in the construction industry in the United States is hampered by an extremely low level of financial support relative to its significance in the gross national product, by both government and private industry. Although some research is done on materials and equipment by private industry, basic research is at a very low level—particularly in areas where interdisciplinary interaction is involved. There is poor coordination of research and development efforts and little in the way of broad dissemination of research results. Typical of the lack of government support has been the failure of Congress to pass the NIBS (National Institute of Building Sciences) bill, even though it was supported generally by industry and the professions, which would have set up a nongovernmental unit in support of research on building standards and codes.

The following summary of problems faced by the construction industry, prepared by Building Technology Inc., reflects the above-mentioned difficulties associated with the conventional construction process.

Fragmentation of Process

The total process which produces buildings is fragmented, and often fragmentary, both in place and in time. The proliferation of independent participants in the process, each entering it at a different point in time and each with private interests and requirements, makes it unlikely that any building resulting from this process will adequately meet the requirements established for it in the beginning.

Fragmentation of Policy

Public policy in the building process, established by government at all its levels and branches, for the purpose of caring for the public's interest in the process and its products, is as fragmented as the building process itself. It is an aggregation of detailed laws and procedures, reflecting the fragmentation of the process, without clear overall direction or purpose.

Public Participation

The public itself, insofar as it has both specific and general interests in the building process and its products, is rarely a direct or an indirect participant in the process. Its rare participations in the process cannot be described as especially effective.

Gap between Need and Demand

Throughout the building process, and particularly in the area of housing, there is a quantitative gap between the need for building as determined by social, psychological, and physical factors, and the translation of that need into effective demand in the market. This disparity often renders public policy decisions ineffective because they are not accompanied by structural changes in the market itself.

Instability

The nearly total dependence of the building process on the flow of money, combined with the acceptance of monetary policy as a major tool in the regulation of the business cycle, has made the building process most sensitive to the least fluctuations in the economy. This irregularity, especially in the area of housing, has probably been the major reason for the inability to implement a consistent, uniform building policy.

Slow Response

There is evident disparity between the rapid rate of progress in the areas of science and technology and the slow pace with which advances are applied in the building process. This disparity causes the building process and its products to be very laggard in responding to rapidly changing needs and requirements.

Product Proliferation

Combined with the fragmentation of the process, there is an ever-growing proliferation of building products at all scales. Together, these factors cause an inability to manage even the traditional building process, due to the professionals' inability to keep up with and assimilate the "progress."

Quality

Fragmentation in the production side of the building process has led directly to a situation where the responsibility for the relationship between the quality of products and the requirements for their use is borne by nobody, generally resulting in a mismatch between needs and product performance.

Leadership

Although there is a growing awareness of some or all of these problems in many sectors, one glaring deficiency stands out above all others—the lack of leadership, both intellectual and practical, in seeking solutions to these problems.

Not only is the traditional approach to construction highly compartmentalized, but communication between the compartments is very formalized and primarily one-directional. The time sequence is also such that decisions are locked in before construction is started, and the schedule becomes obsolete after the start of construction because of the highly stochastic, or random, nature of the construction environment itself.

Much resistance to change is encountered in the construction industry. This resistance is fostered by union quotas, union standby requirements, fixed attitudes ("do it this way only"), lack of motivation by workers, nonparticipation in decisions as opposed to delegation of responsibility to worker, and pressures for production with resultant risk taking and decreased safety.

THE INTERNATIONAL CONSTRUCTION INDUSTRY

Construction abroad suffers from many of the same difficulties as in the United States, but there are important differences from country to country. The existence abroad of vertically integrated construction firms has already been mentioned, these firms carrying out vigorous research programs. Other examples are the use of uniform building codes in some countries, governmental certification of new products by agreement boards, well-rounded public building research agencies, and at least one example of a private research and information agency operating on an international scale.

TRADITIONAL VERSUS CM APPROACH

In the traditional approach to the design and construction process the owner selects an architect/engineer to prepare plans and specifications (bid documents), on which several contractors bid. A contractor is selected through a process of competitive bidding, usually on the basis of a fixed-price low bid for the construction of the project. The contractor may then proceed to subcontract parts of the work to specialty subcontractors, such as fabricators, erectors, plumbers, or electrical suppliers. Because of the numerous tiers of subcontractors, the general contractor—even though he is the prime contractor—often becomes basically a vendor.

The construction management approach, on the other hand, cuts across many traditional lines; it is a professional service relationship between the construction (or project) managers (who are paid a professional fee for their services) and the owners (who retain the manager early in the planning stage of the project). For this the construction (or project) manager coordinates the performance of the general contractor and subcontractors during construction, in accordance with contracts let as in the conventional process; but more importantly, the constructor manager assists the owner in the selection of, and works with, the architect/engineer in the concept planning and design stages to ensure reliable designs to meet the owner's cost, time, and quality constraints. This latter is accomplished by suggesting alternate construction systems and/or bidding packages in the context of economy in life-cycle costs; by developing performance specifications and encouraging introduction of improved methods and materials; by advance procurement of equipment and materials; by promoting early completion and studying the potentials of phased construction; by scheduling and monitoring progress of the project; by managing quality control through site and off-site inspection; and by promoting safety programs and project-wide labor agreements, to ensure harmony on the job site. Thus, construction management views design and construction as a single management effort, rather than as two separate functions, and also as a team effort involving the owner, construction (or project) manager, the architect/engineer, and the contractor.

Not only is the traditional approach to construction highly compartmentalized, but communication between the compartments is very formalized and primarily one-directional. The time sequence is also such that decisions are locked in before construction is started, and the schedule becomes obsolete after the start of construction because of the highly stochastic or random nature of the construction environment itself.

Advantages of CM

From the above it is clear that the CM process has these basic advantages:

1. The construction manager is a professional agent of the owner and is a member of a team effort.

2. The construction manager has an input during the planning and design stages in effecting workable time, cost, and quality schedules and controls, and in providing expertise on market and labor conditions.

3. Involvement of the construction manager during planning and design provides the owner with reliable information about probable costs and schedules.

4. CM achieves a more efficient procurement process, resulting in more effective management of construction budgets.

5. CM permits the use of phased construction or "fast-track" procedures, dovetailing the design and construction phases of the project, thus reducing the time between design and occupancy or use.

6. CM can start construction and order long-delivery material and equipment items before the total design is completed, thus allowing the owner beneficial use of the project at the earliest possible date.

7. CM increases flexibility throughout the entire project, both in design and construction; adjustments to budgets and contracts may be more readily made as they arise.

8. CM permits participation of the owner in decision making for all phases of design and construction, enabling the owner to obtain the desired quality and timing of the end product and the most value for each dollar spent.

9. The architect/engineer and the construction manager can engage in value analyses of alternative design and construction procedures from the early stages of design development. These analyses will enable the architect/engineer to make

major design decisions based upon accurate information relative to cost and time as well as to functional and aesthetic considerations.

10. The interests of the architect/engineer, contractor, and construction manager parallel the owner's, since an adversary relationship does not exist between the construction manager and other team members.

11. In making decisions, options can be considered on the basis of cost, time, and quality factors.

12. Competitive bidding can be used for all subcontracts of the work. Construction management improves competitive bidding under public laws, by providing the coordinating role necessary to implement legislation requiring that subcontractors be selected by competitive bids in the same way as is a general contractor (i.e., bid shopping, auctioning, and similar unfair practices with respect to subcontractors are reduced).

13. CM allows contractors to be selected for their expertise in certain phases of construction, and ensures the availability of interested, competent contractors.

14. The owner retains control of his or her dollar and can plan cash flows to his or her monetary advantage.

15. The latest technology and current marketing conditions are more readily incorporated into the decision-making process.

16. Revisions can be made efficiently to adjust to changes in the owner's needs, or to further control costs or schedules throughout the duration of the project.

17. CM reduces the layering of bonding required; each prime contractor furnishes a bond for his portion of the work. The financial structure is compartmentalized, and financial failure cannot spread.

18. CM permits possible savings in insurance and taxes; a new approach ("wrap-up" insurance) permits the owner to secure insurance on CM jobs; and it is often possible for the owner to buy materials directly, thus avoiding one level of taxation where general contractors pay taxes on materials supplied by the subcontractors.

19. The architect/engineer's relationship and responsibilities to

the owner are not altered by the CM process. In fact, the construction manager actually assists the architect/engineer in many ways in fulfilling his contract requirements.

Disadvantages of CM

1. A guaranteed cost does not exist when the owner begins construction cost commitments; as they do in the traditional process.

2. Costs for all units of work could be established before construction begins but at the penalty of extending the time schedule.

3. Lack of trained construction managers with experience and understanding in the team relationships required by the CM process.

4. Under many public-bidding statutes, construction managers are precluded from performing work with their own forces.

5. The very multiprime nature of the CM process (in certain instances) which replaces the general contractor and the team of subcontractors by a multiplicity of prime contractors may itself be a major drawback because it substitutes a multiplicity of prime contracts for the single, readily and legally enforceable contract between the owner and general contractor. A hierarchy of prime contractors evolves, each with equal contractual status in the eyes of the owner, whereas in the conventional process all subcontractors were subordinate to (and therefore more readily controllable by) the general contractor.

6. The multiprime nature of the CM process, by requiring every contractor to bid and furnish a bond, eliminates a sizable segment of the industry, the nonbondable contractor.

Figure 1-1 illustrates some of the trade-offs sometimes necessary in cost-time-quality factors entering the CM process.

FAVORABLE OUTLOOK FOR CM

Despite the serious difficulty in which the construction industry now finds itself, construction management offers a fresh approach to filling the gaps between construction, engineering, and management as the concepts of the institutions, traditions, and, in essence, the basic fabric of the construc-

The Challenges of Construction

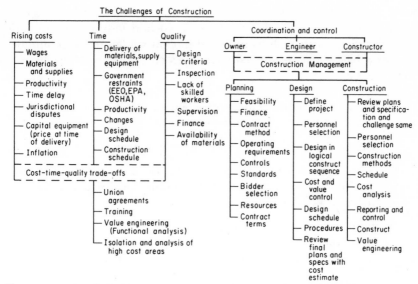

Figure 1-1. The challenges of construction (Developed by Boyd C. Paulson, Sr.; adapted from *Goals for Basic Research in Construction,* by Boyd C. Paulson, Jr.)

tion industry evolves with changing needs. The inexorable growth of the construction industry has been brought about by technological demands for change; by the growth of population and the generated demand for new housing; by new economic development calling for new office buildings, roads, airports, and harbors; by new industrial development associated with new capital investment; by the demand for rebuilding our urban centers; by the need for energy self-sufficiency; by the desire for improved mass transportation; and by the needs of existing facilities for maintenance, repair, and renewal. Future projects will be characterized by a shift to large-scale undertakings, large organizations, and a telescoping of the traditional architect/engineer-contractor relationship in a team attack, aided by social, behavioral, and environmental scientists, to meet the needs of society.

SCIENTIFIC METHOD AND SCIENTIFIC MANAGEMENT

Construction management is an evolving process combining scientific management methodologies having as their objective the control of time, cost, and quality in the design and construction of a new facility.

All the procedures which follow are in essence an application of the scientific method, which is a procedure of research in which a problem is identified, relevant data are gathered, a hypothesis is formulated from these data, and the hypothesis is empirically tested. *Scientific management* in this context (first applied to the construction industry by Frederick Taylor) utilizes such tools as time-and-motion studies, tool optimization, and crew balancing. As applied to modern construction, it involves such techniques as:

1. Modeling, during engineering or field mobilization stages, or both, for design and construction efficiency

2. Detailed preplanning of all construction activities

3. Structural questioning and extensive use of alternate studies to determine and implement the optimum construction method for each field operation

4. Preparation of a detailed plan for each controllable block of field work with each operation assigned a tight but realistic work-hour target based on a fixed set of standards

5. Creation and maintenance of a detailed schedule

6. Periodic control of each craft on each operation by comparison between actual and target work-hours for each piece of work

SCIENTIFIC MANAGEMENT COMPRISES FIVE BASIC FUNCTIONS

Planning, control, organization, coordination, and direction. The first two are difficult in view of the economic problems of the construction industry discussed above. Regarding organization, there are two facets: at the company or office level the problems are no different from those of any other business enterprise; but at the field level the nature of the site and of the project dictates the organizational structure. Coordination in construction projects is unusually complex because of the large number of trades and subcontractors involved. Direction, too, is more difficult because of the temporary connection of the various skilled workers with the contracting company.

Closed System.   In systems building, a closed system is one in which the components are peculiar to that system and cannot be combined with those of any other system.

Component.   A component is any factory or site-produced unit designed to perform specified tasks.

Cost-Benefit Analysis.   Cost-benefit analysis is the systematic evaluation of the costs and benefits associated with a particular policy or project.

Cost Engineering.   Cost engineering is defined by the American Association of Cost Engineers as that area of engineering practice where engineering judgment and experience are utilized in the application of scientific principles and techniques of cost estimation, cost control, profitability, business planning, and management science.

Cost Reduction.   Cost reduction is a programmed system for monitoring dollars saved.

CPM.   The critical path method (CPM) involves network analysis.

Decision Theory.   The logical (scientific) basis for decision making under conditions of uncertainty. The function (decision) to be optimized is known as the *objective function.*

Expediting.   Expediting is the detailed implementation or activation of a construction plan, i.e., of the proposed disposition of labor, materials, and money to be expended on a project.

Life-Cycle Costs.   Life-cycle costs include all costs incident to the planning, design, construction, operation, maintenance, and even demolition of a facility—all in terms of present value.

Modular Coordination.   This is the reduction of the sizes of all building components and buildings to multiples of one basic unit.

Monitoring/Control.   This is the exercise of direction, guidance, or restraining influence in evaluating project progress, identification of potential job problems, and rescheduling of activities at intervals as necessary during the project duration.

Network Analysis.   Network analysis is a graphic procedure of determining the shortest time within which some total project can be completed, by finding a most time-consuming path among its interrelated component activities (Examples: CPM and PERT).

Open System.   In systems building, an open system is one in which the components are interchangeable with those of other systems.

Operations Research.   Related to but not as broadly based as systems analysis, operations research used analytical methods adopted from mathematics for solving operational problems, with the objective of providing management with a more logical basis for making sound predictions and decisions with respect to operations.

PERT.   The program evaluation and review technique (PERT) method of network analysis.

Phased Construction.   Phased construction or "fast tracking" is the deliberate overlapping of the construction phase of a project with the design phase in order to reduce the time for use or occupancy of the project.

Planning (comprehensive planning).   Comprehensive planning is the preparation of a policy guide for a governing body for decisions as to desirable future development. Its characteristics are that it is comprehensive (covers all functional elements bearing on physical, social, and economic development); general (in that it does not get into specific locations or detailed requirements); and long-range (in that it looks beyond the foreground of current issues to the perspective problems and possibilities, say, 10 to 20 years in the future).

Prefabrication.   In systems building, prefabrication includes the factory assembly of structural, mechanical, or electrical components, such as wall panels, or even complete and fully equipped structures, such as mobile homes.

Project.   A project is a specified amount of (construction) work, with a definite beginning and end, which can be divided into component tasks. It includes the totality of all phases from conception through design, construction, operation, and maintenance to eventual demolition.

Rationalized Traditional System.   In systems building, this is a system that depends primarily on conventional skilled trades but which incorporates mechanization and prefabricated components.

Schedule.   A schedule is that combination of resources and task interrelationships which best meets the objectives of management.

Simulation (modeling).   Simulation or modeling is a mathematical, physical, or analog representation of a process, device, or system which permits manipulation of variables as a means of determining how the process, device or system behaves in various situations.

System.   This is an assembly of components (including men, machines, operations and information) united by some form of regulated interaction to form an organized whole. A subsystem would accordingly represent a subassembly of such components.

Systems Analysis. Systems analysis is an inquiry to assist decision makers in choosing preferred future courses of action, by (1) systematically examining and reexamining the relevant objectives and the alternative policies or strategies for achieving them and (2) comparing quantitatively where possible the economic costs, effectiveness (benefits), and risks of the alternatives. Systems analysis applied to building systems is illustrated in Figure 1-2. In this respect, the term "system" must be defined.

Systems Approach. Systems approach is a generic term used for the philosophy of looking at an overall situation rather than the narrow implications of the task at hand; particularly looking for the interrelationships between the task at hand and other functions which relate to it.

Systems Building (industrialized housing). This is the approach to building construction that views a problem as a set of interrelated, interdependent parts working together for the overall objectives of the whole. It integrates the planning, design, programming, manufacturing, scheduling, financing, and management into a disciplined method of mechanized production of buildings.

Systems Engineering. Systems engineering is the implementation of the procedures and plans adopted in a systems analysis of all the elements in a process, problem, or control situation.

The Team. The construction team concept is fundamental to the CM process. The principal actors or participants on the construction team are the owner, the construction (project) manager, the architect/engineer, and the contractor. The first three participate as early as possible in the project; the contractor joins the construction team when his bid for construction is accepted. The owner or client may be a private individual (such as a land developer) or any one of a large number of private and public organizations, including federal, state, county, and municipal agencies of government. The architect/engineer includes not only representatives of architectural and engineering professions, but planners, landscape architect, and other specialists. The contractor or builder may be a general contractor with a complete organization of specialists or may employ subcontractors for specialty tasks.

Technology Assessment. TA is a thorough, balanced analysis of all significant primary, secondary, indirect, and delayed consequences of impact—present and foreseen—of a technological innovation or improvement on society, the environment, and the economy. The Congress of the United States now has an Office of Technology Assessment which attempts such assessments for it.

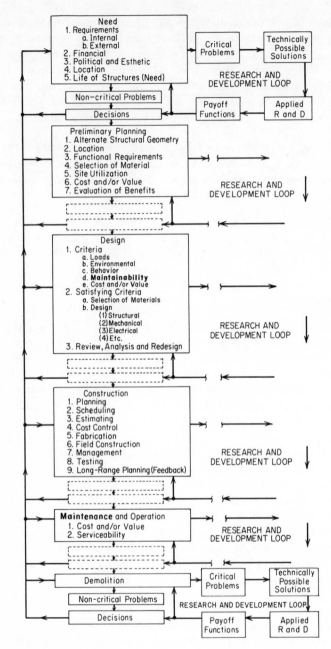

Figure 1-2.   The construction process with research and development subsystems.

Value. Value is the relationship between actual total cost of an item or system and its total worth.

Value Engineering/Value Analysis/Value Management. Value engineering/ value analysis is the systematic effort directed at analyzing the functional requirements of systems, equipment, facilities, procedures, and supplies for the purpose of achieving the essential functions at the lowest total cost, consistent with meeting needed performance, reliability, quality, maintainability, aesthetics, safety, and fire resistance.

Zero Defects. Zero defects is a program intended to motivate employees to eliminate defects attributable to human error.

TOWARD A DEFINITION OF CM

Construction management/project management does not concern itself with the direction of work within a contract or a subcontract but rather deals with the planning for and manipulation of those contracts. Thus, CM does not seek to eliminate the general contractor or to administer a series of separate contracts for a fee. It does focus on the fact that the greatest savings in time, cost, and quality on a construction project can be achieved during the concept and design phase. Nor is CM solely a fast-track system, although the latter can indeed be an appropriate part of the CM process. CM *does* concern itself with a *professional* service to the owner seeking to control time, costs, and quality during the entire project, and the construction manager should be selected to function concurrently with or preceding the planning and design phase of the work and continue his efforts throughout all the subsequent phases of design and construction. The construction manager, of course, may perform other services ancillary to the main objectives stated above, such as scheduling and CPM program maintenance, management of the procurement effort, administration of owner or tenant move-in, coordinator of site and off-site operations, furnishing of operating or maintenance manuals, and other services as called for by the owner.

A definition of construction management may be stated as that group of management activities over and above normal architectural and engineering services related to a construction program, carried out during the conceptual planning, predesign, design and construction phases, that contributes to the control of time, cost, and quality in the construction of a new facility.

REFERENCES

1. Building Technology, Inc., Silver Springs, Md., "Nine Major Problems in the Building Industry in the U.S.," *Professional Engineer,* May 1973, p. 21.

PART

I

THE CONSTRUCTION
PROCESS AND THE
CONSTRUCTION
MANAGER

2
Overview

Through evolution, the construction of a project has become a process with definite and discrete stages. These stages can be described in a number of ways. As shown in Figure 2-1, one broad definition would be: predesign, design, and construction. For reasons which have changed to meet special requirements over the years, the construction industry has become one of specialization, fragmenting the pre–industrial revolution master-builder approach into literally thousands of pieces. These pieces must be orchestrated to make the construction process work. The process is one which must be observed, but the manner in which it is implemented determines whether or not the project is a good one in terms of cost, quality, and timely completion. The concept of construction management is one which provides a means for combining the pieces of the process to the best advantage of all parties—but in particular the owner.

THE PLAYERS

As modern equipment and materials became available, project schedules have continually been compressed. Although the construction phase is the most visible stage of a project, most projects are in the design-and-review phase at least as long as the actual construction period.

As the building process compressed in time, the engineers and architects of projects were able to work on several projects at once. To find the time to do several projects, they gave up many of their construction duties. This evolution led into a specialization of the engineering and architecture for the design phase, relegating construction to contractors.

The design disciplines have been further subdivided during the last 50 years to the point where major engineering disciplines, particularly in

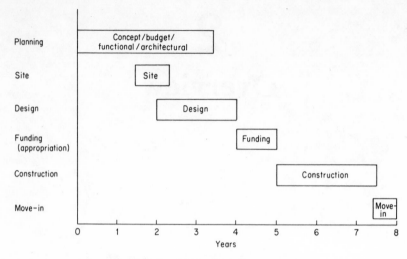

Figure 2-1.   Typical project sequence.

building design, function as separate operations under the general umbrella of "architecture." There are many business and professional reasons for this subdivision of expertise. From the professional viewpoint, it is natural to focus on the individual's area of greatest interest and expertise. This provides the best of any one discipline available to be applied at the optimum point. The smaller groupings provide greater flexibility in weathering recessions and other low-activity periods.

There are a number of excellent design firms that have developed on a total-capability basis—despite the problems introduced by strong decentralization of skills. These firms, however, are not in the majority, and they will always face the problem of maintaining a large work load in order to balance the areas of expertise. There is a load level beyond which the all-purpose firm becomes either noncompetitive, underqualified, or overpriced.

Almost all building projects are constructed by contractors who have had no role in the design phase. Most contracts are awarded by the owner either on a sealed-bid basis, negotiated basis, or cost-plus-fee basis. Usually, the mode of contracting is a function of either legislative restrictions, in the case of government agencies, or prior experience on the part of industry.

Although the cost of the contract is based on the design, in most cases the contractual relationship is between the owner and the contractor. This creates a triangle of interests within which an apparently fixed scope of work can become quite fluid and even a good design can be used as a whipping boy.

Contractor supervision is a key to the success of a project. These managers direct the actual field activities and often control expenditures for materials. On major projects, field superintendents are often engineers or have their own staff of engineers at the job site. Their role is to get the job done at the lowest possible cost within the budget. Most managers recognize that a shorter job is a lower-cost job because it controls the overhead costs which are a direct function of time.

There are two basic types of owners—those who are repeat builders and those who are one-time builders. The experienced owner tends to understand the construction process and the players. The one-time owner has an unfortunate tendency to assume that many assurances and processes are incorporated into the fees which are paid to the designer and the contractor, without understanding that these additional assurances and services would have to be specified.

THE PROCESS

The construction phase is just the tip of the iceberg. There are preconstruction activities which take from one to three times the construction phase itself. While the activities in the preconstruction phase are of much lower cost—on the order of 10 to 20 percent of the construction cost—their impact on total cost is much more important in terms of value decisions.

Figure 2-2 illustrates the characteristic phases of a typical project. Some activities in private industry may have more of an overlap, particularly in the funding phase. Experience indicates that the bureaucratic review process in the private sector is essentially equivalent to that in the public sector—just less visible.

The early stages of the project preconstruction are ones in which the major decisions are made. Conversely, the early stages are the best opportunity for major value analysis. The owner (and/or the project manager) is hampered by a lack of definitive information regarding the project. Accordingly, analysis in the early stages must be directed on a more generic basis than the detailed evaluation during construction.

Figure 2-3 illustrates the funnel effect which occurs regarding the progressive narrowing down of changes of scope which can be tolerated. These more narrow parameters would apply to value analysis.

The predesign sequences include concept planning, budgeting, funding, feasibility studies, programming, and site selection.

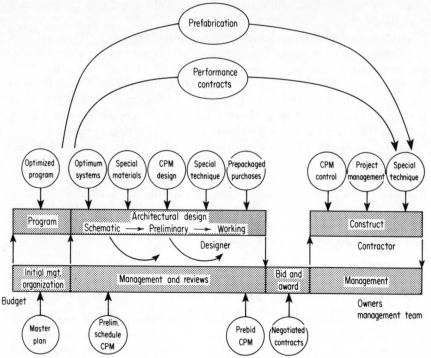

Figure 2-2. *Plan-design-construct project cycle showing systems inputs.*

Concept Planning

This phase may last from weeks to years. It begins with a definition of the project as a possible consideration and is completed with its authorization in the form of a budget backed up by fund appropriation. Projects may continue an existing program—such as a college—or may be developed to solve a specific requirement such as a manufacturing facility. Decisions made as a result of mere conceptual planning are almost always based on insufficient information and represent a beginning stage in the evolution of the project. Value analysis during the stage of conceptual planning should result in emphasis of the positive factors of the project and identification of those which are of obviously poor value or worth.

Budgeting

Each organization has its own procedures for budgetary approval. Generally the complexity of the procedures is directly proportional to the size of the organization, whether corporate or governmental. The budgeting process in these more formalized situations may require many months and may also be tied to specific calendar dates, such as the federal fiscal budget. In terms of the project timetable, the budgeting process is one which should be defined and understood.

Funding

Funding may require separate authorization, such as governmental appropriations, or may be contingent upon the sale of corporate or government bonds. Most organizations have guidelines in regard to how much design work can be accomplished before the appropriation has been assured. Again, this is an important impact upon the project timetable.

Feasibility Studies

As the project takes definitive form, feasibility and/or economic studies of the project and its proposed results should be conducted. This stage is often performed informally, or even omitted. Value-analysis techniques can be utilized to perform a significant portion of the feasibility study. External factors, such as the prime lending rate, are often an important consideration in the economic study.

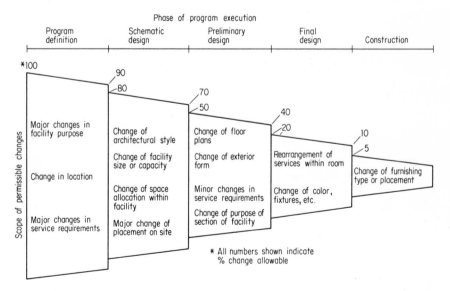

Figure 2-3. Impact of change in scope versus time (funnel effect).

Programming

Programming is an important phase of the project. Unfortunately, it is one which is often omitted. Development of the program is based upon information which was developed during the planning and budgeting stages. It converts the broad generic goals expressed in the budget into specific functional and architectural requirements. It provides the natural basis for design. When omitted, it imposes upon the design team the role of selecting a specific approach. Some owners deliberately omit programming, anticipating that they are getting something for nothing by having their design team perform this very important stage.

Site Selection

Site selection may be in parallel with programming, or may follow it. In some cases, it occurs after the start of design. The comparison of possible sites includes a definite opportunity for the application of value analysis.

Design Phase

The design phase of a project is usually in three phases or stages. It involves a complex interplay between the design disciplines, usually under the direction of the architect—particularly in building projects. The first stage is known as the schematic or sketch design phase. This is sometimes called the conceptual design phase. The next stage is design development or preliminary design. The final stage is design document or working drawings.

Figure 2-4 illustrates the increasing complexity which occurs as the typical project proceeds through the design phases. This figure is a segmented network describing the three stages. Schematic development, in which the major value decisions are being made, is accomplished in eight weeks in this example, while design development takes more than twice as long, and the final stage takes more than 50 percent of the time.

The potential for individual value-analysis evaluations is obviously greatest at the beginning of the design, when there is the least time available for the analysis.

It is obvious that basic changes in design parameters which are imposed during the contract document stage require much more coordination to impose, and the potential for errors is much greater.

Construction

Preconstruction process is oriented toward definition of that which is to be built. Even the names, such as construction document phase in design

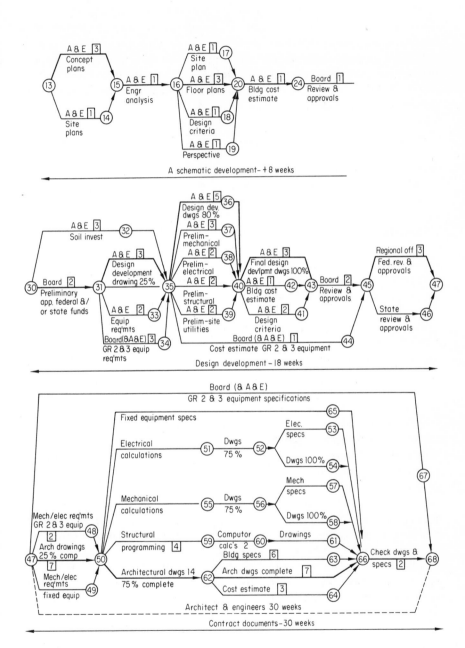

Figure 2-4.

indicates the scoping and definition nature of the preconstruction activities. With the selection of a contractor and the signing of construction contracts, the role of the construction manager changes. There is now a definition and an implementor (or implementors). The emphasis is now upon getting true and optimum value for the owner's investment. Three major areas come under the control of the construction manager: quality, delivery time, and cost.

FAILURE OF THE TRADITIONAL TEAM APPROACH

From the anatomy of a project, there may be the implication of a coordinated team effort in the accomplishment of a typical project. This is almost never the case. Economic objectives of the different parties tend to differentiate their goals and value criteria:

Designers wish to specify a design at the lowest possible cost to themselves—with a parallel objective of providing maximum function to the owner.

The owner wants to purchase a facility of unknown definition at the lowest possible cost, which will produce the greatest functionality.

The contractor desires to deliver the product specified at the lowest cost possible—and of sufficient quality to last through the warranty.

Each participant wants the best product at the lowest price, but views price in terms of his or her own economic requirements. This dichotomy of goals creates adversity between key participants.

At some point in the construction process—the carefully fashioned construction team begins to unravel.

The design usually comes under attack first, because the contractors carefully review all facets in the hard light of their successful acquisition of a contract. No longer suitors, they are now interested in their ability to perform. Any apparent chinks in the armor are examined, probed, and if possible, exploited. The contractor is interested in avoiding areas of potential loss or, conversely, in setting up potential reserves in cost in the form of claims, change of scope, or extensions in time. Often, the contractor does not seriously claim these changes at the start but is only setting up such a potential.

The attack on the design opens a rift between the design team and the contractors. The design team, either confident that it has an airtight and perfectly developed design or concerned that it may be faced with a loss of reputation (or claim by the owner) necessarily goes on the defensive. In the meantime, the project tends to be sidetracked into exchanges of talk and paperwork, rather than real work. Unfortunately, human psychology is the one common thread at this point. All feel that there is time enough to do the job and that the time spent in postcontract negotiations is really available somewhere down the line; but it usually is not.

In this early phase of the construction, the design team also is pressed to review myriad equipment selections and shop drawings. Any delay in the review even when occasioned by improper selection of material, is grist for the time-extension mill.

The owner, too, plays a role in terms of processing contracts, making final approval of materials (if the responsibility is not delegated to the design team) and ensuring the availability of the work site. The owner also has to make these inevitable decisions based on situations that arise or were previously not settled appropriately. When the contractors claim delay, the design team tends to ally itself with the owner.

As the construction work progresses, various suggestions for design modification are inevitably introduced. Delays caused by bad weather and labor disputes crop up, numerous other things occur to bring about change orders or changes in scope.

As these situations arise in the context of a relatively inflexible contractual relationship (between the owner and design team, as well as between the owner and contractors), polarization inevitably develops. Each major party develops its own protective shield made primarily of self-interest, though the interests of the designers and the owner generally tend to be more nearly mutual.

As a result, conflict develops among the owner, the design team, and the contractors. In fact, the antagonism is inherent even before the contractors are selected; usually it is a carryover from prior projects. The feeling of dichotomy is evident in all dealings. Almost ritualistic answers evolve in response to certain stimuli or situations. Each camp sees itself wearing a white hat. The result is that many minor incidents, which could be easily managed, are handled by the old saw, "Don't bother me with the *facts,* my mind is made up."

Solutions

There is no one cure for the problems a construction project must endure. Any improvements must be based on recognition of the project as an entity as well as based on expenditures and actions in terms of their effect on the overall project.

In private industry, one approach has been to use a designer-builder team. These teams have a common business interest in the efficient progress from design stage to construction stage, and the conflict is diminished, though it never totally disappears. Utilities also have used this approach, which is sometimes called "turn key."

Government agencies, usually prevented by law from using the turn-key approach, have utilized project engineers or project managers to follow the project from budgetary estimate to initial startup and operation. In some cases, where sufficient authority is not delegated to the project managers, they at least gather a quantity of information and become the information source for all project concerns. In other cases, either through personality or delegation of authority, or a combination of both, the project manager directs the course of the project throughout its life. This type of project management has saved a substantial amount of time by recognizing the opportunity to overlap or to phase various project activities. The installation of foundations while final design is continuing (dubbed fast track and not really a new technique) is one of the opportunities that can be utilized through project management overview.

A disadvantage of the design-build approach is the deletion of a major area of competition while, at the same time, building in a potential for conflicts of interest. The design and build segments of the turn-key organization tend to consider the organization first and the owner second. However, even under this handicap, a high-quality design-build firm may outperform a contractor selected through the low-bid process.

Construction management can address the problems effectively. However, there are several viable construction management approaches with substantial different methods of performance. These can be categorized as designer CM, contractor CM, and consultant CM.

A/E AS CONSTRUCTION MANAGER

In many talks on the topic, Walter A. Meisen, formerly GSA's assistant director for construction management, has chided design professionals, "Don't tell me what you could do in the field of construction management—I am here to tell you that you haven't done it in the past, and we have to look elsewhere for this type of support."

There are many reasons why the design team should be able to handle the management of the project in the field, but there are easily as many reasons why the design team is psychologically incapable of handling it in most instances. The problem of managing the design itself is often beyond the abilities of the design team because they are designers rather than managers. Even those A/E firms that recognize the construction management field as one in which they choose to practice have organized separate CM groups rather than attempt to utilize their standard functional design groups.

In Ref. 1 L. N. Maloof, operational manager of Heery Associates (CM arm of the A/E firm Heery & Heery) commented on the design-oriented A/E as a construction manager:

> I think we're going to see a very significant change, especially in the private sector, and maybe even in the governmental sector, in the way buildings are delivered in the future. I believe that we as a/es are going to

have to get into the development business in order to be viable during the last quarter of this century. I think we're going to find more and more developers providing buildings even to institutions and government. . . .

The typical a/e-owner agreement has in the past rewarded the architect for poor cost control and penalized him for any efficiencies in getting the project below the budget. He has used it to shield himself from responsibilities in the area of controlling time and dollars. The architect has often said, "I'm a designer. I don't control dollars. I don't price construction, general contractors do that." But during the design phase the building's cost is established, for that is when the quality and quantity of all the components, mechanisms and systems are determined. The general contractor just prices what the a/e designs so that the a/e is really in a position to provide the cost control. If he has no expertise on his staff, or if he doesn't have the proper attitude, the owner is going to suffer, especially if the architect is going to be rewarded because of his percentage-fee contract. For a big overrun, the architect doesn't have to redesign and this creates a problem for the owner. If architects are going to make the problems, owners have to do something to protect themselves. So that's why construction management is coming into its own. . . .

I think that a/e firms ought to have on their staff the expertise to do a good job of cost control. Unfortunately, architects, as a profession, have a very bad reputation. Probably not too bad a track record but a very bad reputation in the area of controlling costs and time. However, you'll find that several large a/e firms in the country have the capability to provide this kind of service. . . .

As an architect, we see construction management in a broader spectrum, closer to project management. I agree that this is a management technique or management service from inception to the earliest planning, through predesign, design into construction and completed with the owner's move into the building. It's an umbrella of management over this whole process. Many owners do not have the expertise or facilities to have project managers. We found ourselves providing more and more services over this entire spectrum, more than just over the design and construction phase that some people define as the construction manager's job. It is a matter of definition. We define CM as those management activities above and beyond the normal a/e services, from predesign through design and construction phases for the purposes of controlling time and cost. The CM is there for the purpose of controlling time and money.

THE GENERAL CONTRACTOR AS CM

The experienced general contractor brings much to a project in terms of real understanding of the way a contractor should approach the project, as well as cost-estimating experience. The contractor is aware of potential labor problems and can provide meaningful ideas about practical construction.

A number of major contractors perform the majority of their work on a negotiated-fee basis as CMs in the construction phase. They offer the additional advantage of having subcontractor relationships and high credibility with subcontractors. They are experienced in buying out a job, and the better firms have experienced management personnel available.

Unfortunately, some firms that would like to enter the construction management field because it is less uncertain have a limited amount of management personnel and can ill afford to share or sell what they have to others. Further, unless CM contractors are particularly well-rounded, as the more capable ones are, their outlook will be that of a general contractor—without a full awareness of the requirements of the mechanical and specialty contractors.

Another problem shared by almost all general contractors acting as preconstruction project managers is their lack of experience as consultants. The consultant-client relationship requires a certain skill not usually developed during the construction stages. Many experienced construction personnel are uncomfortable in the consultant role. Further, many of the experienced construction manager contractors depend on engineers and architects for references—therefore, their livelihood. This, combined with a lack of expertise in actual design process, may limit the managerial scope of the CM contractor in the preconstruction phase.

The Construction Management Guidelines by the Association of General Contractors (AGC) leaves no doubt as to the identity of the CM: "The construction manager is the qualified general contracting organization which performs the construction management under a professional services contract with the owner."

However, the late Saul Horowitz, Jr., AGC president, made it clear that construction management demands above average skills (Ref. 2, preface): "Who should be a construction manager? Perhaps the soundest advice was given at a Construction Manager Seminar held by AGC earlier when contractors were told not to become construction managers if they were less than eminently successful as general contractors."

In Ref. 2 Richard B. DeMars construction company president (Geupel Demars, Inc.) and AGC official warned general contractors that CM requires a different viewpoint:

> To be a construction manager, you must adopt the entirely different attitude that architects are now brothers. That is something I cannot emphasize enough. In our company, this attitude has been instrumental in our getting work. An architect who thinks that we can help him will

urge the owner to give us the job because he knows that we will cooperate, we'll help him, and if he falls down, we'll pick him up and set him on his feet again.

In Ref. 1, Robert A. Marshall, Jr., senior vice president of Turner Construction Company, discussed the role of the general contractor as construction manager:

> In the next five, eight, ten years, the use of construction management is going to expand tremendously, GSA and the Dept. of Housing, Education and Welfare at the governmental level has given the idea tremendous impetus, and in our own business we know that our horizons have been vastly enlarged, from construction management largely on private work to construction management at the state, county and city level. I'm thinking particularly of schools. The last time Turner built a public school was many, many years ago. Now we have several construction management jobs for groups of schools at the county level. We're going to see continued expansion in the use of construction management because of the benefits that the owner receives. . . .
>
> The kind of experience that a general contractor has is extremely important with regard to the qualifications to perform as a construction manager. By this I mean experience in costing and experience in value engineering to determine the relative value of different design costs. We feel that in the construction period the experience with labor, actual experience with the various trades, and the practical approach to construction management is the best way to do CM.

THE CONSULTANT OR PROFESSIONAL CM

A new type of firm is evolving, structured specifically to handle construction management assignments.

Most successful CM consultants have a substantial background in engineering, often having started either in estimating, scheduling, or design. This background gives them a good understanding of the design process. Their experience in working with professional A/E's and owners is an asset in managing the preconstruction phases. In some instances, owners have delegated the entire manager process, including putting together the design team or at least recommending the team to be selected, to the project managers. Needless to say, this substantially increases the managers' influence.

These firms tend to be less knowledgeable in such areas as cost estimating and construction feasibility, but this is mitigated by their consulting experience. This experience makes it possible for them to recognize situations that are sometimes accepted as commonplace by the CM contractor.

In the construction phase, CM consultants tend to be very effective in such specialized areas as scheduling and visibility of results for management; but they are hampered by their lack of working contact with contractors and subcontractors, which can cause problems if the owner wants the CM to break down the project into many small contracts. The few organizations who have been successful in this field have built up successful credibility with contractors.

At the CM roundtable (Ref. 1), one of the authors, a consultant CM, stated:

> Construction management is at its best as project management from the start to finish of the project. The owner, whether he is an experienced owner or, particularly, if he's a one-time builder, needs assistance, and the project manager is the one to furnish this assistance.

> Construction management has three camps. One camp looks to the design team to become the construction manager. Some firms have succeeded but many have failed. In some cases the general contractor has become the construction manager, and he's brought his construction know how back into the design phase, which I think is a vital element. There's a third area developing, the consultant construction manager. . . .

> This view of CM doesn't necessarily knock out the GC. If the owner used a single contractor, the question can be asked is "who needs you as the CM?" With a GC on board, the consultant CM reverts more to a project management level, with the GC partner taking more of a role. A key attribute of the consultant CM is the consulting experience and that experience means getting along with people. Sometimes the GC who's been in the field for 20 or 30 years does not work too well with the design office. But the CM has to sell his ideas whether he's got the authority or not. He's typically a project manager. We hear the constant lament from project managers that they have responsibility but not authority. They claim they need more authority to get the whole job done. The dilemma comes from being both the construction manager and the project manager. Both jobs have the problem of a lot of responsibility, limited authority and they've got to use persuasion, logic and experience to get the job done. A consultant CM can perform in the predesign better than the typical construction guy.

THE PUBLIC POSITION ON CM

Over the last few years, the General Services Administration has spearheaded the national interest in construction management. Already using project managers, but tied through legislative regulations to competitive bidding, the GSA evolved a new role for the CM.

GSA selects a number of qualified teams that are oriented toward general contractors as potential CMs. GSA then negotiates with the selected group of the most qualified teams to pick the final construction manager.

This is done early in the design phase or even before the start of the design. The CM then works as a member of the owner's staff during the design phase, making recommendations on construction feasibility and practicality, contract scopes, cost factors, and other facets of the project. The construction manager provides a contractor's thinking at a point when it can still be utilized as something other than an afterthought. The CM becomes a focus of the value-engineering effort and maintains an overall project schedule viewing not only the construction phase but also the design itself.

The facilities section of the U.S. Department of Health, Education & Welfare has gone even farther in its definition of the construction manager as a general contractor. HEW requires construction managers to submit a binding "upset" price; they must guarantee that the project will not cost more than this amount. In the CM roundtable (Ref. 1), Bert Berube, deputy associate commissioner of PBS (GSA) for project management commented:

> We see construction management as being created to help the owner to save time and money on the project. The owners have developed or have been wanting to go the route of the phased design and construction, or fast-track as it's called in some areas, rather than the traditional process. Phased design and construction causes two basic problems for the owner. During the design phase he doesn't know how to logically break the job up into biddable packages. During the construction phase, with numerous contractors present on the site, the owner normally does not have the expertise to manage these different contractors. In other words, the owner becomes his own general contractor, and he doesn't have the expertise in this area. So for these two basic purposes, he hires someone to do it for him, and this is construction management, from my point of view. . . .

> It also has other secondary benefits that accrue to the owner, such as bringing construction expertise into the design field. Its basic purpose, however, is to bring about the logical breakdown into bid packages and to manage the job in the field. . . .

> GSA builds throughout the country, and one of the real strong benefits that it gets out of a construction manager is his construction expertise in a certain locality. Normally, we'll build a large structure in a certain city—

but won't come back to that locality for another 10 or 15 years to build another one. If we'd have built our own CM team in the area it would be good for the one building, but would not be of any great value thereafter. So GSA prefers to use private industry's expertise. When we're finished with the project we are no longer saddled with the people that would be carried forward.

THE OWNER AS CM

Owners of one-time building projects make poor construction managers because of their lack of expertise and also lack of objectivity. Those who build many projects often have their own project management group available. Most who work in this fashion separate the project management group from the functional or production areas to insulate the project managers from in-house pressures.

In many cases, the best mixture is that of in-house project managers and an outside construction management team that is well qualified to manage a particular project on a project-by-project basis.

As director of the Office of Planning, Design, and Project Management of the University of Pennsylvania, Arthur F. Freedman is one owner who expects to do his own project management and perhaps some construction managing. In the CM roundtable (Ref. 1) he commented:

> The university needs construction management for the implementation of its facilities program—CM is management of an implementation process. Construction management is a management approach starting from the planning cycle through the actual startup of the facility. The techniques the construction manager uses brings his knowledge into the design phase. It is important to manage the actual construction through one method or another, either guaranteed maximum lump-sum bidding when necessary, lump-sum multicontract or time and material contracting. The method should not be mixed up with the definition.

> The owner recognizes that this is a new management concept. The critical criteria from our point of view is flexibility, which allows us to respond to the needs of each project and not be locked in with one mechanism for doing it.

> We never took the attitude that we could stand by and have the a/e proceed totally on his own. In any construction management process there's greater involvement by the owner. This is the prime reason we intend to strengthen and modernize our own capabilities, our procurement specs for services, contracting and our own staff.

> With respect to building up our own forces, we're going to do it for exactly the reasons GSA is not doing it. We build in one place.

Our buildings are constructed on one of two campuses—and we have repetitive problems—if we can build the management expertise then it's more efficient than hiring somebody else to develop that expertise. We're very much the project manager of our own team, but we will buy pieces of a construction management skill spectrum as needed. Each project becomes a different management model utilizing selected tools common to construction management. . . .

Owners are going to react to construction management in many cases by strengthening their own staffs. On modest-size projects, they're going to put themselves in the construction manager's role and continue to work with the GC and with the designer.

There's still a very important role for the designer. He should continue as the prime mover in the construction process.

The industy as a whole will change. Project management is going to become more important. The future manager will be a part of a firm that sells a total package of services to the one-shot owner. We're going to see firms that have the capability to provide different levels of service.

SUMMARY

The concept of construction management is in an evolutionary process. Each major implementer has the capability to perform in a satisfactory manner. The special advantage to an owner offered by one type of construction management tends to preclude the special attributes of another. Doubtless, the competitive marketplace would force the evolution to an almost predetermined configuration *if* the needs of all owners were uniform. While many of the owner's requirements for construction management are in harmony, the controlling requirements are often unique to a category of owners including location, nature of projects, legislative/corporate restraints, financial orientation, type of organization and functions of the project.

REFERENCES

1. *Construction or Project Management—Which is Best?* A CM Roundtable by Actual Specifying Engineer, September 1974, pp. 87–92.

2. *CM for the General Contractor,* Associated General Contractors of America, Inc., 1974, 155 pages.

3
Predesign

In the predesign phase, there is a gestation period within which the project becomes identified as a concept, and a project scope and definition are evolved by an ad-hoc team or an established budgeting group.

Construction management (CM) input at this stage is limited by the obvious precedent action of identifying the concept as a viable project before any selection or assignment of a construction manager (CM) can be made. When that initial selection is made, the choice would probably be the assignment of an in-house project manager.

NEEDS AND OBJECTIVES

Prior to the implementation of any planning in the CM process there first has to be an establishment or identification of a "need." The basic process of decision starts with the recognition that there is a need for a capital improvement or for a new development. This can cover the gamut from the simple desire of a private individual wishing to enlarge his or her quarters to the more complex decision-making process within a major governmental department or segment of industry implementing a long-range master plan for development including the growth and need for expansion and additional facilities. This need may be later identified in the planning process as having been improperly established, overvalued, or false in its basic concept; but the initial process is commenced, and the role of the construction manager is born and exists already at this time. The construction manager, whose specific functions are more readily and traditionally defined in the later aspects of design and construction, may have immediate input at the project's inception. The CM's knowledge of the later project requirements, limitations, and options can influence the results of the earlier decision process. Indeed such input should be sought from a project team member at this early time of development, not only to provide the continuity of having the CM firm involved from the beginning of the project development, but to draw upon the CM's detailed and specific construction and planning knowledge at the inception of the project.

Needs, however, are an outgrowth of the structure of our society and the priorities established within the governmental and political decision-making process. The federal budget has grown from under $100 billion in 1960 to over $400 billion in the 1970s. It continues to grow as do other public, state, and municipal budgets which include funds for development programs that are in the nation's interest. The economic process with both public and private forces at work is, as a result, complex but *needs*— whether arising from basic comsumption demands, consumer marketing factors, or from national policy objectives—are a reflection of all the economic, political, and social forces at work.

The need may be to build additional plant to meet growing consumer demand (until the recession of 1974, a basic concept of our growth economy) or to build adequate housing for all (see Ref. 1). The housing needs and their relationship to the social and political systems were clearly defined. The goal of building 2 million housing units annually was established in this report and underscored by later legislation as essential to the nation's welfare. Since 1968 the units listed in Table 3-1 were actually started.

Recommendations as to methods of financing, new legislative authority, use of federal and local programs, redistribution of funds and numerous methods of implementation were made. The need had been established, the proposed solutions or objectives were identified, and a basis for a

TABLE 3-1*

Year	Units constructed (in thousands)
1969	1,500
1970	1,469
1971	2,085
1972	2,378
1973	2,058
1974	1,352
1975	1,171

*U.S. Department of Commerce, Bureau of the Census.

national policy was formed. However, implementation does not necessarily follow the establishment of the need.

Such needs, although identified in a major policy report such as Ref. 1, must be adopted for implementation within the existing political process. This required not only federal financing but also a commitment on the part of the private sector to harness its resources to meet the demand.

FEASIBILITY

Feasibility can simply amount to an individual's evaluating his financial resources and looking into the marketplace to determine whether there is a home that he can construct or purchase that will satisfy his needs. This is how many basic and initial decisions are made and various alternatives are considered to gain the ultimate objective. Even this analysis of the existing marketplace can be complex. For instance, are the options available—those of owning, renting, investment in a cooperative, or purchase of a condominium? What are the priorities within the financial framework of each one of these options, having different impacts considering cash outlay, interest, and taxes?

The feasibility of the project and evaluation of its practicality, which naturally are dependent upon the extent and scope of the particular project, will identify the comprehensive nature of the feasibility studies that are undertaken. In the basic construction industry most feasibility projects usually are considered and classified as either engineering or economic feasibility studies. In actuality, the feasibility study of a project should consider and evaluate the following aspects:

- *Alternate courses of action:* What are the possible alternative solutions to satisfying or meeting the need?

- *Engineering evaluation or analysis of such alternate solutions:* Practical design solutions, cost estimates, and basic engineering analysis.

- *Economic evaluation of such alternatives:* What is the probable or possible manner of financing? What are the basic revenues? What economic impact will the project have?

- *Social analysis of project:* What is the impact upon society or the community in which the project is under consideration?

- *Political considerations:* The political factor may be considered one of the realities or practicalities of implementation, depending upon different and opposing political points of view that

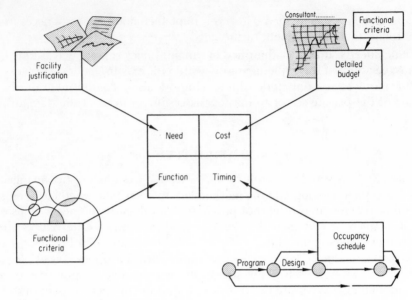

Figure 3-1. Interface between budget and management information.

possibly may change over the period of time and within the area in which the project is being planned and analyzed.

PLANNING

In this phase of the construction project, the various options and methods of implementation must be considered and evaluated. This phase is reached after basic feasibility is established. An evaluation of the feasibility of the project will contribute to the decision-making process leading to this next stage. The planning process in itself may review many of the items considered in the feasibility analysis. The best option or alternative for implementation must be selected. The timing, financing, impacts, and limitations must be considered; and the options available to implement the basic need are again reviewed (see Figure 3-1). At this phase, the beginning of the construction process may already be starting, namely, the planning, architectural and engineering design, and construction. However, the boundaries between these stages are not clearly defined, and the construction process has already been in its formative stage for some time.

The construction process continues and evolves in this early phase; the alternatives of implementation are evaluated and these include the "bricks and mortar" aspects of the project. In order to meet the ultimate objective or satisfy the particular need, what avenues are available? Is the solution to additional housing the construction of:

- Single-family residences?
- Multifamily residences?
- Renovation of existing facilities?
- Better utilization of existing facilities?
- Relocation of families?

All decisions must be made within the framework of the particular need or objective, geographic area, and financial resource or limitation.

The decision process can also relate to the movement of people and goods within a region. Is the solution:

- Mass transit: new facility?
- Mass transit: expansion of an old facility?
- Mass transit: mixed modes?
- Utilization and rehabilitation of an existing facility?
- No new facility because of recognition of changing urban neighborhoods, work patterns?
- No new transit, but construction of new urban cores and relocation of population centers?

Such decisions must be made within the framework of reality, political boundaries, regional plans and needs, and fiscal resources and limitations.

BUDGET APPROVAL

Projects evolve from a vast, intangible array of needs and requirements. (See Figure 3-2.) With the continuing development of operations research and the availability of computers, there has been a positive move toward the systemization of project identification and definition. In the United States, a number of major federal agencies have undertaken to systematize the preparation of the budget. The Department of Defense was the first to evolve the systematic approach to planning, programming, budgeting systems (PPBS). Based on the success in the Dept. of Defense, President Johnson directed that other agencies would also undertake PPBS. The City of New York officially adopted PPBS under John V. Lindsay, and a number of states and cities have expressed interest.

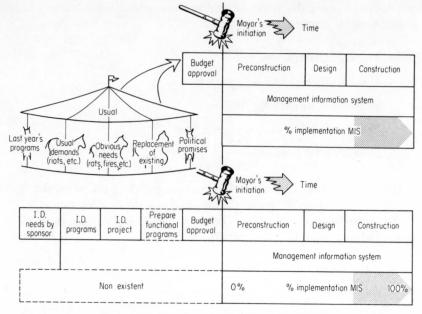

Figure 3-2. Usual methods of input to budget.

More than 10 years later, however, PPBS is more of a concept than a technique or a system. Although it has done much to recognize what might be termed a "mystique" through which a project emerges from areas of need, there has not really been a specific successful systematic development.

The budget is the formal document within which the project is identified, and the point in time at which it is authorized in terms of the ever-important funding phase. The budget must accommodate many types of programs including:

- Continuing programs from prior years

- Debt service on existing capital structure

- Administration funds for existing departments

- Replacement of existing structure

- Meeting of obvious needs (fires, riots, natural disasters)

After the budget structure has addressed itself to the above list, and perhaps others, the amount of resources which can be programmed for new projects is considered. Strong well-defined programs, obviously, have a much better opportunity for selection. Marginal, or poorly expressed, programs usually receive little consideration.

The budget selection process is one which can be continued over years. Until a project has been approved, it has sponsors—but no managers. In most cases, the CM/PM team cannot be selected until the budget for at least the initial planning phase has been approved.

The project manager who has a well-developed project documented with specific goals and objectives is fortunate. He is even more fortunate if the time period between the initial preparation of the complete plan and the present has not changed the planning factors to a degree that the goals and objectives are no longer viable. The initial step of the project plan development must necessarily be to review the goals and objectives and either reaffirm or readjust them.

This initial review can be traumatic. One CM team took over a plan that had been seven years in development. A major university hospital was operating a university medical training and treatment center with an excellent reputation, but in an aging facility. The basic plan had been to revitalize that capital plant, including the demolition of certain very obsolete portions. The project budget had grown from $25 million to $100 million, and had been cut back to $60 million by direction of the university trustees.

After some months of planning for implementation, the project management team reported to the trustees that the $62-million plan did not meet the basic functional guidelines set down. The project was immediately canceled, and over the past several years has been replaced by an incremental project plan geared to the original goals and objectives of the university.

ENVIRONMENTAL IMPACT

Since the passage of the National Environmental Quality Policy Act (PL91-190 42 USC 4321 1969), the construction process has started a new chapter and new course. Although many aspects presently falling within the purview of "environmental analysis" were previously included in general planning, PL91-190 and resulting state and local legislation laid the foundation for a comprehensive environmental planning process. Many states and localities through legislation have defined specific requirements and placed limitations and controls on future development and construction. Court decisions interpreting provisions of the new legislation have identified other requirements as the intent of Congress or of the local legislature when project development or proposed construction has been challenged and the challenges have charged lack of compliance with provisions of the act. Administrative bodies and agencies have drawn up specific requirements that must be followed in the development of an environmental analysis and writing of an impact statement.

As a consequence, the considerations and resulting analysis of environmental impact are broad in scope but detailed and must present all facets—beneficial and harmful—of the impact of a proposed development and project. Without such an analysis, there are increasingly fewer construction projects, whether publicly or privately financed that will be able to proceed to construction.

The application of this law to the federal highway field presents a vivid example of the implications of the law, the development of its scope, and the method of implementation. This itself, more than the fact that in 1969 the interstate highway system was nearing completion and the scarceness of state funds, other than special bond issues, changed forever the construction and development process of highway work. The federal government already had a highly structured procedure administered by a well-trained administrative and technical organization, the Federal Highway Administration (FHWA). The new law was therefore quickly implemented for all projects still in the planning process or, actually, for all projects that had not received FHWA design approval prior to January 14, 1969, subject to certain conditions, the effective date of the federal legislation (FHWA, PPM 90-1). It is not the intention or scope of this volume to describe in detail the scope of the planning and hearing process that is presently in effect and required for project development, but an outline or general overview is illustrative of the environmental planning process as it affects the building development or construction process.

The basic statute 23 U.S.C. (United States Code) 134 pertained to comprehensive planning and established planning requirements for construction of projects in urban areas of more than 50,000 population. This statutory authorization and later amendments led to FHWA regulation (PPM 50-9 issued 11/24/69 and IM 50-3-71 issued 4/13/71) which defined and interpreted the planning process that was required. Guidelines were established and required inventories for:

1. Economic factors affecting development

2. Population

3. Land use

4. Transportation facilities

5. Travel patterns

6. Terminal and transfer patterns

7. Traffic control features

8. Zoning ordinances, subdivision regulations, building codes, etc.

9. Financial resources

10. Social and community value factor

These regulations established the so-called 3-C Process—continuing, comprehensive, cooperation—and no transportation project within such urban areas could be implemented without meeting these specific requirements.

The public hearing requirements emanated from the statutory authority of 23 U.S.C. 128 which established the initial one-hearing process, later amended to the two-hearing process (1) corridor and (2) highway design public hearings (FHWA PPM 20-8 of January 14, 1969).

The planning and public hearing process, and Environmental Impact Study (E.I.S.) requirements as implemented by the various PPMs and IMs, which are periodically revised, established a comprehensive and detailed analysis and study effort required in many instances over an extended time frame and at substantial cost to justify the implementation of construction. The scope of an E.I.S. for a particular project must evaluate impacts of alternatives. In traditional terms the highway engineer considered such factors as land use and regional economic benefits, but in the final analysis he evaluated the cost-benefits of right-of-way relocation, and new construction with ultimate benefits. Such analysis is measurable in value and dollars. Although environmental-impact analysis includes many of the planning elements and cost comparisons it must consider intangibles which, although they may be fully documented and evaluated, cannot necessarily always be quantified. They must, however, be addressed later in the options involved in the decision to build, not to build, or where to build. Such evaluations as required by applicable regulations (Ref. 2) encompass:

1. Detailed descriptions of alternate sites.

2. Identification of appropriate population and growth projections for area.

3. Relationship of project to land use plans and policies of affected area.

4. Probable impact upon the environment including assessment of positive and negative effects on:

  a. Air quality

  b. Water quality

  c. Fish and wildlife

  d. Solid waste

  e. Noise

  f. Radiation

  g. Hazardous substances (such as toxic materials and pesticides)

  h. Energy supply and natural resources development

  i. Land use and management

  j. Protection of environmentally critical areas: flood plains, wetlands, beaches and dunes, unstable soils, steep slopes, aquifer recharge areas

  k. Land use in coastal areas

  l. Redevelopment and construction in built-up areas

  m. Density and congestion mitigation

  n. Neighborhood character and continuity

  o. Impacts on low-income populations

  p. Historic, architectural, and archeological preservation

  q. Soil and plant conservation and hydrology

  r. Outdoor recreation

5. Further analysis to consider secondary effects in form of associated investments and changed patterns of social and economic activities.

6. Alternatives to proposed action: such analysis to be a comprehensive evaluation of all reasonable alternates with sufficient in-depth analysis to make possible an objective evaluation. Such alternative analysis to quantify "no-action" alternate.

7. Definition of probable unavoidable adverse environmental effects.

8. Analysis of short-term impact as differentiated with long

term, as for example, those impacts which occur only during construction.

9. Definition of irreversible and irretrievable commitment of resources.

10. Offsetting interests and considerations of federal policy.

The above is outlined to show the detailed inventory and analysis that precedes the decision-making process. Further, the review process is lengthy and involved. In addition to the multitude of federal agencies and local (state and municipal) bodies given an opportunity to review the draft, there is ample opportunity for the participation and involvement of local citizens. The draft review precedes the public hearing for which there are strict criteria (PPM 20-8), and only after detailed review and analysis—which often results in modification, further study, or consideration of new options—is the final impact statement prepared. This statement essentially incorporates all prior analysis and study and is the best effort and most comprehensive document defining a proposed project.

This final statement must precede the "go" decision before design is implemented. Naturally dependent upon the complexity of the project, the design process may require several months or even a year. During this time there are further reviews, detailed design development, public hearings, and even possibly need to appropriate funds. Only then can construction commence.

Admittedly, the above description and process does not dictate a detailed and comprehensive, time-consuming, and costly process for all projects aided by the FHWA. Many projects may only require what is described as a negative-impact statement for there are no adverse impacts, no alternatives other than the proposed solution, such as an improvement of an existing facility. On the other hand projects in urban areas immediately by their very nature have substantial impact besides their usual controversiality.

The FHWA process is cited as illustrative to the depth and extent that project development may require environmental study. Although the cited example is based on complex and detailed requirements resulting from statutory authority, such requirements and the legislation itself were promulgated for the public interest because this area had been neglected by the highway builder and decision maker in prior years. Recognizing that any construction project has an impact, even before the first spade of earth is turned, it is not surprising that state and local regulations now require more detailed environmental evaluation to obtain building permits or even project approval before design development can proceed.

The construction process and, as a consequence, the construction manager therefore must not only be concerned with the environmental impact of the physical construction itself but with the overall social, economic, regional, and environmental impact with such categories being subject to broad, far-reaching, and detailed definition.

After the project receives approval or the necessary permits licensing construction are obtained, the CM responsibility as well as the design responsibilitity is to ensure that the short-term environmental impacts are controlled. Although this can be considered and to a certain extent is a design function, many other aspects—such as use of equipment and disposal of material—are solely within the control of the contractor. It is not only the recognition of local regulations and ordinances which is fully the contractor's responsibility but also planning and control of combined activities on a job site, which, although being performed as required with the necessary permits, can be structured to minimize impacts.

It is interesting to note that the detailed FHWA process for preparation of E.I.S. analysis recognizes this area which is described as "short-term" impacts and requires preanalysis of this area at this time, long before the start of design or even project approval. Although such short-term-impact analysis would not describe grubbing and clearing operations, it would detail such items as drainage runoff during construction, disposition of waste, erosion control, and noise and air pollution (from construction equipment). All these impacts are essentially variables because, although they have impact, the degree of impact either in volume or range is subject to influence and control during design and actual implementation. Therefore, the role or task of the construction manager is clear in that he or she must recognize the environmental impact of the contemplated and planned work and ensure not only that the project complies with applicable environmental regulations but that all possible instigating action is taken during both the planning-design and construction process.

SITE SELECTION

Traditionally, the most common practice in the overall development of a project is for the owner or ultimate user to establish the site for a new facility. The designer may provide some input by having the option to prepare plans or schematics for alternate sites. But such sites would have been predetermined through the owner's selection process. Although the owner may have utilized the services of a specialist or real estate consultant, the decision making would be essentially complete prior to the implementation of design. The designer's mandate usually is to design and plan a facility on a preselected or predetermined site. The expert or real estate analyst's selection would have been made on sound economic, financial feasibility and valid engineering grounds; but site selection, per se, would have been treated as a separate function or task; the owner would be the only member of the project team being involved in the total project development process.

The need for experts to analyze and evaluate specific site needs exists even more today than in earlier times. Because of urban growth, corporate relocations between urban centers (as, for instance, the movement of various corporate company headquarters occurring in the 1960s from New York City to Houston, Texas) as well as the legislation of new zoning limitations and building restrictions together with growing environmental considerations and increasing local, state, and federal regulations, the evaluation of the appropriate real estate has become a more crucial aspect of the project development process than ever before. As the need for the utilization of experts in the field has grown and become evident, so has the need for a coordinator and manager grown at this phase of project development. This function, often performed by the owner, is a proper coordination and management task of a construction manager. During the real estate phase of the development project, the CM has a specific task to perform.

The CM process, concerned as it is with the life cycle and life-cycle costs, must consider land use and land values. Land as a commodity is generally classified as urban and rural, and the shift of population continues to the urban centers. Of the 200 million people in the United States in 1970, the urban-rural ratio was 73–27 according to the U.S. Bureau of Census. This ratio is increasing with the continuing shift to urban areas and the growth of metropolitan areas. Although inner cities are losing population because of decay and relocation of manufacturing, commercial, and financial companies, such relocations are taking place within urban areas or from one urban area to another. In discussing urban areas, official standards have been established by the United States federal government; they are described as Standard Metropolitan Statistical Areas (SMSAs) consisting of population centers of more than 50,000 and meeting other criteria.

As officially established by the Bureau of the Budget with the advice of the Federal Committee on Standard Metropolitan Statistical Areas (an interagency committee), SMSAs are selected on the basis of the following criteria (Ref. 3):

POPULATION CRITERIA

1. Each SMSA must include at least:

   a. One city with 50,000 or more inhabitants, or

b. Two cities have contiguous boundaries and constituting, for general economic and social purposes, a single community with a combined population of at least 50,000, the smaller of which must have a population of at least 15,000.

2. If two or more adjacent counties each have a city of 50,000 inhabitants or more (or twin cities under 1b) and the cities are within 20 miles of each other (city limits to limits), they will be included in the same area unless there is definite evidence that the two cities are not economically and socially integrated. (Areas may cross state lines.)

3. At least 75% of the labor force of the county must be in the nonagricultural labor force.

4. In addition to Criterion 3, the county must meet at least one of the following conditions:

   a. It must have 50% or more of its population living in contiguous minor civil divisions with a density of at least 150 persons per square mile, in an unbroken chain of minor civil divisions with such density radiating from a central city in the area.

   b. The number of nonagricultural workers employed in the county must equal at least 10% of the number of nonagricultural workers employed in the county containing the largest city in the area, or be the place of employment of 10,000 nonagricultural workers.

   c. The nonagricultural labor force living in the county must equal at least 10% of the number of the nonagricultural labor force living in the county containing the largest city in the area, or be the place of residence of a nonagricultural labor force of 10,000.

5. In New England . . . towns and cities are used in defining SMSA's . . . [and] because smaller units are used and more restricted areas result, a population density criterion of at least 100 persons per square mile is used as the measure of metropolitan character.

CRITERIA OF INTEGRATION

6. A county is regarded as integrated with the county or counties containing the central cities of the area if either of the following criteria is met:

   a. If 15% of the workers living in the county work in the county or counties containing central cities of the area, or

   b. If 25% of those working in the county live in the county or counties containing central cities of the area.

(Where data for Criteria 6(a) or (b) are not conclusive, other related types of information may be used based on such measures as telephone calls, newspaper circulation, charge accounts, delivery service practices, traffic counts, extent of public transportation, and extent to which local planning groups and other civic organizations operate jointly.)

Concurrent with the growth and development of urban areas is the change in the nature and character of real estate. Such change has resulted in the development of detailed regulations, both administrative and legislative, controlling the development and use of real estate. Surprisingly, there is no national uniformity in such regulations, with the possible single exception of those regulations emanating from the passage of the National Environmental Policy Act (NEPA) of 1969. Statutory authority regulating land use and building construction is vested in the state, but the authority of the state legislature gives municipal bodies and governments specific powers (i.e., zoning and building code regulations). The implementation of such powers does not necessarily result in uniform regulations within one SMSA because the boundaries of such an SMSA may encompass a metropolitan city, surrounding suburbs within separate counties with each governmental unit imposing separate restrictions or requirements.

Although the construction manager would not usually be an expert in these areas, the need for a single management and coordination role becomes more significant with the need for proper coordination and control of all the factors that can influence or determine the direction and development of a new project.

The new-town developments in the United States of Reston, Virginia, and Columbia, Maryland, are examples of total planned communities in which a community of homes, factories, business, recreational areas, schools, and institutions comprise the total community as preplanned; the management and coordination role followed the single-community plan. Such instances may occur more frequently in the future with the development of new towns. Although the concept is still in the experimental and formative stage in the United States, it is somewhat more advanced in Europe. Recently, however, the economic crisis in this country, together with the energy "crunch," has brought the new-town movement to a virtual standstill in the United States.

The majority of development, growth, reconstruction, and new construction will be within areas which are existing and developed (to various stages), and thus subject to the complex web of regulations and statutory requirements that can find simplification or at least unified direction in a total planned or new community such as Reston or Columbia. (Both communities utilized CM in modified form.)

In the project coordination role, in order to evaluate land use and function, the following long-range facets must be considered as they will have an influence not only at time of site selection but during various stages of development or even permanently. These are:

Land Characteristics

Not that land is unique and not that parcels with similar characteristics cannot be found, but each project site will presumably have different features and physical attributes. Although the main consideration of a "site" will inherently be in how it is used, the ultimate use may be controlled or at least will be affected by its natural condition.

To identify physical characteristics, one need only consider the following physical features:

- Location: urban or rural

- Size and topography

- Elevation in relation to surrounding areas

- Growth or fertility of soil

- Subsoil conditions and/or mineral deposits

- Water supply and natural water table

- Climatic conditions

- Drainage

Although not physical features, the availability of utility services must be an early consideration in a site analysis. Such services will include:

- Electricity (power)

- Gas

- Sanitary and storm drainage systems

- Public safety: fire and ambulance; police protection

As is patently evident, each of the above-listed "characteristics" and "services" has to be considered and evaluated during the design-construction process. To ensure proper evaluation at the appropriate time during the project development, the construction manager, as part of his involvement in project concept development and planning, should play a key role in site selection.

Value

The immediate consideration of value is property cost. This naturally is the market value which is represented and established in the free marketplace. More readily defined, value is what price a prospective buyer is willing to pay and a seller is willing to accept.

The purchase price is really only the beginning part of the value analysis of a real estate parcel. Every parcel of property is subject to property tax which, although levied by the local governmental body having jurisdiction over the property, may include—in addition to the local municipal tax—county, state, and regional-authority taxes and levies. Local taxes are levied to finance local services, such as the usual housekeeping and public safety costs. The larger governmental unit tax is levied on property to support functions such as county welfare and institutional costs (educational, hospital, correctional) as well as such regional services as sewer construction or cost of transportation facilities.

Property is assessed to establish its value for purposes of raising revenue. Assessment normally separates values of land and buildings, and the assessment is established by the local governmental body. Although each locality—whether village, town or county—has the assessment authority, the basic intent is to establish a fair and equitable basis upon which taxes can be levied to support various governmental costs. Because of the judgment that has to be utilized, which is unavoidable in assigning values, and because of the complexities that are inherent to the process, such as differentiating values between residential, commercial and industrial, the equitable base is often only reached in theory and not practice. This leads to legal challenges and certiorari action, resulting in a complex web of opinion relating to establishment of value.

It is interesting to list the various and different forms and terms for value that exist within the real estate industry. These can include:

- Book value

- Market value

- Sales value

- Use value

- Economic value

- Fair value

- Replacement value

- Depreciated value

- Resale value

In addition to assessment and tax impacts on value, the methods and availability of financing may influence value. Because real estate normally represents a sizable investment, financing through mortgaging the property is the most common method of raising funds to purchase the property.

As nearly every homeowner is aware, mortgage financing is simply the borrowing of funds from a lending institution, whether a bank, insurance company or other institutional group, and placing or conveying the property as security to the lender (the mortgagee). The borrower is the mortgagor and although he is the legal owner of the property, his legal ownership is subject to the rights of the mortgagee in the event that he defaults, is unable to meet the agreed-upon payments within the terms of the mortgage, or cannot repay the loan. The significance of mortgaged property as part of the value and its significance within the CM process is that this may be, and usually is, only part of the total financing required for the project development.

Zoning

With the growth of urban areas, statutory authority has been utilized to zone or control the use of land. Such power is a local one and by way of state legislation is exercised by local municipal governments. The purpose of zoning is to control the orderly growth of property development. Zoning establishes purposes for which property within a governmental boundary may be utilized. Although a tool for regulating urban growth in accordance with preestablished master plan, it is only based upon the states' power to regulate health, safety and general welfare. As a consequence, there are legal boundaries to the use of zoning to achieve "orderly growth," because every locality depending upon the social and economic values dominant within the community or political entity will interpret such powers differently. Also, the scope and extent of the zoning laws will have different implications in highly developed urban areas and developing ones, as well as in the smaller suburban and rural communities.

Programming

A key interface between predesign and design, programming can be subdivided into two categories: *functional* and *architectural*.

During the initial planning and programming stage, the owner has a substantial role—particularly where he has a strong planning staff. In many types of facilities—particularly hospitals—it is almost mandatory that a group of specialists be called in to prepare the program.

The stringent requirements for environmental-impact studies have opened the door to an entirely new field of experts in the preparation of this very specialized statement.

In the power field, nuclear specialists have come into great demand for development of the systems studies for submission to the Nuclear Regulatory Commission (NRC) including related environmental-impact statements.

Consultants, and even entire consulting companies, specialize in economic feasibility studies, particularly in major transportation and development programs.

The role of the consultant as a specialist complicates the implementation of construction. The specialist often exercises his prerogatives of expertise precluding progress. He rarely makes it easier to progress.

In some cases, the obstructionist viewpoint of the specialist is a result of a desire to emphasize the importance of his specialty, while in others it is a failure to realize the need for a coordinated effort. The CM should be a key member of this team.

FUNCTIONAL PROGRAM

The functional program defines the project in terms of purpose, scope, and functions. Based upon a survey, it should set forth clearly the needs to be fulfilled, the specific services to be provided in the building, the organizational structure and staffing pattern, and the proposed operational policies and procedures. Anticipated utilization factors and service loads should be estimated to complete the functional data. The functional program provides the basis for development of the architectural program.

The importance of this phase of the planning process should not be underestimated. It marks the beginning of actual planning. It is an instrument of decision and commitment. It documents and communicates the intent of the project. Subsequent phases of the planning process will depend upon the validity of the functional program. Therefore, it is of paramount importance that this phase of the planning be competently conceived, well considered, and communicated to all concerned for review.

The problem of planning for activities requires that the project be envisioned initially in abstract form.

Since tangible things are more readily understood than abstract concepts, it is a common weakness to start planning in physical terms, rather than to work through to them from principles, purposes, and functions. This tendency to plan facilities before the program is fully evolved should be counteracted by insistence that the functional program be derived first. In short, to plan "functionally," first plan the functions that are appropriate for the particular facility.

This type of planning calls for special expertise—often supplied by planning consultants.

Functional planning requires the availability or assembly of pertinent information regarding the project requirements. If PPBS or other synthesis approach has been used in preparing the budget, information will be readily available. Demographic information sources such as census, or city/state tax records would be reviewed if appropriate. Information should be stored in a manner making it accessible for review in future projects, or reevaluations of this one. Computer data banks lend themselves to this type of storage and also encourage the use of modeling or simulation to exercise different potential solutions.

The functional programming effort should reconfirm the budgetary estimate, and establish the capabilities to be built into the project. Functional program incorporates policy and should be approved by an appropriate level of management.

ARCHITECTURAL PROGRAM

Developed from the functional program, the architectural program is a statement of the design problem that the architect is called upon to solve. Unless the functional program is worked out in advance, the architect will be required to make many assumptions or suppositions. The architect should not be expected to decide the services to be provided in the facility or its methods of operation—this is normally outside the architect's responsibility, although he or she may well assist in reaching conclusions on these matters. Although some allowance should be made for flexibility and professional judgment in the design of the facilities, every functional consideration affecting the architectural program should be resolved and clearly stated.

The written architectural program translates needs and objectives into physical facilities. It forms a transition between the statement of broad functional requirements and detailed architectural planning. All available information relating to the design of the facility should be set forth. Its purpose is to serve as a guide to the architects and as a measure for evaluating the plans. It concerns itself primarily with information which establishes space requirements. The formulation requires thoughtful analysis especially in the early stages.

The architect takes the lead in preparing the architectural program, using the functional program, and is assisted by the owner, construction manager, and any special consultants deemed necessary. As a team they explore many requirements. A list is made of all spaces, however small or unimportant, and of all equipment requiring special housing. Personnel using each space are described. The relationships of rooms and areas are noted as a guide to planning. Special features of lighting, ventilating, communications, color, architectural character, acoustics, and the like are recorded. During this preparation, frequent meetings are held and checklists reviewed to see that all essentials have been considered. Budget limitations, both in dollars and in floor areas, are established, and their effect on the program is studied. The final document gives enough information to establish the size of the facility and its general character.

SUMMARY

The predesign project development phase is an evolutionary process. The time expended is often unaccounted for, since the exact sounding of the "starting gun" may not be until the budget phase has been completed. It is clear that CM input in this very important phase can be significant. It is also, unfortunately, clear that the selection of the CM may not be made until this phase has been completed.

In both government and the private sector, a significant compromise approach has been utilized. As soon as the project is defined as a project, a project manager is assigned. Later, as the project develops and proceeds, the organization retains its project manager in a top-level liaison role, assigning a construction manager to handle the actual CM duties and functions.

Figure 3-3 illustrates the multidisciplinary relationship in a typical major project. The owner interfaces with the professionals and consultants, and they in turn are responsible for solving design problems involving many separate functional areas. (The list shown is schematic only, and the real situation involves many more factors.)

Each major member of the design team accumulates his or her own

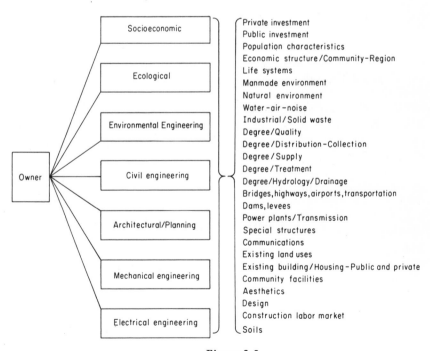

Figure 3-3.

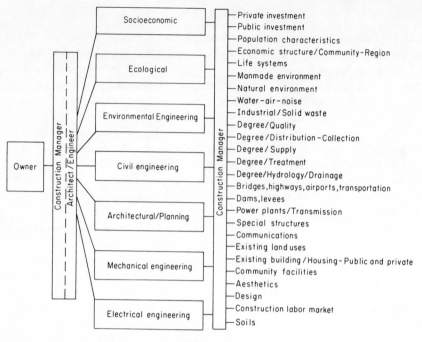

Figure 3-4.

information and formulates his or her own potential solution. These, in turn, should be coordinated with the other primary disciplines.

Figure 3-4 illustrates simplification which can be achieved by the interposition of the construction manager as the owner's representative for interface with all the professional disciplines and as the clearing house for information. Although oversimplified, Figure 3-4 illustrates the strength which managing information can give to the position of the construction managers. They are in a position to act as a filter for information as well as a conduit, disapproving those concepts which appear to be in conflict with the main thrust of the project.

REFERENCES

1. *Building the American City,* Report of the National Commission on Urban Problems to the Congress and the President, December 1968 (known as the Douglas Committee Report).

2. Council on Environmental Quality, "Preparation of Environmental Impact Statements," *Guidelines, Federal Register,* vol. 38, no. 147, Aug. 1, 1973.

3. Bureau of the Budget, Standard Metropolitan Statistical Areas, Washington, D.C., 1961.

4

Planning and Design

In many situations relating to the conventional process of construction of a facility the design phase is all-encompassing and includes feasibility and planning. The designer, who may be either an architect or engineer or an A/E, will, prior to development of a specific design or plan, evaluate alternate concepts and their feasibility. Thus, the traditional relationship between architect/engineer and owner placed the A/E in the lead role from planning through the design phase and continuing with inspection of construction. The A/E can perform the CM role simultaneously during the design phase but with concomitant loss in that certain functions requiring independent judgment from that of the designer (such as the review of design, evaluation of proposed construction systems for material availability, and a survey of availability of specialized labor which may be required by the design) will not be performed by another party other than the designer. Again, each facility, each owner and each circumstance defines the requirements for the extent and scope of CM services that may or may not be required to achieve the ultimate objective.

The design phase, however, is a separate and distinct function in the CM process. Over the years this has been formalized and structured by the design professionals, both architects and engineers, through various professional groups. The basic sequences are schematic, preliminary, and final. Each sequence more specifically defines the concept, culminating in the final set of plans and specifications to be utilized for construction purposes. The American Institute of Architects has formalized the appropriate definitions and scope both as professional functions and in contract terms. The functions are categorized as:

- Schematic design
- Preliminary design

- Final design

- Construction phase (inspection)

The schematic design (or concept) phase defines the concept, evaluates materials to be utilized, and establishes systems and outline specifications for the project or work scope. This phase includes the following:

1. Analysis of functions, services, and planning data (This effort is directly related to programming.)

2. Development of diagrams of functional relationships and service flow

3. Block out by areas of departments, divisions, or functional elements

4. Schematic arrangement of plan elements

5. Adaptation of schematic layout to site plan

6. Schematic traffic-flow exterior

7. Schematic of traffic-flow interior

8. Energy analysis, including selection of primary HVAC solution

9. Evaluation of electrical energy requirements

10. Analysis of structural systems

The schematic design converts program requirements into an architectural solution which best suits the site. Analysis during this stage should be oriented to the type of decisions which are being made. For instance, analysis involving the selection of the types of hardware would be premature during schematic design. In performing value analysis of the conceptual design phase, there is generally no single correct answer to a problem. The creative or speculative phase properly coordinated with the design effort can produce dramatic results at this stage.

DESIGN BUDGET

There are two basic methods of establishing construction budgets. The most popular method is to determine the cost per square foot of a similar facility and apply an escalation factor based on historical information.

The second and more favorable method is to develop a master-plan action program that researches the various subsystems of the proposed facility. This program progresses concurrently with the development design stages.

During the initial (schematic) design phase, the cost estimate would consider the following factors:

Basic scope—study and evaluate basic provisions of the budget relative to the program scope.

Equipment—set aside equipment budget allowance.

Site work—identify special requirements of master-plan action program which may influence site costs.

Basement and special foundations—study and identify probable effect of master plan, soil, and site conditions on foundation and/ or basement design.

Impact of master plan—study and identify the probable effect of the master plan on siting, geometry, acoustics, and links to other parts of the master plan, present and future.

Market abnormality—initiate study of market conditions.

Research—study program and identify areas of design and cost where research is required. Study program and identify unknowns. Initiate research for future phases of development.

Time—initiate study of projected market conditions.

Local market—identify influence of local labor and material costs on choice of materials and systems. Identify market deviations from normal.

Physical design development—develop with the design team layouts of typical spaces to determine if the program function/activity can be accommodated in the area programmed.

Basis for cost evaluation—analysis, research, and experience.

Content of estimate—restatement of program budget.

Detail of estimate—confirm adequacy of the budget for building and site.

The preliminary design (or design development) phase formalizes the adopted scheme and concept into basic plans for all major components of the facility. The plans now include more detailed presentations of architectural, structural, mechanical, and electrical components of the facility. Materials are selected and systems are established. Although this phase is described as "preliminary," certain final determinations as to structure, systems, materials, and architectural treatment are actually made. As a rule of thumb, in the A/E profession the preliminary phase of design is considered to constitute a work effort of 25 percent of the total design. This yardstick is carried over to the determination of value, and the 25 percent factor is used to establish the cost of the fee of the designer's work at completion of this phase. This can often be misleading because of the need to develop or at least initiate many of the final designs and systems during the preliminary phase of design development.

The basic stages in this design phase include:

1. Unit studies of plan elements to determine feasibility of concept

2. Modular analysis of typical spaces to determine constructability and cost practicality

3. Preparation of architectural plan at a scale proper for accurate layout of basic spatial solutions

4. Development of tentative scheme of mechanical and electrical systems

5. Development of personnel and equipment layouts for functional areas

6. Development of exterior design of the structure

7. Preparation of a general outline of materials and finishes (skeleton specification)

8. Preparation of a cost estimate

This stage is in a sense a reiteration of the initial stage. However, the entire operation is based upon the spatial solution which was selected at the end of schematic design. Design development first validates that spatial solution, and then expands the level of detail.

Construction management in this stage should be oriented to the constructability and feasibility aspects. Alternate approaches within the parameters (if possible) of the initial spatial solution should be posed and studied.

During design development, the design team seeks previous modular solutions for incorporation into their overall scheme. Generally, these proven modules are materials or equipment which have been previously utilized, tested, and are available commercially.

In monitoring the design of a structural steel system the construction manager would attempt to impose practical guidelines such as the use of standard structural sizes; limitation on the use of special shapes and the use of standard column sizes where appropriate.

Life-cycle costing is an important consideration during design development. The energy flow and dynamic balance for the building can be evaluated at this stage. The result will affect the roofing and exterior skin, as well as the size of the heating, ventilating, and air conditioning equipment. This, in turn, has direct impact upon the electrical requirements.

During the preliminary phase, outline specifications are prepared and the design is progressed in sufficient detail to make it possible to define costs. Such costs are also "preliminary"; however, they are based on sufficient detail to make it possible to evaluate initial budgets, to make basic changes or decisions within the initial criteria or guidelines for the facility, and to hold budgets or seek budgetary revisions, as may be necessary.

The final design (or contract document) phase of effort formalizes and details all aspects of the facility. All components, systems, and materials are selected and defined. The basic and inherent details for not only a functional facility but for one of aesthetic value and any special requirements or needs of a specific owner are documented and translated into plans and specifications.

Such plans and specifications are the basic part of the contract documents issued to implement the project.

The detailed design phase takes the design concept which has been defined in the design development stage and adds a level of detail which is required for the contractors to construct the facility. This is the development of the documents which will be the basis of the construction contract and which will also instruct the contractor specifically on the quality and quantity of the material which he is to provide and install. Major components of this design include:

1. Layouts of partitions and interior fixtures

2. Engineering design and structural elements

3. Architectural design of construction detail

4. Layout and design of mechanical systems

5. Location of fixtures and utility outlets

6. Chart of materials and finishes

7. Specifications of materials and equipment

8. Layout and design of electrical systems

The CM activity in this stage should emphasize the selection of better values within the spatial solution and modular decisions made in the previous two stages. If a different HVAC system should have been selected or another structural system would have been more appropriate, these decisions should have been made as part of the value analysis at the beginning of the design development stage. Value analysis in the design document stage should be of the type where one material can be directly substituted for another. In a masonry wall, for instance, a larger block might be selected. (Analysis would have to include an evaluation of the labor practices in the area to determine how many of the larger-size block can be laid up under present working conditions.)

A different roofing scheme might be selected within the dimensions of the roof as defined in the previous design phase. Details such as flashing for roofing systems should be studied. Analysis might well indicate that more expensive approaches should be utilized to ensure the integrity of the entire building. Similarly, studies might determine that the life-cycle aspects of maintenance would indicate a better value solution in the use of epoxy-base finishes rather than low-cost acrylic paints in hallways.

OVERVIEW—DESIGN

Figure 2-4 is a network plan showing the three stages of design in a replacement hospital. Each stage becomes more complex, requiring more time and increasing the potential for error. Accordingly construction-management input should be tailored to the increasing inflexibility of the design as it evolves. This effect is illustrated in Figure 2-3 in Chapter 2.

These three phases or sequences of design (schematic, preliminary, and final) are enumerated to identify the evolution of a design whether or not such phases are structured or formalized in the design process. On complex and major design efforts, each of these phases is defined and normally followed by a review and approval process. However, although not necessarily formalized on all projects regardless of their size, these steps of design are followed generally.

The above definition has presented design as a theoretical and total process for an individual facility or project. It does not, however, have to be implemented or progressed from beginning to end, from concept to bidding document (final design). Dependent upon need, the nature of the facility, and budgetary and time restraints, the total design can be "phased."

Phased Design

Also known as "fast track," this term means breaking design into phases or components in such a manner that certain design elements can be suffi-

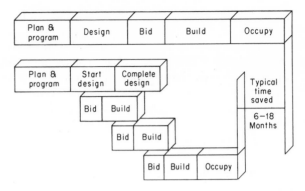

Figure 4-1. **Phased construction versus traditional single contract.**

ciently deferred to permit construction of the facility to commence before final design is complete (see Figure 4-1). As an example, if a project building site requires substantial site work or utility installation or relocation, the scope of this type of work is defined immediately upon siting of the building, plans are issued, and work is commenced while the building plans are being developed. The same could be applied to foundation plans. As soon as loads and sizes are defined, the foundation plan, possibly consisting of a major pile or caisson job, is issued while final architectural, mechanical, and electrical plans are being developed. Or such a foundation plan may be issued to permit work to start in a winter month, thereby gaining construction time while the superstructure design is being completed in time for construction to commence in the spring as soon as the foundations are complete.

The coordination of services through the construction team during the planning and design phases of a project constitutes the essence of the difference between the CM process and that involved in the traditional design services provided by an architect or an engineer. Once again, the primary purpose is to provide the team through the CM process with the professional advisory services which will make possible the control of time, cost, and quality in the construction of the facility. This is the critical time to influence selection of components, materials, and systems because during the planning and design the facility is being created and the decision-making process establishing the components and methods of construction is evolving.

CM SCOPE: PLANNING—SCHEMATIC PHASE

The function of construction management during planning and schematic design is best identified by discussing some tasks that may be included in the CM service.

The CM may assist the owner in the selection of the A/E designer for the contemplated project. Governmental authorities, especially federal, state, and major municipalities, have established procedures for A/E selection, but this procedure is not applicable to all owners, public as well as private. Depending upon the capabilities required, the construction manager is qualified to recommend to the owner the type of design firm that the latter should consider for an assignment. For instance, should the owner seek a primary architect or an engineer? The answer may not be self-evident to a lay owner if his needs are other than standard categories of building (architects) or heavy construction (engineer); the project may be a building in which aesthetics are secondary to function (warehouse— movement of goods); or other factors, such as site conditions (seismic or soils consideration) may outweigh others. In this instance it may be advantageous to the owner to seek engineering/architectural services as differentiated from A/E services.

The construction manager can further comment on or advise the owner on capabilities of specific individual firms being considered by the owner or may draw up lists of qualified firms for an owner's consideration. While the CM can play a significant role in advising, it is almost always the owner who makes the final selection of the A/E designer.

The construction manager should obtain all data relating to the site and surrounding area to enable the designer to implement the design. Such data may include aerial photographs, topographic surveys, property deeds and maps, and subsurface information, including borings.

If such data are not available, the CM may obtain them by subcontracting or by purchase if available from other sources. This in itself may require the taking of competitive bids, as, for instance, for extensive soil borings or testing. Although such data are normally obtained during the design process, the construction manager will have recognized the need for the data in the early stages of project development, and such data will have been obtained in a timely manner when actually required by the designer to develop design details.

As appropriate, together with the A/E, the construction manager should document the owner's objectives. This aspect may only be an amplification of prior activity on the part of the owner and the CM. Again dependent upon the time when the CM is brought into the project development, the scope and extent of such documentation would be appropriately defined. This may only involve documentation for the benefit of the A/E with its purpose limited to obtaining input from the design team to properly define such goals and objectives in light of the functional aspects of the projects.

As appropriate and necessary the construction manager will assist or collaborate with the A/E in a program of evaluation of the owner's requirements, but this program review should be made to assess the scope of program within the budgets and schedules previously prepared. Although this is often a basic-design function, its significance in the CM process is for a strict definition and evaluation in light of budgetary and time constraints, whose significance is not as readily apparent during the formative stage as at later stages when detailed estimates are being prepared.

As appropriate, the construction manager should analyze the program in conjunction with the A/E to assess the costs and benefits of alternative architectural, structural, and mechanical systems at the initiation of and during the schematic stage and report these recommendations to the owner.

The construction manager and architect/engineer should jointly develop a schedule for all A/E work during preconstruction phases. The CM should identify all tasks, milestones, and reviews to be incorporated in the A/E's schedule; identify sequencing and time required to perform during each phase.

The construction manager should prepare cost analysis of systems proposed by the A/E and identify other feasible systems including cost analysis of these alternatives. The CM should prepare narrative reports for all systems being considered, to describe the advantages and disadvantages of each system. (These reports are in addition to the cost analysis.) They can include:

- Area: net to gross ratios
- Structure: tons/cost per square foot
- Lighting & power: watts/cost per square foot/watts per square foot
- Heating: Btu/cost per square foot/Btu per square foot
- Air conditioning: tons/cost per square foot/tons per square foot
- Plumbing: cost per square foot
- Total cost per square foot
- Furniture and fixtures: cost per square foot/total cost

The construction manager should prepare cost analysis of all materials, equipment, fixtures, and methods proposed; identify feasible materials, equipment, fixtures, and methods that have not been suggested; and prepare cost analysis of these alternatives. The CM may prepare narrative reports for materials being considered, to describe the advantages of each material.

CM SCOPE: PRELIMINARY DESIGN PHASE

During design/development the CM should independently investigate costs and availability of building systems proposed by the designer. The construction manager should assume the responsibility to advise the designer or the architect/engineer as to the availability of proposed building systems, his evaluation of such building system cost, and the availability and costs of possible alternate systems.

Independently, the CM should monitor budget and time schedules for the design phase of the project development. This schedule should be reviewed at regular intervals with the A/E's specific project objectives and design requirements.

Dependent upon predetermined time schedules and needs of the owner established in the prior and early stages of project development, the construction manager should assess the design together with the A/E to develop appropriate design packages for construction implementation. Such input will be necessary in the early stages of design to assist the A/E in preparing the appropriate documents for phasing construction if such phasing is deemed appropriate. Dependent upon the project criteria and needs, such phasing—also called fast tracking—may consist of issuing complete documents for certain of the elements prior to total design completion. In early stages it is possible not only to issue contract documents for construction implementation but also to identify long-lead-material items for early purchases. Such purchasing would be initiated and implemented by the CM on behalf of the owner, with the product purchased in this manner turned over to the contractor for installation.

During design development the construction manager performs necessary periodic reviews of the proposed design to monitor with respect to preestablished budgets and cost limitations. If during such review the CM evaluates the design aspects, he should review them with the A/E to formulate appropriate recommendations to the owner. The importance of a review and check of estimates at this time becomes more obvious after a look at the uncertainties of the price structure, evidenced not only by the steep inflationary spiral of the early 1970s but by the dislocation of the supply market in 1974. Such dislocation, which is not limited to petroleum products, has made it impossible to estimate costs with certainty over extended time frames.

The construction manager should review preliminary specifications prepared by the architect/engineer including quality control standards and criteria for site development, architectural, structural, plumbing, electric, and site utilities. The preliminary specifications should describe the following items as a minimum (including economic justification reports where required by owner):

1. Soil conditions (including test boring reports)

2. Footings and foundations

3. Superstructure (type of construction)

4. Exterior walls and trim or features

5. Interior walls and partitions

6. Room finishes, all surfaces

7. Floor construction

8. Roof construction

9. Stair construction and finish

10. Windows

11. Doors

    a. Exterior

    b. Interior

12. Acoustical treatment (type and where used)

13. Heating system, radiation and controls, including design criteria

14. Air conditioning and ventilating system including design criteria and scope

15. Electrical work, including design criteria, source and capacity/demand report

    a. Service

    b. Lighting fixtures, types

    c. Power system, demand and distribution

    d. Provide a brief description of electrical equipment items to be included in the project

    e. Signal and alarm system

16. Plumbing

    a. Pipe materials, all services

    b. Fixtures, all types

    c. Source and disposal systems

    d. Treatment, pumping or other special requirements

17. Waste compaction system

18. Security and life safety systems

19. Elevators and escalators, including design criteria

    a. Capacity

    b. Speed

    c. Platform

    d. Service internal

    e. Type

20. Other work, if in construction contracts, such as kitchen equipment

21. Owner furnished equipment

In accordance with the review of the total design which may include all design aspects such as the architectural, civil, mechanical, electrical, structural plans, the construction manager should consider both construction feasibility and possible economy that may be affected by different choices of proposed materials and possible construction methods. It is assumed that the architect/engineer in the development of a design and performing his assignment in a professional manner will make the most economical, functional, and efficient selections of materials and construction methods. The CM, however, serves as an independent third party to give the benefit of an objective and professional review to develop possible recommendations for consideration.

At the conclusion of the preliminary design phase, the CM makes a very important estimate. This is the first point at which major structural, mechanical, and electrical systems have been defined. This information, combined with the spatial solution of the schematic design, can be cost-estimated with a good degree of accuracy. The cost for each component and system can then be compared with the budget and with standards for the type of construction. Budget variances must be adjusted. This cost information should also be used as the basis for a value-analysis cycle by the construction manager.

CM SCOPE: FINAL DESIGN PHASE

The CM should review the drawings and specifications and continuously make recommendations throughout the design stage concerning the following:

1. Availability of materials and labor

2. Conflicts and overlapping jurisdictions among contractors and subcontractors

3. Coordination among the drawings and between the drawings and specifications

4. Construction detailing, to ensure that the methods, details of wall sections, other sections, etc., shown are easily buildable and adequate to ensure a reliable, permanent, trouble-free installation

5. Quality control standards and criteria

6. A final, detailed review and recommendations of the completed working drawings and specifications

7. On-site temporary facilities necessary to enable the construction manager, architect, and owner to perform their duties

8. Items of a temporary nature necessary for the performance of the contractors

9. Availability of and location of storage and storing area for each contractor and subcontractor

Prior to completion of the final design plans the construction manager together with the architect/engineer should analyze the total design effort and establish the appropriate division of work for the final contract documents and plans and specifications. This is required for the taking of bids or for negotiating of separate contracts. In establishing such bid packages, as these are described, appropriate consideration will have to be given to time of performance, availability of labor, overlapping trade jurisdictions, and related work items. Such review will also ensure that when the plans and specifications are issued to bid and become part of the final contract documents, upon which a contractor submits a competitive price or negotiates a contract, all overlapping functions will have been eliminated. Such review also will ensure that there is no omission of a specific function or specification for the total implementation of the project.

The construction manager prepares a detailed cost estimate of the proposed construction during various stages of planned development. Such work can possibly be limited to an analysis and review of estimates prepared by the architect/engineer who will have prepared such estimates in the normal course of design development. Because of the complexities of the construction marketplace and with the ever-increasing price pressures, an independent detailed take-off based upon a quantity survey of the plans and specifications together with a detailed unit-price estimate fills a useful purpose during the design phase and is readily performed by the CM.

Such detailed cost estimates can be utilized for comparisons with the preestablished budgets prior to the taking of competitive bids; or utilized as a guide with the negotiating of prices with preselected contractors, or may even serve as they do in some instances as a guaranteed outside price if a contracting entity takes on the implementation and construction of the work on such a basis.

In conjunction with the detailed estimate, the CM should review and comment on contract documents prepared by the A/E. These documents are composed of copies of all drawings, specifications, including quality control standards and criteria, necessary for the construction as described by the approved preliminary documents, fully coordinated for bidding of the various contractors and subcontractors. This includes all engineering drawings, plot plans, floor plans, sections, elevations, details, soil exploration data, key construction milestones and other data required to obtain complete bids.

Near the end of the working-drawings preparation, prebid CPM construction networks should be prepared. These networks establish the time of construction, including key milestones, which are very useful for control by the CM during the construction phase.

The construction manager may recommend the purchase of long-lead items. In this case, the CM upon the placement of the early purchase order should assume the function of monitoring the purchase contract. Such monitoring may consist solely of ensuring that all requirements previously established for the specified materials, i.e. a preselected pump or generator requiring lengthy fabrication, are met. It may also include expediting of such prepurchased items. In the traditional construction process expediting becomes the responsibility of the contractor who is furnishing a specified and purchased piece of equipment.

Often, however, construction is delayed because a critical item (one that becomes critical because it is on the critical path of the total construction project) is delayed during the fabrication process. Such delay can be the result of numerous factors beyond the control of a contractor and often only becomes known to him at the time he is seeking its delivery to the job site. The expediting role of the CM may require monitoring the fabrication process of critical fabricated items. The extent of such monitoring will be dependent upon many factors which may include the financial solvency of the manufacturer, and pressures on the fabricator of meeting other deliveries or commitments.

CM Relationship to the Architect

In Ref. 1, Robert A. Marshall, Jr., of Turner Construction comments on the special nature of the CM relationship to the A/E versus the traditional general contractor relationship.

> Some architects, feeling that they have a certain privy relationship with the owner that the contractor does not have, will resent the contractor's going directly to the owner to express his own thoughts during the design period.
>
> Other architects are staunch supporters of CM because they feel it saves them a lot of time and money that would otherwise be wasted finding the most economical way to build through trial and error while the job is already underway.
>
> Most of these architects will tell an owner—"Look, I don't know anything about costing or scheduling and I want to have a contractor with me now."
>
> The architect, of course, must be amenable to operating in the CM way. If the owner already has chosen an architect, he should discuss with him whether to get a construction manager for the job or not. The owner must make sure that the architect agrees with this procedure. If the owner is committed in advance to Construction Management, he must be sure to pick an architect who is willing and cooperative toward that approach.

Critics may ask: "If the architect performs his tasks properly, and the contractor is qualified, why is there a need for an independent third party, namely, the CM?" As evidenced from the definition of the tasks enumerated above (and this comment would also be applicable during the construction phase), the construction manager's role should be complementary to that of a qualified professional performing the architect/engineer's tasks and to that of qualified and competent contractors performing the construction work. The CM during the design role does not usurp or assume any of the roles of the architect/engineer. The design responsibility rests solely on the shoulders of the architect or engineer performing the design. The CM, however, acting as the owner's representative, has a total comprehension of the owner's needs and requirements. This understanding may have developed because of the CM's early selection and participation in the project—far earlier than the design implementation. Even if the CM has not been involved in the early phases, his duties will still have a broader scope because of his mandate and responsibility to monitor and ensure that the owner's needs are met not only within the owner's budget and time schedule but to conform to later requirements with which the designer or architect/engineer may not have as close an involvement.

The traditional design for a building or facility can require an input from the following disciplines:

Architecture

- Landscape
- Building design
- Interior design

Urban Planning

- Site acquisition
- Community factors
- Services

Engineering

- Civil—site work
- Structural
- Mechanical
- Electrical
- Specialties
  Vertical transportation

  Kitchen and hospital equipment

Each of the above disciplines, although performed often in the same design office, involves work by different professionals. Even within the same office there is a requirement for coordination of all disciplines. This is the architect's role and function as the project design captain and leader. The CM role is to assist and to aid the owner and project leader in performing their coordination functions while providing a total overview of the design tasks in light of the relevant project criteria and requirements.

REFERENCES

1. "CM For The General Contractor," Association of General Contractors Inc., p. 10.

5
Construction

Although it is not unusual for the construction manager to enter the picture for the first time in this phase, the construction phase is only one of the many parts of the total construction management tasks. Naturally, this is the critical phase of the CM process since the results of all prior planning, design, coordination, and in fact *all* the elements of the total preconstruction decision-making processes are brought to fruition, and the actual implementation of the project commences. At this point, too, the basic function of the CM undergoes a subtle change and becomes one of control.

In Chapter 4, concerned with the CM design phase, the traditional roles of the architect/engineer and contractor were defined. The basic definition of architectural and engineering services includes certain services during the construction phase. This part of the services is described as the inspection or supervision of construction and is traditionally rendered by the A/E designer. Even during the construction management phase, with an independent professional rendering the service, the designer can fulfill this traditional on-site inspection role, which would be that of the quality control inspector. More commonly than not, however, when there is a construction manager involved in the project, the inspectional phase of the architectural and engineering design responsibility is transferred to the CM. This is a matter of economics, as construction managers can perform the quality control with members of their staff who would also be performing the other CM coordination services during construction, and it represents a logical division of professional responsibility. With the CM performing and assuming responsibility for on-site quality control inspection, the A/E does not become divorced or removed from the project or decision-making process.

Whether a CM is involved and whether the A/E is providing on-site inspection personnel (or even a clerk of the works) or not, the professional responsibility and resulting involvement of the A/E continues during construction. The A/E is the designer, not only because of his contractual relationship but because in his standing as a professional he may be called upon to render consultation during construction by interpreting or clarifying the underlying design documents, if requested and as necessary (see Ref. 1). In addition, the scope of service for any A/E during construction will normally include as a minimum:

1. Review and checking of shop drawings and manufacturer's samples

2. Periodic field site visits for general inspection and observation of conformance of work to design requirements

The contract bid phase is traditionally treated as a separate phase or task. It is by tradition associated with design or planning, because no actual physical construction has commenced and no contractor is selected until bids have been taken or a contract negotiated with a preselected contractor to perform the necessary construction. To place the construction manager's role in proper perspective, however, the bid or prebid tasks culminating in the contract award are best considered as part of the construction phase of the CM activities.

A basic task of the CM is to identify the best contract breakdown for construction implementation. This occurs in early phases of the CM process. There is no magic number of contracts by which the construction of any facility can be performed. In some instances a single general contractor responsibility may be warranted, while in other instances the responsibility split among as many prime contractors as possible might be the most advantageous to accomplish the work within the necessary budgets and time frames. The type of project and facility will dictate the number of specialties and specialized trades required to perform the work; the time frame and budget will control whether any of the work should be accomplished in phases, i.e., fast-tracked. Only after such basic input will the determination be made of the number of separate contracts and their timing for award. In addition many states legislate the number of prime contracts required for the performance of public works. Knowledge of the statutory requirements regulating public construction is part of a CM's input into the bidding phase of any project. Such knowledge is as much a part of the professional construction management service as knowledge of statutory regulations (i.e., building codes) affecting the implementation of the work.

In New York any public contract work in excess of $50,000 requires separate prime contracts for the major elements of the work; these are prime contracts for heating and ventilating, electrical, plumbing, vertical transportation, and general construction. In other states this multiple prime-contract requirement exists, but in different forms. Massachusetts, for example, requires the taking of registered subbids, namely, competitive bids which are opened by the public agency prior to the taking of the general construction bids. These bids are then published and the general contractor in his bid has to name the subcontractors whom he intends to utilize to perform the subcontracts. The Massachusetts legislation lists a total of 18 subtrades including the separate mechanical trades, painting, and plastering (all finish trades). After the taking of the general construction bids, the registered subbids are transferred to the general contractor who then executes subcontracts for the amounts previously bid for the prosecution of the individual categories of work.

THE CM'S FUNCTION BEFORE CONSTRUCTION

Preparation of necessary contract documents and filing of permits to make it possible to take competitive bids for specific work. This can include preparation of complete legal documents, advertising, and taking the necessary steps to ensure that the invitations for bids will bring in competitive proposals. The procedures in public work are clear as to method of advertising for public bids. Naturally, all construction work is not performed through the public bidding process but can be performed by taking of private bids, those bids that may or may not be open publicly by a private owner from a selected group of contractors. Even with negotiated work it is necessary to prepare basic contract documents that will establish the contract terms and requirements between the owner and contractor.

The CM can prequalify potential contractors. Based on their knowledge of the industry and geographic area, construction managers can evaluate the capability of potential contractors. The normal procedure in prequalification is for the contractor to complete a form giving information listing:

1. Past experience

2. Current work load

3. Qualifications of key supervisory personnel

4. Financial statement

5. Statement of equipment ownership

6. Bank or financial credit references

7. Client and architectural references

The CM, even on public works, may submit recommendations to the owner on the capability of prospective bidders and advise whether they should be permitted to bid. On private work the prequalification process leads to the development of lists of selected bidders. Even though selected bidders' lists cannot be used on public work, bids can be limited to prequalified firms. The specifications may require specific experience for a minimum period of time for certain aspects of work (e.g., knowledge and past experience of precasting or particular fabrication methods). Although under the law of all jurisdictions, a public body is obligated to award work to the lowest qualified or bona fide bidder, such bidder has to meet the qualifications and technical requirements as reasonably defined.

An analysis of the marketplace identifies prospective contractors who would be available for the performance of the necessary work. This analysis will more often than not precede the establishment of individual contract or trade breakdowns, if any, that will be recommended to the owner as to the method of division of the construction work and its structuring for implementation.

In the competitive marketplace, it is usually assumed that bid proposals will be received on most construction projects. Dependent upon the economic climate, the timing of the issuance of contract documents for bidding for construction can also be important. Naturally, if the market is depressed there would be no difficulty in obtaining competitive proposals. Conversely, however, in terms of growth, there might already be a great deal of construction work in progress, and contractors might not be available or interested in submitting competitive proposals. In such instances, proposals may be made but would not be as competitive as under normal circumstances. In such situations, the CM should evaluate the possibility of postponing the taking of bids or of restructuring the bid documents into different packages to assure the owner of the most responsive prices.

When competitive bids are sought, the advertisement for bids (which is the notice to prospective contractors and which is prepared by the A/E) will give the requirements to be met. These are the instructions to bidders, which in many instances have been standardized either by professional groups or public agencies. The CM must ensure that these instructions are accurate, that sufficient time is given for contractors to estimate the work, and that the instructions properly relate to the specific contract requirements. A summary of information that should be found in such instructions to bidders is:

1. Site access for inspection and examination of existing conditions

2. Contract documents—procedures for clarification and interpretation during bid period

3. Form for bid and contract

4. Required security or bid bond, amount and time to be held

5. Bid receipt—time and place for delivery (including provision for opening and public reading as applicable)

6. Bid disqualification procedures

7. Owner's rights and time in which to evaluate, accept or reject bids

In addition the construction manager will ensure that sufficient copies of plans and specifications and bidding documents are available for distribution to prospective bidders.

After receipt of bids, the CM will evaluate the bids as to responsiveness and conformance to all requirements; such requirements on public work being a complete and total response to all requested bid information without deviation. This includes completeness of price data (lump-sum, unit, and alternate prices as required) and validity of performance and payment bonds as required. The evaluation process leads to a recommendation of the lowest-qualified and responsive bidder.

Prior to award of contract and recommendation to the owner for award, it is advisable for the construction manager to meet jointly with the successful bidder and the architect/engineer. At this meeting it is possible to review major critical items, not only any possible requirements of the specifications but also the delivery time, to ensure that the contractor interpreted the contract documents or specifications properly and is prepared to supply certain basic equipment and material as intended by the A/E. Although a specification may be clear, the contractor may select to supply an "or-equal" product because of a more competitive price or more favorable delivery time. Critical and major items can be reviewed at a preaward meeting, not to circumvent the normal approval process but to identify the major or specialty areas in order to avoid later surprises, as, for instance, the unavailability of specified material to the contractor or submission of substitute material as equal which would not be acceptable under any circumstances.

Dependent upon the method of contracting for the construction work whether by competitive bidding, negotiated contracts, or guaranteed outside price, the CM's role will vary in the contract award activity. His role may be to recommend award to the low bidder or the CM may award contracts in his own name on behalf of the owner and assume certain contracting responsibilities with his own staff. Such responsibilities in the CM process will be limited to general conditions, and minor construction tasks essentially no more than the coordination of trades and possibly including housekeeping and general cleanup.

CONSTRUCTION PHASE

A preaward meeting has already been held, a meeting probably held in any location other than the field site. Prior to the start of physical on-site work, the CM will initiate a preconstruction meeting. This meeting will be attended by all parties, namely, the general contractor, other prime contractors, the A/E, representatives of the owner and/or operating agency. The purpose of the preconstruction meeting is to establish lines of communication and procedure and to identify specific project and specification requirements; the CM will without fail not only initiate such a meeting, but ensure that there is later follow-up and coordination. More often than not such meetings are either overlooked or if held, do not accomplish their intended aim. The aim of the preconstruction meeting is simply to identify lines of communication and on-site authority. Representatives of all the parties and organization involved meet to review in a checklist manner the critical construction areas, procedures, and owner requirements. Although these are all defined in the specifications and bid documents they have not been previously discussed between the parties who now jointly have the responsibility for implementing the prior planning and design. The checklist might include, as an example, such items as safety requirements, access to the site for construction crews (separate entrances if at a plant because of union and jurisdictional trade considerations or identification), sanitary and medical facilities, critical delivery items, movement of contractor's equipment to the site, and administrative procedures.

The construction manager will probably initially be represented only by a limited staff because he will not yet have provided his full complement of field forces. The CM and his senior representatives are, however, on the job site immediately to properly staff the project. The CM will have to operate within a budget based on his fee or cost quotation for services. As has been previously stressed, each project's needs are unique (e.g., constructing a preengineered warehouse differs from constructing a hospital or institution). The scope of services can be different and can vary greatly depending upon location (urban versus rural; a new site or an expansion of an existing facility) and even dependent upon the timing of the retention of the CM which can be as late as the start of construction. If so, the construction manager may well be reviewing or evaluating matters not listed in this section but identified heretofore as early responsibilities of the CM.

A professional CM scope of services can during the construction phase include the following activities and tasks:

Permits.   Upon or even prior to contract execution, the CM must ensure that all documents necessary for the start of construction are in order and have been obtained. Naturally, most approvals must be and are obtained during the design process, but if the CM was not involved in preconstruction phases, a checklist of items that the CM should consider will include:

1. Zoning conformance—although one would logically assume that if a public body issued a building permit there was compliance with local zoning ordinances, permits may have been issued by oversight or error and in violation of a zoning ordinance

2. Easements—it is necessary to obtain the legal right or permission to cross another's property to relocate utilities temporarily or to use adjoining property temporarily to construct a facility

3. Utility permits (electricity, water, sewer, etc.)

4. Building permit

5. Statutory requirements such as may be required preconstruction by OSHA or EEO as applicable

Insurance Coverage. Although the contractor may have complied with all requirements of contract execution, he is obligated on most projects to file evidence of insurance coverage, as previously spelled out in a contract specification. Such evidence is required prior to the contractor commencing work. The importance of this is identified by the situation that, although any and all contractors carry basic insurance such as statutory workmen's compensation, every contractor depending upon his size and resources will carry different amounts of coverage; an owner may and usually does with the appropriate CM recommendation establish minimum limits of coverage for the basic policies of general and public liability, property damage, and automobile insurance. In addition he may require such special coverages as owner's protective coverage (naming an owner or a party insured) or extra hazard insurance for explosion or nuclear damage.

Coordination. If there is any one word that best describes the role of the CM, during construction, it is that of coordinator. Although this term is as misused as is the term "construction manager," coordination of the total activities of a construction project is the prime function of the CM. By proper coordination of all the various groups that are involved in the construction implementation of a project, the CM will perform his task most efficiently and expeditiously. The construction manager has the responsibility to have not only sufficient, but competent staff on the job site at all times to provide the necessary direction, control, and coordination.

In the traditional construction process the general contractor has been the coordinator for all the various forces on the job site. The general contractor has the responsibility to coordinate the work of his subcontractors and the A/E also has a coordination role as far as design conformance. In the CM process the coordination role for all activities of contractors, A/E designers, separate consultants, specialty contractors, owner, and/or operating agencies is clearly defined. The CM has this responsibility. Coordination does not only require the coordination of the efforts of the various contractors, both prime subcontractors and the general contractor on the job site, but also requires the coordination of the efforts of the other parties who are involved in the construction process. The tools utilized by the CM to perform this function may include schedule monitoring, job, and organizational meetings, administrative procedures of record keeping, progress reports, implementation of management information systems, or any combination thereof to effect a team effort on the construction site.

Scheduling. The most useful and significant control mechanism used by the construction manager is the previously prepared time schedule. During construction the CM will monitor and update the CPM or PERT schedule utilizing input from all contractors and revise as necessary. Although the CM has prepared the initial schedule which may have been included in the contract documents, it is essential for the CM at the beginning of the project, or even at preconstruction, to obtain the contractor's comments, the proposed schedule, and time requirements for the proposed work method. The contractor may have a different approach to performing the work; for instance, there may be idle equipment in the contractor's yard which makes it desirable to move additional bulldozers, scrapers, and trucks onto the job site, thus permitting the acceleration of site clearing and excavation. The resulting impact on the remaining work, as well as sequence of operation on other trades and contractors must be evaluated and scheduled by the CM. Conversely the general contractor or one of the subcontractors may have analyzed the work differently and may only propose to work one crew (e.g., carpenters for form work) instead of the two crews the CM may have assumed in preparing the schedule. It then becomes the CM's responsibility to evaluate the impact of this smaller work force on the overall schedule and to ensure that sufficient crews and work forces are scheduled by various trades and contractors to ensure the meeting of milestone dates within the schedule.

It is imperative that the CM obtain the contractor's interpretation of the required schedule and his projected work-force assignments immediately and evaluate them in light of the total project and previously established target dates. If there are conflicts, they can be evaluated immediately at the early stages of work.

After the initial interpretations have been received and the schedule has been adjusted to reflect this input, the CM has a continuing responsibility to monitor the schedule. It is he who must identify critical areas and ensure that the contractor, the approval agency, the A/E, or whichever party is flagged on the critical path is made aware of his responsibility to meet a scheduled date.

Quality Control and Inspection. As stated previously, this can be a traditional engineering or architectural function. Tradition also includes this responsibility being performed by others than the design A/E; certain major corporations and some public agencies, because of their continuing capital expansion and building programs, maintain staffs who perform on-site inspection service, with the A/E role limited to field consultation. It has also traditionally not been uncommon for an A/E other than the designer to assume the inspection role. In the CM process, however, it is logical for this function and task to be undertaken by the professional serving as the CM. As with the engineering or architectural function, the inspection of work requires the review and supervision of the work to ensure its conformance with the contract plans and specifications. This, as a professional task, does not require, nor is it intended to require, the direction of the contractor's labor forces. Such inspection, therefore, will require on-site staff and qualified inspection personnel to ensure that these criteria are being met. Again dependent upon the nature of the total construction, the extent of the necessary quality control will depend upon the specific work; it may require inspection of (1) concrete in place and at the batch plant, (2) pile driving (under the New York City Building Code pile inspection must be conducted by a registered professional engineer), (3) paving operations, or (4) structural steel operations. Separate tasks may require detailed reports as provided in the specifications prepared by the architect/engineers. The CM, through an inspection staff, will ensure that there is compliance with all these specifications.

Testing: On-Site and Off-Site. As part of the inspection process the CM includes all required testing and inspection procedures. The contract specifications and local building regulations will identify the required laboratory testing to be performed during construction. Certification of construction methods and procedures is coordinated and accomplished through the construction manager. This may, and usually does, require the retaining of services of testing laboratories who are structured to provide the specialized needs for such inspections. These services may include concrete testing (taking of concrete cylinders and concrete strength reports, etc.), soil compaction tests, fill analyses, welding inspection, etc. In addition, these requirements may include off-site inspection. They may also provide the necessary inspection at a concrete or asphalt batch plant, or possibly inspection of a precast or steel fabrication process at a supplier's mill or factory. Necessary inspection would be provided through the CM. This more often than not requires separate contracts which may be placed directly by an owner or be placed as a part of the CM contract and reimbursed through payment to the construction manager.

Organization and Procedures. The CM has to establish his own on-site organization with the responsibility of providing the coordination, inspection, and total services enumerated herein. The on-site organization may be structured as an autonomous staff from the CM's project staff, but if the construction manager has been involved in earlier than construction stages and broader aspects of the project, the field or on-site organization will be an operating arm of the complete construction management organization. A simple table of organization may be structured as shown in Figure 5-1. The CM will define and require on-site procedures affecting all parties. It is therefore the construction manager's obligation to document such procedures properly and to identify the responsibility of his own organization. This is only identified as a separate task under the CM's services to identify its importance. This, naturally, would be a task accomplished in the very earliest stages of construction at which time the procedures to be followed during the construction process would have been defined. Any of these procedures would have already been reviewed at the preconstruction and also possibly at the preawards meetings. The responsibility herein, however, is a total documentation of such procedures for all parties who would be initially involved and who would become involved in the construction of the project.

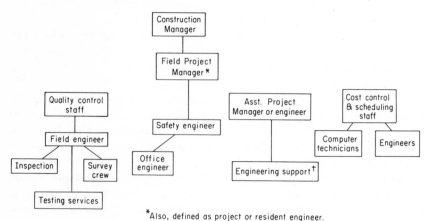

*Also, defined as project or resident engineer.

† Technical support as mechanical or electrical (not necessarily full time).

Figure 5-1. CM table of organization.

Meetings.   The responsibility for conducting meetings is not only a normal requirement for the CM but also for the contractor and the architect/ engineer. The professionals in their scope of services are required to hold meetings and to prepare written reports outlining the content of the meetings. It is listed as a separate task for the CM, not solely to identify that he, as the prime coordinator, is the responsible party for holding the necessary meetings to accomplish his coordination tasks, but also to indicate that the meetings per se are truly part of the coordination process. The meetings are not themselves the basic construction management function, but such meetings—when held and when properly directed with sufficient and scheduled frequency—can attain specific and direct results that move the projects ahead and on schedule. The CM is responsible for preparing detailed agendas for the on-site construction work. Often contractually the construction manager is required to maintain a minimum schedule such as monthly meetings, but actually in performing his task he will establish a schedule of necessary meetings tailored to meet the exigencies of the project. It may be necessary for the CM to direct periodic meetings with specific subcontractors—although under contract to the general contractor—to coordinate and resolve job-site conflicts over such factors as working space at least by bringing the prime parties together. The construction manager has the responsibility to bring all various parts of the project together to move it toward completion. The meetings on the job site are a means to furthering this end.

Shop Drawings.   The designer of record has the responsibility of checking shop drawings for contract compliance. This function often is treated as a secondary matter not just by the designer but by the prime contractor who has the responsibility of preliminarily checking a supplier's or manufacturer's submission.

The importance of shop-drawing procedures, reviews, and compliance cannot be stressed too much. In reviewing any comprehensive CPM schedule or any other schedule, the shop-drawing time for submission and approval is an integral part of such a schedule. The CM has the responsibility in the initial stages of the project for establishing a procedure which will provide for the orderly flow of shop drawings, commencing with the manufacturer to the subcontractor as applicable, and to the general contractor and to the A/E for review for approval. Naturally, if the approval process flows smoothly, no problems arise, because if the manufacturer submits the required and specified piece of equipment or material, the architect/engineer has no difficulty in approving it, and the manufacturer should have no difficulty in providing it within the required time for delivery. The construction manufacturing process, however, is not usually that simple, and more often than not submissions are made that neither match the designer's specifications completely nor are exactly the pieces of equipment that match the catalog numbers proposed by the A/E. The contractor will submit the cut or shop drawing of the manufacturer which meets the specification and offers the best competitive price. This, more frequently than not, is not the same as the exact catalog or manufacturer's model used by the designer for the basis of his specification. As each manufacturer has different components and materials to work with, the designer will have to make a comprehensive review to ensure conformance with the design criteria. With this process, therefore, there are many times in which the approval and checking process of shop drawings becomes time-consuming, because the designer may either reject a submission or may require additional information. The time element cannot be overlooked because, if a critical piece of equipment becomes involved in a lengthy submission, resubmission, approval, and review process, a multimillion dollar project can fall far behind schedule even at such an early stage of work when equipment is being analyzed for conformance with design criteria.

The construction manager, therefore, has the function and the responsibility not only to log and record shop-drawing submissions but continuously to monitor them in light of the schedule requirements of the construction. Part of this function is to eliminate the frequent problem that occurs between the A/E and a contractor when such shop drawings become snarled in the approval process or when a contractor fails even to make the first submission as required by the predetermined schedule prepared by the CM.

Expediting. It is the contractor's responsibility to ensure that equipment and material are delivered to the job site in proper sequence. This includes the contractual responsibility to expedite the delivery of material and equipment from his suppliers and various manufacturers. Why, then, is this responsibility found among the CM's tasks? The answer is simply that the construction manager is the coordinator of all project requirements, and the individual or firm controlling and monitoring the schedule is in the best position to identify critical material items. The contractor may have been assured of deliveries by the suppliers and, because of the expense and other commitments, will not elect to take the time to visit a factory or manufacturing plant some distance away except as a matter of last resort. Usually, by that time, it is too late and the project schedule has suffered. If the CM is concerned with the delivery of certain key items and feels that personal involvement is necessary to ensure the proper timing in the manufacturing process, such as in a scheduled production roll at a steel mill, he has the authority and should assume the responsibility of expediter. The CM is in a position, as the owner's representative, to contact the manufacturer, visit the plant site to make certain that the manufacturer is able to meet the prior commitments, if made, or to establish definite commitments for future delivery. The construction manager may be in a position to identify other material purchases being made by the same owner and therefore deal with a specific manufacturer on broader terms than the general contractor who may be seeking the delivery of one isolated item for this specific job site.

A schedule is meaningless unless there is total knowledge of all its integral parts. The on-site activity can be monitored and controlled; the off-site activity, or lack thereof, can easily be the critical path or weakest link. The added cost of making every possible effort to ensure that scheduled deliveries of material are met are negligible when contrasted with possible added costs resulting from delays and inefficiencies created by the unavailability of necessary material or equipment.

Record Keeping. The CM not unnaturally becomes the prime record keeper on the job site. His records will include not only those relating to the specific items that he is required to accomplish and pursue under his CM tasks, but records that relate to the total project and the activities during construction. As basic as this may seem, it is interesting to draw up a list of all possible records and files that should be maintained during the construction process. This list includes:

1. Daily log—record diary maintained by resident project manager

2. Listing of all contractors, subcontractors, suppliers with names of representatives and suppliers

3. Emergency—first-aid notices

4. Applicable regulations and codes

5. Technical handbooks as references

6. Activity and progress reports—daily, weekly, or monthly (as applicable)

7. Photograph—(progress) records

8. Shop-drawing log

9. Minutes of all meetings, including required periodic meetings

10. Correspondence files: (*a*) Among contractors, (*b*) With owner, (*c*) With architect/engineer, (*d*) With others

11. Construction schedules—original and revised

12. Cost accounting records—for work accomplished by change order or time and materials basis

13. Change-order logs and records

14. Payment estimates—including contractor's requisitions, projected estimates of owner's cash requirements

15. Insurance certificates

16. Progress reports

Payment. The construction manager is responsible for verifying and approving periodic requisitions for payment. In the normal course of business, these requisitions are submitted on a monthly basis by individual prime contractors. It is essential that an orderly procedure for payment to the contractor be established to ensure the contractor's receipt of payment for work previously accomplished without any delay. The first step in the sequence of payment is approval by the owner's on-site representative. This is the construction manager. It is his responsibility to check and verify that all the work for which requisition is being made has been accomplished properly. Based upon such approval, the owner can make payment for the previously approved amount to the contractor.

Change Orders. It is the uncommon project that has no changes during the course of construction. Most changes are incurred for the benefit of all parties. This may be because of an unforeseen field condition or because of a change in a preestablished requirement that arises during construction for which the contractor is justly to be reimbursed. Many contracts in the prebid or negotiation process establish unit prices for extra work. If unit prices for quantities or items of work are not established, the procedures for payment for extra work are specifically defined. Such procedures normally include at least limiting or defining the allowable markup for overhead and profit to which a contractor is entitled. This may be 15 percent, or 10 percent plus 10 percent. It is the CM's responsibility to ensure that all extra work items requested by the contractor are properly analyzed and reviewed. The first review, however, is made by the designer who will analyze such an extra-work or change-order request in light of the specific design or contract requirements. The CM will then review and evaluate the request considering the actual field conditions and the value of work which he believes has been accomplished. The change order then is recommended or not recommended, as the case may be. If recommended, a change-order authorization is issued and the contract amount is revised by the change-order amount. The same procedure for a change order is followed whether it is for additional (extra) work or a reduction (credit).

It is also the CM's responsibility to initiate change orders, if he deems that a change to the basic contract criteria is warranted during the course of construction. Such initiation takes the same course and procedure as an extra work request by the contractor, with the sole exception that the CM requests the contractor to submit a quotation for an extra or anticipated credit for the proposed change or variation in the course of the work.

Claims.   If any disputes or claims for additional compensation are not resolved, the construction manager has an added responsibility. In certain instances a contractor may feel that he should be paid for additional work, but the recommendation by the designer and/or CM has perhaps been contrary to such a request. The contractor may have been directed to accomplish work, and he may have filed a notice that he is accomplishing the work under protest for which he will submit an added claim. The responsibility in this task is not intended to infer that the CM has a legal position or posture; he does, however, have an active and specific role in the analysis of claims if, and as, submitted by a contractor. This role will precede any action upon the claim which may be limited to negotiation and resolution between the parties but can also, if there is no agreement, require the CM's more detailed analysis or even expert testimony if the claim ends in litigation.

All claims are not necessarily resolved by litigation. A not uncommon CM role is that of auditor—not in the strict accounting definition but a construction manager may be called upon to audit costs. Although a CM routinely certifies work for purposes of payment, he may well be required or find it necessary in performing his CM function to review and audit books and records of a contractor to confirm costs and cost allocations. This may be similar in substance to performing an audit for verification of costs incurred, but the essential purpose of the cost review will be to identify costs as properly allocable to specific work functions. This audit or payment certification task is often utilized in the claim process to arrive at negotiated settlements between an owner and contractor.

Plan Interpretation and Corrections.   The CM is implementing the work as designed by another professsional. All architect/engineers, whether required by contract or not, have the professional responsibility to deline-ate the scope and intent of their plans. However detailed a design or however carefully it was prepared, questions as to intent or for clarifica-tion will arise during construction. If a design requirement needs clarifica-tion or interpretation, the CM will confer with the A/E prior to rendering any determinations to the contractor. Architect/engineer, in his professional role, will furnish clarifying sketches or drawings as necessary. The construction manager, however, must also use his professional judgment in aiding the contractor if and when the need arises during the course of the work.

It is not uncommon to find conflicts; for instance, between plan and specification or between structural plan dimension and mechanical plan dimension. The resolution of such conflict is often more than an A/E coordination role but requires coordination by the CM. With several prime contractors or even with one general contractor and the other subcontractors, such design or plan conflicts—or even at times errors—are a logical area for the construction manager to exercise his independent role. He must evaluate the overall impact of the conflict or error and without any vested interest, can resolve such matters in the best interest of the project. Without a CM and his independent role, such matters often become obfuscated by the various parties, who make their interpretations to serve their interests. The designer may wish to avoid embarrassment or even claim of alleged error by blaming the contractor; or contractors may use any possible language to ensure that they are not responsible and that the work required falls in another's section. The CM is in a position to make interpretations and decisions; although they can be challenged, such decisions will more often than not avoid work delay and unnecessary expense.

Final Inspection and Acceptance of Work.   As part of the quality control and inspection function, the construction manager will ensure that prior to the contractor's leaving the job site and prior to final payment all work will be completed, all previously observed deficiencies will be corrected, and no outstanding work or corrective items will remain. Jointly with the architect/engineer the CM will make a full inspection of the site and prepare a detailed report of any and all work items outstanding and remaining. This report, commonly described as the "punch list," is thereafter utilized as the final checklist of outstanding items. Upon completion of all items on the punch list, the contract construction work is considered complete.

There are many different stages of completion, however. Although not actually complete until the punch-list items and all contract matters are taken care of, the project may have already passed through other stages of completion which can include:

- Substantial completion target date for essential completion of work making facility usable

- Beneficial occupancy completion—date at which owner occupies the facility or assumes operating responsibility

- Partial occupancy completion—date at which owner occupies a portion of the facility, such as certain classrooms or a wing of a hospital

The above dates and definitions have significance because dates have to be established to define completion of the work, which can amount to substantial completion, because of a liquidated-damage provision in the contract or time at which the guarantee period for a piece of equipment starts.

The dates for acceptance, occupancy, and takeover of a facility can therefore all be different, and again depending upon the nature of the facility, the duration of time between these dates can vary greatly.

Prior to final acceptance, which normally is tied in to final payment to the contractor, the CM must determine not only that the work is complete but that all outstanding contract matters are settled. These include:

1. Certification of payment subject to receipt of final payment to all subcontractors, vendors, and material suppliers by the prime contractors

2. Waiver of liens by all contractors and subcontractors

3. Filing of all required guarantees for the specified guarantee periods, usually for one year, except for mechanical equipment

4. Submission of all required operating and maintenance manuals, equipment manuals, parts lists, etc.

5. Completion of as-built record drawings, showing details of the project as actually built; this can be a joint effort for contractors, A/E and CM

6. Summary of claims, if any, that remain for resolution by negotiation or through legal or arbitration processes

The functions and tasks enumerated above are intended to describe the potential scope of a CM's range of activity. This is not to suggest that there is any single list of tasks that a construction manager must follow to perform his task, but he may perform any or all of those described. As an example, a CM may fulfill his role and achieve the required result by drawing up and monitoring a schedule; by using the schedule, the A/E and one contractor may be properly guided to perform the work as required. On the other hand the CM may not only perform all the functions described herein but control and coordinate the work being performed by separate contract for all the subdivisions of work which may number up to 40 or more separate contractors, without having to rely on one prime general contractor, who may, in the conventional process, subcontract the majority of the work to others.

The construction manager should conduct the final inspection jointly with the owner and architect/engineer in a manner similar to the following:

1. Inspect the project jointly with the owner and A/E between 30 and 45 days prior to the time the owner is to take over, use, occupy, or operate any part or all of the project, and furnish a detailed report to the owner of observed discrepancies and deficiencies in the work performed by the contractor

2. Inspect the project jointly with the owner and A/E between 10 to 30 days prior to the end of the one-year guarantee period provided in the contracts of the various contractors, and furnish a detailed report to the owner and the A/E of observed discrepancies and deficiencies applicable to such guarantees

3. Prior to final payment, establish that no liens have been filed and that all necessary guarantees, as-built drawings, operating and maintenance manuals, certificates of compliance, etc., have been submitted and that all operating instructions have been given to the owner's personnel consistent with contract requirements

The contractor(s) are usually required to maintain an as-built set of drawings. The CM should arrange for the file to be transferred to the owner. If it has not been properly maintained the construction manager may recommend a backcharge (from the retainage) to meet the contract requirement. As-built information is particularly important in the electrical-mechanical areas. As-built descriptions in these areas should include, but not be limited to:

1. Complete wiring diagrams of all mechanical and electrical systems, such as fire alarm, communication systems, motor controls, supervisory control panel, and temperature controls

2. Complete description of all mechanical and electrical systems, and their proper maintenance, including complete checklists, maintenance programs, and replacement schedules

3. Catalog cuts and shop drawings of all electrical and mechanical systems and equipment such as switchboards, panels, pumps,

air conditioning equipment, fans, air-handling equipment, coils, heating equipment, and duct work

4. Complete valve charts of all mechanical systems, such as cooling, heating, and plumbing. These charts shall indicate location and function of each main valve in these systems

5. Complete set of as-built drawings for all mechanical, electrical, and general construction, checked and approved by the A/E

6. All available manufacturer's catalogs, specifications, installation procedures, and replacement parts lists for building equipment and architectural products installed under the construction contract

SOCIAL & ENVIRONMENTAL CONTROLS DURING CONSTRUCTION

The National Environmental Policy Act (NEPA) PL 91-190 requires environmental analyses on all public construction projects prior to and during design. Recent state and regional legislation, particularly on the West Coast, has extended this regulatory domain to include private as well as public projects, and the trend in this direction will certainly continue.

Besides these general social and environmental concerns during the planning and concept-development phases of the project, the CM will be called upon to exercise certain social and environmental controls in the execution of the construction project. The following is adapted, by permission, from a statement of the Committee on Social and Environmental Concerns of the Construction Division of the American Society of Civil Engineers and defines the critical areas of concern for construction as follows:

Social Areas. These include land use, the visual aspect of the project, including security; avoidance of landscape defacement, such as needless removal of trees; prevention of earth cuts and borrow pits that would deface certain areas for a long time; protection of wildlife, vegetation, and other ecological systems; and visual protection of surrounding residential areas through installation of proper fencing, plantings, etc.

Historical and Archeological. This includes preservation of historical and archeological items of an irreplaceable nature.

Crime. The construction process often creates temporary negative impacts on a community, resulting in a crime increase. This can include local crime as well as fraud and bribing of public officials.

Economics. This includes impact of a project on the economics of region, such as a rapidly increased demand for labor far in excess of supply, with a negative effect on the wage structure in the area and economic harm to the area after construction has been completed.

Community Involvement. This includes hiring practices and dealing with the leadership in the community, whether it be of different ethnic groups, income levels, or organizational affiliations.

Physical Factors in Construction Operations

The effects of construction on land, air, water, and of the release of pollutants and toxic materials on natural resources are of major concern in construction operations. Water is often altered in its purity and temperature, and wildlife often is destroyed on land and water by construction of such projects as dams, power plants, and river and harbor facilities.

Vibrations and Noise from Construction Operations

Vibrations and noise have become of increasing concern through the increasingly large use in buildings of light construction materials. In addition, construction machinery has become larger and more powerful with the result that vibration of this equipment requires strict control.

Identification of noise-producing construction operations and equipment, and control of building construction noise must also be a concern of contractors. Noise-abatement codes for construction exist in many localities. Unless the provisions of these codes are properly understood and enforced, they may result in prohibition of two- or three-shift construction work and delaying of work that requires overtime. Also, some federal agencies have promulgated regulations requiring noise readings on construction projects. In accordance with such readings local officials may place a construction project in one of the following categories: *unacceptable:* noise levels exceeding 80 dB for 1 hr or more per 24-hr period, or 75 dB for 8 hr per 24-hr period; *normally unacceptable* (discretionary): noise levels exceeding 65 dB for 8 hr per 24-hr period, or loud repetitive noise on site; *normally acceptable* (discretionary): noise levels not exceeding 65 dB for more than 30 min per 24-hr period; *acceptable:* noise levels not exceeding 45 dB for more than 30 min per 24-hr period.

Equipment may not be permitted on federal building projects and generally should not be used on other types of projects if it produces a noise level 50 ft away exceeding the limits shown in Table 5-1.

Some jurisdictions prohibit overtime or second-shift work without permission, finding that it may adversely affect the environment of the inhabitants of the area.

Although dust control, noise control, and site runoff were once nuisance factors to the contractors, they are now recognized as environmental

TABLE 5-1
Limits on Noise Levels of
Construction Equipment

Equipment	Maximum noise level at 50 ft, dB(A)
Earthmoving:	
Front loader	75
Backhoes	75
Dozers	75
Tractors	75
Scrapers	80
Graters	75
Trucks	75
Pavers	80
Materials handling:	
Concrete mixers	75
Concrete pumps	75
Cranes	75
Derricks	75
Stationary:	
Pumps	75
Generators	75
Compressors	75
Impact:	
Pile drivers	95
Jackhammers	75
Rock drills	80
Pneumatic tools	80
Other:	
Saws	75
Vibrators	75

factors and can be regulated by government agencies—local, state, or federal.

In addition, the very comprehensive Occupational Safety and Health Act (OSHA) of 1970 has had a tremendous impact upon construction. OSHA is now the basis for most construction safety programs and is covered in Chapter 14 on Labor Relations.

Conservation of Energy in Construction

The environmental factors heretofore delineated are closely interrelated to the concept of energy conservation in the construction process. This is so because emissions from automobiles and power plants foul both air and water resources, because oil spills, drainage from coal mines, and waste heat pollute bodies of water, and because uncontrolled strip mining lays waste to our land resources. Increased use of nuclear power also carries a potential of accidental contamination of the environment by radioactive substances.

Yet five-sixths of the energy used in transportation, two-thirds of the fuel used to generate electricity, and almost one-third of the remaining energy—a total of more than 50 percent of the energy—is discarded as waste heat. Yet little research has been devoted to energy utilization.

In exercising controls on the construction process, the CM will be called upon to exert maximum effort in the control of productivity and costs through resource and energy conservation in both the private and public sectors. Heat-recovery devices and better thermal management can result in savings of energy sufficient to make or break a project's costs.

Aside from these savings in construction efficiency, the construction manager will, of course, have the best opportunity for overall savings in life-cycle costs during the concept development, planning, and design phases of the project wherein improvements in the thermal performance of buildings can be incorporated in accordance with the recommendations of the American Society of Heating, Refrigerating and Air Conditioning Engineers.

REFERENCES

1. A. I. A. Document B131, Contract between Owner and Architect.

II

THE CONSTRUCTION MANAGER

6

Selection of the Construction Manager

Before the selection of a construction manager, the owner must decide that the project is of a size and type which warrants the use of the CM approach. The project size or "critical mass" which warrants construction management is a function of many factors including: the complexity of the project, its location, total projected costs, level of the current value of money (i.e., prime interest rates), and rental rates or other measure of return which might justify crash programs.

From another standpoint, the minimum size of a project which can utilize CM is governed by the costs of putting together the requisite CM team with its diverse skills including management, estimating, budgeting, scheduling, and comprising economists; architects; civil, mechanical, electrical, structural, and construction engineers; planners; legal and real estate specialists; data processors, and other specialists. Clearly, there is a substantial overhead implicit in the construction management approach. Where a firm already is staffed with experienced professionals for the performance of the many required services, and has in-house expertise, it can economically handle projects of diverse sizes. Both construction companies and large interdisciplinary design firms have been orienting themselves toward this type of service and account in part for the major interest and impetus to CM.

On public projects, the critical size of a project in terms of construction management has been generally set by the GSA and other organizations, such as the New York State Health and Mental Hygiene Facilities Improvement Corporation, at about $3 to $5 million. Many of the reports published on the use of CM have concerned projects in the $10-million range.

SELECTION PROCESS STAGES

The process of selection of the construction manager follows a fairly standard series of steps. These steps are, of course, subject to legal requirements in the case of public bodies. These restraints include, but are not limited to, affirmative-action programs, requirements of the Occupational Safety and Health Act (OSHA), competitive bidding requirements, and other legislated factors.

The stages include:

1. *Decision to use construction management:* As noted previously, the size, complexity, and other factors must be considered by the owner in deciding to utilize CM as a form of managing a contract. The experience of the owner in other projects, and/ or the advice of his construction specialists, including the designer, will be factors in this decision.

   It is essential that the construction manager be selected at the earliest practical point. Usually the earliest selection is in the schematic design stage, although it is not uncommon to select a CM before the designer. This permits initial cost estimating to be more effective, and allows the CM to work closely with the architect/engineer in reviewing the owner's needs and requirements. This eases the burden on the A/E for preparation of preliminary budgets and reduces the natural friction which can occur when the CM enters the projects when the design has been well formulated.

2. *Source List:* The owner, in preparation for selection of the CM should prepare source lists of potential CM firms. On public contracts, public invitations to submit qualifications to the responsible agency are one means of accomplishing this goal. The lists may be subdivided by geographical areas as well as by competencies in applicable technical fields. Federal (and local) laws permit a judicious prequalification. This works to the advantage of the firms who might apply, as well as to the owner, by reducing the number of applicants to be considered.

   The source list should consider all types of CM: professional services firms, professional construction management firms, and contractors fulfilling a more extended general contractor relationship. Again, judicious selection by the owner of the form of CM which will best suit his requirements will assist all parties by minimizing the number of firms who may apply.

3. *Solicitation of Proposals:* Solicitations for public proposals usually specify the set of criteria on which the selection is to be based. These criteria usually include prior experience, specific experience, competency in the type of project, availability of qualified personnel, prior CM experience, and other factors as so aptly described in the GSA Qualifications Outline (Exhibit B).

4. *Evaluation of Proposals—technical scope:* Proposals should be first evaluated on a technical basis to eliminate unqualified firms, or more appropriately to select those firms which are best-qualified to perform the task.

5. *Evaluation of Cost Proposals:* The evaluation of the cost proposals by the qualified CM firms can then be used as the final selection process.

GSA PROTOTYPE

The requirements for public and private selection of construction management teams vary because of the legislative constraints under which public organizations must operate. Despite this, the GSA (Public Building Service) approach to the selection of CM teams for specific projects is used in a prototype in private as well as public sectors.

After GSA has identified a project as requiring CM services, the first step is the publication, through a public notice, that the PBS of GSA is interested in starting the procurement process for selection of a construction manager for a specific project. The notice describes the type of experience which will be required, as well as giving specific, but generalized, information on the building name and location, size, and estimated value. (A standard GSA format for this advertisement is included as Exhibit A at the end of this chapter.)

While the GSA has the advantage of the *Commerce Business Daily* for nationwide advertisement, those in the private sector have *Dodge Reports, Engineering News Record,* as well as other media means to reach the specific portions of the construction industry, as desired.

When a prospective CM responds, he is sent a letter, a sample of which is shown in Exhibit B attached to the end of this chapter. This letter is an RFQ, which is a request for qualifications. The qualifications are submitted in two steps. The first key step is the qualification of the firm or joint-venture team. It is submitted separate from the pricing proposal. It is evaluated first and scored. The qualifications are submitted in the 14 categories and subcategories described in the Construction Manager

Questionnaire which is part of Exhibit B. This assists the PBS scoring team in comparing the various sections. Scoring of the questionnaire may be accomplished in two basic ways. In one method, the scoring team is made up of specialists within PBS, who have broad knowledge of the CM process. Each individual scores each questionnaire, so that the final scores rating each questionnaire represent a composite or average.

In the other approach, the specialist in one of the categories scores all the proposals so that the best expertise is focused on the specific part of each questionnaire, but the final score is the result of an averaging. The method to be chosen for marking should be determined by the nature of the selection group, rather than an empirical procedural decision. The request for qualifications includes the standard GSA construction management contract. (This is included in a separate chapter.) The purpose of inclusion of the contract with the RFQ is to give the prospective construction managers an opportunity to review the contract which they will sign if selected.

The PBS may request both qualifications and price proposals simultaneously (but packaged separately). This expedites the process; but on larger projects, the request for price proposal may be limited to those firms which have been deemed to be qualified, or most highly qualified, as a result of the initial submission.

There is usually a scoring breakpoint which is limited either to five highest scores, representing the five most qualified firms, or only those firms exceeding a certain qualification in score (which presumably would be 5 or less). If the pricing proposal has been submitted simultaneously, only the price proposals for those firms who are deemed to be qualified are opened. If the request for price proposal is separate, then those firms deemed to be qualified will be invited to submit proposals. The GSA request for price proposal is attached as Exhibit C at the end of this chapter. It includes a letter format from the proposer to the GSA indicating the term over which the price proposal shall be effective, as well as a breakdown of the lump-sum contract price (for evaluation as well as progress payment purposes), and a listing of the staff which will be included as part of the lump-sum price. A preproposal orientation session is often held, particularly on large projects.

Following the opening and review of proposals by the CM evaluation team, discussions are held with qualified offerers concerning their management plan. The offerers are given an opportunity to identify areas of clarification, explanation, or elaboration of the specifics included in their proposals, but no change in the proposal is permitted.

The evaluation team has the opportunity to meet the key project personnel including the construction executive, construction superintendent, and management system supervisor in these sessions. In addition to permitting the offerers to comprehensively review how they propose to accomplish the project, the management plan contains a listing of deliverable items which make up the lump-sum contract price, and this list is incorporated into the project plan which is implemented soon after the CM contract award. A monthly invoice printout of the payment due the CM is based on an apportionment of the deliverable costs contained in the price proposal.

Although the offerers may not modify their proposal in terms of qualifications, they may submit a written modification of the price and scoping section. (This opportunity is given to all qualified offerers who were invited to meet the CM evaluation team. This invitation, in effect, also functions as an announcement of the finalists for selection.) GSA has a scoring system which gives essentially equal weight to three factors: qualifications, management plan, and price.

CM FOR GOVERNMENT VERSUS PRIVATE OWNERSHIP

The public sector constraints on construction management are different from those in private enterprise. This arises, in part, from safeguards built into the public construction process in relation to award of public contract to qualified lowest bidder. The constraints also recognize the special economics of public construction. Certain factors inherent in public construction do not impact private development. For example, the congressional authorization and appropriation process is unique within governmental establishments. Some federal legislation restricts the use of labor and materials, and other federal procurement regulations limit allowable cost. A GSA study reported that CM appeared to offer greater benefits for large-complex public buildings.

In the private sector, on the other hand, CM has evolved around the general contractor, with whom private enterprise has always been able to negotiate contracts ranging from fixed-fee to cost-plus.

Interestingly, the private sector is now more and more adopting the concept of the construction manager as an agent of the owner. This approach was basically developed in the GSA environment primarily because of its inherent advantages in format and effectiveness. Also, as stated by the GSA, they want no conflict of interest between their CM and his profit motives which can occur if the CM also performs the contracting function.

The nature and extent of the difference between construction operations in the public and private sectors is illustrated in Figure 6-1. This was taken from a comparative study of the GSA practices and private organi-

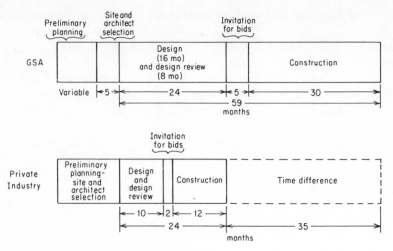

Figure 6-1. Average time for GSA and private industry to design and build a $10-million office building.

zation practices, conducted by the GSA. The illustration indicates that for a $10-million office building, an overall time savings of 35 months out of the project total of 59 months could be achieved in private organizations.

This difference could be achieved through better techniques, but generally it is achieved through the ability of the private sector to be more flexible in its financial negotiations with the contractor. Also, the private sector is able to be more flexible in terms of its internal organization, to more clearly state its owner requirements and needs, and to come to specific conclusions (because of a narrower management range of responsible individuals involved in the decision-making process).

Other factors in the projection of faster production of the private sector are reduced time for initial staffing, reduced time for site selection, greater sense of urgency to complete projects within original schedule, use of phased construction, and the ability to prequalify contractors. The private sector is also better able to utilize performance specifications which shorten the design period and permit the use of selectivity on the part of the contractor in regard to materials, products, and methods.

It is noted that the ability to shorten the project is also reflected in a higher range of fees paid to the design and CM teams in private practice as compared with public work.

The dialogue in the public sector as to the most efficient and economical method of procuring professional services is a continuing one. Because of abuses both by public officials and private practitioners, negotiation without price competition is for good reason questioned. Because of such abuses, the selection of professionals in all fields, not only engineering, architecture, and construction, is under continuous scrutiny. The Brooks Bill is an attempt to protect the public to provide for a competitive selection process while also recognizing that if price became the controlling factor in the selection of services, the level and quality of service available to the public sector would suffer. In July 1976, the General Accounting Office (GAO) of the U.S. government issued a report entitled "Greater Emphasis—Competition is Needed in Selecting A-E's for Federal Projects." The conclusion of this report is contrary to the Brooks legislation stating that there should be more competitive price bidding in the selection process.

TABLE 6-1

**Summary of Federal
Agency Selection Procedures**

Item	D/AG	AID	AEC	DOD	EPA	GSA	HEW	HUD	DOI	NASA	USPS	DOT	D/TR	VA	DOS
Advertise requirements for A/E services	yes	yes	yes	yes	yes	yes	yes		yes	yes	yes	yes		yes	no
Are A/E qualifications maintained?	yes	yes	yes	yes	yes	yes	yes		yes	yes	yes	yes		yes	yes
Preselection board used: (P)Public (S)Staff (N)None	One board (S)	One board (S)	One board (S)	One board (S)	One board (S)	(P)	One board (S)	Grants only	One board (S)	One board (S)	One board (S)	One board (S)	By GSA	One board (S)	(P)
Selection board used: (P) (S) (N)						(S)									(N)
Who selects board members?	Dep. Chief or Sta.Head	Dir. or Ch. Eng'r.	Head of Instal'n.	Head of Organ.unit	Dep. Ass't. Admin.	Admin.	Direct. or Reg.Eng'r.	Grants only	Contr'g Officer	Head of	Postmaster General	Contracting Officer	By GSA	Sta. Head or Asst.Adm.Const	Members nom. successors
Does selection board list firms in order of preference?	yes	yes	one only	yes	yes	no	yes		yes	yes	yes	yes		yes	yes
Does board interview firms?	yes	yes	yes	yes	yes	yes	yes		yes	yes	yes	yes		yes	no
Who is responsible for final A/E selection?	Board of contracts	Head of Proc. Act.	Head of Instal'n.	Head of Organ.unit	Selection board	Admin.	Direct. or Reg.Eng'r.		Contr'g. Officer	Head of Instal'n.	Postmaster General	Contracting Officer	By GSA	Sta.Head or Asst.Adm.Const.	Dep. Under-secretary

Agency

EXHIBIT A*
Construction Management Project Notice for Issuance in the Commerce Business Daily.

Y—Construction Management Services

The General Services Administration seeks construction management services for the proposed *(insert building name and location)* to provide approximately *(insert)* gross square feet within an estimated cost range between $*(insert)* and $*(insert)* million. Design and construction will be concurrently phased with separate construction contracts awarded as segments of the design are completed by the architect-engineer.

Consideration will be given to firms or joint ventures generally meeting the following requirements:

1. Experience as a Construction Manager or potential competence to perform construction management services; 2. Financial ability to provide the services required by the Government; 3. Competence in civil, mechanical, electrical and structural engineering; construction estimating, cost accounting and control; tenant coordination; project management; contract negotiation and administration; construction superintendence and inspection; and other related fields; 4. Experience in constructing buildings in the general geographic area of this project, or good recent knowledge of local conditions in the project area, or ability to retain others with such knowledge; 5. Proven competence in the implementation and maintenance of network—based construction management systems and in the application of systematic cost control throughout the design and construction process; 6. Good professional and business reputation, and an on-time and within budget performance record; and 7. Ability to provide professionally qualified key personnel with a minimum of 12 years satisfactory experience in the design and construction industry. Satisfactory experience should include:

   a. Eight years in work related specifically to the duties to be performed in the designated position for this project; and

   b. Four years in positions with requirements equal to those for the designated position of this project.

Prospective construction management firms or joint ventures who are interested in the project are invited to ask for Request for Qualifications Submission which will be issued by the office below on or by (insert date). Qualifications will be received until (insert date) at the office below, and then evaluated on the basis of the requirements and criteria contained in the Request for Qualifications Submission. Request for Priced Proposal will be subsequently issued to only those firms or joint ventures whose Qualifications have been determined by GSA as being within a competitive range. Only Priced Proposals specifically requested by the Government will be considered.

   General Services Administration, Region *(insert)*
   Director, Construction Management Division
   (insert address and location)
   (insert area code and telephone number)

(Note to GSA writer: Where appropriate, the above format may be expanded or altered)

*Revised: 4-15-75

EXHIBIT B*

Gentlemen:

Subject: Request for Qualifications Submission
Construction Management Contract No. _____

(Project name, location, and *number)*

The Public Buildings Service of the General Services Administration requires the services of a Construction Manager in connection with the project identified above. A copy of the contract which will be awarded is enclosed.

You are invited to submit background data with respect to your qualifications for performing services of the nature that will be required under this contract. Please submit information, responsive to the questions set out in the enclosed questionnaire, in the same order as the questions. Responses should be specific and precise, with as much detail as will accurately disclose your capabilities for performing the services to be required of the successful offeror. You may submit any additional information or data, not called for by the questionnaire, which you believe would be pertinent to the evaluation of your qualifications for performing this contract.

Your response to the questionnaire must be submitted in triplicate to the Project Manager, _____ no later than _____ local time at the foregoing location, on _____ 197___. No submissions received after that time will be considered, except under the conditions set out in the enclosed "Late Proposals, Modifications of Proposals and Withdrawals of Proposals."

The information and data submitted by offerors, as well as that obtained by independent inquiries, will be evaluated competitively.

The offeror having the highest evaluated score, together with all other offerors within a competitive range, will be invited to submit priced proposals. Prior to the preparation of their priced proposals, they will be given an opportunity to attend an orientation meeting at which they will be briefed on contract requirements and be given time to ask any questions. The priced proposals will consist of a lump sum amount for performing the contract (inclusive of profit and all costs, direct and indirect, including overhead, but exclusive of costs that are reimbursable under the terms of the contract), a management plan for performing the services, including a staff listing of nonreimbursable personnel who will be utilized in performance of the contract, and a tentative listing of reimbursable job-site staff by categories and numbers of personnel.

If you have any questions with respect to the questionnaire, please submit them in writing in time to reach the Project Manager at least five days in advance of the date specified for submission of the completed questionnaire.

Sincerely,

Project Manager

Enclosures

    a. "Late Proposals, Modifications of Proposals and Withdrawals of Proposals"

    b. Construction Manager Questionnaire

    c. Copy of proposed contract

*Revised: 4-15-75

Late Proposals, Modifications of Proposals, and Withdrawals of Proposals

(a) Any proposal received at the office designated in the solicitation after the exact time specified for receipt will not be considered unless it is received before award is made, and:

(1) It was sent by registered or certified mail not later than the fifth calendar day prior to the date specified for receipt of offers (e.g., an offer submitted in response to a solicitation requiring receipt of offers by the 20th day of the month must have been mailed by the 15th or earlier);

(2) It was sent by mail (or telegram if authorized) and it is determined by the Government that the late receipt was due solely to mishandling by the Government after receipt at the Government installation;

(3) It is the only proposal received; or

(4) It offers significant cost or technical advantages to the Government, and it is received before a determination of the competitive range has been made.

(b) Any modification of a proposal is subject to the same conditions as in (a) of this provision.

(c) The only acceptable evidence to establish:

(1) The date of a later proposal or modification sent either by registered mail or certified mail is the U.S. Postal Service postmark on the wrapper or on the original receipt from the U.S. Postal Service. If neither postmark shows a legible date, the proposal or modification of proposal shall be deemed to have been mailed later. (The term "postmark" means a printed, stamped, or otherwise placed impression that is readily identifiable without further action as having been supplied and affixed on the date of mailing by employees of the U.S. Postal Service.)

(2) The time of receipt at the Government installation is the time-date stamp of such installation on the proposal wrapper or other documentary evidence of receipt maintained by the installation.

(d) Notwithstanding (a) and (b) of this provision, a late modification of an otherwise successful proposal which makes its terms more favorable to the Government will be considered at any time it is received and may be accepted.

(e) Proposals may be withdrawn by written or telegraphic notice received at any time prior to award. Proposals may be withdrawn in person by an offeror or his authorized representative, provided his identity is made known and he signs a receipt for the proposal prior to award.

General Services Administration
Public Buildings Service
Construction Manager Questionnaire

(Project name, location, and number)

FIRM DATA

1. Present Organization

   If offeror is a joint venture, supply requested information on each involved firm.

   a. *Firm.*

   (1) Name, address, telephone, person to contact?

   (2) Name of parent company (if any)?

   b. *Types of Services.*

   (1) Construction management?

   (2) Project management?

   (3) General construction contracting, with building types?

   (4) Specialty construction contracting?

   (5) Design-build?

   (6) Architect-Engineer?

   (7) Combination, explain?

   (8) Other, explain?

   c. *Legal Form.*

   (1) Individual, partnership, corporation, joint venture, or other?

   (2) Date and location of establishment or incorporation under present name?

   (3) Former names, locations, and dates (if any)?

   (4) Names, titles, and addresses of firm owner, partners, or officers?

   (5) States and categories in which firm is legally qualified to do business?

   d. *Branch Offices.*

   For each branch give:

   (1) City, state, and telephone number?

   (2) Number and type of personnel?

   (3) Person in charge?

   (4) Capability of performing independently of main office?

   e. *Operational Areas.*

List geographic areas of the United States in which firm conducts business and value of construction work put-in-place during the past five years in each area?

f. *Size.*

(1) Present number and type of employees in home office, and in field offices (construction sites)?

(2) Number and type of employees during each of the past five years?

(3) Average annual receipts for the preceding three fiscal years?

g. *Facilities.*

(1) Office space, equipment, and computers?

(2) Field facilities and equipment?

2. Personnel

a. *General.*

(1) Policies?

(2) Recruitment, orientation, training, and development?

(3) Employee benefits and privileges?

(4) Employee relations?

(5) Employee average length of service?

b. *Employee Qualifications.*

Describe design oriented and construction oriented capabilities of personnel of your firm or joint venture, or consultants in the following areas:

(1) Job Cost Control,

(2) Architectural Engineering,

(3) Civil Engineering,

(4) Construction Superintendence,

(5) Contract Law,

(6) Electrical Engineering,

(7) Estimating (architectural, civil, mechanical, electrical),

(8) Construction Inspection,

(9) Labor Relations,

(10) Mechanical Engineering,

(11) Safety,

(12) Structural Engineering,

(13) Testing Facilities,

(14) Value Management,

(15) Management,

(16) Construction Management Control Systems,

(17) Computer Technology, and

(18) Other

c. *Competence.*

In what technical disciplines do you consider your staff to be exceptionally strong? Why? What are the names and specialties of the particular experts.

d. *Design Contact.*

Have your key employees been in personal contact with the designers or your construction projects during the design development? Extent and depth of the contacts?

e. *Continuity.*

(1) What is your capability to sustain loss of key personnel without adverse effect on a project or the firm?

(2) How do you minimize personnel shifts in projects?

(3) Recent history of key personnel turnover with dates, names of personnel and projects, and causes for changes.

3. Construction Management

a. *Organization.*

(1) Team, departmental, combination, permanent, temporary?

(2) Leadership and decision making?

(3) Top management involvement?

(4) Personnel recruitment, within firm or from outside?

(5) Number of personnel normally assigned to project during design, during construction, relationship to construction cost?

b. *Planning.*

(1) Initial

(2) Followup

c. *Design Related Operations.*

(1) Extent?

(2) Personnel involvement?

(3) Working procedures, coordination, followup, and cooperation with Contractors, A-E, and Owner?

(4) Inputting construction know-how?

(5) Market analysis?

(6) Interfacing construction contracts?

(7) Bid packaging and solicitation?

(8) Long range procurement?

d. *Construction Related Operations.*

(1) Extent?

(2) Personnel involvement, full, part time?

(3) Working procedures, coordination, followup, checking, and cooperation with Contractors, A-E, and Owner?

(4) Superintendence?

(5) Inspection?

(6) Technical support and consultants?

(7) Administration?

(8) Handling change orders, shop drawings, materials approvals, samples, as built drawings, and claims?

(9) Labor relations?

(10) Construction facilities, equipment, materials, and manpower?

e. *Overlap of Design and Construction.*

Describe your experience in managing phased construction activities, with particular emphasis on its special problems and their resolution.

f. *Responsibility and Liability.*

Discuss your review of the extent of your responsibility and liability as a Construction Manager under the proposed GSA contract.

g. *Associations.*

With respect to joint ventures or associations with other firms, please describe in detail previous associations on construction projects in sufficient detail to demonstrate your ability to effectively work with and manage a combination of firms. Indicate who the firms were if they are different from the ones proposed for this project.

h. *Improvements.*

What changes have been instituted in the last 5 years to improve your operations? Why were they needed? Have they been successful?

4. Construction Management Control System

Describe your firm's competence in the implementation and maintenance of network-based construction management control systems and in the application of systematic cost control methods. Give answers to the following:

a. Do you use computer generated schedules for construction management?

b. Do you require separate contractors to prepare their own schedules? Explain.

c. What is your experience in scheduling A-E activities?

d. What is your method of estimating construction requirements in pre-construction planning?

e. To what level-of-detail should a construction schedule be defined?

f. Which method of diagramming schedules do you normally employ, activity-on-arrow or precedence diagramming method? Explain.

g. Do you use cost-on-activities as a basis for control and/or payment?

h. To what extent do you rely upon the capabilities of your subcontractors to provide estimating know how?

i. Do you employ computer accounting systems in your work?

j. How do you use your computer systems to forecast work-in-place, manpower requirements, productivity, cash flow, and budget overruns?

k. What relationships do your narrative reporting systems have to your automated systems?

l. Have you ever employed GSA's construction management control system? Where? How? Results?

5. Innovation

Discuss your familiarity, involvement, and application of any of the following techniques or systems:

a. Project Management,

b. Conceptual Estimating,

c. Life Cycle Costing,

d. Specifications System,

e. Building Systems and

f. Value Management.

6. Workload

a. *Present Projects.* List (giving names of projects, locations, owners, estimated construction costs) work your firm responsible for, percent of design completion and construction completion, and firms associated with (if any).

b. *Capacity.* Describe in today's construction dollar the volume of work which your firm can handle at this time with a) your present force and b) with readily available augmentation (i.e. give number and types of additional personnel required).

c. *Long Term Record.* List in today's construction dollars, the volume of work your firm has handled for each of the past 5 years. Discuss reasons for any major fluctuations.

7. Local Knowledge

Show recent knowledge and experience with local construction conditions in the proposed GSA project area.

8. Procedures, Criteria, and Regulations

Discuss your familiarity with GSA's requirements based on your past experience.

9. Socio-Economic

Describe your experience with:

a. Energy Conservation,

b. Environmental Control,

c. Equal Employment Opportunity,

    d. Small Business Utilization,

    e. Utilization of Minority Businesses,

    f. Employment of the Handicapped,

    g. Other?

10. Financial Statement

    Attach statement of financial condition including regular dated statement or balance sheet.

11. Reputation

    Give name, address, telephone number, and person to contact for any of the following references you wish the Government to contact concerning your firm's ability:

    a. Owners,

    b. Bonding Companies,

    c. Financial Institutions,

    d. Public Officials,

    e. Architect-Engineers,

    f. General Contractors,

    g. Major Subcontractors, and

    h. Major Suppliers.

PROJECT DATA

General Note. Base your written answers to the following searching questions on the actual experience of your firm or joint venture during the last five years. The replies should be detailed and informative, and cover all the facets of the questions.

12. Project Experience—General.

    Describe your experience on completed construction projects giving the following information on each project reported:

    a. Project name and location;

    b. Project description;

    c. Construction cost;

    d. Design start and completion dates;

    e. Construction start and completion dates;

    f. Actual work you performed;

    g. Owner's name, address, telephone number, and person to contact; and

    h. Architect-Engineer's name, address, telephone number, and person to contact.

13. Project Experience—Specific.

    For one or more of the above completed construction projects (maximum of three) which you consider similar to or equivalent to the proposed GSA project, provide the following additional information:

a. Discuss any original or unique thinking or judgment exercised by your staff during the design development or construction;

b. Number and subject of addendum issued during bidding; why they were needed;

c. Number and subject of change orders issued during construction; why they were needed; and how they effected the construction progress;

d. The total construction award amount compared to the final prebid estimate;

e. Completed construction cost compared to the initial construction award amount and to the construction estimate when design was initiated;

f. The initial schedule in months for design and for construction compared to the actual time spent;

g. Extent of your involvement in project problems during both design and construction including any design or construction omissions, errors, other deficiencies, or changed conditions;

h. Discuss your relationships with the owner; the architect-engineer and the construction contractors (prime or sub);

i. Describe any post-construction problems in start-up, operation, or maintenance;

j. If you were doing the project again, would you do anything different? Why?

14. Similarities and Differences

In what way were your duties and services on the foregoing projects similar or equivalent to the services required in GSA's construction management contract? How were they different?

EXHIBIT C*

Gentlemen:

Subject: Request for Priced Proposal
Construction Management Contract No. _____

(Project name, location and number)

You are invited to submit a priced proposal for performing the services which will be required under the above-referenced Construction Management Contract (copy of which was previously furnished you). Your priced proposal, consisting of the following, must be submitted in three copies, each bound in a three-ring binder:

a. *Lump sum contract price proposal* (to be submitted on the enclosed forms).

b. *Management plan proposal,* consisting of:

(1) *Narrative* of your strategy for completing the project including both the design and construction phases.

(2) *Network diagram* of the activity-on-arrow type horizontally time-scaled by month and by the three phases (Design, D & C Overlap, and Construct) shown on the lump sum contract price breakdown, and vertically subdivided into bands, one for each of the deliverable categories comprising the lump sum contract price breakdown. The diagram will show the major work items necessary to accomplish the contract services in their logical interrelationships to each other and to major milestones and other intermediate events. The deliverable dollar amounts for each phase and for each category will be subdivided and apportioned to deliverable work items which, when accomplished, result in the delivery of specific services or work products. Offerors are encouraged to show on the network diagram not only the deliverable work items but other work items considered essential to project accomplishment.

(3) *Lump sum contract price breakdown* (to be submitted on the enclosed form).

(4) *Organization chart* for accomplishing the contract services, with names and position categories of all the nonreimbursable staff who will be utilized. The position openings proposed on the tentative reimbursable job-site staff listing will also be shown, but names will be omitted.

(5) *Duties* of all staff personnel, both nonreimbursable and reimbursable, shown on the organization chart, will be described in detail.

(6) *Nonreimbursable staff listing* (to be submitted on the enclosed form). If you do not propose to utilize personnel of any category shown on the form, no entry need be made for that category. However, your attention is drawn to clause "Staff (Nonreimbursable)" of the contract which will require, if you are awarded the contract, that you furnish the services of

not only the personnel shown on the nonreimbursable staff listing submitted as part of your priced proposal but also all other personnel as may be needed (other than reimbursable job-site personnel) for performing the required services. Your construction superintendent and one job-site clerk must be included among the personnel on this list.

(7) *Tentative reimbursable job-site staff listing* (to be submitted on the enclosed form). Give numbers by category and salary level of reimbursable personnel you propose to use under the provisions of clause "Reimbursable Services."

c. *Resumes* of the education, qualifications and pertinent experience of key personnel named in the nonreimbursable staff listing.

d. *Standard Forms 19-B,* Representations and Certifications, and modifications thereto (copies of which are enclosed), fully completed.

An orientation meeting for offerors of priced proposals will be held on _____ at ____ _____ to discuss the contract requirements. You are invited to attend the briefing which will be open to offerors' questions. However, your attendance is not obligatory.

Proposals in triplicate will be received at the GSA Business Service Center, _____ until _____ local time at the place specified for receipt of proposals, _____ 197_____. There will be no public opening.

It is contemplated that, following opening of proposals and review thereof by the Government, discussions will be held with each offeror concerning its management plan. The offerors are required to have their proposed construction executive, construction superintendent and CMCS supervisor in attendance and participating in the discussions. Offerors will also be given an opportunity to identify areas requiring clarification, explanation, elaboration or other modification of their respective proposals. All such modifications will be reduced to writing and submitted no later than a date to be established by the Government.

However, award may be made on the basis of proposals as received, without discussion; therefore you should submit your offer initially on the most favorable terms.

Late proposals will not be considered, except as provided in Enclosure e.

Proposals will be evaluated as to price and substance of the management plan (inclusive of the documents related thereto listed above). Although the successful offeror will not be firmly bound to strict adherence to its tentative reimbursable job-site staff listing, this listing will be taken into consideration in evaluating both your proposed lump sum contract price and your management plan, including the proposed nonreimbursable staff. Award will be made to the offeror having the highest combined evaluated score on (1) qualifications as evaluated previously, (2) management plan, and (3) price. Each of the three evaluation factors will have a maximum weight approximately the same as the others, with slightly greater emphasis on the management plan.

The priced proposal, as modified during negotiations (if applicable), of the successful offeror will be incorporated into and made a part of the contract as awarded. The management plan will be reflected in the implementation of the PBS Construction Management Control System and the work breakdown structure required by the contract.

Copies of the following documents are enclosed for your use in preparing your priced proposal. The successful offeror may retain them for use in carrying out the project. The unsuccessful offerors will be expected to return them to the Government.

   a. The PBS Construction Management Control System User Manual (first edition, amendment one) and PBS-CMCS IBM 360 User Instructions.

   b. GSA Handbook, Value Engineering, PBS P 8000.1.

To prevent opening of your proposal by unauthorized personnel, fill in the bottom portion of the label enclosed herewith and attach the completed label to the lower left corner of the envelope or other wrapper in which you submit your proposal.

Sincerely,

Project Manager

Enclosures:

   a. Priced proposal forms (four copies)

   b. Lump sum contract price breakdown form (four copies)

   c. Nonreimbursable staff listing form (four copies)

   d. Tentative reimbursable job-site staff listing form (four copies)

   e. "Late proposals, modifications of proposals and withdrawals of proposals"

   f. Standard form 19-B and modifications thereto (four copies)

   g. Label (form OF-17)

   h. PBS-CMCS user manual

   i. PBS-CMCS IBM 360 user instructions

   j. GSA handbook, Value Engineering, PBS P 8000.1

General Services Administration
Business Service Center

Gentlemen:

Subject: Priced Proposal
Construction Management Contract No. _____

_____

(Project name, location and number)

In response to your request for a priced proposal on the above-referenced contract, the undersigned hereby offers and agrees, if this proposal is accepted within _____ days after the date specified for receipt of priced proposals, to—

    a. Execute the contract and commence performance promptly after receipt of a letter accepting this proposal; and

    b. Perform all services required under the contract in strict accordance with the terms and conditions thereof, for the lump sum contract price (exclusive of costs which are reimbursable under the terms of the contract) of _____ ____ ($_____).

The undersigned further offers and agrees, if this proposal is accepted, to perform the contract services in the manner set forth in the Management Plan attached hereto, utilizing personnel as shown on the Nonreimbursable Staff Listing and reimbursable job-site staff to the extent indicated.

Enclosed are resumes of key personnel included on the Nonreimbursable Staff Listing, and executed Standard Forms 19-B (including modifications thereto).

The undersigned acknowledges receipt of the following Amendments to the request for priced proposal:

_____   _____

_____   _____

_____

(Offeror's name and address)

By _____

(name)

_____

(title)

_____

Date

Enclosures:
    a. Management plan proposal
    b. Resumes of key personnel
    c. Completed SF 19-B

Lump Sum Contract Price Breakdown

Deliverables	Design (D) phase	D & C overlap phase	Construct (C) phase	Total
1. General Management	$	$	$	$
2. CMCS Narrative Reports				
3. CMCS Schedule Control				
4. CMCS Cost Control				
5. CMCS Financial Control				
6. Design Development/Review				
7. Long Lead Procurement				
8. Separate Contracts Planning				
9. Interfacing				
10. Construction Development/Review				
11. Final Plans/Specifications Review				
12. Market Analysis/Stimulation				
13. Solicitation of Bids				
14. Managing/Inspecting Construction				
15. General Conditions Management				
16. Safety Program				
17. Labor Relations				
18. Construction Changes				
19. Construction Claims				
20. Value Management				
TOTALS	$	$	$	$

Note: The D & C Overlap phase starts with award of the first separate construction contract and ends with award of the last separate construction contract.

Nonreimbursable Staff Listing

Position category	Name	Principal work location	Phases Estimated man hours Design (D)	Overlap	Construct (C)	Hourly wage rate
1. Construction Executive						
2. Construction Superintendent						
3. CMCS Supervisor						
4. Civil Engineer						
5. Mechanical Engineer						
6. Electrical Engineer						
7. Draftsmen						
8. Estimator(s)						
9. Value Engineer						
10. Safety Engineer						
11. Environmental/Energy Specialist						
12. Data Processing Specialist						
13. Accounting/Payroll Specialist						
14. Procurement Specialist						
15. Labor Relations Specialist						
16. Secretary-Typist(s)						
17. Stenographer						
18. Clerks						
19. Other Specialities (list)						

(GSA contract writer may vary position categories to fit project. Leave entries under all other headings blank for completion by offeror.)

Tentative Reimbursable Jobsite Staff Listing

Position category	Number of employees	Employment extent (insert code letter)	Estimated man hours	Estimated hourly wage rate

(GSA contract writer leave entries under all headings blank for completion by offeror.)

Employment Extent Code:
A—Full time for entire construction period; B—Full time for part of construction period; C—Part time; and D—Intermittent.

REFERENCES

1. General Accounting Office, *Greater Emphasis—Competition Is Needed in Selecting A-E's for Federal Projects,* U.S. Government Report LCD-75-313, July 21, 1976.

7

Construction Manager Contract

The contract between the owner and the construction manager is a function of two important conditions: first, the form of contract between the owner and his contractors and, second, the operating mode of the construction manager.

CONSTRUCTION CONTRACTING ALTERNATIVES

In the truest sense of the term it is construction management that is an alternative to other traditional methods of contracting and construction. Construction management is an outgrowth of the needs of owners, public and private, seeking a better product. Because of the failure of the traditional construction methods to meet basic demands within budgetary and time restraints, the construction industry is looking to construction management to provide a better way to build. Construction management can be considered a transitional process adopted by the industry to better utilize available resources and management methods and systems which will achieve the ultimate objective—the finished product—whether it be building, highway, harbor, industrial facility, or residence. As long as the industry remains in its present highly fragmented form, change will be a slow and formative process.

The fragmentation of the industry is a reflection of the private marketplace responding to the basic laws of supply and demand and economic theory. As a consequence, through its evolution and growth the construction marketplace has become highly competitive. This competition together with the need for limited capital for those seeking to enter the marketplace has led to specialization, fragmentation, and geographic limitation. As a national industry, it remains unique with certain strengths, many weaknesses, and resulting inefficiencies. The meeting of its objective of serving the national needs is not a matter of single, unified effort as in the development of a single product or meeting a single objective, as the development of a sophisticated weapons system or the national effort harnessing resources to explore space. Without such single, unified objective requiring a single control, there exist numerous and varied methods of accomplishing construction. Many of these are no more than different methods of contracting for services and the ultimate product.

The numerous methods or alternatives which are utilized within the industry either in part or in whole consist of different approaches to contracting for services or production or different setups created because of different relationships between the owner, ultimate user, or occupant and producer (contractor). Many of these methods are modified depending on the size and complexity of a project, and many can be used as part of the CM process.

A summary of alternate methods of implementing construction would include the following basic approaches and contracting procedures:

Lump-Sum Contract

The traditional method in which a construction project is implemented is the lump-sum method. The owner, having retained an architect/engineer, has a set of definitive documents consisting of design plans and specifications prepared defining the scope of work required. It is necessary for the owner working closely with his A/E to predefine and have a clear understanding of his requirements, whether it be a manufacturing plant, oil refinery, highway, or residence. It is the A/E's function and professional responsibility to define such requirements in the documents prepared by him.

These documents must be complete in all detail and project definition to make it possible for the owner to seek lump-sum bids. This procedure has numerous advantages. Before the start of construction, the total construction cost is defined, and a definite contractual commitment between an owner and contractor is established. This is the most significant advantage as the construction cost is the largest single capital commitment that an owner incurs in developing a project. Other advantages can be summarized:

- Contractual relations between all parties, owner and A/E; owner and contractor are clearly defined

- Project scope and limits are defined preconstruction start

- Best price for work obtained through competitive process with cost for work established and agreed upon

The lump-sum-bid process can be utilized in the open marketplace, soliciting competitive proposals from all interested and qualified parties. The determination of qualifications is within the owner's judgment but subject to legal restrictions as with public bidding which require award to lowest bona fide bidder and consideration of all qualified bidders. The lump sum can also be used by a private owner utilizing a preestablished list of bidders. This is a list of invited bidders, which list is established by the owner usually with the advice of the A/E.

The definitiveness of the lump-sum contract makes it the established method of contracting and in many instances—as with public work—the *only* method utilized because of the statutory requirements.

There are, however, distinct disadvantages that cannot be ignored. This method limits time flexibility and can result in delays of project implementation with resultant cost increases because of cost escalation. In addition the proficiency and competence of the professional A/E are more critical with this method than others because all decisions relating to material and systems are made and fixed during design development. With other methods allowing more flexibility it is easier to implement changes or revisions to affect cost reduction, or necessary modifications to the initial design concept during later stages of work, whether design or construction.

Reimbursable, Cost-Plus, and Negotiated Contracts

The parties involved in this contracting method are the same as in the traditional form of contracting, the lump-sum method. There will be an owner, a separate A/E and the contractor. All the same steps and functions as under the lump-sum contract may be performed with similar requirements and under the same restrictions. The only difference could be in the method of reimbursement for the work performed.

There are numerous variations and adaptations of the reimbursable cost type of contracts. These can include:

1. *Cost Plus Fixed Fee (CPFF).* All costs within predetermined yardsticks or in accordance with specific regulations are reimbursed by the owner to the contractor, with the contractor being paid a fixed sum which represents profit (his fee). This sum is established at time of contract award. A variation on the lump-sum fee is the percentage fee wherein the fee is established as a percentage of the total cost. Although the initial fee may be arrived at by using percentage calculation, it is normally set as a fixed sum. An owner will be seeking the best price and for obvious reasons establishing the contractor's profit as a percentage of cost always will give rise to the

inevitable question: Is the contractor controlling costs as efficiently as he should when he stands to gain by increases in the cost? For this reason the fixed or lump-sum fee is normally used.

2. *Cost Plus Bid Fee.*   Again the costs are to be reimbursed as incurred within predetermined yardsticks. In this instance, however, in lieu of negotiating the fee or profit with one contractor, an owner will issue a request for proposals to a select number of contractors, all of whom he believes are in an equal or at least similar position to build the required facility; or possibly he may include the fee to be charged among several factors including capability, past experience, and performance in the evaluation of the contractors from whom the successful one is selected. The bid fee then is established precontractor selection and is incorporated in the contract between the parties. Naturally, in order to quote a fee, it is calculated on the basis of what is established as the project scope whether from a complete set of bidding documents, as with the lump sum, or from a general description of project magnitude and scope if design parameters remain to be fixed.

Construction can be started before plans and design criteria are completed. Time restraints, such as having a school ready for occupancy or placing a plant in production to meet preestablished dates, may well make it desirable to start construction at the earliest time possible.

Without complete plans and specifications it is not possible to advertise for competitive and fixed lump-sum bids and therefore a cost-plus method of reimbursement becomes a desirable and practical means of meeting the owner's objective.

In many instances in private construction, the project requirements are not fully established nor does the owner wish to make all final decisions required for the issuance of complete and detail bidding documents prior to the start of construction. Such decisions may only relate to finish details but are still ones that would impact the cost. In such instances again the cost-plus method of contracting becomes the logical choice for the owner.

Other situations which make cost-plus methods of contracting desirable include projects which are not readily marketable because of unique requirements and projects to be constructed in remote and not readily accessible locations. In such instances a cost-plus arrangement is utilized to ensure the owner the best and most competitive price. If the contractor had to submit a lump-sum price, he could well have to include contingencies to cover unforeseen expenses and costs which might or might not be incurred, or be given the opportunity to bid with substantial markups because of limited or no foreseeable competition. Although contingencies in bid estimates and prices are not uncommon, both contractor and owner would agree, in unusual situations, that each party's interest would best be served by adopting a procedure obviating this need. The cost-plus method would therefore be the logical choice for both parties.

3. *Guaranteed Maximum (or Outside Maximum Price Including Fee).* This method is one often used as either a direct substitute for a lump-sum, or cost-plus, or modification of either contracting system. No owner wishes or is in a position to issue a blank check for building a new facility; all new building, improvement, maintenance, or repair is accomplished within preestablished budgets. If the budget is exceeded, new appropriations must be sought. In many instances first budgets are final cost ceilings, and if cost increases during design and construction are identified, the project scope must be modified or reduced to effect cost savings.

The maximum or guaranteed price is established before the start of construction with the contractors agreeing to perform the work within the ceiling. If the ceiling is exceeded, the excess cost is borne by the contractor unless there has been an increase in the scope of the project, in which instance a change order would be issued reflecting the cost adjustment, as it would be under the lump-sum form of contract. Conversely, if the work is accomplished below the ceiling, the owner pays no more than actual costs incurred. Many times this method is utilized to provide an incentive; if the costs are less than the agreed-upon ceiling, the savings are shared by owner and contractor in a predetermined ratio. Otherwise it can well be argued: What purpose does the maximum or ceiling achieve? Is it not the same as a lump-sum form without the incentive to the contractor to perform as economically as possible with the basic exception of meeting the upset price?

The reason for use of this method of contracting is usually

to give the owner greater flexibility. The need for flexibility is usually twofold, for purposes of time and lack of definition of project requirements.

In the private sector, the general contractor type of construction manager often has this type of contract, combining the construction and management roles. It would appear to solve the adversarial nature of the owner-contractor interface. The resolution, however, is not automatic. Specific ground rules must be set within the contract to enable the CM to function continually within the owner's interest. This is not always clear-cut. For instance, it may be convenient for the owner to have the prerogative of assigning part of the construction directly to the work force employed by the CM. When this occurs, the CM is wearing two business hats simultaneously and is caught in a definite conflict of interests.

Conversely, if the CM-owner contract precludes use of the construction management forces on the job, it may withhold from the owner one of the principal assets of the CM.

Negotiated Contract (Competitive and Noncompetitive)

Although many elements of the cost-plus method exist in this traditional method of contracting, the negotiated contract is often classified separately within the industry. The end result of the negotiated contract can be any form of contracting previously described, lump-sum or cost-plus. It is dependent, however, upon plan-development status or specific owner or project requirements.

A typical situation might encompass a preselected list of contractors being invited to submit proposals describing:

- Capabilities, past experience in specific area (similar to qualifications considered in selection of design professional)

- Availability of personnel to accomplish work within required time frame

- Estimate (or bid) price

- Proposed method of compensation including amount of fee

The above factors would form the basis of selection of one contractor, leading to negotiation of the contract basis including method of payment for the work. Again, depending upon all circumstances the option exists for selection on a competitive basis in this instance from a limited and preselected (invited) group of contractors or negotiation on a noncompetitive basis.

The relationship among the parties involved in the construction process is the same as in any of the traditional contracting methods. The negotiated contract form is another means utilized to achieve the end result of a completed project.

Design-Build

As the term implies the design-build approach establishes a single administrative, management, and professional responsibility for the two separate functions of design and construction. The owner enters into one agreement for both. The method of contracting can be any of the traditional methods or modifications previously described.

This procedure is utilized only when an owner has in-house staff capability or is able to structure the monitoring of the work for close control having established a definitive program and strict criteria to which the design-build contractor must adhere.

A very simple form and example of the design-build approach is the purchase of a new single residence. The homeowner knows his basic requirements of number of rooms, baths, and types of finishes. His requirements are tailored to his budget and then he enters the marketplace to seek his product. The marketplace is able to respond by offering a predesigned and standard facility which a single contractor can utilize and modify to meet the prospective homeowner's requirements. If a predesigned or standard structure does not meet the requirement, the contractor may modify the plans during construction based upon his know-how and experience or may retain a professional (architect or engineer) to prepare the design and incorporate the revisions in the plan. The homeowner, however, is still only dealing with one party: the home builder performing the design-build function.

Translated into the context and complexity of industrial and heavy construction, many more variable factors must be taken into account in this method.

Having single-contract responsibility is a distinct advantage to an owner. In establishing the contract scope, it is necessary, however, for the owner to have preestablished and definitive design criteria available identifying his requirements. This he may be able to do with his own staff, or if not, it may be necessary for him to retain outside professional assistance to develop the program outline and specification. Such development can well necessitate work effort as extensive as the preparation of preliminary design plans.

This method can also be used to obtain comparative designs and construction approaches from separate teams or groups. This method can be utilized by seeking competitive proposals to meet an owner's preestablished criteria within the preestablished budget. Such proposals will be utilized to establish final design criteria and total project requirements.

Although there is a distinct advantage of single-contract responsibility, the design-build approach—other than in specialty areas such as oil and chemical process work—will require the formation of a project team consisting of a contractor and design professionals who have the expertise and knowledge to prepare plans for the work. Since the main cost of the project is the construction, and the design is only a small fraction of the total cost, the project team is usually created with the contractor being the prime contracting party and the professional groups under subcontract to him. Even though there are instances of associations, joint venture, or joint financial interest, the design group or groups usually have a secondary interest or are under the contract control of the contractor because of their limited financial interest in the total project as a whole. This can create a distinct disadvantage because of the loss of independence of the outside professional check and balance which exists under the traditional separation of contracting in which the A/E is under contract to the owner.

The design-build approach can be employed as a construction management option, wherein the CM is the lead organization in the venture. While any of the three major CM modes could lead in the design-build approach, the GC-CM would probably be the predominant selection.

Owner considerations in the selection of the design-build team should include:

- Owner's staff—internal for project review and control

- Design-build team structure and capability

- Budgetary restraints and controls

The design-build method can be used on a competitive basis. The competition is not based upon the same design or design concept as under the lump-sum bid and contract. This is also true of turn-key construction which broadens the design-build concept.

An innovative approach for the design-build approach is the design-build procedure utilized by the Dormitory Authority of the State of New York which incorporates and takes advantage of the basic element of this approach. Because of the necessity of delivery of a facility (dormitory, hospital, etc.) within a preestablished budget fixed by the preceding bond issue, the D.A. ensures that the work is accomplished within such limitation by using this procedure. It consists of:

1. Establishment of a program of requirements

2. Refinement of program with technical assistance by outside consultant culminating in the development of performance specification

3. Establishment of evaluation criteria for solution to be eventually submitted by design-build teams

4. Definition of cost and establishment of fixed price to be allocated for design and construction

5. Invitation of competitive qualification proposals from architect/builder teams from which three to six teams are selected to enter into the design competition

6. Proposals received in response to the specific request for proposal (RFP) which includes previously prepared performance specification (step 2) and evaluation criteria (step 3); proposals from final competitors include proposed program solution and normally have to be carried through to preliminary plans. (As with competition design, the finalists are paid a fixed sum which partially offsets the costs of the detailed proposal preparation.)

7. Proposals are evaluated and judged in accordance with the preestablished criteria

8. Contract is entered into with successful design/builder team; the contract is based on final design development documents

9. Construction with supervision and control by the owner or his representative

This procedure combines elements of competition within a preestablished price structure. The owner does not define the specific elements and requirements of his program but sets monetary limits on the required performance or function of the proposed facility. He then selects what is proffered to him as the best solution. All these elements are found in turn-key construction.

Turn Key

As with the design-build method, turn-key construction utilizes a single contractor for all functions. There is the one administrative, management, and professional responsibility for design and construction. There is a single party under contract to an owner to fulfill these functions in addition to other functions that may be necessary to implement a project. These may include site selection, land acquisition, and financing all tasks that may be necessary to make the turn key complete. As the term implies, it is an abbreviation for "turn the key," comprising all functions required to enable an owner to turn the key (open the door) and start operating his newly developed and acquired facility.

In the description of design-build functions, reference was made to design-build teams consisting of separate professional and contracting organizations forming associations, joint ventures, or a project team to perform the combined and total service. Although the design-build process can and is performed by the single company with full capability, turn-key service normally is only a single-company function. Such companies, who are most predominant in the oil, chemical, utility industries (Brown & Root, Stone & Webster, Fluor, Foster-Wheeler, EBASCO, etc.), have the in-house capability to render the multifaceted tasks of turn-key construction. This in-house capability is not only technical but includes financial resources that enable a single company to assume multimillion-dollar commitments. Although the owner or ultimate consumer, as the beneficiary of the work to be accomplished, will eventually pay for all costs, interim financing or even arranging financing can be part of the turn-key function and service.

The term "turn key," although as broadly and variedly used within the industry as is "construction management," specifically encompasses the single-contractor responsibility to render and perform all services to bring a plant on line or facility ready for production. Within the turn-key process the single contractor or managing company may be performing many of the tasks of a construction manager. The turn-key contractor, however, has a direct financial interest in the work and final product. He is in the business to build the facility. The cost of construction is the largest single cost incurred in the development of a facility from time of inception to start of operation. The turn-key company's prime business reason and purpose is to build facilities, and its incentive, profit potential, and rate of return on capital investment are related mainly to the construction. The other services are ancillary to the basic purpose of the company although such services and functions may be highly specialized and profitable to the turn-key company in themselves. The services can encompass as wide a range as:

- Site selection

- Site acquisition (the cost of land can be a substantial part of an owner's investment; sometimes as significant a cost as the construction, but it is not customary for a turn-key company to have a financial interest in the real estate itself)

- Financing, short- and/or long-term

- Planning and feasibility analysis

- Design

- Construction

- Equipment procurement

Where design-build may include construction management, the turn-key approach always provides total project management, including CM as a subset.

Leaseback

Leaseback agreements are not methods of contracting but are methods by which an owner can obtain the use of a facility. It is identified as an alternate, although in order to construct the facility, the owner (in this case a developer or contractor) may have utilized the CM process, any of the other alternates discussed, or a variation or modification of any of them.

A leaseback arrangement consists of leasing a completed facility to the ultimate user. This is a common arrangement utilized either by parties who own land and wish to stimulate its development or those who have resources and are in a position to finance construction for another benefit.

The reason that this method of developing a capital plant or facility is utilized is a matter of financing. The ultimate user although requiring additional plant area or warehousing may be in a better position to pay rent than to have to arrange the financing of the total capital plant improvement. The payment of rent for a period of years may be for a myriad of reasons including ability to borrow, convenience (not having to plan, design, and build), availability of facility because of speed of special-ist firms being able to complete the facility.

The leaseback, therefore, is not a construction method but a contracting and financing method between parties to arrange for the construction of a new facility. The relationship of the parties, owner, A/E, contractor, managers becomes different because the owner, in strict legal terms as he retains title to the property, is building to meet demands and needs for others. This will have an impact upon the construction process as this preidentified need will dictate types of construction, speed of erection, and quality of work. These, together with his own skills, will be the determining factors for the owner in selecting the method or alternate of accomplishing the work.

THE CM CONTRACT

Construction management contracts may be of any of the standard types used in construction work. However, CM should be a professional service and, as such, contracts should follow the guidelines which set out the professional nature of such services.

The preferred type of CM contract arrangement is the cost-plus-negotiated-fixed-fee form. Reimbursement is here made for actual costs of all CM services (including salaries, overhead, and defined nonsalary expenses) plus a fixed amount for contingencies, interest on invested capital, readiness to serve, and profit. The contract terms may provide for reimbursement also for specified cost items, or even to provide incentive to seek value engineering or other cost- or time-savings benefits. Where this form of contract is used, it may be the basis for firm fixed-price contracts let by public bid.

Where construction management services are extended to include elements of general contractor services, awards may also be made for service used on CPFF contracts where the general contractor will procure all major construction work from subcontractors.

The question of the construction management fee must be specifically addressed in the CM contract. The method of setting the fee has a direct effect upon the complexity of the contract form. For instance, in the guaranteed-maximum-price (GMP) form of CM-owner relationship, it is necessary to spell out very carefully what is (and what is not) included in the base fee paid to the CM, as well as the method(s) of compensation for nonfee work.

CM FEES

Fees for construction management work may range from 0.5 to 5.0 percent of project cost and vary inversely with the size of the project.

Different state and municipal agencies have developed standard fee schedules for CM work.

The basic fees normally include compensation of officers and principals of the CM firm; home-office salaries (including but not limited to the construction, purchasing, accounting, estimating, and cost control departments of the firm) and related payroll taxes, insurance and pensions; home-office engineers' salaries with related payroll taxes, insurance and pensions; salaries of general supervisory employees who do not devote full time to the project, with related payroll taxes, insurance, and pensions; professional fees (including legal and accounting) and bookkeeping expenses; cost of home-office general-facilities overhead (including but not limited to rent, light, heat and water, insurance related to home office, telephone, telegraph, sales, printing expense, stationery and postage, and miscellaneous office expense); salaries of field inspection personnel and their supervisors, with related payroll taxes, insurance, and pensions; travel and expediting costs; taxes and other than sales and use taxes; interest expense; advertising, dues and subscriptions; electronic data processing services; contributions; recruitment costs; and profit.

On public contracts, costs (exclusive of profit and overhead) for which reimbursement may be authorized in advance include such items as:

1. The costs of all job-site materials used in providing the general condition items.

2. The costs of all job-site labor used in providing the general condition items, including the salaries of foremen and other employees while engaged on the project (but excluding salaries of general supervisory employees, the construction executive, the construction superintendent, or officers) subject to the prior approval of the project manager of all job-site personnel, including the number of such personnel, their job classifications, and salaries.

3. All payroll charges for such job-site personnel, such as FICA and other payroll taxes, workmen's compensation, disability benefits and unemployment insurance as required by law and wage supplements paid to labor organizations in accordance with current labor agreements; vacation expense and sick-leave allowances for such personnel not covered by labor agreements shall be reimbursed in accordance with the policy and trade practices applicable to wages or salaries paid to such employees for work in connection with the project, subject to the prior approval of the owner; provided however, the contractor must comply with the labor standard provisions applicable to the contract.

4. The cost of all plant equipment owned by the CM at rental rates to be determined by the owner in accordance with established principles for the derivation of costs of plant properly chargeable to job-site operations. The CM furnishes its own plant and equipment, if available. For these purposes the rental rate on self-owned equipment should be as listed in

the Associated Equipment Distributor's publication of nationally averaged rates for the appropriate year, for the particular item of equipment. However, the total amount of rental to be allowed by the owner for any item of self-owned equipment should not exceed the fair market value of such item at the time of its first use on the project.

5. Rental costs of equipment rented from others; provided however, that every agreement under which the CM rents equipment from others should contain an option or options for his purchase of such equipment, if available.

6. Transportation costs on equipment and materials.

7. Restricted quantities of small tools and supplies, which include—among other items—all fire extinguishers and all special and protective wearing apparel.

8. The cost of fuel and lubricants, power, light, water, and telephone service if not provided directly by the owner.

9. The cost of premiums on public liability, property damage, or other insurance coverage authorized or required by the owner.

10. The amount of all sales and use taxes paid by the CM in connection with general condition items to be provided by it.

11. The amounts paid in accordance with subcontracts approved in advance by the owner.

12. The cost of all required permits and licenses.

13. The cost of performance and payment bonds.

CONTRACT FORM

The CM-owner contract can incorporate other documents. This can simplify the specific contractual document. This approach is used in Exhibit A, which is a paraphrase of a contract between a consulting CM and a private owner.

Both the American Institute of Architects (AIA) and the Associated General Contractors (AGC) have developed a comprehensive series of guideline contractual documents for use by owners, designers, and contractors. Each has developed its own CM-owner format. The AIA contract standard form B 801 is well-known to all, and AGC document no. 8 is Exhibit B.

The Public Building Service of the GSA has, perhaps, the most comprehensive CM-owner contract form. This blank contract form is appended to the formal RFP (request for proposal) sent to prospective construction managers. The would be construction managers are advised that this contract will be executed with the selected CM. Any exception to the contract form would disqualify the construction manager as unresponsive. (A CM wishing to offer an alternative may do so but only if a responsive base response has been made.) The PBS/GSA CM contract form is Exhibit C.

EXHIBIT A

AGREEMENT

This Agreement made the _____ day of December 1976 by and between the UNIVERSAL UNIVERSITY—State of New York, located in the City of New York, hereafter referred to as THE UNIVERSITY, and KREITZBERG-O'BRIEN ASSOCIATES, INC., Woolworth Building, New York City, New York, hereafter referred to as CONSTRUCTION MANAGER.

WHEREAS, the UNIVERSITY intends to rehabilitate Dormitories A and B and the CONSTRUCTION MANAGER intends to supply consulting and management services as stated in SCOPE OF SERVICES.

SCOPE OF SERVICES

Services to be furnished by the CONSTRUCTION MANAGER are as listed in the attached proposal, as revised 15th day of November 1976.

FEE

The services for Phase I (Preconstruction) of Dormitories A and B as described in the above Scope of Work shall be completed for a lump sum of _____. Payments shall be made on a monthly basis calculated on an estimated percent complete, submitted by the CONSTRUCTION MANAGER and approved by the UNIVERSITY.

TERMINATION

This Agreement, or any part thereof, may be terminated by the OWNER upon twenty days' written notice to the CONSTRUCTION MANAGER. In the event only part of the Agreement is terminated, all the remaining part of the Agreement shall remain in full force and effect. In the event of termination, the CONSTRUCTION MANAGER shall be paid for services performed to termination date.

ASSIGNMENTS

The Agreement may not be assigned by either party without the prior written consent of the nonassigning party.

PROVISIONS OF LAW

Unless otherwise directed by the OWNER, the CONSTRUCTION MANAGER shall comply with all applicable provisions of law or regulations in relation to the design and construction of buildings.

EXTRA WORK

Extra work may be assigned to the CONSTRUCTION MANAGER, and the rate and the fee shall be based either on an agreed lump sum or a man-hour time and material as spelled out in the attached proposal.

This Agreement shall be governed by the laws of the State of New York, both as to interpretation and performance.

IN WITNESS WHEREOF, the OWNER and CONSTRUCTION MANAGER hereto hereunder set their hand and seal the day and year first above written.

KREITZBERG-O'BRIEN ASSOCIATES, INC.

By _____

Title_____

UNIVERSAL UNIVERSITY

By _____

Title_____

EXHIBIT B*

STANDARD FORM OF AGREEMENT
BETWEEN OWNER AND
CONSTRUCTION MANAGER

(GUARANTEED MAXIMUM PRICE OPTION)

(See AGC Document No. 8a for Fixing the Guaranteed Maximum
Price and AGC Document 8b for recommended General Conditions)

*This Document has important legal and insurance consequences; consultation with an attorney is encouraged with
respect to its completion or modification.*

AGREEMENT

Made this _____ day of _____ in the year of Nineteen Hundred
and _____

BETWEEN

_____ the Owner, and
_____ the   Construction   Manager.
For services in connection with the following described Project:
(Include complete Project location and scope)

The Architect/Engineer for the Project is _____

The Owner and the Construction Manager agree as set forth below:

ARTICLE 1
The Construction Team and Extent of Agreement

THE CONSTRUCTION MANAGER accepts the relationship of trust and confidence established between him and the Owner by this Agreement. He covenants with the Owner to
furnish his best skill and judgment and to cooperate with the Architect/Engineer in
furthering the interests of the Owner. He agrees to furnish efficient business administration and superintendence and to use his best efforts to complete the Project in the best

---

*AGC Document No. 8, Owner-Construction Manager Agreement, June 1977, © 1977 Associated General Contractors
of America. All rights reserved. Used with permission.

Certain provisions of this document have been derived, with modifications, from the following documents published
by The American Institute of Architects: AIA Document A111, Owner-Contractor Agreement, © 1974; AIA Document
A201, General Conditions, © 1976; AIA Document B801, Owner-Construction Manager Agreement, © 1973, by The
American Institute of Architects. Usage made of AIA language, with the permission of AIA, does not apply AIA endorsement or approval of this document. This document has been reproduced with the permission of The American Institute
of Architects under application number 77075. Further reproduction, in part or in whole, is not authorized. Because
AIA documents are revised periodically, users should ascertain from AIA the current edition of the document reproduced
above.

and soundest way and in the most expeditious and economical manner consistent with the interest of the Owner.

1.1 *The Construction Team:* The Construction Manager, the Owner, and the Architect/ Engineer called the "Construction Team" shall work from the beginning of design through construction completion. The Construction Manager shall provide leadership to the Construction Team on all matters relating to construction.

1.2 *Extent of Agreement:* This Agreement represents the entire agreement between the Owner and the Construction Manager and supersedes all prior negotiations, representations or agreements. When drawings and specifications are complete, they shall be identified by amendment to this Agreement. This Agreement shall not be superseded by any provisions of the documents for construction and may be amended only by written instrument signed by both Owner and Construction Manager.

1.3 *Definitions:* The Project is the total construction to be performed under Agreement. The Work is that part of the construction that the Construction Manager is to perform with his own forces or that part of the construction that a particular Trade Contractor is to perform. The term day shall mean calendar day unless otherwise specifically designated.

ARTICLE 2
Construction Manager's Services

The Construction Manager will perform the following services under this Agreement in each of the two phases described below.

2.1 Design Phase

2.1.1 *Consultation During Project Development:* Schedule and attend regular meetings with the Architect/Engineer during the development of conceptual and preliminary design to advise on site use and improvements, selection of materials, building systems and equipment. Provide recommendations on construction feasibility, availability of materials and labor, time requirements for installation and construction, and factors related to cost including costs of alternative designs or materials, preliminary budgets, and possible economies.

2.1.2 *Scheduling:* Develop a Project Time Schedule that coordinates and integrates the Architect/Engineer's design efforts with construction schedules. Update the Project Time Schedule incorporating a detailed schedule for the construction operations of the Project, including realistic activity sequences and durations, allocation of labor and materials, processing of shop drawings and samples, and delivery of products requiring long lead-time procurement. Include the Owner's occupancy requirements showing portions of the Project having occupancy priority.

2.1.3 *Project Construction Budget:* Prepare a Project budget as soon as major Project requirements have been identified, and update periodically for the Owner's approval. Prepare an estimate based on a quantity survey of Drawings and Specifications at the end of the schematic design phase for approval by the Owner as the Project Construction Budget. Update and refine this estimate for Owner's approval as the development of the Drawings and Specifications proceeds, and advise the Owner and the Architect/Engineer if it appears that the Project Construction Budget will not be met and make recommendations for corrective action.

2.1.4 *Coordination of Contract Documents:* Review the Drawings and Specifications as they are being prepared, recommending alternative solutions whenever design details affect construction feasibility or schedules without, however, assuming any of the Architect/Engineer's responsibilities for design.

2.1.5 *Construction Planning:* Recommend for purchase and expedite the procurement of long-lead items to ensure their delivery by the required dates.

2.1.5.1 Make recommendations to the Owner and the Architect/Engineer regarding the division of Work in the Drawings and Specifications to facilitate the bidding and awarding of Trade Contracts, allowing for phased construction taking into consideration such factors as time of performance, availability of labor, overlapping trade jurisdictions, and provisions for temporary facilities.

2.1.5.2 Review the Drawings and Specifications with the Architect/Engineer to eliminate areas of conflict and overlapping in the Work to be performed by the various Trade Contractors and prepare prequalification criteria for bidders.

2.1.5.3 Develop Trade Contractor interest in the Project and as working Drawings and Specifications are completed, take competitive bids on the Work of the various Trade Contractors. After analyzing the bids, either award contracts or recommend to the Owner that such contracts be awarded.

2.1.6 *Equal Employment Opportunity:* Determine applicable requirements for equal employment opportunity programs for inclusion in Project bidding documents.

2.2 Construction Phase

2.2.1 *Project Control:* Monitor the Work of the Trade Contractors and coordinate the Work with the activities and responsibilities of the Owner, Architect/Engineer and Construction Manager to complete the Project in accordance with the Owner's objectives of cost, time and quality.

2.2.1.1 Maintain a competent full-time staff at the Project site to coordinate and provide general direction of the Work and progress of the Trade Contractors on the Project.

2.2.1.2 Establish on-site organization and lines of authority in order to carry out the overall plans of the Construction Team.

2.2.1.3 Establish procedures for coordination among the Owner, Architect/Engineer, Trade Contractors and Construction Manager with respect to all aspects of the Project and implement such procedures.

2.2.1.4 Schedule and conduct progress meetings at which Trade Contractors, Owner, Architect/Engineer and Construction Manager can discuss jointly such matters as procedures, progress, problems and scheduling.

2.2.1.5 Provide regular monitoring of the schedule as construction progresses. Identify potential variances between scheduled and probable completion dates. Review schedule for Work not started or incomplete and recommend to the Owner and Trade Contractors adjustments in the schedule to meet the probable completion date. Provide summary reports of each monitoring and document all changes in schedule.

2.2.1.6 Determine the adequacy of the Trade Contractors' personnel and equipment and the availability of materials and supplies to meet the schedule. Recommend courses of action to the Owner when requirements of a Trade Contract are not being met.

2.2.2 *Physical Construction:* Provide all supervision, labor, materials, construction equipment, tools and subcontract items which are necessary for the completion of the Project which are not provided by either the Trade Contractors or the Owner. To the extent that the Construction Manager performs any Work, with his own forces, he shall, with respect to such Work, be bound to the extent not inconsistent with this Agreement, by the procedures and the obligations with respect to such Work as may govern the Trade Contractors under any General Conditions to the Trade Contracts.

2.2.3 *Cost Control:* Develop and monitor an effective system of Project cost control. Revise and refine the initially approved Project Construction Budget, incorporate approved changes as they occur, and develop cash flow reports and forecasts as needed. Identify variances between actual and budgeted or estimated costs and advise Owner and Architect/Engineer whenever projected cost exceeds budgets or estimates.

2.2.3.1 Maintain cost accounting records on authorized Work performed under unit costs, actual costs for labor and material, or other bases requiring accounting records. Afford the Owner access to these records and preserve them for a period of three (3) years after final payment.

2.2.4 *Change Orders:* Develop and implement a system for the preparation, review and processing of Change Orders. Recommend necessary or desirable changes to the Owner and the Architect/Engineer, review requests for changes, submit recommendations to the Owner and the Architect/Engineer, and assist in negotiating Change Orders.

2.2.5 *Payments to Trade Contractors:* Develop and implement a procedure for the review, processing and payment of applications by Trade Contractors for progress and final payments.

2.2.6 *Permits and Fees:* Assist the Owner and Architect/Engineer in obtaining all building permits and special permits for permanent improvements, excluding permits for inspection or temporary facilities required to be obtained directly by the various Trade Contractors. Assist in obtaining approvals from all the authorities having jurisdiction.

2.2.7 *Owner's Consultants:* If required, assist the Owner in selecting and retaining professional services of a surveyor, testing laboratories and special consultants, and coordinate these services.

2.2.8 *Inspection:* Inspect the Work of Trade Contractors for defects and deficiencies in the Work without assuming any of the Architect/Engineer's responsibilities for inspection.

2.2.8.1 Review the safety programs of each of the Trade Contractors and make appropriate recommendations. In making such recommendations and carrying out such reviews, he shall not be required to make exhaustive or continuous inspections to check safety precautions and programs in connection with the Project. The performance of such services by the Construction Manager shall not relieve the Trade Contractors of their responsibilities for the safety of persons and property, and for compliance with all federal, state and local statutes, rules, regulations and orders applicable to the conduct of the Work.

2.2.9 *Document Interpretation:* Refer all questions for interpretation of the documents prepared by the Architect/Engineer to the Architect/Engineer.

2.2.10 *Shop Drawings and Samples:* In collaboration with the Architect/Engineer, establish and implement procedures for expediting the processing and approval of shop drawings and samples.

2.2.11 *Reports and Project Site Documents:* Record the progress of the Project. Submit written progress reports to the Owner and the Architect/Engineer including information on the Trade Contractors' Work, and the percentage of completion. Keep a daily log available to the Owner and the Architect/Engineer.

2.2.11.1 Maintain at the Project site, on a current basis: records of all necessary Contracts, drawings, samples, purchases, materials, equipment, maintenance and operating manuals and instructions, and other construction related documents, including all revisions. Obtain data from Trade Contractors and maintain a current set of record Drawings, Specifications and operating manuals. At the completion of the Project, deliver all such records to the Owner.

2.2.12 *Substantial Completion:* Determine Substantial Completion of the Work or designated portions thereof and prepare for the Architect/Engineer a list of incomplete or unsatisfactory items and a schedule for their completion.

2.2.13 *Start-Up:* With the Owner's maintenance personnel, direct the checkout of utilities, operations systems and equipment for readiness and assist in their initial start-up and testing by the Trade Contractors.

2.2.14 *Final Completion:* Determine final completion and provide written notice to the Owner and Architect/Engineer that the Work is ready for final inspection. Secure and transmit to the Architect/Engineer required guarantees, affidavits, releases, bonds and waivers. Turn over to the Owner all keys, manuals, record drawings and maintenance stocks.

2.2.15 *Warranty:* Where any Work is performed by the Construction Manager's own forces or by Trade Contractors under contract with the Construction Manager, the Construction Manager shall warrant that all materials and equipment included in such Work will be new, unless otherwise specified, and that such Work will be of good quality, free from improper workmanship and defective materials and in conformance with the Drawings and Specifications. With respect to the same Work, the Construction Manager further agrees to correct all work defective in material and workmanship for a period of one year from the Date of Substantial Completion or for such longer periods of time as may be set forth with respect to specific warranties contained in the trade sections of the Specifications. The Construction Manager shall collect and deliver to the Owner any specific written warranties given by others.

2.3 Additional Services

2.3.1 At the request of the Owner the Construction Manager will provide the following additional services upon written agreement between the Owner and Construction Manager defining the extent of such additional services and the amount and manner in which the Construction Manager will be compensated for such additional services.

2.3.2 Services related to investigation, appraisals or valuations of existing conditions, facilities or equipment, or verifying the accuracy of existing drawings or other Owner-furnished information.

2.3.3 Services related to Owner-furnished equipment, furniture and furnishings which are not a part of this Agreement.

2.3.4 Services for tenant or rental spaces not a part of this Agreement.

2.3.5 Obtaining or training maintenance personnel or negotiating maintenance service contracts.

ARTICLE 3
Owner's Responsibilities

3.1 The Owner shall provide full information regarding his requirements for the project.

3.2 The Owner shall designate a representative who shall be fully acquainted with the project and has authority to approve Project Construction Budgets, Changes in the Project, render decisions promptly and furnish information expeditiously.

3.3 The Owner shall retain an Architect/Engineer for design and to prepare construction documents for the Project. The Architect/Engineer's services, duties and responsibilities are described in the Agreement between the Owner and the Architect/Engineer, a copy of which will be furnished to the Construction Manager. The Agreement between the Owner and the Architect/Engineer shall not be modified without written notification to the Construction Manager.

3.4 The Owner shall furnish for the site of the Project all necessary surveys describing the physical characteristics, soil reports and subsurface investigations, legal limitations, utility locations, and a legal description.

3.5 The Owner shall secure and pay for necessary approvals, easements, assessments and charges required for the construction, use or occupancy of permanent structures or for permanent changes in existing facilities.

3.6 The Owner shall furnish such legal services as may be necessary for providing the items set forth in Paragraph 3.5, and such auditing services as he may require.

3.7 The Construction Manager will be furnished without charge all copies of Drawings and Specifications reasonably necessary for the execution of the Work.

3.8 The Owner shall provide the insurance for the Project as provided in Paragraph 12.4, and shall bear the cost of any bonds required.

3.9 The services, information, surveys and reports required by the above paragraphs shall be furnished with reasonable promptness at the Owner's expense, and the Construction Manager shall be entitled to rely upon the accuracy and completeness thereof.

3.10 If the Owner becomes aware of any fault or defect in the Project or non-conformance with the Drawings and Specifications, he shall give prompt written notice thereof to the Construction Manager.

3.11 The Owner shall furnish reasonable evidence satisfactory to the Construction Manager that sufficient funds are available and committed for the entire cost of the Project. Unless such reasonable evidence is furnished, the Construction Manager is not required to commence any Work, or may, if such evidence is not presented within a reasonable time, stop the Project upon 15 days notice to the Owner.

3.12 The Owner shall communicate with the Trade Contractors only through the Construction Manager.

ARTICLE 4
Trade Contracts

4.1 All portions of the Project that the Construction Manager does not perform with his own forces shall be performed under Trade Contracts. The Construction Manager shall request and receive proposals from Trade Contractors and Trade Contracts will be awarded after the proposals are reviewed by the Architect/Engineer, Construction Manager and Owner.

4.2 If the Owner refuses to accept a Trade Contractor recommended by the Construction Manager, the Construction Manager shall recommend an acceptable substitute and the Guaranteed Maximum Price if applicable shall be increased or decreased by the difference in cost occasioned by such substitution and an appropriate Change Order shall be issued.

4.3 Unless otherwise directed by the Owner, Trade Contracts will be between the Construction Manager and the Trade Contractors. Whether the Trade Contracts are with the Construction Manager or the Owner, the form of the Trade Contracts including the General and Supplementary Conditions shall be satisfactory to the Construction Manager.

4.4 The Construction Manager shall be responsible to the Owner for the acts and omissions of his agents and employees, Trade Contractors performing Work under a contract with the Construction Manager, and such Trade Contractors' agents and employees.

ARTICLE 5
Schedule

5.1 The services to be provided under this Contract shall be in general accordance with the following schedule:

5.2 At the time a Guaranteed Maximum Price is established, as provided for in Article 6, a Date of Substantial Completion of the project shall also be established.

5.3 The Date of Substantial Completion of the Project or a designated portion thereof is the date when construction is sufficiently complete in accordance with the Drawings and Specifications so the Owner can occupy or utilize the Project or designated portion thereof for the use of which it is intended. Warranties called for by this Agreement or by the Drawings and Specifications shall commence on the Date of Substantial Completion of the Project or designated portion thereof.

5.4 If the Construction Manager is delayed at any time in the progress of the Project by any act or neglect of the Owner or the Architect/Engineer or by any employee of either, or by any separate contractor employed by the Owner, or by changes ordered in the Project, or by labor disputes, fire, unusual delay in transportation, adverse weather conditions not reasonably anticipatable, unavoidable casualties or any causes beyond the Construction Manager's control, or by delay authorized by the Owner pending arbitration, the Construction Completion Date shall be extended by Change Order for a reasonable length of time.

ARTICLE 6
Guaranteed Maximum Price

6.1 When the design, Drawings and Specifications are sufficiently complete, the Construction Manager will, if desired by the Owner, establish a Guaranteed Maximum Price, guaranteeing the maximum price to the Owner for the Cost of the Project and the Construction Manager's Fee. Such Guaranteed Maximum Price will be subject to modification for Changes in the Project as provided in Article 9 and for additional costs arising from delays caused by the Owner or the Architect/Engineer.

6.2 When the Construction Manager provides a Guaranteed Maximum Price, the Trade Contracts will either be with the Construction Manager or will contain the necessary provisions to allow the Construction Manager to control the performance of the Work.

6.3 The Guaranteed Maximum Price will only include those taxes in the Cost of the Project which are legally enacted at the time the Guaranteed Maximum Price is established.

ARTICLE 7
Construction Manager's Fee

7.1 In consideration of the performance of the Contract, the Owner agrees to pay the Construction Manager in current funds as compensation for his services a Construction Manager's Fee as set forth in Subparagraphs 7.1.1 and 7.1.2.

7.1.1 For the performance of the Design Phase services, a fee of _____ which shall be paid monthly, in equal proportions, based on the scheduled Design Phase time.

7.1.2 For work or services performed during the Construction Phase, a fee of _____ ___ which shall be paid proportionately to the ratio the monthly payment for the Cost of the Project bears to the estimated cost. Any balance of this fee shall be paid at the time of final payment.

7.2 Adjustments in Fee shall be made as follows:

7.2.1 For Changes in the Project as provided in Article 9, the Construction Manager's Fee shall be adjusted as follows:

7.2.2 For delays in the Project not the responsibility of the Construction Manager, there will be an equitable adjustment in the fee to compensate the Construction Manager for his increased expenses.

7.2.3 The Construction Manager shall be paid an additional fee in the same proportion as set forth in 7.2.1 if the Construction Manager is placed in charge of the reconstruction of any insured or uninsured loss.

7.3 Included in the Construction Manager's Fee are the following:

7.3.1 Salaries or other compensation of the Construction Manager's employees at the principal office and branch offices, except employees listed in Subparagraph 8.2.2.

7.3.2 General operating expenses of the Construction Manager's principal and branch offices other than the field office.

7.3.3 Any part of the Construction Manager's capital expenses, including interest on the Construction Manager's capital employed for the project.

7.3.4 Overhead or general expenses of any kind, except as may be expressly included in Article 8.

7.3.5 Costs in excess of the Guaranteed Maximum Price.

ARTICLE 8
Cost of the Project

8.1 The term Cost of the Project shall mean costs necessarily incurred in the Project during either the Design or Construction Phase, and paid by the Construction Manager, or by the Owner if the Owner is directly paying Trade Contractors upon the Construction Manager's approval and direction. Such costs shall include the items set forth below in this Article.

8.1.1 The Owner agrees to pay the Construction Manager for the Cost of the Project as defined in Article 8. Such payment shall be in addition to the Construction Manager's Fee stipulated in Article 7.

8.2 Cost Items

8.2.1 Wages paid for labor in the direct employ of the Construction Manager in the performance of his Work under applicable collective bargaining agreements, or under a salary or wage schedule agreed upon by the Owner and Construction Manager, and including such welfare or other benefits, if any, as may be payable with respect thereto.

8.2.2 Salaries of the Construction Manager's employees when stationed at the field office, in whatever capacity employed, employees engaged on the road in expediting the production or transportation of materials and equipment, and employees in the main or branch office performing the functions listed below:

8.2.3 Cost of all employee benefits and taxes for such items as unemployment compensation and social security, insofar as such cost is based on wages, salaries, or other remuneration paid to employees of the Construction Manager and included in the Cost of the Project under Subparagraphs 8.2.1 and 8.2.2.

8.2.4 The proportion of reasonable transportation, traveling, moving, and hotel expenses of the Construction Manager or of his officers or employees incurred in discharge of duties connected with the Project.

8.2.5 Cost of all materials, supplies and equipment incorporated in the Project, including costs of transportation and storage thereof.

8.2.6 Payments made by the Construction Manager or Owner to Trade Contractors for their Work performed pursuant to contract under this Agreement.

8.2.7 Cost, including transportation and maintenance, of all materials, supplies, equipment, temporary facilities and hand tools not owned by the workmen, which are employed or consumed in the performance of the Work, and cost less salvage value on such items used but not consumed which remain the property of the Construction Manager.

8.2.8 Rental charges of all necessary machinery and equipment, exclusive of hand tools, used at the site of the Project, whether rented from the Construction Manager or other, including installation, repairs and replacements, dismantling, removal, costs of lubrication, transportation and delivery costs thereof, at rental charges consistent with those prevailing in the area.

8.2.9 Cost of the premiums for all insurance which the Construction Manager is required to procure by this Agreement or is deemed necessary by the Construction Manager.

8.2.10 Sales, use, gross receipts or similar taxes related to the Project imposed by any governmental authority, and for which the Construction Manager is liable.

8.2.11 Permit fees, licenses, tests, royalties, damages for infringement of patents and costs of defending suits therefor, and deposits lost for causes other than the Construction Manager's negligence. If royalties or losses and damages, including costs of defense, are incurred which arise from a particular design, process, or the product of a particular manufacturer or manufacturers specified by the Owner or Architect/Engineer, and the Construction Manager has no reason to believe there will be infringement of patent rights, such royalties, losses and damages shall be paid by the Owner and not considered as within the Guaranteed Maximum Price.

8.2.12 Losses, expenses or damages to the extent not compensated by insurance or otherwise (including settlement made with the written approval of the Owner).

8.2.13 The cost of corrective work subject, however, to the Guaranteed Maximum Price.

8.2.14 Minor expenses such as telegrams, long-distance telephone calls, telephone service at the site, expressage, and similar petty cash items in connection with the Project.

8.2.15 Cost of removal of all debris.

8.2.16 Cost incurred due to an emergency affecting the safety of persons and property.

8.2.17 Cost of data processing services required in the performance of the services outlined in Article 2.

8.2.18 Legal costs reasonably and properly resulting from prosecution of the Project for the Owner.

8.2.19 All costs directly incurred in the performance of the Project and not included in the Construction Manager's Fee as set forth in Paragraph 7.3.

ARTICLE 9
Changes in the Project

9.1 The Owner, without invalidating this Agreement, may order Changes in the Project within the general scope of this Agreement consisting of additions, deletions or other revisions, the Guaranteed Maximum Price, if established, the Construction Manager's Fee and the Construction Completion Data being adjusted accordingly. All such Changes in the project shall be authorized by Change Order.

9.1.1 A Change Order is a written order to the Construction Manager signed by the Owner or his authorized agent issued after the execution of this Agreement, authorizing a Change in the Project and/or an adjustment in the Guaranteed Maximum Price, the Construction Manager's Fee, or the Construction Completion Date. Each adjustment in the Guaranteed Maximum Price resulting from a Change Order shall clearly separate the amount attributable to the Cost of the Project and the Construction Manager's Fee.

9.1.2 The increase or decrease in the Guaranteed Maximum Price resulting from a Change in the Project shall be determined in one or more of the following ways:

.1 by mutual acceptance of a lump sum properly itemized and supported by sufficient substantiating data to permit evaluation;

.2 by unit prices stated in the Agreement or subsequently agreed upon;

.3 by cost as defined in Article 8 and a mutually acceptable fixed or percentage fee; or

.4 by the method provided in Subparagraph 9.1.3.

9.1.3 If none of the methods set forth in Clauses 9.1.2.1 through 9.1.2.3 is agreed upon, the Construction Manager, provided he receives a written order signed by the Owner, shall promptly proceed with the work involved. The cost of such work shall then be determined on the basis of the reasonable expenditures and savings of those performing the Work attributed to the change, including, in the case of an increase in the Guaranteed Maximum Price, a reasonable increase in the Construction Manager's Fee. In such case, and also under Clauses 9.1.2.3 and 9.1.2.4 above, the Construction Manager shall keep and present, in such form as the Owner may prescribe, an itemized accounting together with appropriate supporting data of the increase in the Cost of the Project as outlined in Article 8. The amount of decrease in the Guaranteed Maximum Price to be allowed by the

Construction Manager to the Owner for any deletion or change which results in a net decrease in cost will be the amount of the actual net decrease. When both additions and credits are involved in any one change, the increase in Fee shall be figured on the basis of net increase, if any.

9.1.4 If unit prices are stated in the Agreement or subsequently agreed upon, and if the quantities originally contemplated are so changed in a proposed Change Order that application of the agreed unit prices to the quantities of Work proposed will cause substantial inequity to the Owner or the Construction Manager, the applicable unit prices and Guaranteed Maximum Price shall be equitably adjusted.

9.1.5 Should concealed conditions encountered in the performance of the Work below the surface of the ground or should concealed or unknown conditions in an existing structure be at variance with the conditions indicated by the Drawings, Specifications, or Owner-furnished information or should unknown physical conditions below the surface of the ground or should concealed or unknown conditions in an existing structure of an unusual nature, differing materially from those ordinarily encountered and generally recognized as inherent in work of the character provided for in this Agreement, be encountered, the Guaranteed Maximum Price and the Construction Completion Date shall be equitably adjusted by Change Order upon claim by either party made within a reasonable time after the first observance of the conditions.

9.2 Claims for Additional Cost or Time

9.2.1 If the Construction Manager wishes to make a claim for an increase in the Guaranteed Maximum Price, an increase in his fee, or an extension in the Construction Completion Date, he shall give the Owner written notice thereof within a reasonable time after the occurrence of the event giving rise to such claim. This notice shall be given by the Construction Manager before proceeding to execute any Work, except in an emergency endangering life or property in which case the Construction Manager shall act, at his discretion, to prevent threatened damage, injury or loss. Claims arising from delay shall be made within a reasonable time after the delay. No such claim shall be valid unless so made. If the Owner and the Construction Manager cannot agree on the amount of the adjustment in the Guaranteed Maximum Price, Construction Manager's Fee or Construction Completion Date, it shall be determined pursuant to the provisions of Article 16. Any change in the Guaranteed Maximum Price, Construction Manager's Fee or Construction Completion Date resulting from such claim shall be authorized by Change Order.

9.3 Minor Changes in the Project

9.3.1 The Architect/Engineer will have authority to order minor Changes in the Project not involving an adjustment in the Guaranteed Maximum Price or an extension of the Construction Completion Date and not inconsistent with the intent of the Drawings and Specifications. Such Changes may be effected by written order and shall be binding on the Owner and the Construction Manager.

9.4 Emergencies

9.4.1 In any emergency affecting the safety of persons or property, the Construction Manager shall act, at his discretion, to prevent threatened damage, injury or loss. Any increase in the Guaranteed Maximum Price or extension of time claimed by the Construction Manager on account of emergency work shall be determined as provided in this Article.

ARTICLE 10
Discounts

All discounts for prompt payment shall accrue to the Owner to the extent the Cost of the project is paid directly by the Owner or from a fund made available by the Owner to the Construction Manager for such payments. To the extent the Cost of the Project is paid with funds of the Construction Manager, all cash discounts shall accrue to the Construction Manager. All trade discounts, rebates and refunds, and all returns from sale of surplus materials and equipment, shall be credited to the Cost of the Project.

ARTICLE 11
Payments to the Construction Manager

11.1 The Construction Manager shall submit monthly to the Owner a statement, sworn to if required, showing in detail all moneys paid out, costs accumulated or costs incurred on account of the Cost of the Project during the previous month and the amount of the Construction Manager's Fee due as provided in Article 7. Payment by the Owner to the Construction Manager of the statement amount shall be made within ten (10) days after it is submitted.

11.2 Final payment constituting the unpaid balance of the Cost of the Project and the Construction Manager's Fee shall be due and payable when the Project is delivered to the Owner, ready for beneficial occupancy, or when the Owner occupies the Project, whichever event first occurs, provided that the Project be then substantially completed and this Agreement substantially performed. If there should remain minor items to be completed, the Construction Manager and Architect/Engineer shall list such items and the Construction Manager shall deliver, in writing, his unconditional promise to complete said items within a reasonable time thereafter. The Owner may retain a sum equal to 150% of the estimated cost of completing any unfinished items, provided that said unfinished items are listed separately and the estimated cost of completing any unfinished items likewise listed separately. Thereafter, Owner shall pay to Construction Manager, monthly, the amount retained for incomplete items as each of said items is completed.

11.3 The Construction Manager shall promptly pay all the amount due Trade Contractors or other persons with whom he has a contract upon receipt of any payment from the Owner, the application for which includes amounts due such Trade Contractor or other persons. Before issuance of final payment, the Construction Manager shall submit satisfactory evidence that all payrolls, materials bills and other indebtedness connected with the Project have been paid or otherwise satisfied.

11.4 If the Owner should fail to pay the Construction Manager within seven (7) days after the time the payment of any amount becomes due, then the Construction Manager may, upon seven (7) additional days' written notice to the Owner and the Architect/Engineer, stop the Project until payment of the amount owing has been received.

11.5 Payments due but unpaid shall bear interest at the rate the Owner is paying on his construction loan or at the legal rate, whichever is higher.

ARTICLE 12
Insurance, Indemnity and Waiver of Subrogation

12.1 Indemnity

12.1.1 The Construction Manager agrees to indemnify and hold the Owner harmless from all claims for bodily injury and property damage (other than the work itself and other property insured under Paragraph 12.4) that may arise from the Construction Manager's operations under this Agreement.

12.1.2 The Owner shall cause any other contractor who may have a contract with the Owner to perform construction or installation work in the areas where work will be performed under this Agreement, to agree to indemnify the Owner and the Construction Manager and hold them harmless from all claims for bodily injury and property damage (other than property insured under Paragraph 12.4) that may arise from that contractor's operations. Such provisions shall be in a form satisfactory to the Construction Manager.

12.2 Construction Manager's Liability Insurance

12.2.1 The Construction Manager shall purchase and maintain such insurance as will protect him from the claims set forth below which may arise out of or result from the Construction Manager's operations under this Agreement whether such operations be by himself or by any Trade Contractor or by anyone directly or indirectly employed by any of them, or by anyone for whose acts any of them may be liable:

12.2.1.1 Claims under workers' compensation, disability benefit and other similar employee benefit acts which are applicable to the work to be performed.

12.2.1.2 Claims for damages because of bodily injury, occupational sickness or disease, or death of his employees under any applicable employer's liability law.

12.2.1.3 Claims for damages because of bodily injury, or death of any person other than his employees.

12.2.1.4 Claims for damages insured by usual personal injury liability coverage which are sustained (1) by any person as a result of an offense directly or indirectly related to the employment of such person by the Construction Manager or (2) by any other person.

12.2.1.5 Claims for damages, other than to the work itself, because of injury to or destruction of tangible property, including loss of use therefrom.

12.2.1.6 Claims for damages because of bodily injury or death of any person or property damage arising out of the ownership, maintenance or use of any motor vehicle.

12.2.2 The Construction Manager's Comprehensive General Liability Insurance shall include premises—operations (including explosion, collapse and underground coverage) elevators, independent contractors, completed operations, and blanket contractual liability on all written contracts, all including broad form property damage coverage.

12.2.3 The Construction Manager's Comprehensive General and Automobile Liability insurance, as required by Subparagraphs 12.2.1 and 12.2.2 shall be written for not less than limits of liability as follows:

a. Comprehensive General Liability
    1. Personal Injury $_____ Each Occurrence

                                           $_____ Aggregate
    2. Property Damage   (Completed Operations)
b. Comprehensive Automobile Liability $_____ Each Occurrence
    1. Bodily Injury $_____ Aggregate

                                           $_____ Each Person
    2. Property Damage $_____ Each Occurrence

                                           $_____ Each Occurrence

12.2.4 Comprehensive General Liability Insurance may be arranged under a single policy for the full limits required or by a combination of underlying policies with the balance provided by an Excess or Umbrella Liability policy.

12.2.5 The foregoing policies shall contain a provision that coverages afforded under the policies will not be cancelled or not renewed until at least sixty (60) days' prior written notice has been given to the Owner. Certificates of Insurance showing such coverages to be in Force shall be filed with the Owner prior to commencement of the Work.

12.3 Owner's Liability Insurance

12.3.1 The Owner shall be responsible for purchasing and maintaining his own liability insurance and, at his option, may purchase and maintain such insurance as will protect him against claims which may arise from operations under this Agreement.

12.4 Insurance to Protect Project

12.4.1 The Owner shall purchase and maintain property insurance in a form acceptable to the Construction Manager upon the entire Project for the full cost of replacement as of the time of any loss. This insurance shall include as named insureds the Owner, the Construction Manager, Trade Contractors and their Trade Subcontractors and shall insure against loss from the perils of Fire, Extended Coverage, and shall include "All Risk" insurance for physical loss or damage including without duplication of coverage at least theft, vandalism, malicious mischief, transit, collapse, flood, earthquake, testing, and damage resulting from defective design, workmanship or material. The Owner will increase limits of coverage, if necessary, to reflect estimated replacement cost. The Owner will be responsible for any co-insurance penalties or deductibles. If the Project covers an addition to or is adjacent to an existing building the Construction Manager, Trade Contractors and their Trade Subcontractors shall be named as additional insureds under the Owner's Property Insurance covering such building and its contents.

12.4.1.1 If the Owner finds it necessary to occupy or use a portion or portions of the Project prior to Substantial Completion thereof, such occupancy shall not commence prior to a time mutually agreed to by the Owner and Construction Manager and to which the insurance company or companies providing the property insurance have consented by endorsement to the policy or policies. This insurance shall not be cancelled or lapsed on account of such partial occupancy. Consent to the Construction Manager and of the insurance company or companies to such occupancy or use shall not be unreasonably withheld.

12.4.2 The Owner shall purchase and maintain such boiler and machinery insurance as may be required or necessary. This insurance shall include the interests of the Owner, the Construction Manager, Trade Contractors and their Subcontractors in the Work.

12.4.3 The Owner shall purchase and maintain such insurance as will protect the Owner and Construction Manager against loss of use of Owner's property due to those perils insured pursuant to Subparagraph 12.4.1. Such policy will provide coverage for expediting expenses of materials, continuing overhead of the Owner and Construction Manager, necessary labor expense including overtime, loss of income by the Owner and other determined exposures. Exposures of the Owner and the Construction Manager shall be determined by mutual agreement and separate limits of coverage fixed for each item.

12.4.4 The Owner shall file a copy of all policies with the Construction Manager before an exposure to loss may occur. Copies of any subsequent endorsements will be furnished to the Construction Manager. The Construction Manager will be given sixty (60) days notice of cancellation, non-renewal, or any endorsements restricting or reducing coverage. If the Owner does not intend to purchase such insurance, he shall inform the Construction Manager in writing prior to the commencement of the Work. The Construction Manager may then effect insurance which will protect the interest of himself, the Trade Contractors and their Trade Subcontractors in the Project, the cost of which shall be a Cost of the Project pursuant to Article 8, and the Guaranteed Maximum Price shall be increased by Change Order. If the Construction Manager is damaged by failure of the Owner to purchase or maintain such insurance or to so notify the Construction Manager, the Owner shall bear all reasonable costs properly attributable thereto.

12.5 Property Insurance Loss Adjustment

12.5.1 Any insured loss shall be adjusted with the Owner and the Construction Manager and made payable to the Owner and Construction Manager as trustees for the insureds, as their interests may appear, subject to any applicable mortgagee clause.

12.5.2 Upon the occurrence of an insured loss, monies received will be deposited in a separate account and the trustees shall make distribution in accordance with the agreement of the parties in interest, or in the absence of such agreement, in accordance with an arbitration award pursuant to Article 16. If the trustees are unable to agree on the settlement of the loss, such dispute shall also be submitted to arbitration pursuant to Article 16.

12.6 Waiver of Subrogation

12.6.1 The Owner and Construction Manager waive all rights against each other, the Architect/Engineer, Trade Contractors, and their Trade Subcontractors for damages caused by perils covered by insurance provided under Paragraph 12.4, except such rights as they may have to the proceeds of such insurance held by the Owner and Construction Manager as trustees. The Construction Manager shall require similar waivers from all Trade Contractors and their Trade Subcontractors.

12.6.2 The Owner and Construction Manager waive all rights against each other and the Architect/Engineer, Trade Contractors and their Trade Subcontractors for loss or damage to any equipment used in connection with the Project and covered by any property insurance. The Construction Manager shall require similar waivers from all Trade Contractors and their Trade Subcontractors.

12.6.3 The Owner waives subrogation against the Construction Manager, Architect/Engineer, Trade Contractors, and their Trade Subcontractors on all property and consequential loss policies carried by the Owner on adjacent properties and under property and consequential loss policies purchased for the Project after its completion.

12.6.4 If the policies of insurance referred to in this Paragraph require an endorsement to provide for continued coverage where there is a waiver of subrogation, the owners of such policies will cause them to be so endorsed.

ARTICLE 13
Termination of the Agreement and Owner's Right to Perform Construction Manager's Obligations

13.1 Termination by the Construction Manager

13.1.1 If the Project is stopped for a period of thirty days under an order of any court or other public authority having jurisdiction, or as a result of an act of government, such as a declaration of a national emergency making materials unavailable, through no act or fault of the Construction Manager, or if the Project should be stopped for a period of thirty days by the Construction Manager for the Owner's failure to make payment thereon, then the Construction Manager may, upon seven days' written notice to the Owner and the Architect/Engineer, terminate this Agreement and recover from the Owner payment for all work executed, the Construction Manager's Fee earned to date, and for any proven loss sustained upon any materials, equipment, tools, construction equipment and machinery, including reasonable profit and damages.

13.2 Owner's Right to Perform Construction Manager's Obligations and Termination by the Owner for Cause

13.2.1 If the Construction Manager fails to perform any of his obligations under this Agreement including any obligation he assumes to perform work with his own forces, the Owner may, after seven days' written notice during which period the Construction Manager fails to perform such obligation, make good such deficiencies. The Guaranteed Maximum Price, if any, shall be reduced by the cost to the Owner of making good such deficiencies.

13.2.2 If the Construction Manager is adjudged a bankrupt, or if he makes a general assignment for the benefit of his creditors, or if a receiver is appointed on account of his insolvency, or if he persistently or repeatedly refuses or fails, except in cases for which extension of time is provided, to supply enough properly skilled workmen or proper materials, or if he fails to make prompt payment to Trade Contractors or for materials or labor, or persistently disregards laws, ordinances, rules, regulations or orders to any public authority having jurisdiction, or otherwise is guilty of a substantial violation of a provision of the Agreement, then the Owner may, without prejudice to any right or remedy and after giving the Construction Manager and his surety, if any, seven days' written notice, during which period Construction Manager fails to cure the violation, terminate the employment of the Construction Manager and take possession of the site and of all materials, equipment, tools, construction equipment and machinery thereon owned by the Construction Manager and may finish the Project by whatever method he may deem expedient. In such case, the Construction Manager shall not be entitled to receive any further payment until the Project is finished nor shall he be relieved from his obligations assumed under Article 6.

13.3 Termination by Owner Without Cause

13.3.1 If the Owner terminates this Agreement other than pursuant to Subparagraph 13.2.2 or Subparagraph 13.3.2, he shall reimburse the Construction Manager for any unpaid Cost of the Project due him under Article 8, plus (1) the unpaid balance of the Fee computed upon the Cost of the Project to the date of termination at the rate of the percentage named in Subparagraph 7.2.1 or if the Construction Manager's Fee be stated as a fixed sum, such an amount as will increase the payment on account of his fee to a sum which bears the same ratio to the said fixed sum as the Cost of the Project at the time of termination bears to the adjusted Guaranteed Maximum Price, if any, otherwise to a reasonable estimated Cost of the Project when completed. The Owner shall also pay to the Construction Manager fair compensation, either by purchase or rental at the election of the Owner, for any equipment retained. In case of such termination of the Agreement the Owner shall further assume and become liable for obligations, commitments and unsettled claims that the Construction Manager has previously undertaken or incurred in good faith in connection with said Project. The Construction Manager shall, as a condition of receiving the payments referred to in this Article 13, execute and deliver all such papers and take all such steps, including the legal assignment of his contractual rights, as the Owner may require for the purpose of fully vesting in him the rights and benefits of the Construction Manager under such obligations or commitments.

13.3.2 After the completion of the Design Phase, if the final cost estimates make the Project no longer feasible from the standpoint of the Owner, the Owner may terminate this Agreement and pay the Construction Manager his Fee in accordance with Subparagraph 7.1.1 plus any costs incurred pursuant to Article 9.

ARTICLE 14
Assignment and Governing Law

14.1 Neither the Owner nor the Construction Manager shall assign his interest in this Agreement without the written consent of the other except as to the assignment of proceeds.

14.2 This Agreement shall be governed by the law of the place where the Project is located.

ARTICLE 15
Miscellaneous Provisions

ARTICLE 16
Arbitration

16.1 All claims, disputes and other matters in question arising out of, or relating to, this Agreement or the breach thereof, except with respect to the Architect/Engineer's decision on matters relating to artistic effect, and except for claims which have been waived by the making or acceptance of final payment shall be decided by arbitration in accordance with the Construction Industry Arbitration Rules of the American Arbitration Association then obtaining unless the parties mutually agree otherwise. This Agreement to arbitrate shall be specifically enforceable under the prevailing arbitration law.

16.2 Notice of the demand for arbitration shall be filed in writing with the other party to this Agreement and with the American Arbitration Association. The demand for arbitration shall be made within a reasonable time after the claim, dispute or other matter in question has arisen, and in no event shall it be made after the date when institution of legal or equitable proceedings based on such claim, dispute or other matter in question would be barred by the applicable statute of limitations.

16.3 The award rendered by the arbitrators shall be final and judgment may be entered upon it in accordance with applicable law in any court having jurisdiction thereof.

16.4 Unless otherwise agreed in writing, the Construction Manager shall carry on the Work and maintain the Contract Completion Date during any arbitration proceedings, and the Owner shall continue to make payments in accordance with this Agreement.

16.5 All claims which are related to or dependent upon each other, shall be heard by the same arbitrator or arbitrators even though the parties are not the same unless a specific contract prohibits such consolidation.

This Agreement executed the day and year first written above.

ATTEST: ———————————— OWNER: ————————————————————

ATTEST: ———————————— CONSTRUCTION MANAGER: ——————————

EXHIBIT C*

Contract No.__________

GENERAL SERVICES ADMINISTRATION

Public Buildings Service

CONSTRUCTION MANAGEMENT CONTRACT

____

Construction Manager

____

Name of Project

____

Project Number

____

Lump Sum Contract Price

INDEX

1. Project
2. Definitions
3. General
4. Construction management control system
5. Management plan for design and construction
6. Design development and review
7. Long lead procurement
8. Separate contracts planning
9. Interfacing
10. Job-site facilities
11. Weather protection
12. Solicitation of bids
13. Market analysis and stimulation of bidder interest
14. Managing and inspecting construction
15. Monitoring submittals
16. Subcontractor or material vendor recommendations
17. Comprehensive safety program

18. Labor relations
19. Construction contract changes
20. Value management services
21. Claims
22. Meetings and conferences
23. Home office support for job-site staff; relocation costs
24. Reimbursable services
25. General condition items
26. Reimbursable costs
27. Lump sum contract price
28. Payment
29. Staff (nonreimbursable)
30. Subcontracting
31. Federal, State, and local taxes
32. Time for completion
33. Suspension of work—delays
34. Changes
35. Pricing of adjustments
36. Disputes
37. Payment of interest on Construction Manager's claims
38. Termination
39. Partial termination for untimely performance
40. Covenant against contingent fees
41. Officials not to benefit
42. Convict labor
43. Prohibition against bidding
44. Utilization of small business concerns
45. Equal opportunity
46. Certification of nonsegregated facilities
47. Utilization of minority business enterprises
48. Minority business enterprises subcontracting program
49. Listing of employment openings
50. Employment of the handicapped
51. Liability for damage
52. Accident prevention for general conditions work

53. Performance and payment bonds

54. Labor standard provisions

55. Davis-Bacon wage rate decision

56. Home-town or imposed plan—minority hiring practices

57. Buy American

58. Examination of records

59. Cost accounting standards

60. Energy conservation and environmental protection

CONSTRUCTION MANAGEMENT CONTRACT No. _____

On this _____ day of _____, 19____, the United States of America (hereinafter called the Government) represented by the Contracting Officer executing this contract, and _____ (hereinafter referred to as the Construction Manager) mutually agree to perform this contract in strict accordance with the provisions set out herein and in the following documents, all of which are incorporated in and made a part of this contract:

    a. PBS Construction Management Control System (CMCS)

    b. Labor Standards Provisions Applicable to Contracts in Excess of $2,000 (Standard Form 19-A)

    c. _____ (Home-town or Imposed Plan Bid Document)

    d. Construction Manager's Priced Proposal (as modified, if applicable)*

    e. Figure 7-21.5, Chapter 7, GSA Handbook, Value Engineering

    f. Other:

        *In case of any conflict, discrepancy or variance between anything in the Priced Proposal and other requirements of this contract, the latter shall govern.

1. PROJECT

    Name:
    Location:
    Number:
    Description: _____
    _____
    _____
    _____

    Scheduled date for construction completion: _____
    Maximum total project cost: $_____
    Other:

2. DEFINITIONS

    a. The term "head of the agency" as used herein means the Administrator of General Services, and the term "his duly authorized representative" means any person or persons (other than the Contracting Officer) or board authorized to act for the Administrator.

b. The term "Contracting Officer" as used herein means the person executing this contract on behalf of the Government and includes a duly appointed successor or authorized representative.

c. The term "resident engineer" as used herein refers to the technical employee of the Government assigned to the job-site as the direct representative of the Contracting Officer and who has been delegated authority to issue and execute change orders of up to $10,000 each. He will observe the performance of the Construction Manager and his subcontractors (if any) as well as the performance of the separate construction contracts by the respective separate contractors. In addition, he will serve as a common point of contact for the Contracting Officer and the Construction Manager. He will also act as an expediter and trouble shooter. He will work closely with the Construction Manager.

d. The term "Architect-Engineer" and "A-E" as used herein refer to

e. The term "construction executive" as used herein refers to the official of the Construction Manager's firm who shall be designated by the Construction Manager to provide over all direction, coordination, and accomplishment of the Construction Manager's contractual responsibilities in connection with this project. He shall work closely and cooperatively with the Architect-Engineer and the Contracting Officer during the design, design and construction overlap, and construction phases and shall serve as the official within the Construction Manager's organization with lead responsibility for managing the phasing of separate construction contracts during development of the design.

f. The term "construction superintendent" as used herein refers to the Construction Manager's employee, who shall be designated by the Construction Manager for performance of the functions specified in this paragraph. The individual so designated shall have had at least 4 years' supervisory experience in construction activities in the field. He shall work closely with the Architect-Engineer and the Contracting Officer in applying construction know-how to the development of the design and in the division of work into separate construction contract bid packages. Beginning 30 days in advance of award of the first construction contract, he shall be engaged full time at the job-site, managing, directing, inspecting, and coordinating with a view to completion of all construction within the schedule and in accordance with the requirements of each respective separate construction contract.

g. The term "CMCS supervisor" as used herein refers to the employee of the Construction Manager or his CMCS consultant, having experience in the planning, data collection, operation, and control of computer oriented construction management control systems, whom the Construction Manager shall designate to implement the PBS Construction Management Control System. He shall serve full time throughout the life of the contract.

h. The term "separate contractors" as used herein refers to the suppliers of long lead items and to the construction contractors with whom the Government will contract directly for procurement of long lead items and for performance of all construction work other than the general condition items furnished and/or installed by the Construction Manager.

i. The term "general condition items" as used herein shall be deemed to mean provision of facilities or performance of work by the Construction Manager for items which do not lend themselves readily to inclusion in one of the separate contracts. General condition items may include (but are not limited to) the following: watchmen; scaffolding; hoists; signs; safety barricades; water boys; cleaning; dirt chutes; cranes; shanties; preparation for ceremonies including minor construction activity in connection therewith; temporary toilets; fencing; sidewalk bridges; first aid station; trucking; temporary elevator; special equipment; winter protection; temporary heat, water, and electricity; temporary protective enclosures; field office and related costs thereof such as equipment, furnishings and office supplies; progress, final and miscellaneous photographs; messengers; installation of Government furnished items; post and planking; general maintenance; subsoil exploration; refuse disposal; field and laboratory tests of concrete, steel, and soils; surveys; bench marks and monuments; storage on-site or off-site of long lead procurement items; and miscellaneous minor construction work when it is not feasible for the Government to secure competitive bids or proposals thereon.

j. The term "deliverables" is used herein to refer to those services performed by the Construction Manager which will serve as the basis for making installment payments of the lump sum contract amount. The term shall not be deemed to constitute a limitation on the services required of the Construction Manager under this contract. "Deliverables" are the categories comprising the lump sum contract price breakdown, shown as deliverable work items on the network diagram of the management plan submitted as part of the Construction Manager's accepted priced proposal, and subsequently subdivided into detailed deliverable work items on the nonreimbursable work breakdown structure and detailed CMCS schedules.

3. GENERAL

a. By entering into this contract, the Construction Manager undertakes to perform such construction management services as are appropriate, adequate, and necessary to ensure—

(1) that the project will be well designed by the A-E,

(2) that construction will be completed as early as possible, but not later than the scheduled date specified in clause 1 above,

(3) that the construction work is performed in conformity with applicable requirements, and

(4) that the project will be completed at a project cost not more than the maximum amount specified in clause 1 above.

The services which the Construction Manager is required to provide include, but are not limited to, those described or specified herein (including those reflected in the Construction Manager's priced proposal incorporated into this contract by reference). The services described or specified shall not be deemed to constitute a comprehensive specification having the effect of excluding services not specifically mentioned; the Construction Manager is required to furnish all other services as may be necessary to fulfill the undertakings set out in paragraph a of this clause 3.

b. All services will be performed under the direction of the Contracting Officer.

c. The Construction Manager will not be deemed to have failed to meet his contractual undertakings and will not be held responsible for—

(1) Cost overrun, provided the Construction Manager has furnished accurate cost estimates timely, as required by the contract, has kept himself continuously informed as the design developed, has made suggestions and/or recommendations with respect to the design so as to effect cost economies sufficient to ensure construction, together with other project costs, within the overall cost limit specified in clause 1, has evaluated market conditions and stimulated bidders interest, and has recommended separate long-lead procurement in sufficient time to permit the Government to effect procurement for delivery by the time such equipment is needed for installation;

(2) Time overrun, provided the Construction Manager timely developed and maintained a master schedule reflecting all activities having significant impact on scheduling, prepared accurate, timely updates or revisions to the schedule as required by the contract, has taken all reasonable measures to phase the construction work, to eliminate access and availability constraints, to anticipate problems and to eliminate or minimize their adverse impact on the completion of the construction within the time specified in clause 1;

(3) Design deficiencies, provided the Construction Manager has continuously reviewed the design during its development, has taken all reasonable measures to identify defects of commission or omission in the design, has advised the Government with respect to defects identified, and has taken all reasonable precautions to ensure that the separate construction contract bid packages contain no duplication of requirements and that all construction work required is included within one or another construction contract or performed as a general condition item; or

(4) Defective construction, provided that the Construction Manager exercised all due diligence, utilizing competent personnel within authorized limitations, to ensure that construction was performed in conformity with applicable contract plans and specifications.

4. CONSTRUCTION MANAGEMENT CONTROL SYSTEM (CMCS)

a. *General.*

(1) Commencing immediately after contract award, the Construction Manager shall implement and shall utilize throughout the life of this contract all subsystems of the construction management control system required in the PBS CMCS User Manual and Appendices thereto, and in accordance with this clause.

(2) The Construction Manager shall utilize an IBM 360 Computer System, Model 50 or higher model number, with Operating System (OS) to execute the CMCS computer programs and generate computer reports. No substitution, in whole or in part, of any other computer system or programs shall be allowed under this contract.

(3) The reports, documents, and data to be provided shall represent an accurate assessment of the current status of the project and of the work remaining to be accomplished; shall provide a sound basis for identifying variances and

problems, and for making management decisions; and shall be timely prepared and furnished to the Government.

(4) Upon the request of the Contracting Officer, the Construction Manager shall conduct a two day workshop in _____ led by the CMCS supervisor for _____ participants designated by the Contracting Officer. This workshop shall facilitate each participants' and the Government representatives' use and understanding of CMCS; shall support, in part, the function of organizing for the design and construction of the project; and shall establish, in part, procedures for accomplishing the management control aspect of the project.

(5) The CMCS shall be described in terms of the following major subsystems:

    (a) Narrative Reporting,

    (b) Schedule Control,

    (c) Cost Control, and

    (d) Financial Control.

b. *Narrative Reporting Subsystem*

(1) Designated personnel of the Construction Manager shall prepare written reports as described hereunder. No other CMCS narrative reports shall be required.

(2) The narrative reporting subsystem shall include the following reports:

    (a) Construction Executive's report (S-3),

    (b) Chief Estimators report (S-4),

    (c) CMCS Supervisor's report (S-4),

    (d) Project Accountant's report (S-4),

    (e) Daily Diary (S-6),

    (f) Schedule Analysis report. This monthly report shall be prepared by the Construction Manager's CMCS supervisor and shall include an analysis of the schedule, a description of the critical path, and other analyses as necessary to compare planned performance with actual, and

    (g) Construction Superintendent's report (S-3). This monthly report shall include, but not be limited to, the work progress of the separate contractors, long lead contractors, and general conditions work; safety and labor relations programs; job site meetings; problems encountered and recommended actions; and plans for the succeeding month.

(3) Each of the above monthly reports shall contain information up to and including the 25th of the preceding month. Copies of the reports shall be bound together with the required computer reports and estimates and shall be transmitted to the Contracting Officer by the sixth working day of each month.

c. *Schedule Control Subsystem.* The operation of this subsystem shall provide network diagrams, schedule updates, computer generated schedules, and the time related cost data necessary to plan and execute the planning, design, construction, occupancy, and Construction Manager's work within the time specified in clause 1.

(1) *Schedules.* The Construction Manager shall produce and incorporate into the schedule data base, at the required intervals, the following schedules:

  (a) *Master Schedule:* Within 30 days after the award of this contract, the Construction Manager shall submit a master schedule for the planning, design, construction, and occupancy of the project. This schedule shall include all deliverable work items shown on the network diagram submitted as part of the priced proposal. This schedule shall serve as the framework for the subsequent development of all detailed schedules.

  (b) *Construction Manager's Schedule:* At each submission of the Construction Manager's updated Management Plan as specified in clause 5, the Construction Manager shall submit a schedule of all detailed deliverable work items shown on the lowest level of indenture on the work breakdown structure.

  (c) *Design Schedule:* Within 60 days after award of this contract, the Construction Manager shall submit an initial design schedule. Updates thereafter shall reflect not only the design phase activities but also long lead item procurements, and the review, assembly, bid, and award process for separate construction bid packages.

  (d) *Pre-Bid Schedules (Subnetworks):* At least 15 days prior to completion of drawings and specifications for each bid package, the Construction Manager shall prepare a construction schedule for work encompassed in the bid package. The schedule shall be sufficiently detailed as to be suitable for inclusion in the bid package as a framework for contract completion by the successful bidder. It shall show the interrelationships between the work of the successful bidder and that of other separate contractors, and shall establish milestones keyed to the overall master schedule.

  (e) *Construction Schedules (Subnetworks):* Within 30 days after the award of each separate contract, the Construction Manager shall obtain from the separate contractor and recommend approval of a realistic schedule which is more detailed than the pre-bid schedule included in the specifications of the separate contract and which takes into account the work schedule of the other separate contractors. The construction schedule shall include as many activities as necessary to make the schedule an effective tool for construction planning and for monitoring the performance of the separate contract. The construction schedule must also show pertinent activities from the Purchase Order and Shop Drawing Schedules.

  (f) *Purchase Order and Shop Drawing Schedules:* The separate program in the CMCS shall be implemented for control of these activities. The activities, however, must also be shown in the construction schedules under subparagraph (e) above.

  (g) *Occupancy Schedule.* During construction, the Construction Manager shall develop a detailed plan, inclusive of punch lists, final inspections, maintenance training and turn-over procedures, to be used for ensuring accomplishment of a smooth and phased transition from construction to occupancy.

(2) *Integrated and Current Schedule.* The Construction Manager shall provide and monthly maintain a current integrated schedule for the project as follows:

(a) All design, construction and occupancy activities shall be contained in network format in a single computer data base.

(b) Design, pre-construction, construction and occupancy schedules shall be incorporated into the computer data base monthly, as they are developed.

(c) Changes in the planned sequence, interrelationship, or duration of any project activity which occur as a result of project detailed planning, change orders, design revisions, schedule recovery and other actions shall be incorporated into the computer base monthly, as they are identified.

Change order activities shall include the request for proposal, preparation of Government estimates, issuance of the change order plus any negotiations, reviews and approvals of samples, shop drawings, etc., ordering and delivery of materials, and any other activities that take time to perform. The change order shall be logically interrelated to the networks which are affected by the change order.

(d) The activities in the computer base data shall include those listed on page I-3, PBS Information System (PBS/IS) input Report of the CMCS User Manual which are relevant to the project and which have not already been completed. In some cases, the same activities must be repeated several times (for example, once for each design and separate construction contract). Information on these activities shall be reported to the Contracting Officer for inclusion in the PBS/IS as they occur or periodically as requested by the Contracting Officer. In addition, the Construction Manager shall report the percent of design and construction completion with reporting dates and anticipated completion dates.

(3) *Network Diagrams.* The Construction Manager shall prepare a network or subnetwork logic diagram in activity-on-arrow format for each of the master, construction management, design, pre-construction, construction and occupancy schedules developed. All changes in the planned sequence, interrelationship, description, or duration of any activity shall be diagrammed or re-diagrammed as they are determined. The Construction Manager shall make prints of the diagrams and distribute them as required by the Contracting Officer.

d. *Cost Control Subsystem.* The operation of this subsystem shall provide sufficient timely data and detail to permit the Construction Manager, the Contracting Officer and the A-E to control and adjust the project requirements, needs, materials, equipment, and systems so that construction will be completed at a cost which, together with all other project costs, will not exceed the maximum total project cost specified in clause 1. The systems cost data shall serve as meaningful design parameters. Requirements of this subsystem include the following submissions at the following phases of the project life:

(1) *Estimates.*

(a) *Concepts:* This submission will be an estimate which will be used for cost control.

(b) *Tentatives:* The tentatives submission shall expand upon the estimate developed for the concepts submission. It will be used to verify cost criteria.

(c) *Fifty Percent Bid Package Estimates:* During the working drawings stage of design, the Construction Manager shall prepare and submit a comprehensive cost estimate for each bid package, when the design for the package is 50% complete.

(d) *Monthly Current Working Estimates:* The fifty percent estimate for each bid package shall be updated monthly thereafter.

(e) *Contract or Bid-Cost Estimates:* Prior to the receipt of bids for each bid package when the working drawings and specifications are complete, the Construction Manager shall update the previous monthly estimate on the basis of a comprehensive quantitative material take-off with current local costs.

(2) Other reports based on construction cost estimates developed by the Construction Manager and the A-E shall be prepared and up-dated at intervals in the formats indicated in the CMCS User Manual and Appendices, to detail, summarize, and update costs first, by building systems and second, by trades when required for bid and change order reviews.

e. *Financial Control Subsystem.* The operation of this subsystem shall enable the Contracting Officer, and Construction Manager to plan effectively and to monitor and control the application of funds available for the project, cash flow, costs, change orders, payments, claims, and other major financial factors, principally by comparison of funds available, funds expended, funds committed but not yet expended, and funds required for commitment in the future. These reports must be such as will serve as a basic accounting tool and an audit trail.

(1) *Computer generated reports.* The Construction Manager shall furnish computer produced reports, based on data files (such as project, contract, allotment of funds, invoices, change orders, vendors, etc.), updated at intervals indicated in the CMCS User Manual and Appendices to integrate the most recent data, to provide detail and summary data as necessary to provide a complete accounting record of all transactions.

(2) *Progress Payments.*

(a) The contractor payment approval printout provided in the (CMCS) User Manual and Appendices will be used for evaluation and processing of separate construction contractor payment requests. Use of GSA Forms 184, 184-A, and 184-B, Construction Progress Report will not be required.

(b) A monthly invoice printout of the payment due the Construction Manager based on detailed deliverable work items contained in the CMCS detail schedule will be furnished using Report No. F6.

(3) *Books of Account.* The Construction shall provide and maintain manual

books of account as required in this contract and as necessary to supplement the operation of this subsystem.

5. MANAGEMENT PLAN FOR DESIGN AND CONSTRUCTION

a. *Management Plans.* The Construction Manager shall develop, for each of the three principal phases of the design and construction of the project, a detailed Management Plan for accomplishing the services set forth in this contract. These plans shall further delineate and expand the applicable portions of the management plan included as part of the Construction Manager's accepted priced proposal and shall provide the single comprehensive plan for the control, direction, coordination, and evaluation of the work performed during the phase. The Management Plan for the design phase shall be submitted within 30 days after contract award, for the design and construction overlap phase shall be submitted no later than the date on which the invitation for bids for the first separate contract is issued, and for the construction phase shall be submitted no later than the date on which the invitation for bids for the last separate contract is issued. Three copies of each plan and of the updates thereto, shall be submitted to the Contracting Officer who will bind the material in a three ring binder provided by the Construction Manager.

b. *Contents of Management Plans.* Each plan shall describe in detail the program of and requirements for executing the work planned for the phase, and the organizations participating in the phase. To achieve desirable uniformity in preparation and use, each plan shall include the sections and structures described below:

(1) *Project Definition:* The known characteristics of the project shall be described in general terms which provide participants a basic understanding of the project.

(2) *Project Objectives:* The Government's schedule, budget, physical, technical and other objectives for the project shall be defined or updated.

(3) *Work Statement:* A narrative description of the program of work to be performed by the Construction Manager, the A-E, and the Government during the phase.

(4) *Work Breakdown Structures:*

(a) *Nonreimbursable work.* This box-type chart shall describe the total work program of the Construction Manager for the phase of the project. Level one shall equal the lump sum contract price for the phase. The second level of indenture shall contain each of the deliverable categories comprising the lump sum contract price breakdown. The third level of indenture shall contain the deliverable work items for the phase shown on the network diagram accepted as part of the priced proposal. Each deliverable work item shall be further subdivided to the fourth or fifth level of indenture as necessary to define detailed deliverable work items, either of not greater than 30 calendar days in duration whose accomplishment shall result in the provision of a specific management service or of shorter duration whose accomplishment will result in a specific work product. The price for performing each detailed deliverable work item shall be indicated and summarized at each higher level of indenture.

(b) *Other work.* The major work items to be performed by the A-E and the Government shall be subdivided to the fourth or fifth level of detail as necessary to provide a comprehensive description of the detailed work items to be executed during the phase.

(5) *Organization Charts.* A summary chart showing the interrelationships between the Contracting Officer, the Construction Manager, the A-E, and the GSA supporting organizations. Detailed charts, one each for the Construction Manager, the A-E and the Government, showing organizational elements participating in the phase.

(6) *Duties* of all Construction Manager staff personnel, both nonreimbursable and reimbursable participating in this phase, shown on the organization chart, shall be described in detail. The duties of each organizational element of the A-E and the Government, shown on the organization chart, shall be described.

(7) *Linear Responsibility Charts.* These charts shall display in matrix format the functional role of each position category shown on the Construction Manager's organization chart, and the role each organizational element shown on the A-E and Government organization chart shall have in executing the detailed work items contained at the lowest level of indenture shown on the work breakdown structures. By use of an appropriate graphic symbol each of the following responsibilities shall be displayed for each work item:

(a) Direct responsibility for executing the work,

(b) Direct responsibility for supervising the completion of the work,

(c) Technical responsibility for quality of the work produced,

(d) General management responsibility of the work, and

(e) Recipient of the work product. This relationship involves the transfer of information and not any coordinative responsibility.

(8) *Schedules.*

(a) Tabulation of Major Milestones,

(b) CMCS Master Schedule or update thereto,

(c) Construction Manager's Schedule, and

(d) Detailed schedules for A-E and government work.

(9) *Written Procedures* for coordinating the project among the Construction Manager, the A-E, the Government, and the separate contractors.

c. *Approval of the Management Plans for Design and Construction.*

(1) The non-reimbursable work breakdown structures and detailed schedules of all deliverable work items submitted for each phase will be reviewed by the Contracting Officer who shall have the right to approve or disapprove the price and/or schedule for performing each detailed deliverable work item. The sum of the prices for each detailed deliverable work item shall not vary from the price for the higher-level deliverable work items shown on the network diagram of the accepted priced proposal management plan. The

schedule for performing the detailed deliverable work items shall not vary substantially from the time of performance indicated upon the network diagram. The written approval of the price and schedule for performance of each detailed deliverable work item shall establish the specific basis for monthly payment for work accomplished.

(2) The management plans submitted for each phase will be reviewed by the Contracting Officer who shall have the right to approve or disapprove the recommended plan. The Contracting Officer's approval of each plan shall provide the Construction Manager the basis to execute the program of work for each phase.

(3) The CMCS shall be adjusted to reflect any changes necessitated by implementation of this clause.

d. *Management Plan Updates.*

The Construction Manager shall continuously update and revise the major aspects of the management plans which are necessary to maintain the plans as a viable management tool.

e. *Recommendations for Reimbursable Job-Site Staff.*

Included in the Construction Manager's submission of the management plan for the design and construction overlap phase shall be the Construction Manager's recommendations for the reimbursable job-site staff.

(1) The Construction Manager shall review the management plan in his accepted priced proposal and the elements of the above detailed management plan.

(2) The Construction Manager will develop his recommendations for reimbursable job-site staff to supplement the nonreimbursable job-site staff in carrying out the detailed schedule of all deliverable work items. The recommendations will be based upon the tentative reimbursable job-site staff listing in his accepted priced proposal management plan and shall not vary substantially therefrom with respect to numbers, ratio of higher-salaried to lower-salaried positions, man-hours or other factors disclosed in the tentative reimbursable job-site staff listing of the accepted priced proposal management plan. He shall submit the recommendations to the Contracting Officer, together with resumes of the qualifications of the full-time reimbursable job-site staff proposed. The Construction Manager is encouraged to propose utilization of personnel of the Architect-Engineer who were involved in design development to the extent they became available for employment as inspectors by the Construction Manager.

(3) The recommendations will be reviewed by the Contracting Officer who shall have the right to approve or to disapprove deviations from the tentative reimbursable job-site staff listing submitted with the Construction Manager's priced proposal as well as the right to approve or disapprove the reimbursable job-site staff personnel proposed.

6. DESIGN DEVELOPMENT AND REVIEW

a. The Construction Manager shall familiarize himself thoroughly with the evolving architectural, civil, mechanical, electrical, and structural plans and specifications and shall continuously follow the development of design through concepts, tentatives and working drawings. He shall make recommendations with respect to the site, foundations, selection of systems and materials, and cost reducing alternatives. He shall furnish pertinent information as to the availability of materials and labor that will be required. He shall submit to the Government such comments as may be appropriate concerning construction feasibility and practicality. He shall call to the Government's attention any apparent defects in the design.

b. As the A-E completes his work on each bid package for each separate contract, the Construction Manager shall perform a specific review thereof, focussed upon factors of a nature encompassed in paragraph a above and on factors set out in the clause "Interfacing." Promptly after completion of the review, he shall submit to the Contracting Officer a written report covering action taken by the A-E with respect to suggestions or recommendations previously submitted, additional suggestions or recommendations as he may deem appropriate, any comments he may deem to be appropriate with respect to separating the work into separate contracts, and all comments called for under the clause "Interfacing."

7. LONG LEAD PROCUREMENT

During the concept design phase and each phase thereafter, the Construction Manager shall review the design for the purpose of identifying long lead procurement items (machinery, equipment, materials and supplies) which can or must be separately procured by the Government ahead of the time required for installation in order to assure completion of the project within the time specified in clause 1. As each item is identified, the Construction Manager shall notify the Contracting Officer and the A-E of the required procurement and schedule. As soon as the A-E has completed drawings and technical specifications, the Construction Manager shall prepare invitations for bids in conformity with applicable Government procurement statutes, regulations and policies. The Construction Manager shall keep himself informed of the progress of the respective contractors manufacturing or fabricating such items and advise the Contracting Officer of any problems or prospective delay in delivery.

8. SEPARATE CONTRACTS PLANNING

a. The Construction Manager shall continuously review the design development with the Architect-Engineer and make recommendations to the Contracting Officer and to the Architect-Engineer with respect to dividing the work in such manner as will permit the Government to take bids (or proposals) on and to award separate construction contracts on a phased basis while design is being completed. He shall take into consideration such factors as natural and practical lines of severability, sequencing effectiveness, access and availability constraints, total time for completion, construction market conditions, availability of labor and materials, community relations and any other factors pertinent to saving time and cost by overlapping design and construction.

b. He shall give particular attention to planning the separation of work into separate contracts in such a way as to enable the Government to award contracts to the Small Business Administration for performance by economically disadvantaged small business firms under the SBA's 8(a) program. To this end, he shall make active inquiries as to the identity of such prospective firms, the categories of work which they are qualified to perform and the maximum size of contract they are capable of undertaking.

9. INTERFACING

    a. The Construction Manager shall take such measures as are appropriate to ensure that all construction requirements will be covered in the separate contracts for procurement of long lead items, the separate construction contracts and general condition items to be performed by the Construction Manager, without duplication or overlap, sequenced to ensure completion of all work by the time required under the provisions of this contract. Particular attention shall be given to ensuring that each bid package clearly identifies what work is included in that particular separate contract.

    b. The Construction Manager shall include in the reports required under paragraph b of the clause "Design Development and Review" comments on overlap with any other separate contract, omissions, lack of correlation between drawings, and any other deficiencies noted, in order that the Contracting Officer may arrange for necessary corrections.

10. JOB-SITE FACILITIES

The Construction Manager shall ensure that provision is made for (1) all of the temporary facilities necessary to enable contractors to perform their work and (2) all job-site facilities necessary to enable the Construction Manager and the Government representatives to perform their duties in the management, inspection, and supervision of construction.

11. WEATHER PROTECTION

The Construction Manager shall ascertain what temporary enclosures, if any, of building areas should be provided for and may be provided as a practical matter, in order to assure orderly progress of the work in periods when extreme weather conditions are likely to be experienced. He shall submit to the Contracting Officer his recommendations as to needed requirements of this nature and as to the contract or contracts in which they should be included (or, alternatively, his recommendation that such facilities be furnished as general condition items under the provisions of this contract).

12. SOLICITATION OF BIDS

    a. The Construction Manager shall prepare for Government issuance invitations for bids (or requests for proposals, when applicable) for all procurements of long lead items and for separate construction contracts.

    b. As part of such preparation, he shall review the specifications and drawings prepared by the Architect-Engineer. Ambiguities, conflicts or lack of clarity of language, use of illegally restrictive requirements, and any other defects in the specifications or in the drawings shall be brought to the attention of the Contracting Officer.

    c. The Construction Manager shall prepare all additional forms and provisions, required by applicable statutes, Government procurement regulations and GSA policies, as will constitute invitations for bids suitable for reproduction and issuance by the Government. Applicable Government procurement regulations include, but are not limited to, the Federal Procurement Regulations and the General Services Procurement Regulations.

    d. For each separate construction contract, the Construction Manager will conduct a pre-bid conference with prospective bidders. In the event questions are raised which require an interpretation of the bidding documents or otherwise indicate a need for clarification or correction of the invitation, the Construction Manager shall prepare an amendment to the invitation, suitable for issuance by the Government.

e. The Construction Manager shall review bids, if requested to do so by the Contracting Officer, provide the Contracting Officer with assistance during any negotiations under the negotiated procurement procedures, and, if requested by the Contracting Officer, submit information or recommendations concerning an award.

13. MARKET ANALYSIS AND STIMULATION OF BIDDER INTEREST

a. The Construction Manager shall continuously monitor conditions in the construction market to identify factors that will or may affect costs and time for completing the project; he shall make analyses as may be necessary to (1) determine and report on availability of labor, material, equipment, potential bidders, and impact of any shortages or surpluses of labor or material, and (2) in the light of such determinations, make recommendations as may be appropriate with respect to long lead procurement, separation of construction into bid packages, sequencing of work, use of alternative materials, equipment or methods, other economies in design or construction, and any other matter that will promote cost savings and completion within the time specified in clause 1.

b. Within 30 days after receiving notice to proceed, the Construction Manager shall submit a written "Construction Market Analysis and Prospective Bidders Report" setting out the above-required determinations and recommendations and providing information as to prospective bidders. Once each month thereafter, until award of the final separate construction contract, the Construction Manager shall submit an updated report.

c. The Construction Manager shall carry out an active program of stimulating interest of qualified contractors in bidding on the work and of familiarizing those bidders who are not experienced in Government contracting with Federal government procurement requirements.

14. MANAGING AND INSPECTING CONSTRUCTION

The Construction Manager shall coordinate and provide general direction of the work of the separate construction contractors; he shall inspect the work performed by the separate contractors to ensure conformity with requirements of their respective contract. In the event any differences arise between the Construction Manager and any separate construction contractor, the Construction Manager shall inform the Contracting Officer promptly in writing, giving both the details of pertinent facts and applicable contract provisions and his recommendation as to action to be taken by the Contracting Officer. Promptly after receipt of the Contracting Officer's written interpretation, the Construction Manager shall transmit it to the separate construction contractor.

15. MONITORING SUBMITTALS

The Construction Manager will monitor the time of submission and the processing of shop drawings, samples and other separate contractor submittals. If submittals are not being timely received, he shall ascertain the reason therefore and either take such action, or direct the field staff to take such action, as may be appropriate to eliminate lags and delays in such processing. He shall notify the Contracting Officer promptly of any delays of the A-E in processing.

16. SUBCONTRACTOR OR MATERIAL VENDOR RECOMMENDATIONS

Whenever any separate contract requires advance approval of proposed subcontractors or material vendors, the Construction Manager shall review the competitive proposals received by the separate contractor, the prospective subcontractor's or supplier's qualifications and financial ability to complete the work (if applicable) and shall recommend to the Contracting Office the appropriate action to be taken on the request for approval.

17. COMPREHENSIVE SAFETY PROGRAM

The Construction Manager shall review the safety programs developed by each of the separate contractors and prepare and submit to the Contracting Officer a recommended comprehensive safety program. (Performance of such services will not be regarded by the Government as relieving the separate contractors of their respective responsibilities for the safety of persons and property or from compliance with all applicable statutes, rules, regulations, or orders.) During construction, the Construction Manager shall monitor compliance by the separate contractors with their contractual safety requirements and report deficiencies. He shall cooperate to the extent appropriate with officials of other agencies (Federal and/or State) who are vested with authority to enforce the requirements of the Williams-Steiger Occupational Safety and Health Act of 1970.

18. LABOR RELATIONS

The Construction Manager shall make recommendations and render assistance as necessary for the development and administration of an effective labor relations program for the project and the avoidance of labor disputes during construction.

19. CONSTRUCTION CONTRACT CHANGES

The Construction Manager shall furnish assistance to the Contracting Officer in the administration of changes to separate contracts, including but not limited to the following services:

a. The Construction Manager shall recommend a change to a construction contract whenever a change appears to be necessary. Upon receipt of any change suggested by a separate contractor, the Construction Manager shall review the merit thereof and either reject the suggestion or forward it to the Contracting Officer with his recommendation thereon.

b. Whenever the Contracting Officer so directs, the Construction Manager shall request a proposal from the affected separate contractor(s) for performing a change contemplated, prepare a cost estimate, review applicable drawings and specifications (whether prepared by the A-E or by the affected contractor or contractors), estimate additional performance time that may be required in the event a change order is issued, review the proposal received, and make such recommendation to the Contracting Officer as the Construction Manager may, in the exercise of sound judgment, deem appropriate.

c. For any change order on which agreement has not been reached as to the amount of equitable adjustment prior to commencement, the Construction Manager shall observe performance by the separate contractor, make detailed records of equipment, material, and labor utilized and of the impact on unchanged work, together with records of any other data or information pertinent to a determination of the amount of equitable adjustment of the separate contractor's contract price and time of performance.

d. All changes shall be reflected in the CMCS.

20. VALUE MANAGEMENT SERVICES

The Construction Manager shall perform all Value Management services required of a Construction Manager under the provisions of Chapter 7, Figure 7-21.5, GSA Handbook, Value Engineering, PBS P 8000.1. Paragraph 220 of Figure 7-21.5 is amended to delete "A-E" from the second line thereof and to substitute "CM".

21. CLAIMS

Whenever any claim arises under or out of any contract awarded by the Government in furtherance of this project, the Construction Manager shall diligently render all assistance which the Government may require, including the furnishing of reports with supporting information necessary to resolve the dispute or defend against the claim, participation in meetings or negotiations with the claimant or its representatives, appearance before the Board of Contract Appeals or court of law, and other assistance as may be appropriate; Provided, however, that the Construction Manager shall not be obligated under this contract to provide such services after all construction work has been completed and accepted by the Government.

22. MEETINGS AND CONFERENCES

The Construction Manager shall take minutes at meetings; transcribe the minutes; and furnish a copy to each participant. The Construction Manager shall also conduct pre-bid conferences and a pre-construction conference with the successful bidder on each separate construction contract; he shall also conduct job-site meetings with separate contractors and representatives of the Contracting Officer, as necessary, to discuss such matters as procedures, progress, problems, schedules, equal employment opportunity and any other matters that may arise.

23. HOME OFFICE SUPPORT FOR JOB-SITE STAFF; RELOCATION COSTS

The Construction Manager shall provide all home office support and relocation costs for the nonreimbursable job-site staff and the approved reimbursable job-site staff.

24. REIMBURSABLE SERVICES

The Construction Manager shall perform the following services utilizing approved reimbursable job-site staff except to the extent otherwise provided:

a. *Coordination and Inspection:* Assist the non-reimbursable job-site staff in performing the requirements of the clauses "Managing and Inspecting Construction" and "Monitoring Submittals" and in monitoring the separate contractors' adherence to their respective schedules.

b. *Safety:* Assist the non-reimbursable job-site staff in monitoring the separate contractors' compliance with the safety requirements of their respective contracts in the context of the Construction Manager's comprehensive project safety program.

c. *Meetings and conferences:* Assist the non-reimbursable job-site staff in conducting pre-bid and pre-construction conferences; schedule and either conduct or assist the non-reimbursable job-site staff in conducting job-site meetings with separate contractors and representatives of the Contracting Officer, to discuss procedures, progress, problems, scheduling and other appropriate matters; take minutes of each such meeting, transcribe, and distribute copies to all those who attended.

d. *Contractor personnel, equipment and supplies:* Assist the nonreimbursable job-site staff in monitoring the adequacy of the separate contractors' personnel and equipment and availability of necessary materials and supplies.

e. *CMCS data:* Assist the nonreimbursable staff in obtaining and assembling data for incorporation into the CMCS data base.

f. *Records:* Under the direction of the non-reimbursable job-site staff, maintain at the job-site, on a current basis, records of all contracts (including all correspondence received or issued by the Construction Manager and the Contracting Officer's authorized representatives); all change orders and documents related thereto; all records relating to shop drawings, samples, purchases, sub-contracts; material, equipment; applicable handbooks, and Federal, commercial and technical standards and specifications; daily diary; and all other documents related to this contract and the construction work. These records will be delivered to the Contracting Officer prior to final payment under this contract.

g. *Time and material records:* Assist the non-reimbursable job-site staff in making the observations and records required under paragraph c of the clause "Construction Contract Changes;" and make similar observations and records of time and material in connection with any other contract work which is performed on a time and materials basis, unit cost basis, or other basis necessitating such observation and record-keeping.

h. *Daily diary; progress records; reports:* Under the direction of the nonreimbursable job-site staff, keep accurate and detailed written records of the progress of the project during all stages of construction. Maintain a detailed daily diary of all events which occur at the job-site or elsewhere which affect or may be expected to affect progress of the project. The diary shall be available to the Contracting Officer at all times and shall be turned over to him upon completion and approval of all construction.

i. *Contractors' Payments:* Under the direction of the nonreimbursable job-site staff, review and process all applications by separate contractors for progress payments and final payments, and submit recommendations concerning approval thereof to the Contracting Officer in accordance with the current printout of the CMCS.

j. *Changes to Separate Contracts:* Assist the nonreimbursable job-site staff in evaluating proposed changes, securing proposals, preparing estimates, reviewing proposals, making recommendations to the Contracting Officer, and observing performance of changes pursuant to the clause "Construction Contract Change."

k. *Claims:* Under the direction of the nonreimbursable job-site staff, review claims from separate contractors; furnish information to be included in the reports required under the clause "Claims"; and, when requested by the Contracting Officer, participate in meetings or negotiations with the claimant or its representatives and/or appear before the Board of Contract Appeals or court of law; Provided, however, that the Construction Manager shall not be obligated under this clause to provide the services required hereunder after all construction work has been completed and accepted by the Government.

l. *Overall Dimensions and Elevations:* Prepare and submit to the Government certified records in duplicate of building and approach lines; elevations of bottoms of footings, floor levels, and approaches made as the work progresses. Each record shall be certified by the Construction Manager (or by an employee of the Construction Manager if the Construction Manager is not eligible, as a firm, to certify) and by the resident engineer if a resident engineer has been designated by the Government.

m. *As-Built Drawings:* Maintain at the job-site a current marked set of the working drawing prints and specifications. Upon completion of construction, transcribe all changes on a set of plastic reproducibles of the drawings and turn over to the Contracting Officer a complete set of the plastic reproducibles as well as the marked set of working drawings and specifications.

n. *Storage of Long Lead Items:* At the direction of the Contracting Officer, make arrangements for accepting delivery and for on-site or off-site storage, protection and security until the items of material or equipment are turned over to separate contractors for installation.

o. *General Condition Items:* When required by the Contracting Officer under the provisions of clause "General Condition Items," perform general condition items of work or, if performance of the item by subcontract is authorized, supplement the services of nonreimbursable personnel in securing quotations and administering the subcontract.

p. *Inspection:* Assist Government personnel and nonreimbursable job-site staff in performing pre-final and final inspections of the work of separate contractors; prepare detailed reports to the Contracting Officer covering observed discrepancies, deficiencies and omissions in the work performed by any of the separate contractors.

25. GENERAL CONDITION ITEMS

a. The Construction Manager shall, from time to time and without notice to any surety during the course of construction, recommend to the Contracting Officer general condition items for performance by the Construction Manager.

b. In addition, the Government shall have the right to require the Construction Manager to perform general condition items as determined by the Contracting Officer.

c. If the Contracting Officer elects to approve a recommendation for, or direct, performance of a general condition item by the Construction Manager, he shall so notify the Construction Manager in writing, describing the services to be performed and providing any applicable specifications, drawings and any other necessary details. The Construction Manager shall comply promptly upon receipt of any such approval or directive. In addition, the Contracting Officer shall have the right to make changes in any such approval or directive.

d. The Government shall reimburse the Construction Manager for all costs and expenses (but without mark-up for profit and overhead) incurred in performing general condition items authorized or required under the provisions of this clause, as follows:

    (1) The costs of all job-site materials used;

(2) The costs of all job-site labor and supervision (except supervision by the Construction Manager's nonreimbursable staff and supervision by reimbursable job-site staff for whom the Construction Manager is being reimbursed under other provisions of this contract), inclusive of wages or salaries, payroll taxes thereon, fringe benefits required pursuant to the Secretary of Labor's Wage Rate Decision made applicable under this contract, and fringe benefits for supervisors (such as vacation and sick leave allowances) in accordance with established company policies;

(3) The costs of renting equipment from others; Provided, however, that every agreement under which the Construction Manager rents equipment from others shall contain an option or options for purchase of such equipment by the Construction Manager. A copy of each such agreement shall be filed with the Contracting Officer promptly after execution. At the request of the Contracting Officer, the Construction Manager shall exercise the option and in such event, the Government shall reimburse the Construction Manager for the purchase price. The Construction Manager shall dispose of such equipment as directed by the Contracting Officer and shall credit the proceeds to the Government;

(4) A rental rate on equipment owned by the Construction Manager and used in the performance of a general condition item, computed in accordance with the provisions of the latest edition of the "Contractors' Equipment Ownership Expense" prepared by the Associated General Contractors of America, Inc. The rental shall be computed starting with the date equipment is placed in operation at the site and terminating when the equipment is no longer required for use in performing the general condition item, excluding any time the equipment is out of service for major repairs or overhauling;

(5) Costs of transporting equipment and materials to and from the site;

(6) Costs of expendable supplies consumed in performing the work; (such as fuel, lubricants, water, electricity, fire extinguishers, etc.).

(7) Expenditures for permits, licenses and privileges which are necessary for performance of the general condition items and would not otherwise be required;

(8) Sales and use tax on equipment, materials, supplies and/or services for which the Construction Manager is reimbursed hereunder, except to the extent such taxes are included in an equipment rental rate and except when an exemption is available under the provisions of the tax statute.

(9) Amounts paid subcontractors on approved subcontracts;

(10) The cost of performance and payment bonds;

(11) Premiums on any additional insurance which the Construction Manager would not otherwise have obtained, to the extent reasonable; and

(12) Such additional costs of performing a general condition item as determined by the Contracting Officer to constitute a necessary and actual cost of performing the work, which costs would not have been incurred but for the authorization or directive to perform the general condition item.

e. Reimbursement to the Construction Manager under the foregoing provisions shall be reduced by the amount of (1) discounts for prompt payment of invoices,

(2) the salvage value of materials, equipment or supplies for which the Construction Manager has been reimbursed, to the extent the Construction Manager retains them for its own use when no longer needed in connection with this contract; and (3) any rebates, refunds, returned deposits or other reductions of costs for which the Construction Manager has been reimbursed.

f. The Construction Manager shall remove and replace any work or materials found to be defective, without cost to the Government.

26. REIMBURSABLE COSTS

a. *Reimbursement:* The Government shall reimburse the Construction Manager for costs and expenses (without mark-up for overhead and profit) for the following, provided that the Contracting Officer has authorized the Construction Manager in advance in writing to incur such costs:

(1) Costs of reproducing and distributing the CMCS reports and network diagrams;

(2) Amounts paid special consultants under subcontract (except the CMCS and Value Management consultants or specialists);

(3) Costs incurred in performing general condition items in accordance with the provisions of clause "General Condition Items";

(4) Salaries paid reimbursable job-site staff as authorized under the provisions of the clause "Management Plan for Design and Construction", payroll taxes thereon, the actual costs of fringe benefits (such as vacation and sick leave, court leave, military leave, pension or retirement plan contributions, and the like) to the extent allowable under FPR Part 1-15 and not in excess of amounts payable under established policies of the Construction Manager;

(5) The cost of premiums for insurance such as builders risk insurance, general liability insurance, or other appropriate types of insurance exclusively for this project, as determined jointly by the Contracting Officer and the Construction Manager to be necessary for the project;

(6) Travel expenses and per diem in lieu of subsistence (except for intra-joint venture travel, if any), in accordance with the Standardized Government Travel Regulations, as amended, in effect at the time the travel is performed; and

(7) Office facilities at locations other than the Construction Manager's home office, branch office or job-site, when jointly determined by the Construction Manager and the Contracting Officer to be necessary for the project.

b. *Records, Accounts and Audit:*

(1) Requests for reimbursement of identified costs under the provisions of this contract shall be accompanied by such supporting evidentiary documentation as the Contracting Officer may require.

(2) The Construction Manager agrees to keep books of account, records, documents, and other evidence of costs for which reimbursement is claimed under the provisions of this contract. The method of accounting employed by the Construction Manager shall be subject to the approval of the Contracting Officer and shall segregate or permit ready identification of costs for which reimbursement is requested.

c. *Replacement of Reimbursable Personnel:* If the Contracting Officer directs removal from the work of any personnel of the reimbursable job-site staff or the removal from the work of any personnel employed on general condition items, the Construction Manager shall promptly replace such personnel with personnel acceptable to the Contracting Officer, at no change in reimbursable costs.

27. LUMP SUM CONTRACT PRICE

a. Except to the extent that the Construction Manager is entitled to be reimbursed for costs incurred, under the provisions of this contract, payment of the lump sum contract price as provided herein shall constitute full compensation for all costs (direct or indirect, including overhead) and profit.

b. The Construction Manager agrees that all services will be performed by nonreimbursable personnel except to the extent otherwise provided under, or authorized pursuant to, the provisions of this contract. In the event the Construction Manager elects to locate nonreimbursable personnel at the job-site in order to facilitate the performance by them or for other reasons, the Construction Manager will not be entitled to be reimbursed for their services under the terms of the clause "Reimbursable Services" or for any costs incurred in such transfer, location or relocation. The Construction Manager shall not be entitled to be reimbursed under the provisions of clauses "Reimbursable Services" and "Reimbursable Costs" to the extent he utilizes otherwise authorized reimbursable job-site staff to perform services or functions outside the scope of services to be performed by such personnel under the terms of this contract. In the event that services, other than as authorized under or in accordance with the terms of this contract, are performed by reimbursable job-site staff, the Construction Manager shall credit the amount of any reimbursement which he has received but which he is not entitled to receive against future payments due under the contract or remit the amount to the Government.

28. PAYMENT

a. The lump sum contract price of $_____, including $_____ for the design phase, $_____ for the design and construction overlap phase, and $_____ for the construction phase shall be paid in monthly installments based upon detailed deliverable work items which are shown on the approved nonreimbursable work breakdown structures and CMCS Report F6 and which have been completed as of the end of the month, less all prior monthly payments. Installment payments made on the foregoing basis shall be deemed to constitute payment for all services rendered up to the date of payment including services not within the definition of deliverables (except services which are reimbursable).

b. The Government shall reimburse the Construction Manager for all expenditures during the billing month for which he is entitled to be reimbursed under the provisions of the clause "Reimbursable Costs".

c. Prior to final payment under the provisions of this clause, the Construction Manager shall furnish the Contracting Officer a release of all claims against the Government, other than claims in stated amounts as may be specifically excepted by the Construction Manager from the operation of the release.

29. STAFF (NONREIMBURSABLE)

a. The Construction Manager shall utilize the personnel named and/or otherwise identified in its priced proposal as well as any additional personnel as may be necessary in order to meet the performance requirements of this contract. The Construction Manager will not be entitled to any increase in the lump sum contract price for furnishing such additional personnel. Reimbursable personnel will be used only to the extent permissible or authorized under clauses "Reimbursable Services", "General Condition Items" and "Reimbursable Costs".

b. The Contracting Officer shall have the right to require the Construction Manager to remove from the work any employee determined by the Contracting Officer to be unqualified, incompetent, uncooperative or otherwise unacceptable for valid reasons.

c. In the event that any of the personnel named in the priced proposal are unable to perform because of death, illness, resignation from the Construction Manager's employ, the Contracting Officer's request for removal, or similar reasons, the Construction Manager shall promptly submit to the Contracting Officer, in writing, the name and qualifications of a proposed replacement. No substitution shall be made without the prior written approval of the Contracting Officer. Any such approved substitutions shall be made at no increase in the lump sum contract price.

d. If the Contracting Officer directs removal from the work of any personnel, identified other than by name in the Construction Manager's priced proposal, performing services necessary for accomplishment of the performance requirements of this contract, the Construction Manager shall promptly replace such personnel with a staff member acceptable to the Contracting Officer, at no change in the lump sum contract price.

30. SUBCONTRACTING

a. In subcontracting for performance of general condition items, the Construction Manager shall solicit competitive bids (not less than three unless otherwise authorized by the Contracting Officer).

b. Except as provided above with respect to subcontracts for general condition items, the services to be performed hereunder shall be performed by the Construction Manager's own staff, except to the extent (1) otherwise authorized or required herein, or (2) otherwise authorized by the Contracting Officer. The employment of, contract with, or use of the services of any other person or firm by the Construction Manager, as a consultant or in any other capacity, except as an employee, shall be subject to the prior written approval of the Contracting Officer. Such approval shall not be construed as constituting an agreement between the Government and any such person or firm.

c. The Construction Manager agrees to physically include in all authorized or approved subcontracts (including subcontracts for performance of general condition items) all clauses of this contract which, by their terms, are required to be included in such subcontracts (as, for example, the clause "Equal Opportunity") and all clauses, which, by their nature, must be carried forward into the subcontract (for example, "Accident Prevention for General Conditions Work").

31. FEDERAL, STATE, AND LOCAL TAXES

a. Except as may be otherwise provided in this contract, the contract price includes all applicable Federal, State, and local taxes and duties.

b. Nevertheless, with respect to any Federal excise tax or duty on the transactions or property covered by this contract, if a statute, court decision, written ruling, or regulation takes effect after the contract date, and-

(1) Results in the Construction Manager being required to pay or bear the

burden of any such Federal excise tax or duty or increase in the rate thereof which would not otherwise have been payable on such transactions or property, the contract price shall be increased by the amount of such tax or duty or rate increase: Provided, that the Construction Manager if requested by the Contracting Officer, warrants in writing that no amount for such newly imposed Federal excise tax or duty or rate increase was included in the contract price as a contingency reserve or otherwise; or

(2) Results in the Construction Manager not being required to pay or bear the burden of, or in his obtaining a refund or drawback of, any such Federal excise tax or duty which would otherwise have been payable on such transactions or property or which was the basis of an increase in the contract price, the contract price shall be decreased by the amount of the relief, refund, or drawback, or that amount shall be paid to Government, as directed by the Contracting Officer. The contract price shall be similarly decreased if the Construction Manager, through his fault or negligence or his failure to follow instructions of the Contracting Officer, is required to pay or bear the burden of, or does not obtain a refund or drawback of, any such Federal excise tax or duty.

c. No adjustment pursuant to paragraph b. above will be made under this contract unless the aggregate amount thereof is or may reasonably be expected to be over $100.

d. As used in paragraph b. above, the term "contract date" means the date set for the bid opening, or if this is a negotiated contract, the date of this contract. As to additional supplies or services procured by modification to this contract, the term "contract date" means the date of such modification.

e. Unless there does not exist any reasonable basis to sustain an exemption, the Government, upon request of the Construction Manager, without further liability, agrees, except as otherwise provided in this contract, to furnish evidence appropriate to establish exemption from any tax which the Construction Manager warrants in writing was excluded from the contract price. In addition, the Contracting Officer may furnish evidence to establish exemption from any tax that may, pursuant to this clause, give rise to either an increase or decrease in the contract price. Except as otherwise provided in this contract, evidence appropriate to establish exemption from duties will be furnished only at the discretion of the Contracting Officer.

f. The Construction Manager shall promptly notify the Contracting Officer of matters which will result in either an increase or decrease in the contract price, and shall take action with respect thereto as directed by the Contracting Officer.

32. TIME FOR COMPLETION

a. As provided in clause "General" and other clauses of this contract, the Construction Manager is to perform this contract in such a manner as to ensure that construction will be completed as early as possible, but not later than the date set out in clause 1; he will not be responsible for time overrun in the event that construction is not completed by the scheduled date for reasons beyond his control and without his fault or negligence.

b. In any event, however, services required under this contract shall be considered complete only when all construction work has been completed and accepted by the Government.

33. SUSPENSION OF WORK—DELAYS

a. The Contracting Officer may order the Construction Manager in writing to suspend, delay, or interrupt all or any part of the Construction Manager's work or services under this contract for such period of time as he may determine to be appropriate for the convenience of the Government.

b. If the performance of all or any part of the Construction Manager's work services under this contract is, for an unreasonable period of time, suspended, delayed, or interrupted by an act of the Contracting Officer in the administration of the project, or by his failure to act within the time specified in this contract (or if no time is specified, within a reasonable time), an adjustment shall be made for any increase in the cost of performance of this contract (excluding profit) necessarily caused by such unreasonable suspension, delay, or interruption and the contract modified in writing accordingly. However, no adjustment shall be made under this clause for any suspension, delay, or interruption to the extent (1) that performance would have been so suspended, delayed, or interrupted by any other cause, including the fault or negligence of the Construction Manager or (2) for which an equitable adjustment is provided for or excluded under any other provision of this contract.

c. No claim under this clause shall be allowed (1) for any costs incurred more than 20 days before the Construction Manager shall have notified the Contracting Officer in writing of the act or failure to act involved (but this requirement shall not apply as to a claim resulting from a suspension order), and (2) unless the claim, in an amount stated, is asserted in writing as soon as practicable after the termination of such suspension, delay, or interruption, but no later than the date of final payment under the contract.

d. In the event work on the project is suspended or otherwise delayed the Government shall reimburse the Construction Manager for the costs of its reimbursable job-site staff as provided for by this agreement for the first 30 days of such delay. The Construction Manager shall reduce the size of its reimbursable job-site staff for the remainder of the delay period as directed by the Contracting Officer and, during such period, the Government shall reimburse the Construction Manager for the costs of such reduced staff plus the actual cost of fringe benefits as prescribed in clause 26a(4). Upon the termination of the delay the Construction Manager shall restore its reimbursable job-site staff to its former size, subject to the approval of the Government.

34. CHANGES

a. The Contracting Officer may, at any time, by written order, make changes within the general scope of this contract in the services to be performed. If such changes cause an increase or decrease in the Construction Manager's cost of performance of any services under this contract, whether or not changed by any order, an equitable adjustment shall be made and the contract shall be modified in writing accordingly. Any claim of the Construction Manager for adjustment must be asserted in writing within 30 days from the date of receipt by the Construction Manager of the notification of change unless the Contracting Officer grants a further period of time before the date of final payment under this contract.

b. No services for which an additional payment will be claimed under this clause by the Construction Manager shall be furnished without prior written authorization of the Contracting Officer.

35. PRICING OF ADJUSTMENTS

When costs are a factor in any determination of a contract price adjustment pursuant to the "Changes" clause or any other provisions of this contract, such costs shall be in accordance with the contract cost principles and procedures in Part 1-15 of the Federal Procurement Regulations (41 CFR 1-15) or section XV of the Armed Services Procurement Regulation in effect on the date of this contract.

36. DISPUTES

a. Except as otherwise provided in this agreement, any dispute concerning a question of fact arising under this agreement which is not disposed of by agreement shall be decided by the Contracting Officer, who shall reduce his decision to writing and mail or otherwise furnish a copy thereof to the Construction Manager. The decision of the Contracting Officer shall be final and conclusive unless within 30 days from the date of receipt of such copy, the Construction Manager mails or otherwise furnishes to the Contracting Officer a written appeal addressed to the Administrator of General Services. The decision of the Administrator of General Services or his duly authorized representative for the determination of such appeals shall be final and conclusive. This provision shall not be pleaded in any suit involving a question of fact arising under this contract as limiting judicial review of any such decision to cases where fraud by such official or his representative or board is alleged; Provided, however, that any such decision shall be final and conclusive unless the same is fraudulent or capricious or arbitrary or so grossly erroneous as necessarily to imply bad faith or is not supported by substantial evidence. In connection with any appeal proceeding under this clause, the Construction Manager shall be afforded an opportunity to be heard and to offer evidence in support of his appeal. Pending final decision of a dispute hereunder, the Construction Manager shall proceed diligently with the performance of the contract and in accordance with the Contracting Officer's decision.

b. This "Disputes" clause does not preclude consideration of questions of law in connection with decisions provided for in paragraph a above. Nothing in this agreement, however, shall be construed as making final the decision of any administrative official, representative, or board on a question of law.

37. PAYMENT OF INTEREST ON CONSTRUCTION MANAGER'S CLAIMS

a. If an appeal is filed with the Construction Manager from a final decision of the Contracting Officer under the "Disputes" clause of this contract, denying a claim arising under the contract, simple interest on the amount of the claim finally determined owed by the Government shall be payable to the Construction Manager. Such interest shall be at the rate determined by the Secretary of the Treasury pursuant to Public Law 92-41, 85 Stat. 97, from the date the Construction Manager furnishes to the Contracting Officer his written appeal under the "Disputes" clause of this contract, to the date of (1) a final judgment by a court of competent jurisdiction, or (2) mailing to the Construction Manager of a supplemental agreement for execution either confirming completed negotiations between the parties or carrying out a decision of a board of contract appeals.

b. Notwithstanding a. above, (1) interest shall be applied only from the date payment was due, if such date is later than the filing of appeal, and (2) interest shall not be paid for any period of time that the Contracting Officer determines the Construction Manager has unduly delayed in pursuing his remedies before a board of contract appeals or a court of competent jurisdiction.

38. TERMINATION

a. The Contracting Officer may, by written notice to the Construction Manager, terminate this contract in whole or in part at any time, either for the Government's convenience or because of the failure of the Construction Manager to fulfill his contract obligations. Upon receipt of such notice, the Construction Manager shall: (1) immediately discontinue all services affected (unless the notice directs otherwise) and (2) deliver to the Contracting Officer all estimates, schedules, reports, records, summaries, data and such other information and materials as may have been accumulated by the Construction Manager in performing this contract, whether completed or in process.

b. If the termination is for the convenience of the Government, the Construction Manager will be paid an installment of the lump sum contract price for completed deliverables, in accordance with all applicable provisions of this contract, for which payment has not already been made, an equitable adjustment for all activities in process not covered by the last installment payment hereunder, and any settlement costs to which the Construction Manager may be entitled under the provisions of FPR 1-8 of the Federal Procurement Regulations (41 CFR 1-8) in effect on the date this contract was executed. The Construction Manager shall not be entitled to be paid any amount as profit on unperformed work or on settlement costs.

c. If the termination is due to the failure of the Construction Manager to fulfill his contract obligations, the Government may take over the work and prosecute the same to completion by contract or otherwise. In such case, the Construction Manager shall be liable to the Government for any additional cost occasioned to the Government thereby.

d. If, after notice of termination for failure to fulfill contract obligations, it is determined that the Construction Manager had not so failed, the termination shall be deemed to have been effected for the convenience of the Government and the Construction Manager shall be paid in accordance with the provisions of paragraph b above.

39. PARTIAL TERMINATION FOR UNTIMELY PERFORMANCE

In lieu of any other right of termination, if the Construction Manager fails to complete any activity under the clause "Management Plan for Design and Construction", which activity is within the definition of deliverables, by the time shown in the applicable phase, the Government shall have the right to reject the late performance (whether completed or not) and terminate the Construction Manager's right to proceed with that activity and the lump sum contract price shall be reduced on the basis of the ratio which the terminated activity bears to the whole of the services required under this contract, regardless of whether or not the Construction Manager had incurred costs in connection therewith prior to the termination. The Government's rights under this clause may be invoked only when performance, if untimely, is of little or no value to the Government as determined by the Contracting Officer.

40. COVENANT AGAINST CONTINGENT FEES

The Construction Manager warrants that no person or selling agency has been employed or retained to solicit or secure this contract upon an agreement or understanding for a commission, percentage, brokerage or contingent fee, excepting bona fide employees or bona fide established commercial or selling agencies maintained by the Construction Manager for the purpose of securing business. For breach or violation of this warranty the Contracting Officer shall have the right to annul this agreement price or consideration, or otherwise recover, the full amount of such commission, percentage, brokerage, or contingent fee.

41. OFFICIALS NOT TO BENEFIT

No member of or delegate to Congress, or resident commissioner, shall be admitted to any share or part of this agreement, or to any benefit that may arise therefrom; but this provision shall not be construed to extend to this agreement if made with a corporation for its general benefit.

42. CONVICT LABOR

In connection with the performance of work under this contract, the Construction Manager agrees not to employ any person undergoing sentence of imprisonment except as provided by Public Law 89-176, September 10, 1965 (18 U.S.C. 4082(c)(2)) and Executive Order 11755, December 29, 1973.

43. PROHIBITION AGAINST BIDDING

Neither the Construction Manager nor any firm of which any officer, director, supervisory employee or principal stockholder of the Construction Manager is an officer, director, supervisory employee or principal stockholder or owner, or of which the Construction Manager is a principal stockholder or owner, shall during the term of this contract and until final payment for the services provided for herein is made by the Government, make or cause to be made any bid on the project referred to in this contract unless otherwise authorized by the Contracting Officer. For purposes of this provision the term "principal stockholder or owner" shall mean any stockholder holding ten percent or more of the capital stock of such corporation in his or its own name or which is held directly or indirectly for his or its account.

44. UTILIZATION OF SMALL BUSINESS CONCERNS

a. It is the policy of the Government as declared by the Congress that a fair proportion of the purchases and contracts for supplies and services for the Government be placed with small business concerns.

b. The Construction Manager agrees to accomplish the maximum amount of subcontracting to small business concerns that the Construction Manager finds to be consistent with the efficient performance of this contract.

45. EQUAL OPPORTUNITY

(The following clause is applicable unless this contract is exempt under the rules, regulations, and relevant orders of the Secretary of Labor (41 CFR, ch. 60).)

During the performance of this agreement, the Construction Manager agrees as follows:

a. The Construction Manager will not discriminate against any employee or applicant for employment because of race, color, religion, sex, or national origin. The Construction Manager will take affirmative action to ensure that applicants are employed, and that employees are treated during employment, without regard to their race, color, religion, sex, or national origin. Such action shall include, but not be limited to, the following: Employment, upgrading, demotion, or transfer; recruitment or recruitment advertising; layoff or termination; rates of pay or other forms of compensation; and selection for training, including apprenticeship. The Construction Manager agrees to post in conspicuous places, available to employees and applicants for employment, notices to be provided by the Contracting Officer setting forth the provisions of this "Equal Opportunity" clause.

b. The Construction Manager will, in all solicitations or advertisements for employees placed by or on behalf of the Construction Manager, state that all qualified applicants will receive consideration for employment without regard to race, color, religion, sex or national origin.

c. The Construction Manager will send to each labor union or representative of workers with which he has a collective bargaining agreement or other contract or understanding, a notice to be provided by the agency Contracting Officer, advising the labor union or workers' representative of the Construction Manager's commitments under this "Equal Opportunity" clause, and shall post copies of the notices in conspicuous places available to employees and applicants for employment.

d. The Construction Manager will comply with all provisions of Executive Order No. 11246 of September 24, 1965, and of the rules, regulations, and relevant orders of the Secretary of Labor.

e. The Construction Manager will furnish all information and reports required by Executive Order No. 11246 of September 24, 1965, and by the rules, regulations, and orders of the Secretary of Labor, or pursuant thereto, and will permit access to his books, records, and accounts by the contracting agency and the Secretary of Labor for purposes of investigation to ascertain compliance with such rules, regulations, and orders.

f. In the event of the Construction Manager's noncompliance with the "Equal Opportunity" clause of this agreement or with any of the said rules, regulations, or orders, this agreement may be cancelled, terminated, or suspended, in whole or in part, and the Construction Manager may be declared ineligible for further Government contracts in accordance with procedures authorized in Executive Order No. 11246 of September 24, 1965, and such other sanctions may be imposed and remedies invoked as provided in Executive Order No. 11246 of September 24, 1965, or by rule, regulation, or order of the Secretary of Labor, or as otherwise provided by law.

g. The Construction Manager will include the provisions of paragraphs a. through g. in every subcontract or purchase order unless exempted by rules, regulations, or orders of the Secretary of Labor issued pursuant to section 204 of Executive Order No. 11246 of September 24, 1965, so that such provisions will be binding upon each subcontractor or vendor. The Construction Manager will take such action with respect to any subcontract or purchase order as the contracting agency may direct as a means of enforcing such provisions, including sanctions for noncompliance: Provided, however, that in the event the Construction Manager becomes involved in, or is threatened with, litigation with a subcontractor or vendor as a result of such direction by the contracting agency, the Construction Manager may request the United States to enter into such litigation to protect the interests of the United States.

46. CERTIFICATION OF NONSEGREGATED FACILITIES

[Applicable to (1) contracts, (2) subcontracts, and (3) agreements with applicants who are themselves performing federally assisted construction contracts, exceeding $10,000 which are not exempt from the provisions of the "Equal Opportunity" clause."

By submission of this bid, the bidder, offeror, applicant, or subcontractor certifies that he does not maintain or provide for his employees any segregated facilities at any of his establishments, and that he does not permit his employees to perform their services at any location, under his control, where segregated facilities are maintained. He certifies further that he will not maintain or provide for his employees any segregated facilities at any of his establishments, and that he will not permit his employees to perform their services at any location, under his control, where segregated facilities are maintained. The bidder, offeror, applicant, or subcontractor agrees that a breach of this certification is a violation of the "Equal Opportunity" clause in this contract. As used in this certification, the term "segregated facilities" means any waiting rooms, work areas, rest rooms and wash rooms, restaurants and other eating areas, time clocks, locker rooms and other storage or dressing areas, parking lots, drinking fountains, recreation or entertainment areas, transportation, and housing facilities provided for employees which are segregated by explicit directive or are in fact segregated on the basis of race, color, religion, sex, or national origin, because of habit, local custom or otherwise. He further agrees that (except where he has obtained identical certifications from proposed subcontractors for specific time periods) he will obtain identical certifications from proposed subcontractors prior to the award of subcontracts exceeding $10,000 which are not exempt from the provisions of the "Equal Opportunity" clause; that he will retain such certifications in his files; and that he will forward the following notice to such proposed subcontractors (except where the proposed subcontractors have submitted identical certifications for specific time periods)]:

NOTICE TO PROSPECTIVE SUBCONTRACTORS OF REQUIREMENT FOR CERTIFICATIONS OF NONSEGREGATED FACILITIES

A Certification of Nonsegregated Facilities must be submitted prior to the award of a subcontract exceeding $10,000 which is not exempt from the provisions of the "Equal Opportunity" clause. The certification may be submitted either for each subcontract or for all subcontracts during a period (i.e., quarterly, semi-annually, or annually).

NOTE: The penalty for making false statements in offers is prescribed in 18 U.S.C. 1001.

47. UTILIZATION OF MINORITY BUSINESS ENTERPRISES

a. It is the policy of the Government that minority business enterprises shall have the maximum practicable opportunity to participate in the performance of Government contracts.

b. The Construction Manager agrees to use his best efforts to carry out this policy in the award of his subcontracts to the fullest extent consistent with the efficient performance of this contract. As used in this contract, the term "minority business enterprise" means a business, at least 50 percent of which is owned by minority group members or, in case of publicly owned businesses, at least 51 percent of the stock of which is owned by minority group members. For the purposes of this definition, minority group members are Negroes, Spanish-speaking American persons, American-Orientals, American-Indians, American-Eskimos, and American Aleuts. The Construction Manager may rely on written representations by subcontractors regarding their status as minority business enterprises in lieu of an independent investigation.

48. MINORITY BUSINESS ENTERPRISES SUBCONTRACTING PROGRAM

a. The Construction Manager agrees to establish and conduct a program which will enable minority business enterprises (as defined in the clause entitled "Utilization of Minority Business Enterprises") to be considered fairly as subcontractors and suppliers under this contract. In this connection, the Construction Manager shall—

(1) Designate a liaison officer who will administer the Construction Manager's minority business enterprise program.

(2) Provide adequate and timely consideration of the potentialities of known minority business enterprises in all "make-or-buy" decisions.

(3) Assure that known minority business enterprises will have an equitable opportunity to compete for subcontracts, particularly by arranging solicitations, time for the preparation of bids, quantities, specifications, and delivery schedules so as to facilitate the participation of minority business enterprises.

(4) Maintain records showing (i) procedures which have been adopted to comply with the policies set forth in this clause, including the establishment of a source list of minority business enterprises, (ii) awards to minority business enterprises on the source list, and (iii) specific efforts to identify and award contracts to minority business enterprises.

(5) Include the "Utilization of Minority Business Enterprises" clause in subcontracts which offer substantial minority business enterprises subcontracting opportunities.

(6) Cooperate with the Contracting Officer in any studies and surveys of the Construction Manager's minority business enterprises procedures and practices that the Contracting Officer may from time to time conduct.

(7) Submit periodic reports of subcontracting to known minority business enterprises with respect to the records referred to in subparagraph (4), above, in such form and manner and at such time (not more often than quarterly) as the Contracting Officer may prescribe.

b. The Construction Manager further agrees to insert, in any subcontract hereunder which may exceed $500,000, provisions which shall conform substantially to the language of this clause, including this paragraph b., and to notify the Contracting Officer of the name of such subcontractors.

49. LISTING OF EMPLOYMENT OPENINGS

(This clause is applicable pursuant to 41 CFR 50-250 if this contract is for $2,500 or more.)

a. The Construction Manager agrees, in order to provide special emphasis to the employment of qualified disabled veterans and veterans of the Vietnam era, that all suitable employment openings of the Construction Manager which exist at the time of the execution of this contract and those which occur during the performance of this contract, including those not generated by this contract and including those occurring at an establishment other than the one wherein the contract is being performed but excluding those of independently operated corporate affiliates, shall be offered for listing at an appropriate local office of the State employment service system wherein the opening occurs and to provide such reports to such local office regarding employment openings and hires as may be required: Provided, that if this contract is for less than $10,000 or if it is with a State or local government the reports set forth in paragraphs c. and d. are not required.

b. Listing of employment openings with the employment service system pursuant to this clause shall be made at least concurrently with the use of any other recruitment service or effort and shall involve the normal obligations which attach to the placing of a bona fide job order, including the acceptance of referrals of veterans and nonveterans. This listing of employment openings does not require the hiring of any particular job applicant or from any particular group of job applicants, and nothing herein is intended to relieve the Construction Manager from any requirements in any statutes, Executive orders, or regulations regarding nondiscrimination in employment.

c. The reports required by paragraph a. of this clause shall include, but not be limited to, periodic reports which shall be filed at least quarterly with the appropriate local office or, where the Construction Manager has more than one establishment in a State, with the central office of the State Employment service. Such reports shall indicate for each establishment (i) the number of individuals who were hired during the reporting period, (ii) the number of those hired who were disabled veterans, and (iii) the number of those hired who were nondisabled veterans of the Vietnam era. The Construction Manager shall submit a report within 30 days after the end of each reporting period wherein any performance is made under this contract. The Construction Manager shall maintain copies of the reports submitted until the expiration of one year after final payment under the contract, during which time they shall make available, upon request, for examination by any authorized representatives of the Contracting Officer or of the Secretary of Labor.

d. Whenever the Construction Manager becomes contractually bound by the listing provisions of this clause, he shall advise the employment service system in each State wherein he has establishments of the name and location of each such establishment in the State. As long as the Construction Manager is contractually bound to these provisions and has so advised the State employment system, there is no need to advise the State system of subsequent contracts. The Construction Manager may advise the State system when it is no longer bound by this contract clause.

e. This clause does not apply to the listing of employment openings which occur and are filed outside of the 50 states, the District of Columbia, the Commonwealth of Puerto Rico, Guam, and the Virgin Islands.

f. This clause does not apply to openings which the Construction Manager proposes to fill from within his own organization or to fill pursuant to a customary and traditional employer-union hiring arrangement. This exclusion does not apply to a particular opening once an employer decides to consider applicants outside of his own organization or employer-union arrangement for that opening.

g. As used in this clause:

(1) "All suitable employment openings" includes, but is not limited to, openings which occur in the following job categories: Production and nonproduction; plant and office laborers and mechanics; supervisory and nonsupervisory; technical; and executive, administrative, and professional openings which

are compensated on a salary basis of less than $18,000 per year. The term includes full-time employment, temporary employment of more than 3 days' duration, and part-time employment. It does not include openings which the Construction Manager proposes to fill from within his own organization or to fill pursuant to a customary and traditional employer-union hiring arrangement.

(2) "Appropriate office of the State employment service system" means the local office of the Federal-State national system of public employment offices with assigned responsibility for serving the area of the establishment where the employment opening is to be filled, including the District of Columbia, the Commonwealth of Puerto Rico, Guam, and the Virgin Islands.

(3) "Openings which the Construction Manager proposes to fill from within his own organization" means employment openings for which no consideration will be given to persons outside the Construction Manager's own organization (including any affiliates, subsidiaries, and parent companies), and includes any openings which the Construction Manager proposes to fill from regularly established "recall" or "rehire" lists.

(4) "Openings which the Construction Manager proposes to fill pursuant to a customary and traditional employer-union hiring arrangement" means employment openings for which no consideration will be given to persons outside of a special hiring arrangement, including openings which the Construction Manager proposes to fill from union halls, which is part of the customary and traditional hiring relationship which exists between the Construction Manager and representatives of his employees.

(5) "Disabled veteran" means a person entitled to disability compensation under laws administered by the Veterans Administration for disability rated at 30 percentum or more, or a person whose discharge or release from active duty was for a disability incurred or aggravated in line of duty.

(6) "Veterans of the Vietnam era" means a person (A) who (i) served on active duty with the Armed Forces for a period of more than 180 days, any part of which occurred after August 5, 1964, and was discharged or released therefrom with other than a dishonorable discharge, or (ii) was discharged or released from active duty for service-connected disability if any part of such duty was performed after August 5, 1964, and (B) who was so discharged or released within the 48 months preceding his application for employment covered by this clause.

h. If any disabled veteran or veteran of the Vietnam era believes that the Construction Manager (or any first-tier subcontractor) has failed or refuses to comply with the provisions of this contract clause relating to giving special emphasis in employment to veterans, such veteran may file a complaint with the veterans' employment representative at a local State employment service office who will attempt to informally resolve the complaint and then refer the complaint with a report on the attempt to resolve the matter to the State office of the Veterans' Employment Service of the Department of Labor. Such complaint shall then be promptly referred through the Regional Manpower Administrator to the Secretary of Labor who shall investigate such complaint and shall take such action thereon as the facts and circumstances warrant consistent with the terms of this contract and the laws and regulations applicable thereto.

    i. The Construction Manager agrees to place this clause (excluding this paragraph (i)) in any subcontract directly under this contract.

50. EMPLOYMENT OF THE HANDICAPPED

(This clause applies to all nonexempt contracts and subcontracts which exceed $2,500 as follows: (1) Part A applies to contracts and subcontracts which provide for performance in less than 90 days. (2) Parts A and B apply to contracts and subcontracts which provide for performance in 90 days or more and the amount of the contract or subcontract is less than $500,000, and (3) Parts A, B, and C apply to contracts and subcontracts which provide for performance in 90 days or more and the amount of the contract or subcontract is $500,000 or more.)

PART A

a. The Construction Manager will not discriminate against any employee or applicant for employment because of physical or mental handicap in regard to any position for which the employee or applicant for employment is qualified. The Construction Manager agrees to take affirmative action to employ, advance in employment and otherwise treat qualified handicapped individuals without discrimination based upon their physical or mental handicap in all employment practices such as the following: employment, upgrading, demotion or transfer, recruitment or recruitment advertising, layoff or termination, rates of pay or other forms of compensation, and selection for training, including apprenticeship.

b. The Construction Manager agrees that, if a handicapped individual files a complaint with the Construction Manager that he is not complying with the requirements of the Act, he will (1) investigate the complaint and take appropriate action consistent with the requirements of 20 CFR 741.29 and (2) maintain on file for three years, the record regarding the complaint and the actions taken.

c. The Construction Manager agrees that, if a handicapped individual files a complaint with the Department of Labor that he has not complied with the requirements of the Act, (1) he will cooperate with the Department in its investigation of the complaint, and (2) he will provide all pertinent information regarding his employment practices with respect to the handicapped.

d. The Construction Manager agrees to comply with the rules and regulations of the Secretary of Labor in 20 CFR CH VI. Part 741.

e. In the event of the Construction Manager's noncompliance with the requirements of this clause, the contract may be terminated or suspended in whole or in part.

f. This clause shall be included in all subcontracts over $2,500.

PART B

g. The Construction Manager agrees (1) to establish an affirmative action program, including appropriate procedures consistent with the guidelines and the rules of the Secretary of Labor, which will provide the affirmative action regarding the employment and advancement of the handicapped required by P. L. 93-112, (2) to publish the program in his employee's or personnel handbook or otherwise distribute a copy to all personnel, (3) to review his program on or before March 31 of each year and to make such changes as may be appropriate, and (4) to designate one of his principal officials to be responsible for the establishment and operation of the program.

h. The Construction Manager agrees to permit the examination by appropriate contracting agency officials or the Assistant Secretary for Employment Standards or his designee, of pertinent books, documents, papers and records concerning his employment and advancement of the handicapped.

i. The Construction Manager agrees to post in conspicuous places, available to employees and applicants for employment, notices in a form to be prescribed by the Assistant Secretary for Employment Standards, provided by the Contracting Officer stating Construction Manager's obligation under the law to take affirmative action to employ and advance in employment qualified handicapped employees and applicants for employment and the rights and remedies available.

j. The Construction Manager will notify each labor union or representative of workers with which he has a collective bargaining agreement or other contract understanding, that the Construction Manager is bound by the terms of Section 503 of the Rehabilitation Act, and is committed to take affirmative action to employ and advance in employment physically and mentally handicapped individuals.

PART C

k. The Construction Manager agrees to submit a copy of his affirmative action program to the Assistant Secretary for Employment Standards within 90 days after the award to him of a contract or subcontract.

l. The Construction Manager agrees to submit a summary report to the Assistant Secretary for Employment Standards, by March 31 of each year during performance of the contract, and by March 31 of the year following completion of the contract, in the form prescribed by the Assistant Secretary, covering employment and complaint experience, accommodations made and all steps taken to effectuate and carry out the commitments set forth in the affirmative action program.

51. LIABILITY FOR DAMAGE

All liability for damage to property or injury or death of persons resulting directly or indirectly from the Construction Manager's furnishing general condition items shall be borne by the Construction Manager and the risk of loss for all general condition items furnished hereunder shall be borne by the Construction Manager until accepted by the Government. The Construction Manager, however, shall not be responsible for damage resulting from faulty designs furnished by the Contracting Officer or the Architect-Engineer. The Construction Manager shall maintain adequate protection of general condition items furnished by it hereunder and shall also protect the Government's property and all adjacent property from injury arising out of the furnishing of general condition items. If the Construction Manager believes that any general condition items shown by the working drawings or specifications will not, when executed, procure safe and substantial results, or if any discrepancy appears, it shall be the Construction Manager's duty to notify the Contracting Officer immediately, in writing, stop work thereon and await the Contracting Officer's written instructions. The Construction Manager shall not load or permit any part of the structures to be loaded with any weight that will endanger safety.

52. ACCIDENT PREVENTION FOR GENERAL CONDITIONS WORK

The Construction Manager shall comply with the requirements of the Handbook, Accident and Fire Prevention—Construction and Alteration Work—PBS P 5900.3, dated February 16, 1962, and any revisions thereto in effect on the date of this contract issued by the General Services Administration, as well as applicable provisions of the regulations issued by the Secretary of Labor pursuant to section 107 of the Contract Work Hours and Safety Standards Act, entitled "Safety and Health Regulations for Construction" (29 CFR Part 1518, renumbered as Part 1926). Where there may be conflict in requirements, the more stringent one will apply.

53. PERFORMANCE AND PAYMENT BONDS

At least thirty days before the start of any construction, the Construction Manager shall submit to the Contracting Officer an estimate of the cost of general condition items it intends to recommend be provided by the Construction Manager during the course of construction. Promptly, upon approval of the estimate by the Contracting Officer, the Construction Manager shall furnish to the Contracting Officer a Performance Bond (Standard Form 25) and a Payment Bond (Standard Form 25-A) covering general condition items, with good and sufficient surety or sureties acceptable to the Government. The penal sum of the Performance Bond shall be 100% of the approved estimate for general condition work and the penal amount of the Payment Bond shall be 50% of the approved estimate. Bonds shall be furnished by the Construction Manager prior to the performance of any construction work. If the cost of general condition work provided by the Construction Manager exceeds the approved estimate, the Contracting Officer, at his option, may require the Construction Manager to provide additional security increasing the penal amounts to cover the increased cost. If any surety upon any bond furnished in connection with this agreement becomes unacceptable to the Government, the Construction Manager shall promptly furnish such additional security as may be required from time to time to protect the interests of the Government and of persons supplying labor and materials in the prosecution of the work contemplated by this agreement.

54. LABOR STANDARD PROVISIONS

The Labor Standards Provisions set forth in Standard Form 19-A, attached to this agreement, are incorporated herein by reference for use on general condition items.

55. DAVIS-BACON WAGE RATE DECISION

When the Contracting Officer authorizes the Construction Manager to perform one or more general condition items, he shall furnish the Construction Manager with the current applicable wage rate decision of the Secretary of Labor, containing wage rates and fringe benefits for categories of labor to be utilized in performing the general condition item or items. The Construction Manager agrees to be bound by such wage decision and, if all or part of the general condition item or items is to be performed by subcontract, to include the wage rate decision in each such subcontract.

56. HOME-TOWN OR IMPOSED PLAN—MINORITY HIRING PRACTICES

Before the Contracting Officer authorizes the Construction Manager to perform one or more general condition items involving the employment of construction labor, the Construction Manager shall execute either the "Bid Conditions—Affirmative Action Requirements—Equal Employment Opportunity" or the imposed plan, an unexecuted copy of which was incorporated in and made a part of this contract. The

Construction Manager shall ensure that each subcontractor (if any) implements the requirements of such plan. In the event that the Labor Department has not issued a home-town plan or an imposed plan at the time this contract was executed but subsequently issues such a requirement, the Construction Manager shall be bound to execute and implement the plan in the same manner and to the same extent as set forth above.

57. BUY AMERICAN

   a. *Agreement.* In accordance with the Buy-American Act (41 U.S.C. 10a-10d) and Executive Order 10582, December 17, 1954 (3 CFR, 1954-58 Comp., p. 230), as amended by Executive Order 11051, September 27, 1962 (3 CFR, 1959-63 Comp., p. 635), the Construction Manager agrees that only domestic construction material will be used (by the Construction Manager, subcontractors, materialmen, and suppliers) in the performance of general condition items under this agreement, except for non-domestic material listed in this agreement.

   b. *Domestic Construction Material.* "Construction Material" means any article, material, or supply brought to the construction site for incorporation in the building or work. An unmanufactured construction material is a "domestic construction material" if it has been mined or produced in the United States. A manufactured construction material is a "domestic construction material" if it has been manufactured in the United States and if the cost of its components which have been mined, produced, or manufactured in the United States exceed fifty percent (50%) of the cost of all its components. Components means any article, material, or supply directly incorporated in a construction material.

   c. *Domestic component.* A component shall be considered to have been "mined, produced, or manufactured in the United States" (regardless of its source in fact) if the article, material, or supply in which it is incorporated was manufactured in the United States and the component is of a class or kind determined by the Government to be not mined, produced, or manufactured in the United States in sufficient and reasonably available commercial quantities and of a satisfactory quality.

58. EXAMINATION OF RECORDS

   a. The Construction Manager agrees that the Comptroller General of the United States, the Contracting Officer, or any of their duly authorized representatives shall, until the expiration of three years after final payment under this contract or such lesser time specified in either Appendix M of the Armed Services Procurement Regulation or the Federal Procurement Regulations Part 1-20, as appropriate, have access to and the right to examine any directly pertinent books, documents, papers, and records of the Construction Manager involving transactions related to this contract.

   b. The Construction Manager further agrees to include in all his subcontracts hereunder a provision to the effect that the subcontractor agrees that the Comptroller General of the United States, the Contracting Officer, or any of their duly authorized representatives shall, until the expiration of three years after final payment under the subcontract, or such lesser time specified in either Appendix M of the Armed Services Procurement Regulation or the Federal Procurement Regulations Part 1-20, as appropriate, have access to and the right to examine any directly pertinent books, documents, papers, and records of such subcontractor, involving transactions related to the subcontract. The term "subcontract'' as used in this clause excludes (1) purchase orders not exceeding $2,500 and (2) subcontracts or purchase orders for public utility services at rates established for uniform applicability to the general public.

c. The periods of access and examination described in a. and b., above, for records which relate to (1) appeals under the "Disputes" clause of this contract, (2) litigation or the settlement of claims arising out of the performance of this contract, or (3) costs and expenses of this contract as to which exception has been taken by the Comptroller General, the Contracting Officer, or any of their duly authorized representatives, shall continue until such appeals, litigation, claims, or exceptions have been disposed of.

59. COST ACCOUNTING STANDARDS

a. Unless the Cost Accounting Standards Board, or the General Services Administration in the case of nondefense contracts, has prescribed rules or regulations exempting the Construction Manager or this contract from standards, rules, and regulations promulgated pursuant to 50 U.S.C. App. 2168 (P. L. 91-379, August 15, 1970), or other statutory authority, the Construction Manager, in connection with this contract shall:

(1) By submission of a Disclosure Statement, disclose in writing his cost accounting practices as required by regulations of the Cost Accounting Standards Board. The required disclosures must be made prior to contract award unless the Contracting Officer provides a written notice to the Construction Manager authorizing postaward submission in accordance with regulations of the Cost Accounting Standards Board. The practices disclosed for this contract shall be the same as the practices currently disclosed and applied on all other contracts and subcontracts being performed by the Construction Manager and which contain this Cost Accounting Standards clause. If the Construction Manager has notified the Contracting Officer that the Disclosure Statement contains trade secrets and commercial or financial information which is privileged and confidential, the Disclosure Statement will not be released outside of the Government.

(2) Follow consistently the cost accounting practices disclosed pursuant to (1) above, in accumulating and reporting contract performance cost data concerning this contract. If any change in disclosed practices is made for the purposes of any contract or subcontract subject to Cost Accounting Standards Board requirements, the change must be applied prospectively to this contract, and the Disclosure Statement must be amended accordingly. If the contract price or cost allowance of this contract is affected by such changes, adjustment shall be made in accordance with subparagraph a(4) or a(5), below, as appropriate.

(3) Comply with all Cost Accounting Standards in effect on the date of award of this contract or if the Construction Manager has submitted cost or pricing data, on the date of final agreement on price as shown on the Construction Manager's signed certificate of current cost or pricing data. The Construction Manager shall also comply with any Cost Accounting Standard which hereafter becomes applicable to a contract or subcontract of the Construction Manager. Such compliance shall be required prospectively from the date of applicability to such contract or subcontract.

(4) (A) Agree to an equitable adjustment (as provided in the Changes clause of this contract, if any) if the contract cost is affected by a change which,

pursuant to (3) above, the Construction Manager is required to make to his established cost accounting practices whether such practices are covered by a Disclosure Statement or not. (B) Negotiate with the Contracting Officer to determine the terms, and conditions under which a change to either a disclosed cost accounting practice or an established cost accounting practice, other than a change under (4)(A), above, may be made. A change to a practice may be proposed by either the Government or the Construction Manager, provided, however, that no agreement may be made under this provision that will increase costs paid by the United States.

(5) Agree to an adjustment of the contract price or cost allowance as appropriate, if he or a subcontractor fails to comply with an applicable Cost Accounting Standard or to follow any practice disclosed pursuant to subparagraphs a(1) and a(2), above, and such failure results in any increased costs paid by the United States. Such adjustment shall provide for recovery of the increased costs to the United States together with interest thereon computed at the rate determined by the Secretary of the Treasury pursuant to P.L. 92-41, 85 Stat. 97, or 7 percent per annum, whichever is less, from the time the payment by the United States was made to the time the adjustment is effected.

b. If the parties fail to agree whether the Construction Manager or subcontractor has complied with an applicable Cost Accounting Standard, rule, or regulation of the Cost Accounting Standards Board and as to any cost adjustment demanded by the United States, such failure to agree shall be a dispute concerning a question of fact within the meaning of the "Disputes" clause of this contract.

c. The Construction Manager shall permit any authorized representatives of the head of the agency, the Cost Accounting Standards Board, or the Comptroller General of the United States to examine and make copies of any documents, papers, or records relating to compliance with the requirements of this clause.

d. The Construction Manager shall include in all negotiated subcontracts which he enters into the substance of this clause except paragraph b. and shall require such inclusion in all other subcontracts of any tier, except that this requirement shall apply only to negotiated subcontracts in excess of $100,000 where the price negotiated is not based on:

(i) Established catalog or market prices or commercial items sold in substantial quantities to the general public; or

(ii) Prices set by law or regulation.

NOTE:

1. Subcontractors shall be required to submit their Disclosure Statements to the Construction Manager. However, if a subcontractor has previously submitted his Disclosure Statement to a Government Contracting Officer he may satisfy that requirement by certifying to the Construction Manager the date of such Statement and the address of the Contracting Officer.

2. In any case where a subcontractor determines that the Disclosure Statement information is privileged and confidential and declines to provide it to the Construction Manager or higher tier subcontractor, the Construction Manager may authorize direct submission of that subcontractor's Disclosure Statement to the same Government offices to which the Construction Manager was required to make submission of his Disclosure Statement. Such

authorization shall in no way relieve the Construction Manager of liability as provided in paragraph a(5) of this clause. In view of the foregoing and since the contract may be subject to adjustment under this clause by reason of any failure to comply with rules, regulations, and Standards of the Cost Accounting Standards Board in connection with covered subcontracts, it is expected that the Construction Manager may wish to include a clause in each such subcontract requiring the subcontractor to appropriately indemnify the Construction Manager. However, the inclusion of such a clause and the terms thereof are matters for negotiation and agreement between the Construction Manager and the subcontractor, provided that they do not conflict with the duties of the Construction Manager under its contract with the Government. It is also expected that any subcontractor subject to such indemnification will generally require substantially similar indemnification to be submitted by his subcontractors.

e. The terms defined in Sec. 331.2 of Part 331 of Title 4, Code of Federal Regulations (4CFR 331.20) shall have the same meanings herein. As there defined, "negotiated subcontract" means "any subcontract except a firm fixed-price subcontract made by the Construction Manager or subcontractor after receiving offers from at least two firms not associated with each other or such Construction Manager or subcontractor, providing (1) the solicitation to all competing firms is identical, (2) price is the only consideration in selecting the subcontractor from among the competing firms solicited, and (3) the lowest offer received in compliance with the solicitation from among those solicited is accepted.

60. ENERGY CONSERVATION AND ENVIRONMENTAL PROTECTION

During construction, the Construction Manager shall designate one member of his job-site staff as "Energy and Environmental Control Officer". The assigned additional duties shall include responsibility for enforcing compliance with all energy conservation and environmental protection requirements of the specifications, requirements of the Occupational Safety and Health Act, and other applicable Federal, State, and local standards.

IN WITNESS WHEREOF, the parties hereto have executed this agreement as of the day and year first above written.

_____

Name of Construction Manager

By _____
            (Signature)

_____

(Title)

UNITED STATES OF AMERICA
GENERAL SERVICES ADMINISTRATION

By _____
    Contracting Officer

*Revised: 4-15-75

8

Legal Aspects

No single formula or set of legal rules is applicable to construction management or to the construction industry of which CM is a part. Throughout the text the construction manager has been referred to as an individual. However, in conducting his business the CM can take the form of any number of different business organizations. Such business organizations include individuals, individual proprietorships, partnerships, limited partnerships, and corporations, both publicly and privately held. The construction manager conducts his business in the commercial marketplace and is subject to all the regulations and statutory requirements that control the conduct of any business.

ORGANIZATION

Most business is conducted in the corporate form but this does not negate individual and partnership structures. The size of a firm may control the selection of the type of entity under which a CM may elect to conduct his business although, even with a relatively small business operation, the corporate form is normally utilized. In the eyes of the law a corporation is a separate entity and thus an individual conducting his business in the corporate form can separate his business activities and resultant obligations, liabilities, and tax consequences from that of his personal activities, assets, and holdings.

Business organizations and entities are formed under the laws of the various states. If incorporated, a business will usually incorporate (organize) under the governing laws of the state in which it is located or where it maintains its prime place of business or main office. The state of Delaware, however, more often in the past than at present was a favored state for corporations to use as the state of incorporation rather than their own domicile. Delaware initially developed the most concise and comprehensive statutes governing corporate practice before many of the other industrial states and for this reason new groups forming business organizations adopted Delaware as their state of incorporation. As most states have modernized and updated their corporate rules, this practice no longer continues.

As states prescribe rules under which business groups can conduct business they also place limitations on groups that can conduct business in the corporate form. The New York Education Law identifies licensing requirements for professions including limitation on the conduct of business in a corporate form until the passage of legislation permitting the formation of professional service corporations (PCs). These regulations are applicable to the medical, legal, and accounting professions as well as to engineering and architecture. As construction management is practiced by many engineering and architectural firms, this corporate limitation applies to their overall conduct of business, not to the practice of construction management per se.

Construction management is practiced by many different groups within the construction industry. Some firms have been formed specifically for this business reason, others include construction companies, industrial firms, computer specialists as well as professional engineering or architectural firms.

If the professionals practice construction management as part of their architectural or engineering business, as for example through a separate division, then in New York State these firms would have to conduct their business as partnerships or newly formed PCs. The exception to this would be those firms who held "grandfather" corporate charters and were thus able to conduct business under the general corporate statutes.

The purpose of such legislation as applicable to various professions is to protect the public and general welfare from the possibility of unauthorized professional practice. Some states (and New York was among them until 1970 when legislation was enacted permitting the formation of professional corporations) prohibit or restrict corporate practice. Others permit limited corporate practice. An overview of the varying legislation affecting the practice of engineering in the various states would be as follows:

1. States not prohibiting the practice of engineering in corporate form. Such states have no specific legislation governing the conduct of engineering or architecture, and therefore the rules governing such conduct are established as a result of court decisions or rules laid down by state authorities including state boards of licensing.

2. States by statute prohibiting corporate practice.

3. States, such as New York, that retain restrictive grandfather clauses.

4. States permitting corporate practice if certain specific requirements are met. New York would also fall into this category with the provision for professional corporations. The specific requirements range from one that requires all officers and directors of the corporations to be registered engineers in the state (Michigan) to the requirement that the work performed within the state be under the direction of one registered professional within the state (New Jersey, Massachusetts, etc.).

Although at present (1977) there are no statutory definitions for professional construction managers, the practitioners in this field are mainly members of existing professions or construction firms. Their conduct of business therefore is subject to such existing regulation. Although contracting is not governed by the strict rules that control professional practice, various states require the licensing of contractors or licensing of those individuals placed in responsible charge of construction projects. The logic and rationale for establishing statutory requirements is the same as with the practice of professions, namely, the protection of the public interest and safety and welfare. For the same reason various states also license the mechanics in the building trades (electricians, plumbers, mechanics).

In addition to professional licensing laws, the majority of states have specific requirements that control the construction process. Minimum amounts are established above which public bidding for the implementation of the work is required. In actuality, unless work is accomplished under an emergency order, it is fair to state that essentially all public construction is accomplished through the taking of competitive bids.

The dialogue concerning the legal status of construction managers—whether they are professionals or are performing a construction function subject to the various regulatory requirements—started with the growth and development of the CM approach. This dialogue is expected to continue for some time and result in the recognition of their status as rendering a professional service. As such they are subject at present to existing legal regulations and to the competitive requirements of the marketplace.

CONTRACTS

Before agreements are signed and obligations incurred by two parties, there are usually discussions and negotiations before commitments are made. The conduct of the two parties leads to the eventual contract that they enter into or execute. Their conduct, however, as well as interpretations of the contract or agreement, are governed by the law of the state or jurisdiction in which they reside, conduct their business, or elect to be the governing jurisdiction.

Obligations of parties to each other stem from their contract agreements. Although each party is subject to the same laws, the contracting parties define their understanding, commitments, and obligations in a contract between them. Normally, this takes the form of a written document signed by both parties, but it can be an oral contract (agreement by a handshake) or a written document signed by one party and accepted by the conduct of the second party.

There are numerous parties involved in a construction development performing various tasks. They will be working under various separate contract agreements. The web of agreements that can be found on a particular project can form this typical index:

- Property owner and real estate agent

- Property owner and buyer

- Bank and owner (mortgage—financing)

- Owner and architect

- Owner and CM

- Owner and contractor, or CM and contractors

- Contractor and subcontractor (labor and material)

- Contractor and supplier (material only)

- Architect and engineer

- Owner and operating company

- Operating company and leasing company

- Leasing company and tenant

- Tenant and manufacturer

- Owner and utility company

- Contractor and utility company

A contract has been described as the writing containing the agreement of parties with specified terms and conditions and serving as a proof of the obligation. For every contract there has to be an offer, an acceptance, and some consideration between the parties. As an example, the offer can be the contractor's bid; the acceptance follows as a letter of acceptance of such a bid or the issuance of the written contract between owner and contractor. Strictly speaking, however, the contract itself when signed by all parties contains the final offer and acceptance. The bid, per se, may have no further legal consequence after contract execution unless there is a dispute or litigation and it is used or admitted in evidence to show the intent of the parties on a particular point where the contract terms are not clear. Consideration between the parties consists of the agreement by the owner to pay a specified sum for the performance of the agreed amount of work. This is the legal base upon which a contractual agreement is built. Contract documents therefore can consist of one sheet of paper documenting the agreement between the parties and signed by both parties, or can consist of several hundred pages documenting the detailed obligations, conditions, and various considerations that have to be enumerated, to cover all possible situations, contingencies, and related obligations that must be considered in the complex marketplace of the twentieth century. The purpose of the document is to set forth as completely as possible the full understanding between the parties and to document the specific conditions that must be met or the various conditions that must be followed.

In the event of a disagreement or a dispute, it is a first step to look at the document or contract between the parties to determine what was contemplated in the basic agreement. Disputes, however, are not always that simple to be subject to resolution by a reading of the agreement or a document. Complex and even simple agreements are subject to a variety of interpretations depending not only upon surrounding conditions but also the attitude of the parties involved. Even with complex agreements and detailed documentation, courts of law will often look to the intent of the parties to resolve the dispute that is brought before them; the intent of the parties being utilized to determine what really was intended by the parties if there is a contention that a specific provision is not clear, that is, was not covered in the written contractual agreement or that a misinterpretation is being made by one of the parties.

Further, although the contract may seem to be a simple document, it must be within the purview of the governing laws. If a contract is in conflict with existing statutory provisions or with basic public policy, it may be voided by a court of law. Also this could apply to a single provision in a contract that was contrary to statutory requirement within a specific jurisdiction. The most common situation to which such a restriction would apply would be a matter of public safety, welfare, or policy. If a contract provision required a portion of work to be done in an unsafe manner, such as without shoring in a deep excavation or without protective barriers at exposed and elevated areas, such contract provisions would be superseded by applicable regulatory provision implemented by law.

Another example that may fall into this category is the handling of provisions for liquidated damages that may be considered to be punitive, per se, and may then if challenged be held void unless shown to be other than punitive. Such proof would require the showing of actual damages having been incurred by the failure of the contractor to perform on time thus resulting in actual loss or damage to an owner, as for instance, loss of rent or increased operating expenses by his inability to occupy the building, within the time required by the contract specifications. This would make the liquidated damage provision enforceable. Courts will look to the language of the agreement (but that in itself is not determinative) and to the intent of the parties in establishing such provision. Then they will look to the amount involved in relation to the delay as well as to project value and cost. Because of this reasoning some contracts now include bonus provisions to offset the liquidated clauses, thus eliminating the penal aspect of the liquidated-damage provision. If a contractor, therefore, entered into a contract which enabled him to receive a bonus for finishing ahead of schedule as well as making him subject to a penalty for his failure to perform within a period of time, such a provision would become acceptable in the eyes of the law because the unilateral and punitive aspect of the contract would be eliminated by the contractor having an equal opportunity to realize a gain by early performance. This would be a clear intent of the contracting parties.

OBLIGATIONS—LEGAL

Although the contract establishes the basis of agreement with resulting obligations, the relationship between the two contracting parties is not limited to the written contract. Each party has obligations to perform the work, render services, perform professional tasks, and meet contractual commitment, with a duty of care. This duty has been categorized into three main areas:

- Slight care

- Ordinary care

- Great care

Such definitions of care are established as a result of negligent action and cases of damages being incurred because of another's negligence. The main areas of care that are of concern in the CM process are ordinary and great. Slight care is usually limited to such care as persons of ordinary prudence usually exercise in the conduct of their own affairs of slight importance.

Ordinary or reasonable care is such a degree of care, or precaution, as may fairly and properly be expected or required, having regard for the nature of the action or the subject matter, and the circumstances surrounding the transaction. It is such care as ordinarily prudent persons would exercise under the conditions existing at the time they are called upon to act. The courts, however, will be more interested in the area of great care which is such as persons of ordinary prudence usually exercise about affairs of their own which are of great importance, or to the degree of care which a very cautious and prudent person would exercise under the same or similar circumstance. Distinction in such degrees is significant because most of the parties that are involved in the construction process are in the eyes of the law more than ordinary people. The contractor is considered to have knowledge and experience and capability in his field of endeavor. The architect and engineer are professionals, as is the construction manager. All these parties, therefore, in the performance of their tasks as required of them under the basic contract terms, will under the eyes of the law, be required to exercise greater care than might be required of an ordinary person.

Professionals in general, and those who undertake any work calling for special skill, are required not only to exercise reasonable care in what they do, but also to possess a standard minimum of special knowledge and ability.

RESPONSIBILITIES—PROFESSIONAL

The engineer and architect are held to such responsibility, as is the CM in the performance of his tasks. A general contractor in the conduct and execution of his work can also be held to this degree of care and skill. The significance of the degree of care applicable to the performance of the CM's tasks naturally is in the determination of the CM's responsibility in the event of a dispute, accident, or claim. This significance is even more material when one considers the extent of claims and litigation that exist within the construction industry. Not that the construction industry, per se, is litigation prone. It is not surprising, however, that there is a large volume of litigation, when one considers the numerous parties involved in the construction process, namely all the separate subcontractors, material suppliers, and the numerous subdivisions of the work itself. In addition as compared to other labor intensive activities there is a much higher degree of risk in the performance of the work itself. There can be tunneling and underground work, excavation, work on high elevations and in open areas with moving equipment, conditions with loose material and numerous workmen with a variety of tools and work aids all in one concentrated area, the construction site. It is not surprising therefore, that there is not only a higher frequency of accident than in other industries but also there are numerous potential causes for disputes, disagreements, and contract problems—many of which find their way into the legal process.

The CM, although involved in the entire construction process to coordinate activities and to bring greater efficiency through better management control, is another party or legal entity thrust into the construction process. As a consequence, therefore, there is no question that the CM as all others involved in the construction development (the owner, contractor, subcontractor; architect, engineer, material supplier) will find himself involved in adversary proceedings resulting from claims originating in one way or another either directly or indirectly from the construction process.

Because the CM, identifiable as a separate profession from that of engineer, architect, or contractor, is a relative newcomer to the construction site, it is quite possible that he will be responsible for a new body of case law arising that will set standards to govern his conduct and identify the extent of his legal responsibility. At present (1977), the CM is not treated by the law in any jurisdiction as a separate profession or trade, as are engineers, architects, and contractors. The standard of conduct to which a CM is to be held is no different from that of any other professional. He is not a guarantor of services, but he must conduct himself at a minimum to fall within the legal definition of an "undertaking in profession or trade" as summarized in the *Restatement of the Law of Torts,* 2d ed. by Prosser (Ref. 1): "Unless he represents that he has greater or less skill or knowledge one who undertakes to render services in the practice of a profession or trade is required to exercise the skill and knowledge normally possessed by members of that profession or trade in good standing in similar communities."

The CM is governed by the law applicable to his trade or profession, but depending upon contractual terms and the scope of services for which he is engaged, the CM in the performance of his work is assuming responsibility in three basic areas: First, he is assuming certain tasks previously undertaken by the professional designer; second, he is undertaking certain contractor functions; and third, he is serving in new areas not previously defined. This last area is the most significant, and will be influenced both by the manner in which CM practice evolves over the years and by future statutory and judicial interpretations.

The CM process has been shown to bridge and encompass the numerous phases and tasks that are inherent and integral to the end product, the completed project. Because the construction manager through his contractual commitment undertakes tasks that cover this wide range and sphere of activity it is not surprising that his function and resulting professional responsibility will be subject to differing scrutiny in the eyes of the law. Legal precedents evolve slowly; there is no separate or new body of law applicable to CM per se, as there are precedents and legal authorities that have evolved that are applied to the practices within the construction industry affecting the role of professionals and contractors. The CM is subject to these same rules, but because of his expanded role, is he assuming greater professional responsibility?

The construction process is like the fitting of a myriad and multitude of pieces into a jigsaw puzzle. The completed puzzle is the finished product, the completed facility.

The CM has undertaken to coordinate the proper fit of the pieces in the puzzle. If a piece fits improperly because of the failure or improper performance of one of the contractors working on the one piece alone, the CM may find himself in a new area of legal exposure because he has contracted to coordinate all parts to obtain the proper fit of puzzle, the final product. Without a CM involvement the responsibility for an improper fit for a portion of the project would trace directly to the one contractually bound for that piece of work, and he would be responsible for the results of his failure as it might affect the entire project.

As defined previously, the CM has assumed the significant role of "coordination." The specific and exact tasks will be defined in his contract but will be subject to the pressures of the construction project and practices within the industry itself. Construction in the public sector is governed by long-established precedents and statutory requirements.

A substantial portion of public construction is subject to federal controls not only by direct contract with federal agencies but also on contracts awarded both by private and other (state, municipal, etc.) public agencies because of federal aid or funding. Specific and strict criteria for federal contracting and procurement apply to such public work. The taking of competitive bids for public improvements and construction is only the basis of establishing the procedure of purchasing within the free market-place. Detailed requirements are established for the entire design/specification/bid/contract award/implementation procedures. Specification cannot be proprietary. Minimum salary scales are established, award must be to the lowest bona fide bidder, contract review procedures are firmly established, etc.

LEGAL CONTROLS

The reference to such federal procurement is made to indicate that strict procedures and contracting requirements exist, and the CM entering the industry does not change such procedures. It becomes his function to administer and coordinate many of these existing procedures. For instance, New York State requires separate contracts or specifications (prime contracts for general construction, plumbing, electrical, HVAC, and vertical transportation) for purchases over $50,000. This usually results in a minimum of five separate prime contracts on a public project in New York State. Other states have similar requirements pertaining to construction as separate bids for subcontracts or other practices to give opportunities to smaller contractors or subcontractors to bid or contract directly with the public authority or agency.

Although the CM is not performing any physical work and each individual contractor has the contractual responsibility for his contract, the construction manager in situations such as this where there are numerous contracts can assume legal responsibility for coordination previously held to be that of the owner.

As the law states, no professional is a guarantor of his services; the CM is not a guarantor nor can he guarantee the work of others but he, as a professional implementing and overseeing the performance of work assumes a responsibility that previously did not exist in the normal owner-architect-engineer-contractor relationship.

CM AS AGENT

As stated previously, the CM's conduct and responsibility is not limited to the contract agreement and specific contract terms. Nearly without exception all the relationships among the various and numerous parties involved in the total construction process are relationships between independent contractors. Standard contract language, especially in professional contracts, defines that the professional party is a separate entity or independent contractor. The purpose of such provisions is to define the legal relationship between the contracting parties and to establish that they are separate entities and that the hired party (the architect or contractor) is not an agent. An agent can act under a contract but is the representative of another and acts on his behalf. In law an agency relationship is substantially different from a contractual relationship between two independent parties.

Of interest is the AIA approach identifying the CM as the agent of the owner in rendering the defined services in the standard form contract. Even with contract language defining a relationship between the parties, the role and function undertaken as well as the manner in which it is performed can govern the actual relationship between the parties; whether that of an independent contractor or agent. Conversely normal contract language identifying a party as an independent contractor does not necessarily eliminate the possibility of an agency relationship between the two parties occurring as far as a third party is concerned.

An agent acts on behalf of another but also has powers and authority that are recognized by law that inure to him because of the agency relationship. Such authority can be specific, limited or general but the agent represents and acts on behalf of the owner. People dealing with him rely on his authority and ability to commit the owner, in the conduct of business.

The significance of the agency relationship is the reliance by an individual or company dealing with the CM. The CM is a professional, and contractually is defined an independent contractor and therefore by contract he is not an agent of the owner. However, he acts on behalf of the owner and represents the owner and his interests in the CM progress. Persons dealing with the CM may because of the CM's action assume the CM has certain authority and rely on certain of CM's actions. If the CM exceeds his contractual authority because of his temporary or accidental position, as for instance in the field as an inspector directing certain work not contractually under his jurisdiction, he may create an agency relationship. If a party in good faith without being bound by contravening contractual authority relied on the CM's directive, this party could contend that because of the CM's position and apparent authority he was justified in relying on the CM's action. If there were a dispute he could seek recovery for costs or damages on the grounds of his reliance on the CM's apparent authority because of his position as the owner's representative. This would be an alleged agency relationship, although contractually none existed.

INSURANCE

One of the most troublesome areas facing any contemporary professional, regardless of the field of practice is insurance coverage. The conduct of any business and profession regardless of scale requires insurance to cover the business practice and activity of the firm. The CM, therefore, is no different. Possibly as the practice evolves, the CM will find that the writing by insurance carriers of policies presently not in use may have been initiated. As his conduct of business impacts both professional design and construction contracting, as defined within the insurance industry, the question of extent of coverage and/or applicability of the standard professional liability (error and omissions) can arise.

Insurance coverage for a business firm simply represents that firm's participation in a plan that pools (or spreads) risk within an industry or over a wider base. It is the mechanics of providing relief from uncertainty. The cost (premium) to the single entity is not only a worthwhile investment but actually essential to protect it from a single or series of claims or incidents that it could not afford to meet with its own resources.

The basic concept of insurance is well established within the marketplace. In 1933, when the first states legislated compulsory employer's workmen's compensation, the necessary coverage was underwritten and provided by insurance companies. A portfolio of insurance for a firm can include the following types of coverages:

1. Workmen's compensation (mandatory by statute)

2. General public liability

3. Property damage

4. Comprehensive fire and theft casualty coverage

5. Automobile insurance coverages

6. Owner's protective insurance (naming an owner occupant or ultimate user of facility as an added insured under other basic insurance coverages)

7. Specialized forms of insurance, i.e.:

   a. *Umbrella*—providing excess coverage for underlying policies

   b. *Builders risk*—contractor's insurance to cover construction in progress if not insured by owner

8. Professional liability (errors and omissions)

The above categories are illustrative of the types of insurance with which a CM will become involved. Of most significance in this field is the area of professional liability insurance coverage, also referred to as errors-and-omission insurance.

The "malpractice" debate has been raging in the medical field since the mid-1970s. Malpractice insurance to the doctor is the same as errors and omissions to the professional in the construction industry. Because of the upsurge of claims, litigation, and high-court awards, the medical field has recently been faced with insurance policy cancellations, nonrenewal of policies at expiration, and rapidly accelerating premiums. The nature of the problem relating to professional insurance coverage or lack thereof for the medical practitioner is best exemplified by such incidents as certain doctors limiting their practice to avoid high-risk areas, doctors slowdown or strike as occurred in California in late 1975, the cancellation of all insurance and transfer of personal assets to fully protected trusts and proposed legislation to place limits on legal liability for malpractice.

This reference to the medical field is made to point to the ever-increasing problem in financial terms that professionals will find in protecting their interests as they pursue their professional endeavors. Design professionals, both architects and engineers, since the mid-1970s and especially during the years of 1974–1976, have felt this impact through substantial premium increases as well as in the limiting of the availability of such coverage from established insurance carriers (i.e., The Travelers Insurance Company ceased the writing of renewals and new policies in New York State as of December 1975).

The construction manager rendering a professional service can expect to encounter similar problems. During the evolution of CM practice he has found that his activity and resulting insurance coverages fall under the purview of basic existing policies, whether he is primarily also engaged in other fields of endeavor, such as design or construction. Depending upon the scope and nature of service the CM undertakes, it may be necessary to revise the insurance portfolio. The CM may, for instance, find the need to seek insurance protection for professional liability exposure when previously the general and public liability policies were sufficient to cover the contracting operation. The CM may have undertaken by contract to perform tasks or various services which fall under the definition of requiring a degree of care of a professional, such exposure not being considered by the insurance carrier as an insured risk under the general insurance coverage.

As the construction management process evolves and is used more as a distinct process from the traditional methods of contracting, legal rules and precedents applicable to the CM and his activities will evolve. The CM, whether a contractor, professional, or industrial group, is by his basic tasks crossing boundary lines previously established by practice and precedent between professionals, between professional and contractor or materialman and between owner and all the parties with whom he contracts. The CM is not a new professional, but is applying new methods and procedures to an established industry. He is also following established practices and using existing tools of the trade.

Because of all these factors the CM, as a professional, will find his legal responsibility to be greater than that of his counterparts who are performing their tasks within the standard framework of the industry. He will be held to the same high degree of care by the court as any professional, and he will be involved "legally" with the *total* project since he will not be able to limit his responsibility to one specific function such as planning, or design, or construction as is the case within the traditional framework of reference utilized within the construction industry.

LITIGATION

In addition to being a part of the construction industry and one of the members or groups that can find themselves a party to litigation, either as claimant or defendant, the CM can well find himself in the role of "claim prevention." A construction project involves numerous separate parties and in the legal sense, independent contractors, each with separate and defined responsibilities or functions. The combination of all results in a finished product, a building, a new transportation system, a rehabilitated facility, or any new or capital improvement. The path to reaching the end result or product can often be strewn with legal pitfalls and entanglements.

Because of the CM's role in the construction management process encompassing involvement from the beginning to the end, the CM will not be a stranger to legal action. Such action may result because of a basic dispute or differences with his client, the owner, as resulting from any commercial transaction. Of greater significance, however, can be the possible allegations holding the construction manager accountable for failures in any part of the CM process. Although his contractual relationship (privity of contract) is with one party, the owner, his exposure is to any one of the participants in the CM process. This can include the designer (architect and/or engineer), contractor, subcontractors, material suppliers, and vendors. Will the industry look to the construction manager for greater results as he has placed himself in a position of team leader, coordinator, expediter, and efficiency (time-and-cost) expert? What is the CM's professional responsibility to these other parties?

The determination of such responsibility is predicated upon an evaluation of what is the party's contract obligation. But in measuring such obligations, the courts will reach judgments on the basis of that party's standing within his industry or profession. What is the measure of reasonable professional responsibility that a third party can expect from one who holds himself out as a CM? The guidelines will evolve around existing yardsticks respecting contractors and professionals, but it is reasonable to expect that a new body of case law establishing the degrees and levels of responsibility can evolve from the construction management process.

It is not surprising that the term "litigation prone" is often applied to the construction industry. Because of the multiplicity of relationships together with the significant volume of economic activity (over 15 percent of the gross national product), it is not surprising that numerous disputes and disagreements eventually end up in the courts or other impartial tribunals.

The American Arbitration Association has administered commercial cases since its founding. Although its main involvement in dispute settlement was in the labor field for many years, growth of activity in construction claims has been growing rapidly in recent years. Not only has this association administered a larger case volume, but the dollar case load has grown appreciably as evidenced by statistics given in Table 8-1 applicable to construction related cases.

TABLE 8-1

Year	Number of cases
1966	460
1967	504
1968	559
1969	759
1970	1,009
1971	1,053
1972	1,113
1973	1,333
1974	1,618
1975	1,793

Year	Dollar volume
1973	63,607,000
1974	105,903,000
1975	108,932,000

Without the evolution of the CM process bringing more control, coordination, and efficiency to the construction, this growth of litigation would have been even greater: For the CM's purpose is to perform tasks and establish controls that were previously missing in the total construction process.

SUBCONTRACTS

Common to any of the contracting methods is the subcontract. The various types of contracts between an owner and prime contracting party accomplishing the construction have been defined previously. Alternative types of prime contracting methods were summarized in seven categories as follows:

1. Lump-sum contract
2. Reimbursable/cost-plus-negotiated contract
   a. Cost plus fixed fee
   b. Cost plus with bid fee
   c. Guaranteed maximum price
3. Negotiated contract (competitive and noncompetitive)

4. Design-build contract

5. Turn-key contract

6. Leaseback

7. CM contract

In each and every one of these approaches the privity of contract is between the owner, the ultimate user of the facility as one party, a contractor, construction manager, design professional or developer as the other or second party. Under any of the prime contracting systems, all construction projects of any size have, in addition, a multitude and multilevel of subcontracting arrangements.

Any construction regardless of the size or nature of work ranging from a wooden-frame single-story residence to a major heavy-construction project such as a power plant, is not performed by one company. No *one* contractor has all the skills, material, equipment, and/or labor to accomplish the entire task. As a consequence, on any one specific project, even utilizing the residential example, more than one company will be physically on the job site at the same time. Several levels or tiers of subcontractors and/or manufacturers will also be under contract to furnish components for use at the site. The usual situation on any project of any consequence is that several companies (independent employers) are at work on a project site simultaneously. These companies are all the various subcontractors who are required to implement the total construction process.

The prime contract between owner and, for instance, general contractor will establish all the basic criteria for the project. These are made applicable to all the various subcontractors through a separate contract agreement: the prime contractor or developer (one party) and the subcontractor (the second party). The subcontract entered into between the general contractor and individual subcontractor will establish and carry over many of the same conditions and obligations that the general contractor has assumed in his prime contract. It is not totally uncommon for there to be incorporated in a subcontract many of the documents that constitute the basic prime contract. In actuality, this is normal practice. Therefore, as an example, the payment terms may be similar to that of the prime contract or the amount of payment to the subcontractor will be controlled by the total prime-contract amount. Many of the conditions are similar but a separate contract document is executed between the subcontractor and prime contractor; they are the new contracting parties who have "privity." No privity exists between an owner and a subcontractor. Privity is the legal term that forms the basis of the relationship between two contracting parties. For instance, using the payment provision as an example, a subcontractor is paid for his work by the contractor; if a subcontractor performs, and the contractor does not pay, the subcontractor cannot seek payment on the basis of his contract directly from the owner. He has legal rights, such as filing liens, which involve the owner on legal grounds other than contract obligation.

The significance of the subdivision of work among numerous subcontractors and their lower-tier manufacturers and suppliers, whose tiers can reach numerous lower levels (see Figure 8-1), is exemplified by the fact that the single prime contract which the owner of the facility executes is essentially subdivided into numerous components for its actual prosecution. As an example, for a simple commercial building requiring site work, utility work, general construction, and numerous possible finish trades, the numbers of subcontracts and lower-level tiers can number up to 100 if one takes into account the various supply or purchase contracts that are required by each individual subcontractor to accomplish his segment of work.

The contract documents, therefore, have great significance. Also of great significance is the manner in which the division of the work among these various tiers of subcontractors is established. One of the prime

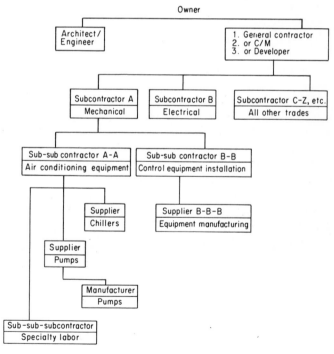

Figure 8-1.   Example of tier of subcontractors.

reasons and accomplishments of the CM process is the coordination of the numerous contractors and labor organizations who are required to implement the final construction product. Taking the document, however, alone, the main and most critical aspect of the subcontract document is to properly establish the subcontractor's scope of work and responsibility. Without the proper establishment of scope of work among each individual subcontractor—as, for instance, between the mechanical and electrical trades—problems frequently arise. These are ones that plague the industry and are described as "jurisdictional," and often result in disputes and litigation. Although part of the whole project, a party to such a dispute will assert that he has limited responsibility contending that it is another contractor's (no privity between them) responsibility to accomplish the work that may be in question. For example, the installation of a piece of mechanical equipment is incorporated in the total design and designated in the total contract documents which are part of the basic prime contract. When the work is subcontracted, it may occur that through improper contract draftsmanship and contract division of work, this piece of equipment is not properly identified in any specification division. Although clearly designated on the design plans, it may not have been properly identified in a specification section. The prime contractor may have believed that he had subcontracted the installation of this equipment, but upon its need for installation, he may discover that the party whom he believed had the responsibility for the specific piece of work disclaims responsibility because of its lack of proper identification in the contract. A dispute, resulting possibly in a claim or delay in the work, may follow.

The legal doctrine of privity of contract must be considered in the discussion concerning subcontracts and the relationship among the various parties. Privity of a contract is a long-established doctrine and states that relationship is between the party of the first part and the party of the second part. A third party, namely a subcontractor, is not and cannot be bound by the conditions of the contract to which he is not a party or a signatory. The doctrine of privity is of the greatest significance when one is concerned with the incorporation of the prime-contract documents within subcontracts. Such incorporation of prime documents cannot be made in total disregard for the specific activity of the subcontractor. The general statement that the subcontractor shall be bound by any and all provisions as applicable to his work as found in the general contract documents attached to the subcontract does have legal significance. Such significance is applicable (and will be so interpreted by the courts) only to the specific segment of work for which the subcontractor has responsibility. Such reference cannot be utilized by a general contractor to pass on obligations to a subcontractor which are not specifically referenced and defined as being that subcontractor's responsibility.

The significance of the subcontract is overlooked too frequently in the CM process. One of the reasons that the CM process has evolved is the need for the'proper subcontract coordination and definition of subcontractor relationships. Though the contract relationship may be between general contractor and contractor, the construction manager in the execution of his work and performance of his professional task undertakes the additional role of ensuring proper coordination, scheduling, and identification of the subcontractor's activities in relation to one another. Although he may not necessarily have privity of contract with individual subcontractors, he will review plans and coordinate the total project to ensure that the subcontract work, as contracted, encompasses the total project as designed and planned by the professional A/E.

Without a monetary interest in the contract (as general contractor to a subcontractor), the construction manager has the advantage of not being in an adversary role as in relation to the contractors. This facilitates the CM's function in coordinating the total work process.

REFERENCES

1. Prosser, *Restatement of the Law of Torts,* 2d ed., ¶ 299A.

III

PROJECT CONTROL BY THE CONSTRUCTION MANAGER

9

Project Management Concepts

The project manager concept is the fundamental basis for the role of the construction manager. This concept has evolved because it has had to. Although project management is utilized in projects for large and varied segments of government, institutions and industries, it is particularly well recognized and utilized in construction.

A dictionary definition of *project* is "an undertaking requiring concerted effort." More informative definitions by those in project management tend to add conditions such as: projects are complex efforts to achieve specified results within a schedule and budget; projects typically cut across organizational and functional lines; projects are unique and not completely repetitive of some previous effort.

Eric Jenett, vice president of Brown & Root and a past chairman of Project Management Institute, gives an explicit definition of project management:

> PM is the planning and scheduling and subsequent management and direction of the time phased pattern of application of resources (time, dollars, people, equipment, material), skills and knowledge to the execution (completion) of the various components and segments of a project. This must be done in an orderly economical manner and sequence so that the project objectives as to time, dollars, and technical end results are successfully met. In day to day practice, project management in large measure actually is interface or conflict management; it must almost continually curb, direct, counter or if necessary override almost everyone's self-interest. Information, response times, structural relationships, communication channels, techniques and tools are either themselves very temporal in nature or keyed to the temporary nature of projects. PM can be likened to management of a just-formed company whose sole objective

223

is to go out of business as rapidly and economically as possible while still reaching a given goal of accomplishment—project completion on cost/schedule—via an unknown and usually undefined route.

Project management is a new term for an organizational situation created to meet an ad hoc problem. Today's major organizational management structure has evolved from two great institutions: the church and the military. The entire concept is oriented toward order and stability. One of the primary motivations is the continuation of the functions of the organization with a minimum of change.

Within this broad, and rather inflexible, framework the founding institutions and their successors have had the problem of projects to be accomplished. To meet this challenge, project teams led by missionaries and task force commanders were created.

The fact that the task or mission did not fall within traditional lines of authority and function tends to frustrate the management coterie, since the mission or task cannot be accomplished within the standard management framework.

The unique nature of the project team tends to set it apart from the parent organizational structure. This tends to alienate those in the parent organization responsible for maintaining the equilibrium, while attracting to the project a special type of person with either the inclination or the special capabilities to implement the requirements of the task.

FACTORS AFFECTING SUCCESS

The Management Institute of Boston College undertook a broad-based study for the National Aeronautics and Space Administration (NASA) to investigate the interactions of project characteristics in terms of project performance. Basic information was collected through a very complete survey to which 646 responses were received. Of the respondants, more than 80 percent had been part of major project teams, and more than 10 percent had been the direct management superior of a project manager.

The questionnaire addressed more than 200 individual items of which 116 were shown to be significant. Fifteen items were found to strongly affect success, while 34 tended to affect success, and 25 appeared to be associated with success. The investigators reported (Ref. 1) that 34 independent and significant factors were uncovered.

The investigators concluded:

> Project management is a complex mechanism containing numerous variables significant to project success. There is no simple approach to insure project effectiveness. Many factors contribute to project success. . . .

The determinants of success are multiple in number; and many success determinants are factors which lie within the control of those who are managing a project. . . .

The presence of negative determinants tends to cause failure, but the absence of negative determinants is not a sufficient condition for success. The presence of positive determinants is necessary for success, but will not insure against failure.

The reviewers concluded: "To achieve the potential of a project, it is necessary to both encourage positive determinants; and *simultaneously* discourage negative determinants." They go on to note that this conclusion is not particularly startling but is, perhaps, more meaningful when considered in terms of specifics from their analysis of data.

An example which they give relates to team spirit on the project team:

A high degree of team spirit, good coordination and rapport between the project team, the client and the parent organization and adequate administrative, social and technical skills on the part of the project manager are ingredients often assumed to be highly related to project success. The analysis showed, however, that while the absence of these ingredients predicts project failure, their presence insures only mediocrity not success. Success requires avoidance of failure factors plus ingredients such as appropriate project team structure, adequate control procedures, commitment to budgets, schedules and performance goals which is shared by the using agency, the parent organization and the project team.

ORGANIZATION STRUCTURES

All management authorities agree that there is no ideal organizational structure. Several make the observation that given the choice between a good or bad manager or organization, the better chance for success was with the good manager in the bad organization.

Figure 9-1 is a typical upper portion of an organization chart for a company which produces a product for a profit. The particular organization described also develops, designs, and builds its own facilities for production. The example is taken from the petrochemical industry, which has developed well-rounded project engineers and project managers who are prototypical of the best results of project management principles.

It is typical for the hierarchical structure in this type of organization to be function-responsibility oriented.

Figure 9-2 is the matrix problem which faces the individual project manager. To complete his assigned project, he must run the gauntlet— not once but several times—through the authority of six vice presidents and three senior vice presidents.

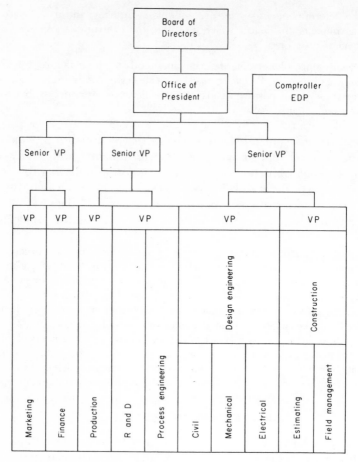

Figure 9-1.   Upper segment of petrochemical organization.

Within the traditional functional structure, an individual within the mechanical engineering group passes his problems upward for resolution. Should a particular project produce a conflict between two functional areas, the project manager—generally at a much lower rank—is suddenly face to face with a senior vice president or his representative. Since stability (and often tranquility) is the goal of the traditional vertically organized structure, conflicts and disputes produce negative reactions.

In a management journal, a leading management academician (Ref. 2) expressed concern about the "bonfire bonanza man," describing an individual who manages to get himself promoted by putting out bonfires. The concern expressed by that article was bona fide, but to many higher-level managers, any disruptive influence appears to be a bonfire bonanza man. The project manager who has stepped on functional toes in the process of getting his project through the vertical oriented structure may find himself categorized as unruly.

R. B. Archibald (Ref. 2) discussed the management of projects:

> Managing projects is without question a difficult job. It is a rare organization these days that is satisfied with its performance on projects in meeting schedules and budgets, achieving desired quality of end results, and controlling the effort without too much management infighting. . . .
>
> Managing projects is considerably more complex than managing stable organizations. The traditional concepts learned in graduate business schools do not apply very well in project management. In fact, severe conflicts usually exist between organizational or functional line management on one hand and the project management team on the other.

The NASA team (Ref. 1) concluded that:

> Less controllable factors such as legal-political difficulties, the on-going nature of the parent organization, and the behavior of the client need not

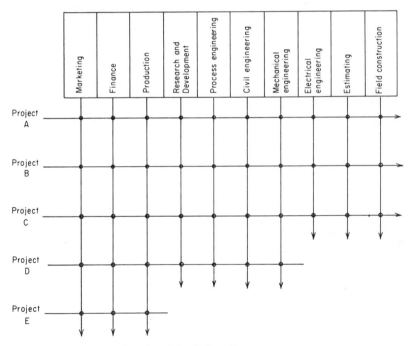

Figure 9-2. Project-fraction. Matrix interface.

necessarily be fatal obstacles to the success of a *well-managed* project, nor are they factors which can, by their presence or absence, make a success of a poorly managed project. . . . Many determinants of success are established prior to the time period during which a project is conducted. As a result, the potential success of a project is established prior to its undertaking. . . . Many potentials for success or lack of success are established by parties external to the project team. As a result, the potential success of a project is established by agents external to the team. The influence of the project manager and project team is therefore limited.

The team suggested some major variables which affect the success of projects as follows:

PARENT ORGANIZATION

- Coordinative efforts
- Structural flexibility
- Strategic dynamics
- Maintenance of rapport
- Past experience
- External buffering
- Prompt and accurate communications
- Enthusiasm

CLIENT ORGANIZATION

- Coordinative efforts
- Maintenance of rapport
- Reasonable and specific goals
- Prompt and accurate communications
- Commitment
- Lack of red tape
- Prompt decision making

Dr. Cleland (Ref. 3), a leading matrix organizational specialist, viewed the problems of the vertical organizational structure, noting that this organizational arrangement deals decisively with problems of efficiency and control in current operations. However, the organization is generally unable to deal effectively with task-oriented problems for two basic reasons: organization parochialism and disciplinary parochialism.

Organizational Parochialism

There is a tendency for each manager to view his organization as the center of affairs particularly if his department has had past successes. If the manager has responsibility for the profit center, this form of parochialism is usually reinforced. There is unfortunately little recognition either in merit increases or promotional opportunities for task-oriented performance versus functional-traditional performance.

Disciplinary Parochialism

Managers tend to perform (often unknowingly) in a narrow, specialized function which was the basis of their education and first work experiences. Many of their basic managerial disciplines and views were shaped through this combination of education and early experience. To the extent that the manager is inclined to become overinvolved with those areas with which he is familiar, he neglects interdisciplinary approaches and overall effectiveness of strategy.

PROJECT MANAGEMENT AS A STRUCTURE

Alvin Toffler (Ref. 4) comments on project management as a structure:

> We are witnessing not the triumph, but the breakdown of bureaucracy. We are, in fact, witnessing the arrival of a new organizational system that will increasingly challenge, and ultimately supplant, bureaucracy. This is the organization of the future. . . . The high rate of turnover (in organizational relationships) is most dramatically symbolized by the rapid rise of . . . "project" or "task force" management. . . . Indeed, project management has, itself, become recognized as a specialized executive art.

A major problem in the implementation of project management assignments is that interorganizational and intraorganizational conflict. These are forms of conflict which usually develop when groups of professionals in different organizations and working units must interface on a regular basis and are expected to coordinate their activities in the implementation of a project.

INTERFACE BETWEEN PROJECT
MANAGER AND ORGANIZATION

Almost without exception, the project manager sees himself as an individual with great responsibility and limited authority. Generally, he is quite correct. For a variety of reasons, management chooses to assign responsibility to the project manager. For a different variety of reasons, management is always reluctant to delegate authority on a broad basis.

The project manager who expects to have his authority clearly documented in a written charter or in the form of a crisp organization chart will be disappointed in either of two ways. Generally, he will not get the clear, crisp charter which he desires. Should he be fortunate (or unfortunate) enough to achieve his apparent clear authority, he will often find it difficult to enforce.

In the vertical hierarchy, authority through established position or office is a finite commodity. (Typically, once assigned, the individual tends to enhance his authority through his actions or to diminish it in the same manner.)

By definition, the project manager has to perform on a horizontal path through various established organizations including his own and, in some cases, client and regulatory organizations. His true influence is derived from the nature of his project, and the manner in which his own and the other organizations perceive the desired results. In Ref. 2, the project manager is compared with the noncommissioned officer in the infantry. Although low in the organizational structure, this is the individual who leads at the implementation level. Although the importance of sergeants is implicitly recognized, the recognition by the officer corps has a substantial element of reluctance about it. Much of the recognition is by default, because the senior levels really do not care to lead patrols or missions, however important they might be. Recognition of the noncommissioned project manager is at its height just before and during the actual mission. The noncommissioned project manager has other problems besides authority and recognition. Limited resources are certainly one of these. A mission has to be accomplished with the resources assigned, and because of his limited authority, the noncommissioned project manager is unable to call upon reserves unless the situation is in extremis—often too late to do any good.

These limitations on the military project manager encourage development and exercise of innovation and ingenuity in accomplishing assigned missions.

Because of his limited rank, he has command of only his own team in the field, and yet in the confusion of a mission, the need often arises to direct others. The successful noncommissioned project manager solves this problem through the application of leadership, using tact, persuasion, diplomacy, and guile. The sergeant gets his job done.

In the military analogy, the sergeant understands the basic command structure, and the latitude—if any—which he can take in a given situation. Further, if he has proper intelligence information, he has an appraisal of the forces with which he is interfacing—friend and foe alike. He then carries out his mission within those very inflexible parameters.

The project manager would do well to emulate this approach. First, understand the organizational structure of the parent, the client, and any other groups which have a mandatory interface for the project. In organizational terms, the project has a relatively short life. In most cases, it is impractical to expect an inflexible organization to change. Further, even if the organization is willing to change, the machinery to change grinds much slower than the pace of a project.

THE PROJECT MANAGER: KEY TO SUCCESS

Having examined the various relatively inflexible structures which influence, in an external sense, the potential of a project in the form of the parent organization, the client organization, regulatory or auxiliary organizations, and the locus or environment in which the project is to proceed, the question can well be raised: What is the positive potential for a project?

Without question, the project management team is the key to its success potential. Granted, some projects have no opportunity for success because they start with too many implicit (and sometimes explicit) liabilities against them. For those that could succeed, the project management team has to be the key to success. It exists because it represents flexibility and a means to accomplish an end.

In Ref. 6, Morton sees the project manager as a catalyst to change. He points out:

> Management is getting things done through people. Technical knowledge is not enough, for every managerial decision has behavioral consequences. . . . The project manager finds himself in most instances in a unique job within a complex environment, interacting with people of many disciplines and functions. . . . Acting as a catalyst, the project manager with his single point of responsibility and centralized planning and control can more efficiently and effectively respond to the constant rapid changes in external and internal environment, molding individuals into a team to obtain project objectives. The very nature of the project management organization often produces conflict with the functional organization and in many instances, the project manager must coerce people into getting the work done since he may not have the legitimate authoritarian power to direct the work.

While the project manager lacks the stability of the traditional organization, he has the opportunity to innovate. Where the typical functional manager has been taught to standardize all operations, the project manager must think in terms of dynamic change. If he is prepared to cope with change of this nature, he may have a substantial psychological advantage over those in traditional organizational structures.

The project manager must package and assign work relationships to members on his team so that the changing nature of the assignments are isolated or minimized in terms of the individual, so that they can continue to perform effectively. The following are some of the personal attributes to be sought in an effective project manager:

Integrity of Character

Foremost should be an uncompromising emphasis on integrity of character. Exercising a high level of ethical and professional standards enables the project manager to assume a leadership role. By setting an exacting example himself to focus on people's strengths, not their weaknesses, he aids in the development and utilization of the human resources under his supervision.

The project manager must be inwardly motivated toward self-development, with his own personal performance standards, goals, and objectives sufficient to stimulate by example the development of all under him. This is important in the construction industry where technological and management changes occur so rapidly as to outpace the available human skills necessary to keep abreast of them.

Teamwork Attitude

The ability of a project manager to perform well on a construction project is almost directly proportionate to the amount of teamwork that can be generated within his organization. Projects generally are so large and complex now that each individual member of the team must have not only the desire to do his job well but the esprit de corps to inspire other members of the team.

Problem-Solving Ability

A crucial factor in the project manager's performance is his thorough comprehension of the principles underlying the systems approach to problem solving, including not only the simple logical elements of arriving at a solution but the identification of the problem itself and of the factors which caused the problem.

Mental Discipline

A tough-minded approach to the conclusion of a task is a necessary requisite for the construction project manager, since many roadblocks, caused by external forces, will be thrown at the person trying to accomplish the CM tasks. The ability and the mental discipline required to affix priorities to tasks and to follow through on those tasks in order of the priorities is one of the most valuable traits of any manager.

Emotional Maturity

The project manager must be willing to accept responsibility for his decisions and actions. Some exposure to the elements of good management practice is desirable in terms of the management tools of planning, directing, coordinating, and follow-up.

Enthusiasm

Certainly nothing is more contagious than a great degree of personal enthusiasm. The woods are full of people who are capable of doing a job, but the ability to be enthusiastic about one's work can often spell success or failure for the construction project.

People-mindedness

Machines and money are not the only things that make the work go around. *People* are still primarily what it's all about. The translation of owner/client needs into social and human criteria during the conceptual and planning stages of the project is one of the most important elements of the CM process. The human relations aspect continues until completion because it is the CM who must deal with, coordinate, and direct activities of the professional firms, contractors, and reviewing agencies— all represented by people of diverse background and differing objectives.

Inquisitiveness

A project manager must have a built-in desire to continue his own education, for only when he realizes that he has but scratched the surface of his learning curve will he be able to progress to better things. A major mistake in the higher-learning process has been the impression that once having learned all the latest techniques, theory, and approaches, a student's education is complete. It is really only beginning and must be a continuing process.

Leadership

The project manager must exhibit leadership which motivates the individuals and the team as a whole toward the ideal conception of a cohesive, compatible, and efficient group. In order to integrate the various disciplines, the project manager must be capable of understanding, utilizing, and managing the technological complexities required by the project.

Since, in many instances, the project manager will not have a specific charter of authority covering all the requirements for the project, he must lead the team through persuasion, example, conflict in a controlled sense, and coercion in a controlled sense.

REFERENCES

1. Baker, Fisher, and Murphy, "Factors Affecting Project Success," *PMI 6th International Seminar Proceedings,* Washington, 1974, pp. 165–188.

2. O'Brien, James J., "The Project Manager: Not Just a Firefighter," *SAM Advanced Management Journal,* January 1974, pp. 52–56.

3. Cleland, "Matrix Management in Long-range Planning," *PMI 4th International Seminar Proceedings,* Philadelphia, 1972.

4. Toffler, Alvin, *Future Shock,* Random House, New York, 1970, pp. 125–133.

5. Cleland, "The Impact of Horizontal Hierarchy," *PMI 6th International Seminar,* Washington, 1974, pp. 203–213.

6. Morton, "Project Manager, Catalyst to Constant Change," *PMI 6th International Seminar Proceedings,* Washington, 1974, pp. 430–460.

10
Value Control

Value analysis has been an established technique for more than 20 years, and many in the construction field—designers and contractors—have been trained in the concepts and techniques of value analysis and value engineering. Only about half of those in the industry are aware of value analysis, perhaps less than 5 percent realize its potentials, and only about 1 percent are actively utilizing value-analysis techniques. This is an incredible situation. There are definite reasons for this apparent apathy, and the value analyst needs to understand and empathize with the balance of the team in order to turn them *on,* rather than off, to value analysis.

Constructors are almost constantly aware of project situations in which poor value judgments were made during the design phase. Even though most of the actual implementations of value analysis have been in the construction phase, the real potential lies in the ability of experienced constructors to participate in value analysis during the design phase. The increasing recognition of the potential of construction management is simultaneously opening the door to more value analysis. One of the problems in the construction field has been the dichotomy between design and construction.

The role of the design team is vital to the successful application of value analysis. It is during this phase that most consistent opportunities for major value-analysis implementation occur. Architects and engineers are constantly involved in value judgments during design, and value analysis offers the construction manager a specific technique for participation in the process.

Background

Value analysis developed as a specific technique after World War II. The development work was done at the General Electric Company, where it was observed that some of the substitute materials and designs utilized as a necessity because of wartime shortages offered superior performance at lower cost. An in-house effort to improve product efficiency by intentionally developing substitute materials and methods to replace the function of more costly components was directed and assigned in 1947 to Lawrence Miles, staff engineer. Miles researched the techniques and methodology available and utilized a number of proven approaches in combination with his own procedural approach to analysis for value. The value-analysis technique was accepted as a GE standard, and gradually other companies and governmental organizations adopted the new approach as a means of reducing costs.

Other major firms in private industry followed GE in the establishment of value-analysis departments, including: RCA, Minneapolis-Honeywell, Lockheed, Joy Manufacturing, and others.

In 1954, the Navy Bureau of Ships became the first Department of Defense organization to set up a formal value-analysis program, and Lawrence Miles was instrumental in the development of that program. The program was retitled "value engineering" to reflect the engineering emphasis of the Bureau of Ships.

In 1956, the Army Ordnance Corps initiated a value-engineering program, again with the assistance of GE personnel. This program has continued over the years, and the Army Management Engineering Training Agency offers value-engineering training as part of its curriculum.

In 1961, the Air Force became interested in the potential of value engineering as a result of the effectiveness of applications by Air Force weapons-systems contractors such as GE. This interest was one of the building blocks which, in 1962, led Secretary of Defense McNamara to place his prestige behind the use of value engineering, calling it a key element in the drive to reduce defense costs. (In that same year, Secretary McNamara gave great impetus to the development of network-based planning systems such as PERT and CPM by his mandate that these techniques be utilized in all project and program planning for the Department of Defense.)

To implement the directive of Secretary McNamara, value engineering was included as a mandatory requirement by the Armed Services Procurement Regulations (ASPR). The Armed Forces' definition of value engineering is: "A systematic effort directed at analyzing the functional requirement of the Department of Defense systems, equipment, facilities and supplies for the purpose of achieving essential functions at the lowest total cost, consistent with the needed performance, reliability, quality, and maintainability."

VALUE ANALYSIS IN CONSTRUCTION

Prior to the introduction of value engineering into ASPR, applications in the construction field were random and infrequent. Although the adoption of value engineering by the Department of Defense was oriented principally toward the purchase of materials, equipment, and systems, the change in ASPR automatically introduced value engineering to two of the largest construction agencies in the country: the U.S. Army Corps of Engineers and the U.S. Navy Bureau of Yards and Docks. In the first 10 years of use, the Corps of Engineers estimated savings of almost $200 million, with most of the savings the result of its own reevaluations of major projects. In that time period, 2,200 contractors had submitted cost-cutting value-engineering suggestions, of which 1,400 were accepted with the cash-shared savings of $7 million.

As the success of value engineering, principally in the construction phase, was documented, other federal agencies began tentative steps toward the adoption of value engineering. In 1965, the Bureau of Reclamation undertook value-engineering training for its engineering staff and in 1966 placed a value-engineering incentive clause in its construction contracts.

In 1967, the Post Office Department set up a value-engineering staff in its Bureau of Research and Engineering. In that same year, the Senate Committee on Public Works held hearings on the use of value engineering in the government at which many of the major agencies exchanged information on their utilization of value engineering. In 1969, the Office of Facilities of the National Aeronautics and Space Administration (NASA) began formal value-engineering studies and training. The U.S. Department of Transportation published a value-engineering incentive clause to be used by its agencies. In that same year, the Public Building Service of the General Services Administration (PBS/GSA) set up its value-engineering staff.

Until 1972, the construction industry, in general, had only limited interest in value analysis or value engineering. In 1972, the twelfth annual conference of the Society of American Value Engineers (SAVE) emphasized the application of value analysis in the construction industry. Chartered in 1959, SAVE has had much to do with the evolution of value analysis, particularly in the federal government. Key SAVE members in the Washington chapter are predominantly from federal departments. The SAVE conference provided a forum where some 400 engineers, architects, and other industry members could hear the specifics of progress which had been made.

Where the Department of Defense was responsible in 1962 for the first major introduction of value engineering to the construction industry, in 1972 the GSA, under Administrator Arthur Sampson, clearly took leadership of a positive program to expand dramatically the utilization of value analysis in both design and construction. Under Administrator Sampson, GSA actively undertook the evaluation and implementation of several improved management techniques to be applied to the implementation of design and construction for federal nonmilitary building facilities. As the purchaser of hundreds of millions of dollars in annual construction value, these efforts toward improved management demanded the attention of the entire construction industry. One of these was a broad-based use of construction management.

On March 1, 1972, the GSA required that most new architectural, engineering, and construction management contracts contain value-engineering clauses.

The GSA requirements call for basic value-engineering services where construction costs range from $200,000 to $3 million, more extensive value-management services when over $3 million, and special value-management services for construction management contracts. The detailed requirements are spelled out in a manual published by the Public Buildings Service (PBS) of GSA (Ref. 1).

What's in a Name?

Value-analysis specialists use the terms "value analysis" and "value engineering" interchangeably. However, the term "engineering" has a very definite preestablished meaning in the design and construction fields. Its application to value analysis would imply a narrow operation not touching many of the activities of the owner, the architect, and the contractor. For that reason, a conscious effort has been used by many construction managers to select the term "value analysis" which is all-encompassing.

In a few instances, use of the term "value engineering" is inescapable—such as the VECP (value-engineering change proposal), which is a term well established in the various federal organizations.

Because of the dichotomy in the two well-established terms value analysis and value engineering in their application to design and construction, there is another trend toward the use of a new term. As a result, the Public Building Service has renamed its office of value engineering the office of Value Management.

Value is, of course, a relative term, not an absolute one. There are many components, most common of which are:

Use value—The properties and qualities which accomplish a use, work, or service compared to a base. Use value is equal to the value of the functions performed and is synonymous with worth or total worth.

Cost value—The summation of the labor, material, overhead, and all other elements of cost required to produce an item or provide a service compared to a base.

Esteem value—The properties, features or attractiveness which create a desire to possess the article but are not necessarily required so far as functional performance is concerned.

Exchange value—The properties or qualities which will remain attractive enough to other people to permit market resale in the future.

Social value—The properties or qualities contributing generally to the quality of life.

Psychic value—Qualities associated with human well-being.

Certainly in the context of the application of value to construction management, value engineers (and construction managers) would be concerned primarily with use values, which are fairly objective and for which definitive indicators are available. For the other components of value, a broad unexplored domain of value methodology remains to be sounded. These will provide major challenges to the construction manager, as they underlie much of the concerns of society at the present time.

If a building or facility is to be evaluated only on its use value, the worth described would be that of an engineered shelter. However, the human interaction to and with a building is a subtle but very significant consideration. It is a relationship which may, in many ways, determine the volume of utilization of the facility. In the life cycle of a facility, the amount of utilization has a high impact upon the true worth. For instance: two similar buildings are compared and have similar purposes and functions; one building has been constructed at the lowest first cost with no intentional aesthetic value added, while its companion has had aesthetic treatment designed to attract more users. If it is assumed that perhaps twice as many people will utilize the more attractive facility over its lifetime, and the additional cost of the aesthetics is less than the initial cost of the engineered shelter, a true quantitative value could be assigned to the cost of the aesthetics.

Aesthetic value might also be termed attractiveness value, wherein attraction is considered a real dollar-and-cents return. A supermarket which attracts no customers is a very expensive investment, regardless of how low the initial cost has been.

FUNCTION ANALYSIS

Value is the basic dimension to be analyzed, and the basic analytical process is termed "function analysis."

Lawrence Miles describes value analysis as "a disciplined action system, attuned to one specific need: accomplishing the functions that the customer needs and wants" (Ref. 2). He further indicates that "the basic function is straightforward to determine, and any work done before that has been accomplished is wasted effort."

The Public Building Service describes function analysis in this way:

> A user purchases an item or service because it will provide certain functions at a cost he is willing to pay. If something does not do what it is intended to do, it is of no use to the user and no amount of cost reduction will improve its value. Actions that sacrifice needed utility of an item actually reduce the value to the user. On the other hand, expenditures to increase the functional capacity of an item beyond that which is needed are also of little value to the user.

The Value Management Office of PBS sees anything less than the necessary functional capability as unacceptable—and anything more as unnecessary and wasteful. A project or part of a project which is to receive function analysis is addressed with the six basic questions of value analysis:

- What is it?
- What does it do?
- What is its worth?
- What does it cost?
- What else would work?
- What does that cost?

What Is It?

A prerequisite to function analysis is the selection of the function to be analyzed. Figure 10-1 shows a work-breakdown analysis for a weapons system. Selection of the optimum function for analysis depends upon the state of development of the project as well as the relative value of the different components.

At a very early stage, the weapons system could be evaluated on a

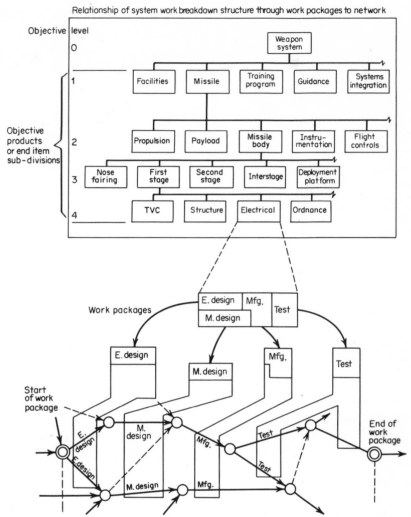

Figure 10-1. Work structure network (U.S. Navy Special Projects Office, Government Printing Office).

functional-analysis basis as an overall concept. However, if the development of the system is well advanced, the opposite end of the spectrum would be available for analysis, such as the different work packages which make up the electrical portion of the first stage of the missile body.

Within the area to be analyzed, selection of the functions which should be considered can be guided by the Pareto distribution shown in Figure 10-2. Pareto's law of distribution, often referred to by value analysts,

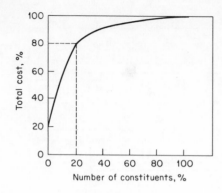

Figure 10-2. Pareto's law of distribution (Public Building Service GSA Manual P 8000.1 **Value Engineering).**

suggests that 20 percent of the items in any complex thing account for 80 percent of the cost. As will be noted on the section on cost, this distribution does not exactly hold for construction projects. However, it is axiomatic that a minority of the components of a project make up the majority of the cost. Within this minority of high-cost areas, the best opportunities can be found for value analysis. The identification of the high-value items narrows the number of viable opportunities for value analysis which remain in a project. Analysis of the high-value areas produces the "best bang for the buck." Standard cost-breakdown models for types of projects can be utilized in identifying the potential areas for best results.

It is the consensus of value specialists that the most productive areas of opportunity should be selected for analysis, and these areas are inherently the most expensive ones.

Knowledgeability regarding the cost makeup of components of a project is important. Without this, an uninformed analyst might assume that "mechanical work" at 25 percent of the project cost is a more opportune area for functional analysis than "superstructure" at 16 percent. However, mechanical work breaks down into subpackages which would require multiple functional analysis—while the superstructure may be analyzed in one single study.

What Does It Do?

This is the key value analysis question. It requires definition of the function of the item under study. The method of this definition is prescribed by established value analysis procedure as two words, a noun and a verb.

The simplicity of the approach is deceptively simple. Selection of the proper two-word description is often quite difficult, requiring comprehensive understanding of the item under study.

The functional description is not necessarily correct when it is the most obvious, and therein lies the potential for successful analysis. The analyst is not limited to a single two-word description. In fact, a series of descriptions can apply to the same item. However, only one of these descriptions is the basic function. The other descriptions, necessarily, become secondary functions. Secondary functions may be important, but they are not controlling.

It is quite usual to find that many have assumed that the basic function is really one which had always been considered a secondary one.

VERBS

Some typical verbs which can be used to describe construction functions are:

absorb	enclose	protect
amplify	filter	reduce
apply	generate	reflect
change	hold	reject
collect	improve	separate
control	increase	shield
conduct	insulate	support
create	interrupt	transmit
decrease	prevent	

NOUNS—MEASURABLE

circuit	force	power
contamination	friction	pressure
current	heat	protection
damage	insulation	radiation
density	light	repair
energy	liquid	voltage
flow	noise	water
fluid	oxidation	weight

NOUNS—AESTHETIC

appearance	effect	prestige
beauty	features	style
convenience	form	symmetry

The difficulty of identifying in a two-word phrase is often substantial.

Accordingly, nouns such as thing, part, article, device, or component generally indicate a failure to conclusively define. The noun should be measurable or capable of quantification. For instance, a water service line to a building could have the function "provide service," but the term "service" is not readily measurable. A better definition would be "transport water." The noun in this definition is measurable, and alternatives can be determined in terms of the quantity of water to be transported, or in special situations such as laboratories, in terms of the quality of water being transported.

The functional definition must concern itself with the type of use as well as the identification of the item. A piece of wire might "conduct current," "fasten part," or "transfer force," depending upon the specific utilization.

The spartan restraint involved in holding the description to two words can be difficult to apply. There is often a temptation to utilize a slightly broader definition by insertion of additional adjectives to condition the noun. Some value analysts permit this variation, but the tried and tested approach insists upon the two-word abridgment. The rigorous application of the two-word functional definition often discloses a factual view of the project category which was subconsciously available but not consciously realized.

For instance, one perception would be that it is not the door itself but the doorway or the accessway which is the true basic purpose for the specification of a door at a given location. The overall context of the application has to be considered. In an office building, the basic purpose of a doorway is to "provide access," while in a prison, this might be to "control access." An interior door at a fire wall does "provide access," but its basic purpose is to "control fire." A doorway at a classroom entrance might be there to "control noise."

At a detail level, doors throughout a building would be separate categories. To evaluate the generic category, the subbreakdown would be an important factor. Figure 10-3 describes some of the function definitions for doorways in a complex courthouse structure. The cost of certain doors, such as the elevator-shaft doors, would be included in other systems. However, a subset of the system of doors is the door bucks in which they mount. That system would be included in the hollow metal or miscellaneous metal subcontract.

The item under study can, and should, have different levels of indenture as identified in the work-breakdown structure. Figure 10-4 illustrates a breakdown structure for a fire alarm system prepared by PBS. The second level of indenture breaks down the system into two sectors: person and equipment. This identifies the system as semiautomatic. The table in Figure 10-4 shows the functional definition developed with these various levels of indenture. At the third, or detailed, level the basic function of the

VALUE ENGINEERING FUNCTIONAL ANALYSIS WORKSHEET

PROJECT *Courthouse* NAME

ITEM *Doors* TEL. NO.

BASIC FUNCTION *Control Access* DATE

QUAN-TITY	UNIT	ELEMENT DESCRIPTION	FUNCTION VERB	NOUN	KIND	EXPLANATION	WORTH	COST
		Exterior doors	*Provide*	*Security*	B	*Control of access mandatory*		
			Exclude	*Weather*	S	*Alternates possible*		
			Express	*Prestige*	S	*Image to the public*		
			Provide	*Visibility*	S	*Entry doors*		
		Office doors	*Exclude*	*Noise*	B	*Judge's chambers*		
			Contain	*Noise*	B	*Typing pool*		
			Enclose	*Space*	B	*Public areas*		
		Area doors	*Provide*	*Visibility*	S	" "		
			Exclode	*Fire*	B	*Exit passageways*		
			Contain	*Fire*	B	*Mechanical rooms*		
			Control	*Air*	B	*HVAC zone perimeter*		
			Control	*Traffic*	B	*Key zone points*		
		Security doors	*Control*	*Prisoners*	B	*Secure passage to courtrooms*		
			Contain	*Prisoners*	B	*Cell doors; cell block*		
			Exclude	*Public*	B	*Doors from public areas*		
			Exclude	*People*	B	*Elevator Shaft doors*		
		Other	*Provide*	*Privacy*	B	*Bathroom doors*		

Figure 10-3. *Functional definitions for doorways in a complex courthouse structure.*

bell was selected as "make noise," which would permit a greater latitude in the development of alternative ways of effectively making noise not limited to the bell.

What Is It Worth?

Worth is a measure of value and represents the least expenditure required to provide the function required as defined by the functional definition. The evaluation may be specific but is quite often subjective. A method of deriving worth is identification of the cost of comparable items which would provide a similar service.

Many value analysts use the seven classes of value defined by Aristotle: economic, moral, aesthetic, social, political, religious, and judicial. The definition used by Mudge (Ref. 3) is: "Value as used in the systematic approach is defined as: the lowest cost to reliably provide the functions of service at the desired time and place and with the essential quality." He provides a number of subcategories: use value, esteem value, cost value, and exchange value. Within these categories, only use value is capable of a quantitative evaluation. However, in a facilities project, esteem value

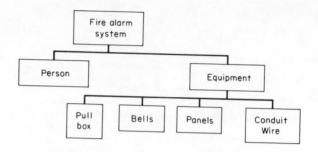

Figure 10-4.   Breakdown structure for a fire alarm system. (Public Building Service/GSA, Manual P 8000.1 Value Engineering).

would be equivalent to aesthetic value and is a very important consideration.

In the value analysis of a major project, the construction manager found the aesthetic value difficult to incorporate. After one value analysis seminar, the construction manager was quoted as saying that suggestions made as part of the value analysis could save the GSA $1.4 million on an $11.5 million project, or about 12 percent. He then went on to say that "although limestone will cost $250,000 more, it would be aesthetically more pleasing than precast concrete . . . and we would still be saving over $1 million." The construction manager appeared to recognize the value of attractiveness but relegated it to a secondary function.

Proper application of value analysis should add to the willingness of well-informed owners to invest in attractiveness as a function.

What Does It Cost?

When the area has been defined enough to identify quantities, the costs can be estimated and compared with worth. The result is a value index found as follows:

$$\text{Value index} = \frac{\text{worth}}{\text{cost}} = \frac{\text{utility}}{\text{cost}}$$

Accordingly, value may be increased by improving utility with no change in cost, retaining the same utility for less cost or combining an improved utility with a decrease in cost.

The choice of worth may be reconsidered when the cost of the area under study is established. In discussing something as basic as the worth of a bolt (Ref. 4), Heller suggests the results may be affected when the analysts are advised that this particular bolt holds on the wings of a transport plane. Engineers who would assign a certain dollar value to the worth of a bolt tend to increase the worth when they are asked to consider that they are passengers on an airplane in which that particular bolt holds on the wings. However, their original evaluation included a requirement that the item meet functional requirements. Implicit in this requirement is the understanding that the bolt is not allowed to fail on the service stated. Accordingly, the worth value for this bolt should not include an emotional value of the consequences of possible failure of the bolt.

The worth figure should be kept as basic as possible so that the value index theoretically cannot be above 1. In fact, if a cost figure of less than the worth can be achieved, and it is a viable figure, the initial worth figure was incorrect. The value index provides a reasonable indication of the premium which an alternative approach is costing.

Some analysts attempt to hold the worth at the very lowest possible minimum—at a point which is below that which would be acceptable or feasible. One example in evaluating a pencil equates its worth to a nail which "makes marks." If the pencil is a drafting pencil, this can hardly be a realistic comparison. A more reasonable comparison would be the lowest acceptable quality of drafting pencil at the proper weight purchased in suitable quantities compared with, for instance, a lead holder. The cost of the lead holder, which is refillable, would be compared on a life-cycle basis with the cost of the number of equivalent pencils to determine a value index.

A common example used for worth in value analysis is the worth of a tie clip. If the function is really "hold tie," the value is perhaps equivalent to that of a paper clip. However, tie pins and tie clips usually cost much more than a paper clip. The worth is really in the appearance of the tie pin or tie clip, having a prestige value to the purchaser. For those users, however, who are really interested in "hold tie," a cloth loop sewn to the inner face can be used to hold the two sections of tie together when it is tied, at a cost of not much more than a paper clip. The function must be considered in terms of whether the user is really interested in prestige as a basic function or in "hold tie" as the basic function.

What Else Would Work?

After the establishment of the functional definition and assessment of its worth and cost, the next key stage is the application of creativity to determine alternatives which would also perform the same function.

Creativity is one of the essential techniques of value analysis. It is one of those existing attitudes important to value analysis which value analysts have incorporated into the total value-management approach.

It is human nature for people to resist change—to resist either stopping things which they are doing or adopting new ideas. The development of alternative approaches to meet functional analysis requires a breakdown of this inertial resistance to change.

A key technique in the development of creative alternatives is the use of a think-tank or brainstorming approach. The group is used to develop ideas without evaluating them. The creative session is not limited to ideas which will probably work, but to a free-form type of idea listing. The idea is to break through typical inhibitions and restraints and list even outlandish ideas. Rube Goldberg would feel right at home in this kind of creative session.

In brainstorming, the starting point is the two-word abridged functional definition. Ideas which are abstract, even humorous, are encouraged, because through stream-of-consciousness thinking and free associating, these ideas may lead to more practical considerations.

The creative session has its own set of ground rules to encourage free and open thinking. Not only is evaluation and judgment deferred, but also critical response is discouraged until the entire listing has been developed.

THE JOB PLAN

In the words of L. E. Miles (Ref. 2): "Value analysis is a system, a complete set of techniques, properly arranged, for the sole purpose of efficiently identifying unnecessary costs before, during or after the fact. Some of the techniques are familiar, some modified, some new. . . . It is a disciplined action system."

The job plan is the disciplined system which combines the special technology of value analysis with other procedures and techniques to result in the complete analysis.

The six basic phases in the job plan as identified by the Department of Defense are:

1. Orientation

2. Information

3. Speculation

4. Analysis

5. Development

6. Presentation and follow-up

Table 10-1 lists the job-plan descriptions as described by four Dept. of Defense and GSA handbooks and three experts in the field.

Orientation

Orientation actually precedes the development of the job plan, and so it has been omitted as the first phase of job planning in many considerations. To orient is to "place or arrange relative to an external reference frame." In a properly established value-analysis situation, this would include the selection of appropriate areas to be studied and the appropriate team to accomplish the study. In an organization which has been conducting value analysis, policies will have been established which assist in these determinations.

The greatest potential for net-cost savings occurs in the earlier stages of a project so that, given a choice, the value analysis team would select study areas in projects in the earlier stages of the project cycle. Naturally, this is controlled by the nature and number of projects which can be considered for study. If the organization has under its control only projects which are in construction, these represent the only area of opportunity. Conversely, the question may not even be one of selecting projects. If, in fact, the organization has one major project, the value-analysis team has the initial assignment of orienting its studies to the area of greatest potential return.

Information

The information phase is a fact-finding phase. The purpose is to accumulate all the factual information available in regard to the proposed area of study. If the information phase is the initial one, this may require collection of information on the entire project so that the selection of the most opportune area for value analysis can be made. If this area has already been selected, the factual collection can focus upon that one phase of the project for this sector of the value-analysis study.

In a construction project, the facts available will depend to a great degree upon the phase of design or construction. Collection of the facts should include assembly of the best available program parameters, design specifications, and flow diagrams and/or drawings available at the time.

Background information should be assembled and subdivided into the facts and assumptions.

TABLE 10-1
Value Engineering Job-Plan Categories

L. D. Miles* (3) 1961	DOD HANDBOOK 5010.8-4 (1963)	DOD (USA META) 1968	E. D. Heller† (1) 1971	A. E. Mudge‡ (2) 1971	GSA-PBS P 8000.1 1972	L. D. Miles§ (4) 1972	PBS VM workbook 1974
Orientation		Orientation		Project selection	Orientation	Information	Information
Information	Information	Information	Information	Information	Information	Analysis	Function
Speculation	Speculation	Speculation	Creative	Function	Speculation	Creation	Creative
Analysis	Analysis	Analysis	Evaluation	Creation	Analysis	Judgment	Judicial
Program planning	Development	Development	Investigation	Evaluation	Development	Development	Development
Program execution	Presentation	Presentation and follow-up	Reporting	Investigation	Presentation		Presentation
			Implementation	Recommendation	Implementation		Implementation
Summary and conclusion					Follow-up		Follow-up

*L. D. Miles, *Techniques of Value Analysis and Engineering,* 1st ed., McGraw-Hill, New York, 1961.
†E. D. Heller, *Value Management: Value Engineering and Cost Reduction,* Addison-Wesley, Reading, Mass., 1971.
‡Arthur E. Mudge, *Value Engineering,* McGraw-Hill, New York, 1971.
§L. D. Miles, *Techniques of Value Analysis and Engineering,* 2d ed., McGraw-Hill, New York, 1972.

250

The information phase is not one of evaluating or judging. The maximum amount of pertinent information should be gathered in the minimum amount of time.

In addition to facts and assumptions, any information required for further analysis but not available should be delineated. The team should sort out extraneous matter in preparation for the analytical phase.

Function Analysis

This step is included as part of the information phase in many job plans (see Table 10-1). However, it is the very heart of the value-analysis effort, and both Miles and Mudge—two of the leading experts—single out the function analysis as a separate phase. When this is not done, the function analysis would necessarily be the latter portion of the information phase.

The key value questions are addressed to the area under study at this point:

- What is it?
- What does it do?
- What does it cost?
- What is it worth?

The function of the key area under study is described in a two-word phrase consisting of one noun and one verb. Any number of secondary functions may also be described.

Creative-Speculative Phase

The purpose of this phase is the generation of ideas for alternative solutions to the function being analyzed. The emphasis is on imagination, and free-form think-tank approaches or brainstorming are very successful. Miles suggests a group of three to ten people as the optimum.

The purpose is to generate ideas—not to judge them. Nothing should be done to stifle a creative process, for the thought-association process may generate feasible ideas in response to abstract solutions which may seem ridiculous when listed.

Judicial Analysis

Those ideas developed in the creative phase are screened to eliminate those which do not meet the functional requirements. The viable alternatives are identified and ranked according to feasibility and cost. Various techniques can be used, most based on a matrix comparison, to develop and select the best solution.

Development

The alternatives selected for potential implementation are now reviewed in depth. The ideas are checked out with purchasing departments, vendors, and other specialists in the field. Cost factors are verified. Ideas are reviewed for flaws or problem areas, and a development plan is established. The plan is based upon the alternative or alternatives which are economically viable.

Blast-Create-Refine

In Ref. 2, a special technique is described which can be used to reach value objectives in specific problems. The technique is carried out in the following stages:

1. *Blast*—As described in the DOD manual, blast means to get off the beaten path. Basic functions are identified, but alternatives which are suggested may cover only part of the function. The approach may be traumatic to the originator of a design or plan, but it does tend to help the team break away from the status quo or inertia.

2. *Create*—Creativity as described by the DOD is reaching for an unusual idea or a totally new approach. As described by Miles, it is the use of intense creativity to generate alternative means by which concepts revealed by the blasting can be modified to accomplish a large part of the function.

3. *Refine*—In the DOD parlance, refining involves strengthening and expanding ideas which suggest a different way to perform the function. Miles suggests that the necessary created alternatives be added to the functions which would be accomplished by the blasted product and the total sifted and refined until the refined product fully accomplishes the total function.

The blast-create-refine technique incorporates all the methods and procedures of value analysis, but focuses them more specifically on a single area and uses a team approach to generate results perhaps more rapidly. The blast-create-refine approach should be applied with judgment. The very

term "blast" suggests a brute-force breakthrough of roadblocks and inertia. Necessarily, negative feelings will be set up either with part of the
organizational structure or within the team itself. Accordingly, the organizational groundwork has to be properly laid when this high-powered-
focus type of value analysis is applied. Further, the "blast" approach
applied without an overview consideration of the power factors within an
organization can result in the winning of a battle and the loss of a war.
Where the value-analysis purpose can be achieved without the blast stage,
the normal routine of value analysis should be used. Using an elephant
gun to kill an ant is an overinvestment—and poor value.

Value Assurance

The term "value assurance" has been used by the GSA (Ref. 1) to apply
specifically to the design phase as follows:

> *Value Assurance*—Value engineering applied during the initial creative
> phase of a design or procedure, intended to assure a high value item
> when released for procurement or when placed in service.

While traditional value engineering developed in the construction field as
an intentional reexamination of existing designs or hardware, usually on
the part of the contractor on an incentive basis, use in the design stage
goes far beyond such restricted application. In the more comprehensive
approach, focus is on function analysis and on applied creativity to
generate alternative solutions serving the required functions; this logically
takes place during the planning and design stages of the project.

This broader application now mandated by GSA extends the concepts
of value analysis to what could be termed "value architecture" and "value
planning." That such a broad equivalence is possible is not surprising;
the congruence with value analysis of the many new, modern concepts
application to construction (such as systems analysis and systems building)
has been noted by many writers. Certainly value engineering is also a
powerful catalyst to systems engineering and to the development of the
performance concept in construction practice.

Although the application of value analysis to design is a straightforward and rational application of systems analysis, its implementation,
in the federal agencies at least, was found beset by procedural difficulties
in the value-engineering symposium in 1969, the principal factors in the
structuring of value-engineering proposal efforts being:

1. How value-engineering study proposals are generated

2. How proposals are screened and selected

3. Who actually performs selected studies

4. How studies are paid for

5. How those performing the studies are trained in value engineering methodology

6. How such training is paid for

7. How study costs are controlled

8. How results are implemented

9. How benefits are measured

10. How the overall value engineering program is stimulated

At that time, however, the only federal agencies having value-engineering-in-design programs were the Army Corps of Engineers and the Naval Facilities Engineering Command, with only limited formal organization in the Bureau of Reclamation and the Postal Service. Since the GSA action on value-in-design, however, the organizational difficulties with the above factors have largely been resolved, and a more universal application of value-in-design is expected, by the GAO and legislators—as well as the agencies themselves.

Figures 10-5 and 10-6 illustrate the relatively insignificant proportion of total or life-cycle costs represented by the design process, and the very major potential influence the client or using agency (who sets standards and criteria) and the architect engineer have in reducing life cycle. On the other hand, the opportunities for savings by the contractor after the design has been set, or later by the operation and maintenance personnel once the facility has been built, diminish rapidly with time.

These figures point up the desirability of coordinated value-analysis

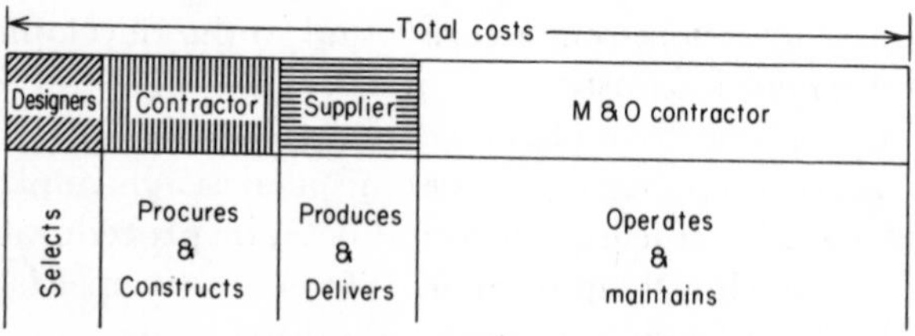

Figure 10-5. Distribution of costs for a facility (Public Building Service/GSA, Manual P 8000.1, Value Engineering).

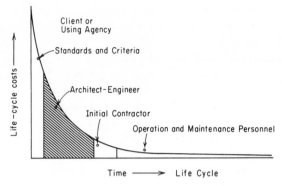

Figure 10-6. Decisionmakers influence on cost (P 8000.1)

services at the client or user agency level (at which needs and criteria are formulated), and this is best achieved by close cooperation with the design professionals involved—the planners, architects, and engineers who will implement these concepts in their preliminary and final designs. This is accomplished by a continuing process of functional cost analysis, consideration of alternatives improving functional values, and in the final stages eliminating restrictive detail, insuring standardization, and minimizing quantities of different types of components. When the construction manager has been selected early in the project cycle, he can play a leading role in the application of value analysis. In addition to his experience and leadership qualities, he offers a vital component—cost data.

VALUE SAVINGS DURING CONSTRUCTION

In the construction phase of the life cycle there is still ample room for value savings, (1) by the internal A/E organization, using value reviews and change orders where money savings are indicated and (2) by the contractor, using the VECP (value engineering change proposal) procedure, which is a specific cost-reduction proposal developed and submitted pursuant to a value-engineering contract provision, by a contractor, and which requires a change to the contract if approved.

Operation and maintenance of the facility offers potential for life-cycle cost improvement by virtue of the extended period over which even modest savings may accumulate. Value engineering is particularly applicable to this phase where new technology has developed or where functional analysis indicates that user needs have changed.

The above phase considerations point up the primary advantage of the early and timely application of value engineering principles if the basic purpose of eliminating excessive or unnecessary costs is to be achieved. The value engineering methodology without question fosters simplification of design and procurement methods.

Value engineering also fosters use of new advances in technology, new test data, new information resulting from feedback from users, and even encourages reexamination of user needs which are subject to change with time. Secondary, but important advantages also arise from the value engineering process through improved reliability, maintainability, performance, life safety, fire protection, and human factors considerations. The latter are of importance in relation to job satisfaction and the general professional development of staff.

VALUE MANAGEMENT IN CONSTRUCTION MANAGEMENT (GSA)

Special value-management services are required by the Public Buildings Service (PBS) of the U.S. General Services Administration (GSA) in all construction management contracts (see Exhibit A). These include the filing of value management qualifications of employees, associates, principals, and consultants used on the value-management work, and certification of education, training, and experience, equivalent to that required by the Society of American Value Engineers (SAVE) for certified value specialists, for all those individuals performing value-management services at the levels of workshop leader, seminar lecturer, or task team leader. Other agencies such as the EPA, have also adopted value engineering for their projects.

Cost of Value Management

The cost of value-engineering effort in construction management necessary to achieve satisfactory results is in the order of 0.1 to 0.3 percent of the construction cost of the project. This is relatively insignificant in comparison with cost savings of up to 10 percent in a well-managed value engineering effort. On selected project areas having high costs, however, value-engineering effort can result in savings of up to 50 percent.

The ultimate savings, life cycle as well as initial, may be even greater when value analysis identifies a project as nonfeasible at an early point in its development.

GSA suggests that a candidate for value analysis should have the potential for at least a 10 to 1 return (i.e., savings at least ten times the cost of the study).

EXHIBIT A
VE Services for Construction Manager Contracts

A. Design Phase

201. The CM shall examine all criteria for each of the various disciplines of work; i.e., site, architectural, structural, mechanical, and electrical for the purpose of identifying and questioning constraints to achieving the required task at the lowest overall cost consistent with desired performance requirements.

    a. Based upon this examination, the CM shall submit a report to the Contracting Officer identifying areas where criteria changes are considered desirable to develop maximum savings in structures, equipment, materials, or methods, even though such recommendations may be at variance with existing GSA criteria or instructions provided concerning the design in question.

    b. Recommended criteria modifications, together with the magnitude of savings, therefor, should be included in the report. Use of GSA Form 2692, Design Review Ideas, is suggested.

    c. This report shall be submitted with the design concept review.

202. The CM shall host a 40-hour VE Workshop using a qualified VE Consultant. The Workshop shall be held after completion of the A-E's design tentative submittal.

    a. The Workshop shall be attended by a suitable number of employees of the CM's firm. In addition, it will be attended by employees of the A-E's firm and his design consultants. The CM shall also invite the attendance of representatives from the Government and the various using agencies of the facility under design to provide for an optimum attendance of 25-30 people.

    b. The CM, in concert with the Government and the A/E, shall identify areas in the design for value study during the Workshop. The CM shall complete the information phase of the VE Job Plan referenced in the VE Handbook and shall prepare a data package for each VE study to be used in the Workshop.

    c. The Workshop schedule, project studies and program of instruction shall be submitted to the Contracting Officer for approval at least 3 weeks in advance of the proposed commencement of the Workshop.

    d. The closing portion of the Workshop involving team project presentations shall be held in a suitable location to facilitate attendance by Government management officials. The A/E shall provide the Government with a copy of each teams' VE Workbook and Executive Brief developed during the Workshop.

    e. The CM shall provide suitable facilities, programs, and loose-leaf notebook binders for participants in the Workshop session.

203. The CM shall continue to utilize the individuals of his firm who have received VE experience under this contract as a special value review team to provide comments, ideas and recommendations for value improvement through the rest of the design effort.

204. The CM shall perform a task team effort to review the intermediate working

drawing design for VE ideas and cost effectiveness. This review should concentrate on high volume use items provided in the design such as doors, valves, finishes, etc. where the cost to make a change is minimal compared to the potential savings. Use of GSA Form 2762, Design Review Ideas, is suggested.

B. Construction Phase

210. The CM shall encourage the Separate Construction Contractors on the project to participate in the VE program by submitting Value Engineering Change Proposals (VECPs) in accordance with the VE Incentive Clause in their construction contracts.

   a. As field representative of the Government, the CM will initially receive all VECPs submitted.

   b. The CM shall promptly review all VECPs and submit his recommendations regarding acceptance to the Contracting Officer. The CM shall suggest modifications to VECPs, when appropriate, in order to make the idea acceptable. The CM shall provide constructive, technical reasons for disapproval when he makes such a recommendation.

C. Standard Services

220. The conducting of VE Workshops as required by this contract shall be performed by an outside VE Consultant. The A/E shall submit for approval of the Contracting Officer the name(s) of the VE Consultant (with their record of education and experience) whom he proposes to provide the workshop leadership required by this contract. The VE Consultant shall be qualified by education, training, and experience equivalent to that required by the Society of American Value Engineers for certified value specialists and shall have a recognized background in the field of Value Engineering.

221. The VE task team required by this contract shall be composed of at least one architect, structural engineer, mechanical engineer, and electrical engineer with other support as necessary. The CM shall submit for approval of the Contracting Officer the names of the members of the VE task team (with their record of education and experience) whom he proposes to perform the VE design reviews required by this contract. The CM can meet this requirement by one of the following three options:

   a. Utilize employees of the CM and his design consultants, all of whom have completed a 40-hour VE Workshop course accredited by the Society of American Value Engineers or its equivalent.

   b. Engaging a qualified VE Consultant to work with and guide the inexperienced employees of the CM Firm and his design consultants. In this option the VE Consultant would serve as team leader.

   c. Engaging a qualified VE Consultant to provide the full service. The VE Consultant shall be qualified by education, training, and experience equivalent to that required by the Society of American Value Engineers for certified value specialists and shall have a recognized background in the field of Value Engineering.

222. The Government will furnish VE Handbooks, Executive Briefs and all other referenced forms for the information and use of the CM as necessary.

223. The Government will provide guest speakers for Workshop sessions as desired, provide VE Handbooks as reference material, and will provide Workshop certificates for each participant.

G. Handbooks

230. VE Handbook, PBS P 8000.1, will be issued for the information and use of the CM.

H. Fee and Payment

240. With regard to VE services, no incentive payments to or sharing of savings with the CM will be made by the Government in connection with this contract.

SOURCE: GSA Manual P8000.1, 1972.

REFERENCES

1. Public Buildings Service of the GSA, Manual P8000.1, 1972.

2. Lawrence D. Miles, *Techniques of Value Analysis and Engineering*, 2d ed., McGraw-Hill, New York, 1972.

3. A. E. Mudge, *Value Engineering*, McGraw-Hill, New York, 1971.

4. Edward D. Heller, *Value Management, Value Engineering, and Cost Reduction*, Addison-Wesley, Reading, Mass., 1971.

11
Time Control

TRADITIONAL METHODS

In the early 1900s Henry L. Gantt and Frederick W. Taylor developed graphical representations of work versus time. Their "Gantt charts" were the basis for today's bar graphs or bar charts. The work of Taylor and Gantt was the first scientific consideration of the problem of work scheduling. Although this consideration was originally aimed at production scheduling, it was readily accepted for planning construction and recording its progress. The bar graph was, and is, an excellent graphic representation of activity. It is easily read and understood by all levels of management and supervision.

If the bar graph is so well suited to construction activity, why look for another planning aid? The reason lies in the fact that the bar graph is limited in what it can present. In the preparation of a bar chart, the scheduler is almost necessarily influenced by desired completion dates, often actually working backward from the completion dates. The resultant mixture of planning and scheduling is often no better than wishful thinking.

If the bar graph is carefully prepared, the scheduler goes through the same thinking process that the network planner does. However, the bar graph cannot show (or record) the interrelations and interdependencies which control the progress of the project. At a later date, even the originator is often hard-pressed to explain his plan using the bar graph. Figure 11-1 is a simplified bar chart of the construction of a small one-story office building. Suppose that, after this 10-month schedule has been prepared, the owner asks for a 6-month schedule. By using the same time for each activity, the bar chart can be changed as shown in Figure 11-2.

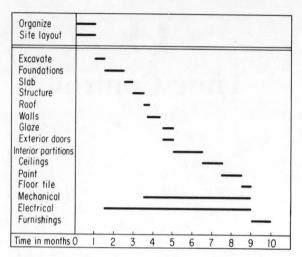

Figure 11-1.   Bar chart, small office building.

Although this looks fine, it is not based upon logical planning; it is merely a juggling of the original bar graph.

The overall construction plan is usually prepared by the general contractor. This is sensible since the schedules of the other major contractors depend upon the general contractor's schedule. Note that in Figures 11-1 and 11-2 the general contractor's work is broken down in some detail, while the mechanical and electrical work are each shown as a continuous

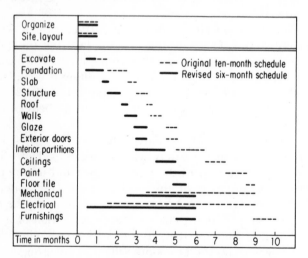

Figure 11-2.   Revised bar chart, small office building.

line starting early and ending late. In conformance with the bar-graph "schedule," the general contractor often pushes the subcontractors to staff the project as early as possible with as many mechanics as possible, while the subcontractors would like to come on the project as late as possible with as few mechanics as possible. The general contractor often complains that the subcontractor is delaying the project through his lack of interest in project progress. At the same time, the subcontractor complains that the general contractor is not turning working areas over to him and that he, the subcontractor, will have to go into a crash effort to save the schedule. As in most things, the truth of the matter is somewhere between the extremes, but not readily identified through the bar graph.

Although progress can be plotted directly on the schedule bar chart, the S curve has become popular for measuring progress. The usual S curve consists of two plots (see Figure 11-3): scheduled dollar expenditures versus time, and actual expenditures versus time. Similar S curves can be prepared for work-hours, equipment and material acquisitions, concrete yardage, etc. Although this presentation can be interesting, it does not give a true indication of project completion. For instance, a low-value critical activity could delay the project completion far out of proportion to its value.

NETWORK-BASED SYSTEMS

The network-based system is one of the most powerful tools available to the project manager for planning, scheduling, evaluation, monitoring, and control of his progress. Most of the network-based systems used in construction are Critical Path Method (CPM). The precedence diagram method (PDM) has gained in popularity and some aerospace/military construction systems are still using the Navy-developed Program Review

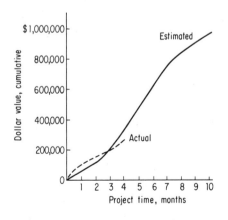

Figure 11-3. Typical S curve.

and Evaluation Technique (PERT). Any of the systems should give essentially the same results, with varying formats.

Networking has been applied principally in the complex construction phase. Many major owners or construction agencies require the use of networking on all major projects. These agencies, which include the U.S. Army Corps of Engineers, the Naval Facilities Command, the U.S. Postal Service, the General Services Administration, the EPA, and other major agencies, are requiring CPM. Many private-sector owners, as well as states and cities, are also requiring network analysis.

A number of the agencies require the general contractor to prepare the CPM for the construction phase. Although the contractor input is vital to an effective network, better success has been obtained where the contractors provide the information, but either the construction manager or a consultant undertakes the preparation of the CPM working plan and schedule. This is the approach followed by the New York State Dormitory Authority on many of its projects.

Networks and Construction Management

The recent popularity of construction management has encouraged reexamination of all available project management tools. The one most frequently utilized by the construction manager, whether consultant or contractor, is CPM. After all these years of being around the construction industry, it is much less a stranger than might have appeared in the recent past.

The construction manager who utilizes CPM does so for one or a combination of the following reasons:

- CPM improves the quality and quantity of the initial project scheduling.

- It can be used as a means of communication to identify and evaluate problems or potential problems in the progress of the project.

- It is a convenient means for monitoring the rate of progress, as well as the physical progress, in terms of its effect on the overall schedule.

- It can evaluate the time impact of unusual delays, such as strikes or bad weather, and also can evaluate the time effect of change orders.

- The owner may require CPM because he sees it as a means of accomplishing some or all of the above as well as providing a basis for reports from the construction manager to the owner.

- CPM may be used by the construction manager to convey to the owner that he is utilizing the latest and best project management techniques.

Obviously, some of the reasons are better than others. But whichever path leads to the use of CPM, there are often cases of good results occurring for less than the best reasons. Conversely, CPM has been used many times with the best intent, but the results were of limited benefit. Unfortunately, the case of the successful operation where the patient dies has its equivalent in project management with CPM.

Not all construction managers are leaping at the opportunity to use CPM. In describing the use of project management on the $150 million Sears Tower in Chicago, the *Wall Street Journal* noted that

> Sears keeps track of the costs required to make all material, deliver it to site and arrange it in the building. It uses a computer program called the Critical Path Method of Job Scheduling. A master plan was issued, and each subcontractor is interviewed every 2 to 4 weeks to update the printouts. While Sears thinks the method is "important" to its monitoring of the project, the construction manager tends to downplay it. "The Critical Path Method works well in everything but sex and construction," says the construction manager. "I don't need a computer to tell me when the job is slipping."

CPM can, and has, worked without the cooperation or enthusiasm of the project manager, just as a tree can survive in adverse conditions—but both do better in a favorable climate.

DEVELOPMENT OF THE NETWORK

The logic network is the key component in CPM and other network-analysis systems. How is the actual network preparation initiated? There is no one correct method. The conference approach is an effective way to prepare the diagram. Key persons involved in the project take part in the conference. These should include people from the construction manager, architect, engineers, contractor's offices and field groups, as well as representatives from the owner. The size of the group must be kept small enough to permit it to work. The group must also have the authority to make commitments on the sequence of work. If the decisions of the group are not upheld in the implementation of the work, the network becomes worthless.

Once the planning group meets, the routine is simple. The project is talked through from start to finish. As each portion is discussed, the arrows representing that portion are drawn. This first try at a diagram must be viewed and discussed by the group. For these reasons, the first network is usually drawn in rough form on a blackboard. When the group agrees on the work sequence, the information is transferred from the blackboard to tracing paper or cloth.

The CPM plan prepared must be the one which the consensus expects to be used to implement the project. This is particularly important since the contractor is usually delegated broad powers in the scheduling of his work. Since the owner is purchasing the contractors' experience and know-how, nothing in the CPM plan should preclude the use of this background.

The conference approach is not suitable for all projects. In some situations there are too many *key* people to make a conference approach manageable. In others there are too few for a full-blown conference. In both situations, an executive approach is effective. The planning group is limited to two or three people. A typical group would be the general contractor's superintendent and project manager plus the construction manager's scheduling staff. With the smaller group, the diagram preparation can go faster; of course, there is a commensurate loss in communication among key personnel.

The diagram is prepared as the project is talked through. A blackboard can be used for drawing the diagram; however, with the smaller group a long sheet of paper can also be used. This saves the step of transferring the information from the blackboard to the paper. The backs of old blueprints or brown wrapping paper can be used for this first network. The use of either gives mute testimony that this first step is a rough cut. Of course, if the diagramer expects the first effort to be correct, tracing paper or linen can be used. However, there is rarely an initial network which would not be much improved if it were redrawn. Also, the rough diagram can be drawn two to three times as fast as a finished network. This minimizes the time demands on the group.

There is an inherent danger in committing the plan to paper. This is the tendency of people to try to make the project suit the network, rather than to have the network suit the best planning. A network must be flexible; do not allow it to lock in your thinking. The network should be altered if better ideas are offered after the network has been prepared. This is, in fact, one of the prime advantages of CPM. Most people, understanding something clearly, assume that all others view it with the same clarity. The CPM plan is the communication medium which can demonstrate this clarity, or lack of it, to the various planners.

A modified version of the executive approach is the consultant approach. In this approach the construction management staff talks the project through with the general contractor's superintendent and key people and then prepares the diagram. This method is the least demanding on the time of the people involved in the project. It can be effective but it must be applied with care. The primary problem is that project people do not accept the diagram as their plan as readily as a diagram which they helped to prepare.

Also, a 1,500-arrow diagram can be more than a little overwhelming (even to an experienced CPM planner). The project people must be properly oriented in CPM fundamentals if this approach is used. This consultant approach can be very effective when the project people have participated in at least one previous CPM-planned project and have developed confidence in CPM.

The work of some subcontractors is independent of the work of the general contractor after the site has been prepared for them. This category would include operations such as structural steel erection, cooling tower erection, and tank erection. All these are essentially package units. However, major subcontracts such as electrical, mechanical, heating, and plumbing are entirely dependent upon the progress of the general contractor's work. It is not usually practical to prepare a separate network to show the subcontractors' work (except for the package units). Experiments in this regard have resulted in disjointed, disconnected failures unless the general work is also indicated on the diagram. When this is done, the network is no longer separate. Even if it were practical to draw the subcontractors' work on a separate network, the result would be self-defeating since the purpose of CPM is to show a coordinated plan of work for all contractors.

During the later stages of a project, the subcontracts often include much of the critical work. If the conference approach is used, key subcontractor personnel can be included in the conference group. In the executive approach, the general contractor assumes a sequence of work and time estimates for subcontractors' work. These assumptions are then reviewed with the applicable subcontractors and revised as necessary. It is quite important that subcontractors point out those areas where they need special consideration. For instance, a school kitchen-equipment subcontractor might need complete control of the kitchen area for his equipment installation. The kitchen work by other subcontractors (electrical, plumbing, plaster, painting, quarry tile, etc.) must be coordinated to recognize this requirement for space. The general contractor often does not allot sufficient time for the subcontractors' work, because he is necessarily preoccupied with his own responsibilities. Through the network, proper work sequences and time estimates can be made before the coordination problems ever get to the field. The diagram can be used to demonstrate to the general contractor that the subcontractor does not need workers on the job at certain times and could not use them effectively if they were there. Of course, this is a two-way street; the diagram may show the subcontractor that his work is critical during certain phases and that he must man his work accordingly.

EXAMPLE PROJECT

The following example shows a comprehensive building project of the industrial park, light industrial, multiple-use type (Figure 11-4 is the John Doe Building exterior, while Figure 11-5 shows floor plans, and Figure 11-6 elevations):

Site Preparation

The site is in a low area, overgrown with scrub timber and bushes; the soil is a sand-and-gravel mixture overlaid by clay. Cast-in-place piles will be driven and concrete filled to about 30 feet for the plant and warehouse foundations. The office building will be on spread footings. As there is no water supply available, a well and 50,000-gallon elevated water tower will be installed. Sewage and power trunk lines are 2,000 feet away. Power connections will be by overhead pole line up to 200 feet from the building; from that point in, the power line will run underground. The sewer will pass under part of the power line. The activities representing the above work are: survey and layout, clear site, rough grade, excavate for electrical manholes, install electrical manholes, set pole line, drill well, install well pump, install underground water supply, excavate for sewer, install sewer, pull in power line. The resulting logic diagram is shown in Figure 11-7 and has the following rationale:

Event 0: The Project Start

0–1   Clear site: necessary before any survey work can start.

1–2   Survey and layout: cannot start before the site is cleared; otherwise many of the survey stakes would be lost in the clearing operation.

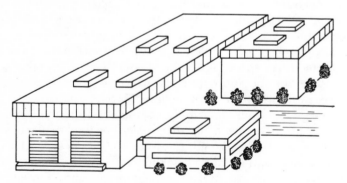

Figure 11-4.   Building, John Doe Company.

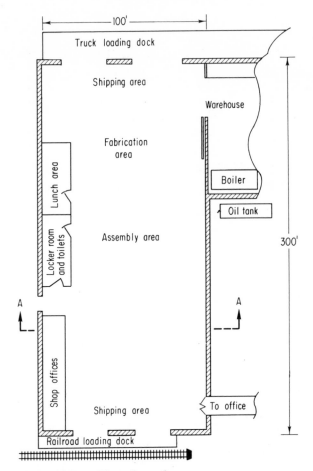

Figure 11-5a.   Plant floor plan.

2–3   Rough grade: cannot start until the area has been laid out. This activity ties up the whole site with earth-moving equipment.

3–4   Drill well: cannot start until the rough-grading operation is completed.

4–5   Install well pump: cannot be done until well is completed and cased.

5–8   Underground water piping: although this might be started earlier, the site contractor prefers to work from the pump toward the building site.

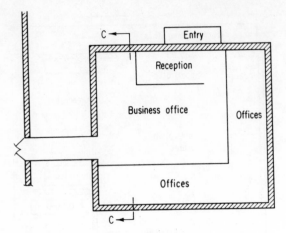

Figure 11-5b.   Office floor plan.

3–6   Water tank foundations: after the rough grading, these simple foundations can be installed.

6–7   Erect water tank: obviously the water tank cannot be erected until its foundations are poured.

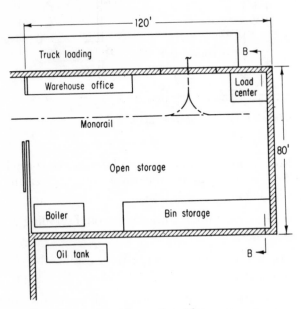

Figure 11-5c.   Warehouse floor plan.

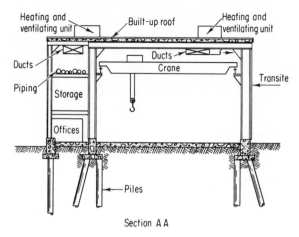

Figure 11-6a.

7–8 Tank piping and valves: cannot be fabricated and erected until the tank is completed.

8–13 Connect piping: the water piping cannot be linked up until both sections are completed.

3–9 Excavate for sewer: can be started after rough grading.

9–11 Install sewer and backfill: immediately follows the sewer excavation, working from the low point uphill.

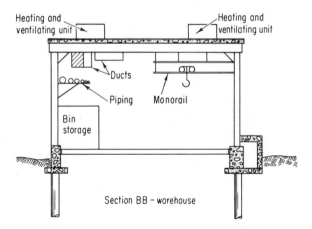

Figure 11-6b.

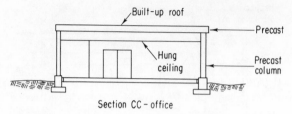

Figure 11-6c.

3–10 Excavate for electrical manholes: can start after rough grading.

10–11 Install electrical manholes: cannot start until the excavation is completed.

11–12 Install electrical duct bank: is started after the electrical manholes are complete. The start of this also depends upon the completion of the sewer line since that line is deeper than the duct bank.

3–12 Overhead pole line: can be started after the site is rough-graded.

12–13 Pull in power feeders: can start after both the duct bank and the overhead pole line are ready to receive the cable.

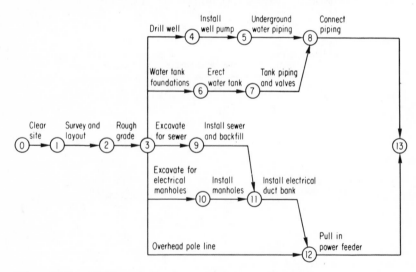

Figure 11-7.   CPM network, site preparations and utilities.

Event 13: The Site Preparation and Utilities Work Are Complete.

Foundations

Following site preparation, excavation, piles, and foundations are to be accomplished as a package. The required work sequence is shown in Figure 11-8. The logical rationale is as follows:

13–14 Building layout: necessary before foundation work can start.

14–15 Drive and pour piles: after layout, this is the first step in the plant and warehouse foundation work.

15–16 Excavate: follows piling. This is fine grading to finish grade.

16–17 Pour pile caps: starts after fine grading.

17–18 Form and pour grade beams: these are poured across the exterior pile caps in this project.

18–21 Form and pour railroad loading dock: this dock is essentially an extension of the grade beams.

18–22 Form and pour truck loading dock: this dock at the opposite end of the building also backs on the grade beams.

18–19 Backfill and compact: cannot start until the grade beams are ready to contain the fill.

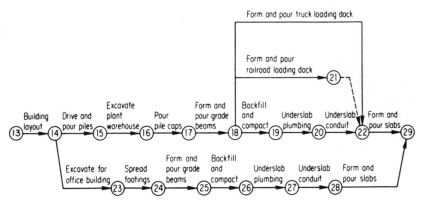

Figure 11-8. CPM network, foundation contract.

19–20 Underslab plumbing: cannot be installed until the backfill is complete.

20–22 Underslab conduit: is installed after the plumbing because the plumbing lines are deeper.

22–29 Form and pour slabs: the loading dock sides and underslab preparation must be completed before the slabs are poured.

14–23 Excavate for office building: can start after the building layout work is complete.

23–24 Spread footings: can be placed after the excavation is done.

24–25 Form and pour grade beams: are poured on top of the spread footings.

25–26 Backfill and compact: is done after the grade beams are finished.

26–27 Underslab plumbing: is installed in the backfill.

27–28 Underslab conduit: is installed on top of the plumbing lines.

28–29 Form and pour slabs: can be done after the underslab preparations are complete.

Event 29:   The Foundations and Concrete Contract Is Completed.

Structure

The plant and warehouse structures are to be structural steel, with high-tensile bolted connections. The plant will have an overhead craneway running the length of the building; the warehouse will have a monorail. The roof system will be bar joists and precast concrete planks covered with 20-year built-up roofing. The siding of both buildings will be transite with translucent upper panels to admit light.

The owner expects to finance the building from current income; he wants the warehouse and plant areas completed before any work starts on the office building. Steel erection is to start after the slabs are poured. The office will be temporarily located in the warehouse while the office building is in construction.

The rationale is as follows (as in Figure 11-9):

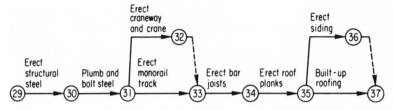

Figure 11-9. CPM network, close-in, plant and warehouse.

29–30 Erect structural steel: follows the completion of foundations.

30–31 Plumb and bolt steel: of course, this cannot be done until the steel has been erected.

31–32 Erect craneway and crane: can be done after the steel is bolted up; and to make rigging easier, is planned before the installation of the bar-joists system.

31–33 Erect monorail track: although this is not as difficult to erect as the craneway, it is convenient to erect it before the bar joists.

33–34 Erect bar joists: can start after structural steel and major rigging.

31–35 Erect roof planks: cannot be done until the bar joists system is complete.

35–37 Built-up roofing: goes on top of the roof planks.

35–36 Erect siding: follows the roof planking for safety reasons and because the flashing detail makes it more practical.

Event 37:   The Building Is Closed In, and Interior Work Can Start.

Interior—Plant and Warehouse

Figure 11-10 represents the interior work for the plant and warehouse. At this point the general, mechanical, and electrical contractors can each initiate activities.

37–38 Set electrical load center: is located on the slab in the warehouse. This is a package unit.

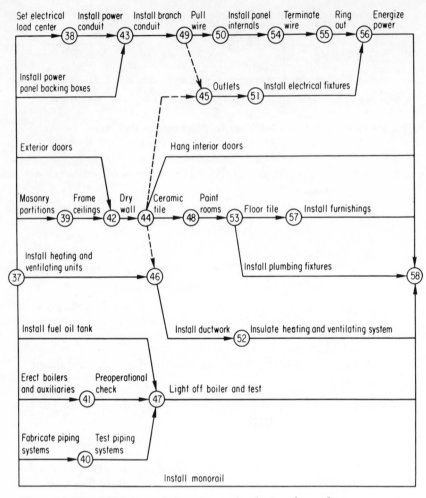

Figure 11-10. CPM network, interior work, plant and warehouse.

37–43 Power conduit: main runs start after the electrical load center is set in place.

43–49 Install branch conduit: these runs follow the installation of the main conduit runs and the backing boxes for the power panels.

49–50 Pull wire: follows completion of the conduit system.

50–54 Panel internals: are installed after the panel wires are pulled in.

54–55 Terminate wires: these are terminated after the panel internals are in place.

55–56 Ringout: after the wiring is connected, the circuits are checked out.

45–51 Room outlets: start after branch conduit and dry wall are complete.

Logical restraints 49–45 and 44–45 operate as spreaders. If 44–45 were not there, "ceramic tile" would depend on "branch conduit." If 49–45 were not there, "pull wire" would depend on "dry wall."

51–56 Install electrical fixtures: follows the completion of the room outlets.

37–39 Masonry partitions: start as soon as the building is closed in.

39–42 Frame ceiling: is supported upon the masonry partitions.

37–42 Exterior doors: can be hung after the building is closed in but must be prior to the dry wall.

42–44 Dry wall: cannot start until the building is weathertight and the partitions framed out.

44–58 Hang doors: can follow dry wall installation.

44–48 Ceramic tile: can follow dry wall.

48–53 Paint rooms: follows the dry wall and ceramic tile installation.

53–57 Floor tile: should be held off until the room painting is complete.

57–58 Furnishings: are installed last.

53–58 Plumbing fixtures: are installed after painting.

37–46 Install heating and ventilating units: can be installed after the built-up roofing, as they are on the roof.

46–52 Ductwork: can be installed after the heating and ventilating units and room dry wall are complete.

52–58 Insulate heating and ventilating ducts: cannot be done until the ductwork is in place.

37–41 Erect boiler and auxiliaries: is in the warehouse and is best done after the warehouse is closed in. The unit is small enough to move through the regular shipping door opening.

41–47 Preoperational check: is a routine check after the boiler is installed.

37–40 Fabricate piping systems: can be done after the building is closed in.

40–47 Test piping: follows completion of the piping systems.

37–47 Install fuel oil tank: is planned to start after the building siding is on so that the excavation will not interfere with the siding work.

47–58 Light off the boiler: cannot be done until the piping systems are tested, boiler checked out, and fuel oil tank ready.

37–58 Install monorail: can be done any time between the close in and completion of the building.

The Office Building

Figure 11-11 shows the logic plan for the office building. The office building is designed as a precast concrete structure with masonry walls. The roof system is designed as precast planks with built-up roofing. The partitions are to be metal lath with plaster. The ceiling is to be hung. The building will have a self-contained air-conditioning unit. At the owner's request, this follows the completion of the plant and warehouse, which occurs by event 58.

58–59 Erect precast: is the first operation in the office building, since the foundations were prepared previously.

59–60 Erect roof: naturally must follow the erection of the structure. Since it uses the same crane rigging, it follows closely.

60–61 Exterior masonry: follows the roof erection.

60–76 Package air conditioning: can be set as soon as the roof is completed.

61–77 Ductwork: can commence when the building is closed in. If started earlier, this operation would interfere with the masonry scaffolds.

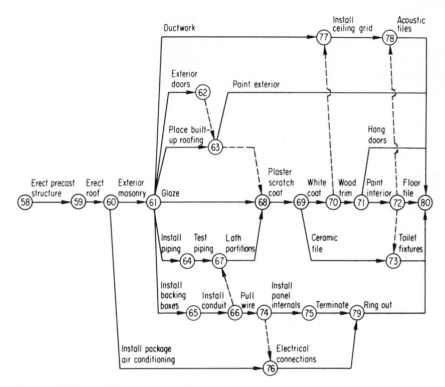

Figure 11-11.   CPM network, office building.

61–63   Built-up roofing: follows masonry so that the roofers are not mopping tar on the masons. This might be called preferential logic, since this operation could physically commence at event 60.

61–62   Exterior doors: installation must wait for the door bucks which go up with the masonry.

61–68   Glazing: is done in the windows which went up with the exterior masonry.

61–64   Piping installation: can start after the exterior masonry is closed in.

61–65   Install backing boxes: as they mount on the masonry and structure, can start after the masonry is placed.

63–80   Paint exterior: starts after the roofing is on and the doors are installed.

64–67 Test piping: follows the piping installation.

65–66 Install conduit: follows backing boxes since this is smaller branch conduit rather than main feeders.

66–74 Pull wire: is done after the conduit is in place.

67–68 Lath partitions: follow the piping tests and the conduit installation since portions of these systems are embedded in or behind the lath.

68–69 Plaster scratch coat: cannot start until the building is weathertight ("glaze," "roofing," and "exterior doors") and the lath is installed.

69–70 Plaster white coat: follows the scratch coat.

69–73 Ceramic tile: also follows the scratch coat.

70–71 Wood trim: is placed after the plaster white coat.

71–72 Paint interior: follows the wood trim.

72–80 Floor tile: follows the painting in order to protect the tile.

73–80 Lavatory fixtures: are installed after the interior painting and ceramic tile in order to protect the fixtures.

74–75 Install electric panel internals: follows the pulling of wires.

75–79 Terminate wires: follows the installation of panel internals.

76–79 Electrical connections (air conditioning): follow the air-conditioning equipment installation and the electrical panel installation.

77–78 Install ceiling grid: is preceded by ductwork and the plaster white coat.

78–80 Acoustic tiles: can be installed after the ceiling grid is installed and the interiors painted.

79–80 Ringout: of electrical systems comes after the systems are complete.

Site Work

Figure 11-12 represents the site work which starts when the foundation work is completed (event 37). Note that random numbering was used for

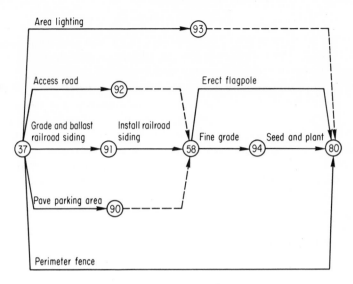

Figure 11-12. CPM network, site work.

this diagram since all digits up to 80 had been used in previous sections of the diagram. The following can all commence when the foundation contractor moves off the site.

37–93 Area lighting.

37–92 Access road.

37–91 Grade and ballast railroad siding.

37–90 Pave parking areas.

37–80 Perimeter fence.

91–58 Railroad siding: follows grading and ballast of the bed.

The access road, parking, and railroad siding have to be ready by the completion of the plant and warehouse (event 58). The final activities for the office building include:

58–80 Erect flagpole.

58–94 Fine-grade.

94–80 Seed and plant.

TIME ESTIMATES

The time dimension used for CPM analysis may be project time or calendar time. Any convenient unit can be used, but it must be consistent throughout the network. The unit usually used is days.

One method of estimating activity durations is to estimate work-hour requirements for the activity and divide that figure by the assumed work crew (see Table 11-1). Work-hour requirements are usually not available by activity. This is to be expected since almost all construction estimates are prepared by taking off the work quantities by physical category. An activity will often include more than one work category but rarely includes all of a major category.

For the application of basic CPM, this is not the problem it might appear to be. It is, of course, not possible to make an accurate time estimate for the entire project on an off-the-cuff basis. However, when the project is properly broken down into its discrete activities, very accurate

TABLE 11-1
Informal Time Estimates for the John Doe Site Preparation

Activity		Brief description	Assumed crew	Project time, days
0–1	Clear site	Four acres, four bulldozers	5	3
1–2	Survey and layout	Four acres, benchmarks available	3	2
2–3	Rough-grade	One acre, two bulldozers	3	2
3–9	Excavate for sewer	Average depth 5 feet, 2,000 feet long	5	10
9–11	Install sewer and backfill		5	5
3–10	Excavate for electrical manholes	Two manholes, 5 feet deep	2	1
10–11	Install electrical manholes	Poured in place	4	5
11–12	Install electrical duct	200 feet long by 5 feet deep 4-inch conduit, straight run	7	3
3–12	Overhead line	1,800 feet	4	6

time estimates can be made informally if the estimator is experienced in the type of project being planned.

In certain situations it is not practical to forecast the time requirement. For instance, in subgrade work unusual situations may develop, or weather conditions may be a big factor. In any case, the estimator makes his best judgment of the probable time factor. In this situation, it is quite proper to add some contingency time. The more uncertain the conditions, the more contingency time is included. Here again, the breakdown of the overall project into well-defined activities helps to reduce the contingency required.

EARLY EVENT TIME

The basic calculation in CPM is the early event time. In the site-work network shown in Figure 11-7, between events 0 and 3 are three activities. The network logic indicates that these must be done in serial order. Accordingly, assuming a start time at 0, the earliest time at which event 3 can be started is the sum of the times for the activities "clear site," "survey and layout," and "rough-grade." This is the sum of 3 + 2 + 2, or 7. The early event time is shown in a square over the circle.

The arithmetic process which the computer is required to go through is the same as this manual technique. The computer program sets up a matrix from the network as an intermediate step. By utilizing this more direct approach, the manual technique described here can be used to compute networks ranging from 100 to 500 activities. Larger networks can be calculated, but this rapidly becomes uneconomical.

As long as the arrow paths are diverging, the question of early event time is very obvious, and the answers fall right into place. In the network in Figure 11-13, there are three points of arrow convergence: events 8, 11, and 12. A problem occurs at these junction points—the fact that there are two answers at each point of juncture. In performing the calculations, one of these answers must be chosen. Reflection on the meaning of the logical network will indicate which is the correct answer. The arrow convergence shows that both paths must be completed before the logic can continue from a junction event. Thus, the earliest event time at which the project may proceed from a junction event is the latest or longest path into that event. Accordingly, the lesser answers are deleted, the longer answer becomes the early event time at the junction event. In the example in Figure 11-13 the lesser answers are shown and crossed out. These are usually not shown on the network, but are indicated here as an aid in understanding the approach. At event 13 the longest path is 34 days, and this becomes the shortest reasonable time in which this project can be

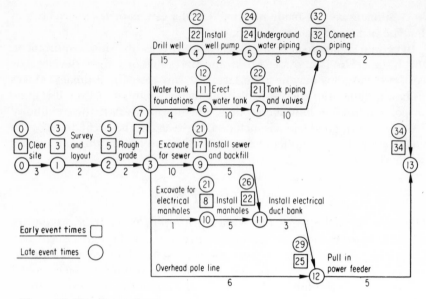

Figure 11-13. Event times.

accomplished according to this logic and these time estimates. Naturally, any variation in either the logic or the time estimates may affect the end point. The fact that these may affect the end answer and not necessarily will affect the end answer, provides one of the key insights into the value of CPM; that is, all paths are not equally critical, and changes on certain paths can be made without affecting the overall project time. These paths with scheduling flexibility are termed *float paths*, and their value can be specifically calculated.

LATE EVENT TIME

Late event times are also intuitively obvious. However, the concept is slightly more difficult than that of early event times. Late event times start with the assumption that the early completion time for the last event is also the latest allowable event time. This assumption can be varied to suit the actualities of the project after the initial evaluation. However, to define the critical path, this assumption that early completion time equals late event time is a necessary starting point.

Late event times are usually shown on the network in a circle either above or beside the early-event-time box. By definition the late event time for the last event equals the early event time for that event. Accordingly, in Figure 11-14, the event times for event 13 are both 34. Late event time is defined as the latest time at which an event can start without preventing the final event from occurring later than its earliest event time. Accordingly, the late event time for an event can be calculated by subtracting the longest path of duration times between the terminal event and the event in question. In making the calculation, the approach is quite straightforward and analogous to the early event calculation as long as the paths are diverging. In calculating late event times, of course, the activity durations are subtracted. In the network shown in Figure 11-14, all paths diverge until event 3 is reached. Accordingly, there is no decision point until event 3. At event 3, there are four choices or path durations as they come into event 3. The latest time at which event 3 can be completed without delaying the project is the earliest time calculated. This rule appears paradoxical, but on consideration is quite logical. The path running through event 3 to event 13 is 27 days long after it leaves event 3. Thus the late event time of 7 plus the 27 days remaining establish the 34-day overall project time. This, then, is the controlling path or, as described later, the *critical path.*

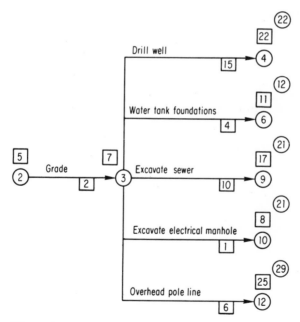

Figure 11-14.   Late event times.

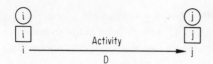

Figure 11-15. Typical activity *(Source: CPM in Construction Management used with permission of McGraw-Hill Book Co.).*

ACTIVITY TIMES

Event times are important and form the basic CPM calculation. Figure 11-15 shows the typical activity i–j in schematic form. The earliest time at which this activity can commence is its early start (ES). The early start is intuitively equal to the early start time, or T_E for the i event.

The latest time at which activity i–j can be completed without delaying the overall network is the late event time at the j event. Thus, the late finish time (LF) for event j is the T_L at event j.

The activity-time information for the first nine activities in the site preparation network (Figure 11-14) is summarized in activity form in Table 11-2.

Two additional important activity information items can easily be computed from the previous table. The first of these is the early finish time (EF), which is the early start time plus the duration ($ES + D$). The other item is the late start (LS), which is computed by subtracting the duration from the late finish time ($LF - D$). Making these simple calculations, the nine activities from the previous table are summarized in Figure 11-16.

CRITICAL PATH

Identification of the critical path in the network is the main feature of CPM. Since the critical path determines the length of the project, it is

TABLE 11-2

Activity	Duration	Description	ES	LF
0–1	3	Clear site	0	3
1–2	2	Survey and layout	3	5
2–3	2	Rough-grade	5	7
3–4	15	Drill well	7	22
3–6	4	Water tank foundation	7	12
3–9	10	Excavate sewer	7	21
3–10	1	Excavate electrical manholes	7	21
3–12	6	Pole line	7	29
4–5	2	Well pump	22	24

Activity	Duration	Description	ES	EF	LS	LF
0–1	3	Clear site	0	3	0	3
1–2	2	Survey and layout	3	5	3	5
2–3	2	Rough-grade	5	7	5	7
3–4	15	Drill well	7	22	7	22
3–6	4	Water tank foundation	7	11	8	12
3–9	10	Excavate sewer	7	17	11	21
3–10	1	Excavate electrical manholes	7	8	20	21
3–12	6	Pole line	7	13	23	29
4–5	2	Well pump	22	24	22	24

Figure 11-16. Summary.

necessarily the longest connected path between the beginning event and the terminal event. There must be at least one critical path through any network. It may be a single arrow running from the starting event to the terminal event, or it may be any number of connected arrows. The path must be continuous, but it may branch into any number of parallel paths. It is possible for a network to be entirely critical, although this is quite unusual.

Figure 11-17 indicates the critical path for the site preparation network. Determination of the critical path cannot readily be made only from inspection of the network. In this case, the late event times from Figure 11-14 are the basis for the determination. It is obvious that the activities running through events 0-1-2-3 must be critical since this is the only path from event 0 to event 3. At event 3, any or all of the five paths branching out could be critical.

There are three rules of criticality:

1. The early and late event times at the activity start must be equal:

$$i = i$$

2. The early and late event times at the activity completion must be equal:

$$j = j$$

3. $LF - ES$ must equal the duration.

The first two conditions are easily recognized when the network has T_E and T_L values posted. However, the third rule is often not tested for.

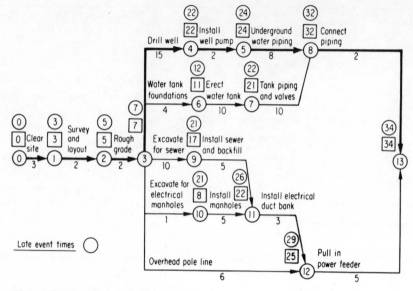

Figure 11-17.   Critical path site net.

If there were one activity 3 directly to activity 8 (3-8) of duration 24, it would not be critical. This activity would be in parallel with the critical path, but would be one day shorter. Accordingly, it would not be critical. If, however, the path 3-8 were 25 days in length, it would be critical. If it were 26 days long or longer, the path which originally was critical (3-4-5-8) would no longer be critical.

FLOAT

Those activities which are not critical have some scheduling flexibility. In CPM this flexibility is termed "float time." It is the quantitative measure of the flexibility available in assigning the actual start within the early- and late-start range. Intuitively, float equals the difference between early and late start. It also equals the difference between late finish and early finish. These values can be determined algebraically as follows:

$$\text{Float} = F = (LF - ES) - D$$

$$\text{Since } EF = (ES + D) \text{ and } ES = (EF - D),$$

$$\text{Float} = (LF - (EF - D) - D)$$

$$= (LF - EF)$$

$$\text{Since } (LF = LS + D) \text{ and } (EF = ES + D),$$

$$\text{Float} = (LF - EF)$$

$$= (LS + D) - (ES + D)$$
$$= (LS - ES)$$

This measure of float is referred to as *total float*. The CPM originators defined a variety of floats. However, only two of these have proved at all practical: total float and free float. Free float is still computed in some computer approaches, but has not been utilized to any extent. Accordingly, total float is usually synonymous with float. Using the event-time information given in Figure 11-14, the floats shown in Table 11-3 are computed:

TABLE 11-3

Activity	$LF -$	Formula: $F = LF - ES - D$ $ES -$	$Duration =$	*Float*
0–1	3	0	3	0
1–2	5	3	2	0
2–3	7	5	2	0
3–4	22	7	15	0
3–6	12	7	4	1
3–9	21	7	10	4
3–10	21	7	1	13
3–12	29	7	6	16
4–5	24	22	2	0

Activity	$LF -$	Formula: $F = LF - EF$ $EF =$	*Float*
5–8	32	32	0
6–7	22	21	1
7–8	32	31	1
8–13	34	34	0

Activity	LS	Formula: $F - LS = ES$ $(LF - D)$	$- ES =$	*Float*
9–11	21		17	4
10–11	21		8	13
12–12	26		22	4
12–13	29		25	4

TABLE 11-4

Activity	ES	LS	Float
3–9	7	11	4
9–11	17	21	4
11–12	22	26	4
12–13	25	29	4

Total float is a shared commodity. The path from event 3-9-11-12-13 in Figure 11-17 has a float value of 4, as shown in Table 11-4.

Now consider the span of activities from 3 to 11 along this path. The early start at 3 is 7, and the late start at 11 is 26. This provides a total time span of 19 (26 − 7). However, the duration for these two activities combined is 15, indicating an overall float for the two activities of 4. Now consider the longer path from event 3 along this path to event 12. The difference between early and late starts is 29 − 7, or 22. The total sum of the work durations is 18, so that the overall net float is 4. Along this path, the float value 4 can be utilized at any point. There is an unlimited number of combinations of float utilization which might be made.

COMPUTERIZATION

Most of the major data centers, such as Computer Sciences Corporation, Infonet and SBC, have available proprietary network packages which can be utilized to do the basic network calculations. If an organization has its own in-house computer, the network analysis package is usually part of the standard software made available. For instance, project scheduling system (PCS by IBM) is one of the most commonly utilized software packages and is available through IBM for IBM users.

The General Services Administration, as part of its construction management program, has made available its CMCS program system which operates either on an IBM 1130 or IBM 360.

The system, complete with operating manual and computer tape, is available at a nominal fee from the construction management group at GSA headquarters.

One of the most comprehensive network programs is the McDonnell Automation MSCS (see Figure 11-18) which is offered through its nation-wide data centers. The program has many additional capabilities such as cost control and resources control, and special output formats such as bar graphs. MSCS is also available through lease arrangements and by remote batch at satellite centers.

Another comprehensive system is Project 2 which is the proprietary product of Project Software and Development Inc. This system is available for lease or can be utilized through data centers which offer it on a per-run basis. The system is currently available at more than 30 computer installations.

The cost of processing a network varies dramatically with the program, the machine, the basic machine-cost factors (i.e., leased or per run), the complexity of the network, the basic number of activities, the numbering system, the amount of output, the number of edits, and other factors. There are some basic rules of thumb. The number of activities, which is the basic control, is generally 1.6 times the number of events.

The cost of calculating a network usually is in the range of 10¢ to 30¢ per activity for basic information on time calculations including float. Cost per run tends to increase with size of network, but cost per activity drops.

It is even possible to draw the network by computer. In the initial setup of this approach, it is necessary to have all the activities and interconnections. Experience indicates that it is easy to make mistakes in attempting to do this from a rough network which is not well laid out. However, in replanning or reprogramming a network, the computer could be used to redraw. In redrawing, using a system such as EZPERT by Systonetics, the time-scaling effect can be gained at no additional cost. Of course, the cost

NETWORK REPORT SORT KEYS ARE IJ					POLLUTION CONTROL FACILITIES EXPANSION CPM: J.J. O'BRIEN,P.E. INITIAL RUN				PAGE 2 DATA DATE 14JAN77	
I NODE	J NODE	ACTIVITY DESCRIPTION	ORG DUR	REM DUR CODES	EARLY START	EARLY FINISH	LATE START	LATE FINISH	TOTAL FLOAT	
352	356	DEMO SLUDGE HEATR BLDG EB-7	5.0	5.0 SITE	11APR77	18APR77	11APR77	18APR77	0.0	
354	366	FR&P CONC SLAB SUBSTA #2	10.0	10.0 SITE	11APR77	25APR77	09JUN77	23JUN77	42.0	
355	370	ELEC REMOVALS EB-2	5.0	5.0 SITE	18APR77	25APR77	18APR77	25APR77	0.0	
356	370	DEMO CHLORINE BLDG EB-2	5.0	5.0 SITE	18APR77	25APR77	18APR77	25APR77	0.0	
357	366	U/G ELEC SUBSTA #2	5.0	5.0 SITE	11APR77	18APR77	16JUN77	23JUN77	47.0	
358	374	SCHEDULED LAG	20.0	20.0 SITE	31MAY77	28JUN77	29AUG77	27SEP77	63.0	
360	364	EXCAV PERSONNEL BLDG B-8	5.0	5.0 B-8	18NOV77	28NOV77	25MAY78	02JUN78	130.0	
362	378	EXCAV B/O DISC BLDG B-2	15.0	15.0 B-2	18NOV77	12DEC77	18NOV77	12DEC77	0.0	
366	372	SET SUBSTATION #2	2.0	2.0 SITE	25APR77	27APR77	23SEP77	27SEP77	106.0	
366	380	EXCAV VAC FLTR BLDG B-3	10.0	10.0 B-3	25APR77	09MAY77	23JUN77	08JUL77	42.0	
368	382	EXCAV FOR MOD ET-4A&4B&ET-5	5.0	5.0 ET-4 A&B	25APR77	02MAY77	11JUL77	18JUL77	53.0	
370	376	EXCAV CONTROL BLDG B-4	5.0	5.0 B-4	25APR77	02MAY77	25APR77	02MAY77	0.0	
374	390	START U/G ELEC QUAD A&D	40.0	40.0 SITE	28JUN77	24AUG77	27SEP77	23NOV77	63.0	
374	392	START U/G MECH QUAD A&D	40.0	40.0 SITE	28JUN77	24AUG77	27SEP77	23NOV77	63.0	
376	388	DRIVE PILES SUBSTATION #1	5.0	5.0 SITE	02MAY77	09MAY77	21APR78	28APR78	246.0	
378	428	EXCAV OPER BLDG B-7	5.0	5.0 B-7	12DEC77	19DEC77	29DEC77	06JAN78	12.0	
382	384	DRIVE PILES ET-4A & ET-4B	2.0	2.0 ET-4 A&B	17MAY77	19MAY77	02JAN79	04JAN79	410.0	
382	386	INST TEMP CL2 FACILITIES	5.0	5.0 SITE	17MAY77	24MAY77	18JUL77	25JUL77	42.0	
386	402	PLANT OPER TEMP FACILITIES	420.0	420.0 SITE	24MAY77	23JAN79	25JUL77	23MAR79	42.0	
388	403	U/G ELEC SUBSTA #1	5.0	5.0 SITE	09MAY77	16MAY77	05MAY78	12MAY78	251.0	
388	404	FR&P SLAB SUBSTATION #1	10.0	10.0 SITE	09MAY77	23MAY77	28APR78	12MAY78	246.0	
390	396	COMPL U/G ELEC QUAD A&D	60.0	60.0 SITE	24AUG77	18NOV77	23NOV77	21FEB78	63.0	
392	398	COMPL U/G MECH QUAD A&D	60.0	60.0 SITE	02SEP77	30NOV77	23NOV77	21FEB78	56.0	

Figure 11-18.

of machine generation of a network as opposed to manual preparation has to be evaluated on the basis of its economics. A factor will be the frequency with which the organization utilizes this type of equipment. Large companies such as Rockwell International and NASA have their own in-house installations, and the cost is much lower per unit of material graphed. Present data center charges for networking by computer cost about $1.50 per activity, with this unit cost decreasing somewhat for large networks.

Output.   The basic CPM format is shown in Figure 11-19. The results are arranged in order of the *i-j* identifying event numbers. In Figure 11-20, the work is listed in the early start order. This is an optimistic listing, and

I	J	DUR-ATION			DESCRIPTION	START		FINISH		TOTAL FLOAT
						EAR	LAT	EAR	LAT	
0	1	3	1	1	CLEAR SITE			3	3	0
1	2	2	1	2	SURVEY AND LAYOUT	3	3	5	5	0
2	3	2	1	1	ROUGH GRADE	5	5	7	7	0
3	4	15	1	7	DRILL WELL	7	7	22	22	0
3	6	4	1	3	WATER TANK FOUNDATIONS	7	8	11	12	1
3	9	10	1	1	EXCAVATE FOR SEWER	7	11	17	21	4
3	10	1	1	1	EXCAVATE ELECTRICAL MANHOLES	7	20	8	21	13
3	12	6	1	4	OVERHEAD POLE LINE	7	23	13	29	16
4	5	2	1	5	INSTALL WELL PUMP	22	22	24	24	0
5	8	8	1	5	UNDERGROUND WATER PIPING	24	24	32	32	0
6	7	10	1	6	ERECT WATER TOWER	11	12	21	22	1
7	8	10	1	5	TANK PIPING AND VALVES	21	22	31	32	1
8	13	2	1	5	CONNECT WATER PIPING	32	32	34	34	0
9	11	5	1	5	INSTALL SEWER AND BACKFILL	17	21	22	26	4
10	11	5	1	4	INSTALL ELECTRICAL MANHOLES	8	21	13	26	13
11	12	3	1	4	ELECTRICAL DUCT BANK	22	26	25	29	4
12	13	5	1	4	PULL IN POWER FEEDER	25	29	30	34	4
13	14	1	2	2	BUILDING LAYOUT	34	34	35	35	0
14	15	10	2	7	DRIVE AND POUR PILES	35	35	45	45	0
14	23	3	2	1	EXCAVATE FOR OFFICE BUILDING	35	65	38	68	30
15	16	5	2	1	EXCAVATE FOR PLANT WAREHOUSE	45	45	50	50	0
16	17	5	2	3	POUR PILE CAPS PLANT-WAREHSE	50	50	55	55	0
17	18	10	2	3	FORM + POUR GRADE BEAMS P-W	55	55	65	65	0
18	19	3	2	1	BACKFILL AND COMPACT P-W	65	65	68	68	0
18	21	5	2	3	FORM + POUR RR LOAD DOCK P-W	65	73	70	78	8
18	22	5	2	3	FORM + POUR TK LOAD DOCK P-W	65	73	70	78	8
19	20	5	2	5	UNDERSLAB PLUMBING P-W	68	68	73	73	0

Figure 11-19.   John Doe output with i-j sort; computer CPM output.

I	J	DUR-ATION			DESCRIPTION	START		FINISH		TOTAL FLOAT
						EAR	LAT	EAR	LAT	
20	22	5	2	4	UNDERSLAB CONDUIT P-W	73	73	78	78	0
21	22	0			DUMMY	70	78	70	78	8
22	29	10	2	3	FORM + POUR SLABS P-W	78	78	88	88	0
23	24	4	2	3	SPREAD FOOTINGS OFFICE	38	68	42	72	30
24	25	6	2	3	FORM + POUR GRADE BEAMS OFF	42	72	48	78	30
25	26	1	2	1	BACKFILL + COMPACT OFFICE	48	78	49	79	30
26	27	3	2	5	UNDERSLAB PLUMBING OFFICE	49	79	52	82	30
27	28	3	2	4	UNDERSLAB CONDUIT OFFICE	52	82	55	85	30
28	29	3	2	3	FORM + POUR OFFICE SLAB	55	85	58	88	30
29	30	10	3	6	ERECT STRUCT STEEL P-W	88	88	98	98	0
30	31	5	3	6	PLUMB STEEL AND BOLT P-W	98	98	103	103	0
31	32	5	3	6	ERECT CRANE WAY AND CRANE P-W	103	103	108	108	0
31	33	3	3	6	ERECT MONORAIL TRACK P-W	103	105	106	108	2
32	33	0			DUMMY	108	108	108	108	0
33	34	3	3	6	ERECT BAR JOISTS P-W	108	108	111	111	0
34	35	3	3	6	ERECT ROOF PLANKS P-W	111	111	114	114	0
35	36	10	3	7	ERECT SIDING P-W	114	114	124	124	0
35	37	5	3	7	BUILT UP ROOFING P-W	114	119	119	124	5
36	37	0			DUMMY	124	124	124	124	0
37	38	2	3	4	SET ELECTRICAL LOAD CENTER PW	124	124	126	126	0
37	42	5	3	6	ERECT EXTERIOR DOORS P-W	124	147	129	152	23
37	43	10	3	4	POWER PANEL BACKFILL BOXES P-	124	136	134	146	12
37	39	10	3	7	MASONRY PARTITIONS P-W	124	137	134	147	13
37	46	15	3	5	INSTALL H + V UNITS P-W	124	147	139	162	23
37	40	30	3	5	FABRICATE PIPING P-W	124	157	154	187	33
37	41	25	3	5	ERECT BOILER + AUXILIARY P-W	124	167	149	192	43
37	47	3	3	5	INSTALL FUEL TANK P-W	124	194	127	197	70

Figure. 11-19 (continued).

mixes high and low priority items without reference to their available float.

The float sort (with critical work first) is very useful for analysis of the output. Figure 11-21 is the John Doe output in this form.

The output can also be sorted by work package, as demonstrated in Figure 11-22.

PERT

PERT is event-oriented but has some activity formats quite similar to CPM.

I	J	DUR-ATION			DESCRIPTION	START EAR	START LAT	FINISH EAR	FINISH LAT	TOTAL FLOAT
37	58	5	3	7	INSTALL MONORAIL WAREHOUSE	124	197	129	202	73
37	80	10	5	7	PERIMETER FENCE	124	276	134	286	152
37	90	5	5	7	PAVE PARKING AREA	124	197	129	202	73
37	91	5	5	1	GRADE+BALLAST RR SIDING	124	187	129	192	63
37	92	10	5	7	ACCESS ROAD	124	192	134	202	68
37	93	20	5	4	AREA LIGHTING	124	266	144	286	142
38	43	20	3	4	INSTALL POWER CONDUIT P-W	126	126	146	146	0
39	42	5	3	8	FRAME CEILINGS P-W	134	147	139	152	13
40	47	10	3	5	TEST PIPING SYSTEMS P-W	154	187	164	197	33
41	47	5	3	5	PREOPERATIONAL BOILER CHECK	149	192	154	197	43
42	44	10	3	8	DRYWELL PARTITIONS P-W	139	152	149	162	13
43	49	15	3	4	INSTALL BRANCH CONDUIT P-W	146	146	161	161	0
44	45	0			DUMMY	149	186	149	186	37
44	46	0			DUMMY	149	162	149	162	13
44	48	10	3	7	CERAMIC TILE	149	167	159	177	18
44	58	10	3	8	HANG INTERIOR DOORS P-W	149	192	159	202	43
45	51	5	3	4	ROOM OUTLETS P-W	161	186	166	191	25
46	52	25	3	7	INSTALL DUCTWORK P-W	149	162	174	187	13
47	58	5	3	5	LIGHTOFF BOILER AND TEST	164	197	169	202	33
48	53	5	3	7	PAINT ROOMS P-W	159	177	164	182	18
49	45	0			DUMMY	161	186	161	186	25
49	50	15	3	4	PULL WIRE P-W	161	161	176	176	0
50	54	5	3	4	INSTALL PANEL INTERNALS P-W	176	176	181	181	0
51	56	10	3	4	INSTALL ELECTRICAL FIXTURES	166	191	176	201	25
52	58	15	3	7	INSULATE H+V SYSTEM P-W	174	187	189	202	13
53	57	10	3	7	FLOOR TILE P-W	164	182	174	192	18
53	58	10	3	5	INSTALL PLUMBING FIXTURES P-W	164	192	174	202	28

Figure 11-19. *(continued).*

Looking over the John Doe networks, milestone events are given in Table 11-5.

This table singles out 11 of the 85 events for names. Actually all the events could be named, although it is difficult to name some events since they concern so many diverse activities.

The emphasis on events made PERT event-oriented, while CPM has always been activity-oriented. This difference in emphasis does not make the systems incompatible.

The PERT group took the position that a single time estimate was not practical for research and development work. For this reason, PERT uses three time estimates:

m—is the most likely time interval between two events. This is the same as the CPM estimate you would make for an activity.

a—is the optimistic time. This is the shortest time interval which could be expected between the events. A more informal definition is that there is a one-in-a-hundred chance that you might hit this estimate.

b—is the pessimistic estimate. This is the time between events if everything goes at its worst. The informal definition here is that there is only a one-in-a-hundred chance that things will go this badly.

I	J	DUR-ATION			DESCRIPTION	START		FINISH		TOTAL FLOAT
						EAR	LAT	EAR	LAT	
54	55	10	3	4	TERMINATE WIRES P-W	181	181	191	191	0
55	56	10	3	4	RINGOUT P-W	191	191	201	201	0
56	58	1	3	4	ENERGIZE POWER	201	201	202	202	0
57	58	10	3	7	INSTALL FURNISHING P-W	174	192	184	202	18
58	59	5	4	6	ERECT PRECAST STRUCT. OFFICE	202	202	207	207	0
58	94	5	5	1	FINE GRADE	202	276	207	281	74
58	80	5	5	7	ERECT FLAGPOLE	202	281	207	286	79
59	60	5	4	6	ERECT PRECAST ROOF OFFICE	207	207	212	212	0
60	61	10	4	7	EXTERIOR MASONRY OFFICE	212	212	222	222	0
60	76	5	4	5	INSTALL PACKAGE AIR CONDITR	212	272	217	277	60
61	62	5	4	8	EXTERIOR DOORS OFFICE	222	236	227	241	14
61	63	5	4	7	BUILT UP ROOFING OFFICE	222	236	227	241	14
61	77	15	4	7	DUCTWORK OFFICE	222	256	237	271	34
61	68	5	4	7	GLAZE OFFICE	222	236	227	241	14
61	64	10	4	5	INSTALL PIPING OFFICE	222	222	232	232	0
61	65	4	4	4	INSTALL ELEC BACKING BOXES	222	222	226	226	0
62	63	0			DUMMY	227	241	227	241	14
63	68	0			DUMMY	227	241	227	241	14
63	80	5	4	7	PAINT OFFICE EXTERIOR	227	281	232	286	54
64	67	4	4	5	TEST PIPING OFFICE	232	232	236	236	0
65	66	10	4	4	INSTALL CONDUIT OFFICE	226	226	236	236	0
66	67	0			DUMMY	236	236	236	236	0
66	74	10	4	4	PULL WIRE OFFICE	236	256	246	266	20
67	68	5	4	7	LATH PARTITIONS OFFICE	236	236	241	241	0
68	69	5	4	7	PLASTER SCRATCH AND BROWN	241	241	246	246	0
69	70	10	4	7	PLASTER WHITE COATS	246	246	256	256	0
69	73	10	4	7	CERAMIC TILE OFFICE	246	271	256	281	25

Figure 11-19 (continued).

I	J	DUR-ATION			DESCRIPTION	START		FINISH		TOTAL FLOAT
						EAR	LAT	EAR	LAT	
70	77	0			DUMMY	256	271	256	271	15
70	71	10	4	8	WOOD TRIM OFFICE	256	256	266	266	0
71	72	10	4	7	PAINT INTERIOR OFFICE	266	266	276	276	0
71	80	5	4	8	HANG DOORS OFFICE	266	281	271	286	15
72	80	10	4	7	FLOOR TILE OFFICE	276	276	286	286	0
72	78	0			DUMMY	276	276	276	276	0
72	73	0			DUMMY	276	281	276	281	5
73	80	5	4	5	TOILET FIXTURES OFFICE	276	281	281	286	5
74	76	0			DUMMY	246	277	246	277	31
74	75	5	5	5	INSTALL PANEL INTERNALS OFFICE	246	266	251	271	20
75	79	10	4	4	TERMINATE WIRES OFFICE	251	271	261	281	20
76	79	4	4	4	AIR CONDITIONING ELEC CONNECT	246	277	250	281	31
77	78	5	4	8	INSTALL CEILING GRID OFFICE	256	271	261	276	15
78	80	10	4	7	ACOUSTIC TILE OFFICE	276	276	286	286	0
79	80	5	4	4	RINGOUT ELECT.	261	281	266	286	20
90	58	0			DUMMY	129	202	129	202	73
91	58	10	5	7	INSTALL RR SIDING	129	192	139	202	63
92	58	0			DUMMY	134	202	134	202	68
93	80	0			DUMMY	144	286	144	286	142
94	80	5	5	7	SEED + PLANT	207	281	212	286	74
					END					

Figure 11-19 (continued).

The PERT group assumed that these three estimates would fall on a bell-shaped (beta) curve (Figure 11-23). There was no proof available for this assumption, but then nothing to disprove it either. The following formula is used to convert these three times into one time t_e equivalent to the beta distribution:

$$t_e = \frac{a + 4m + b}{6}$$

Time t_e can be in any consistent unit but is often in weeks. One decimal place is also usual. Through the formula, the three times estimates have now been reduced to one for the purpose of computing event times.

However, another use is made of the a and b times. A variance is computed for each activity; this is a function of the difference between the estimate extremes $(b - a)$. Intuitively, if $b - a$ is small, there is more certainty of meeting the time estimate; and if $b - a$ is large, there is less chance. With the sum of these $b - a$ differences, a standard deviation is computed for the entire project. By using the standard deviation, the probability of meeting a schedule event time is calculated on the following basis:

$$\frac{\text{Schedule date} - \text{expected date}}{\sqrt{\text{Variance of event involved}}}$$

I	J	DUR-ATION			DESCRIPTION	START		FINISH		TOTAL FLOAT
						EAR	LAT	EAR	LAT	
0	1	3	1	1	CLEAR SITE			3	3	0
11	2	2	1	2	SURVEY AND LAYOUT	3	3	5	5	0
2	3	2	1	1	ROUGH GRADE	5	5	7	7	0
3	4	15	1	7	DRILL WELL	7	7	22	22	0
3	6	4	1	3	WATER TANK FOUNDATIONS	7	8	11	12	1
3	9	10	1	1	EXCAVATE FOR SEWER	7	11	17	21	4
3	10	1	1	1	EXCAVATE ELECTRICAL MANHOLES	7	20	8	21	13
3	12	6	1	4	OVERHEAD POLE LINE	7	23	13	29	16
10	11	5	1	4	INSTALL ELECTRICAL MANHOLES	8	21	13	26	13
6	7	10	1	6	ERECT WATER TOWER	11	12	21	22	1
9	11	5	1	5	INSTALL SEWER AND BACKFILL	17	21	22	26	4
7	8	10	1	5	TANK PIPING AND VALVES	21	22	31	32	1
4	5	2	1	5	INSTALL WELL PUMP	22	22	24	24	0
11	12	3	1	4	ELECTRICAL DUCT BANK	22	26	25	29	4
5	8	8	1	5	UNDERGROUND WATER PIPING	24	24	32	32	0
12	13	5	1	4	PULL IN POWER FEEDER	25	29	30	34	4
8	13	2	1	5	CONNECT WATER PIPING	32	32	34	34	0
13	14	1	2	2	BUILDING LAYOUT	34	34	35	35	0
14	15	10	2	7	DRIVE AND POUR PILES	35	35	45	45	0
14	23	3	2	1	EXCAVATE FOR OFFICE BUILDING	35	65	38	68	30
23	24	4	2	3	SPREAD FOOTINGS OFFICE	38	68	42	72	30
24	25	6	2	3	FORM + POUR GRADE BEAMS OFF	42	72	48	78	30
15	16	5	2	1	EXCAVATE FOR PLANT WAREHOUSE	45	45	50	50	0
25	26	1	2	1	BACKFILL + COMPACT OFFICE	48	78	49	79	30
26	27	3	2	5	UNDERSLAB PLUMBING OFFICE	49	79	52	82	30
16	17	5	2	3	POUR PILE CAPS PLANT-WAREHSE	50	50	55	55	0
27	28	3	2	4	UNDERSLAB CONDUIT OFFICE	52	82	55	85	30

Figure 11-20. John Doe output early-start sort (partial).

I	J	DUR-ATION			DESCRIPTION	START		FINISH		TOTAL FLOAT
						EAR	LAT	EAR	LAT	
0	1	3	1	1	CLEAR SITE			3	3	0
1	2	2	1	2	SURVEY AND LAYOUT	3	3	5	5	0
2	3	2	1	1	ROUGH GRADE	5	5	7	7	0
3	4	15	1	7	DRILL WELL	7	7	22	22	0
4	5	2	1	5	INSTALL WELL PUMP	22	22	24	24	0
5	8	8	1	5	UNDERGROUND WATER PIPING	24	24	32	32	0
8	13	2	1	5	CONNECT WATER PIPING	32	32	34	34	0
13	14	1	2	2	BUILDING LAYOUT	34	34	35	35	0
14	15	10	2	7	DRIVE AND POUR PILES	35	35	45	45	0
15	16	5	2	1	EXCAVATE FOR PLANT WAREHOUSE	45	45	50	50	0
16	17	5	2	3	POUR PILE CAPS PLANT-WAREHSE	50	50	55	55	0
17	18	10	2	3	FORM+POUR GRADE BEAMS P-W	55	55	65	65	0
18	19	3	2	1	BACKFILL AND COMPACT P-W	65	65	68	68	0
19	20	5	2	5	UNDERSLAB PLUMBING P-W	68	68	73	73	0
20	22	5	2	4	UNDERSLAB CONDUIT P-W	73	73	78	78	0
22	29	10	2	3	FORM+POUR SLABS P-W	78	78	88	88	0
29	30	10	3	6	ERECT STRUCT STEEL P-W	88	88	98	98	0
30	31	5	3	6	PLUMB STEEL AND BOLT P-W	98	98	103	103	0
31	32	5	3	6	ERECT CRANE WAY AND CRANE P-W	103	103	108	108	0
32	33	0			DUMMY	108	108	108	108	0
33	34	3	3	6	ERECT BAR JOISTS P-W	108	108	111	111	0
34	35	3	3	6	ERECT ROOF PLANKS P-W	111	111	114	114	0
35	36	10	3	7	ERECT SIDING P-W	114	114	124	124	0
36	37	0			DUMMY	124	124	124	124	0
37	38	2	3	4	SET ELECTRICAL LOAD CENTER PW	124	124	126	126	0
38	43	20	3	4	INSTALL POWER CONDUIT P-W	126	126	146	146	0
43	49	15	3	4	INSTALL BRANCH CONDUIT P-W	146	146	161	161	0

Figure 11-21. John Doe output total-float sort (partial).

This value is then used for a statistical probability table. If an answer of 0.5 is achieved, there is a reasonable probability that the date will be met. A high probability of meeting the schedule is not necessarily good, for it indicates that the schedule is unrealistic. Of course, a low probability of meeting the schedule is not good either.

The PERT time calculation is similar to the CPM event-time calculation. It can be done either manually or on a computer. The early-event-time (T_E) and late-event-time (T_L) calculations are made in a similar manner. The total-float value is referred to as slack, but is computed in the same manner as total float. Figure 11-24 is the John Doe project site-preparation work in PERT form.

The fourteen activities could theoretically require about 35 events to describe them completely, since the start and completion of each activity is described in redundant fashion. However, if this redundant method is not used, the network can require too much inference on the part of the reader. This is one of the most unfortunate facets of the event-oriented network and has resulted in almost all networks being activity-oriented. In Figure 11-24, only 19 events are identified, but 12 of these are dual events, describing both the completion and the start. Essentially, then, 31 events were really required to describe the 17 activities in the John Doe network.

Figure 11-25 is a severely summarized version, which is much simpler in appearance but much more difficult to interpret. Since this version is more analogous to the activity-oriented CPM network, it is utilized in the following comparison. The t_e times are shown in Table 11-6.

I	J	DUR-ATION			DESCRIPTION	START		FINISH		TOTAL FLOAT
						EAR	LAT	EAR	LAT	
49	50	15	3	4	PULL WIRE P-W	161	161	176	176	0
50	54	5	3	4	INSTALL PANEL INTERNALS P-W	176	176	181	181	0
54	55	10	3	4	TERMINATE WIRES P-W	181	181	191	191	0
55	56	10	3	4	RINGOUT P-W	191	191	201	201	0
56	58	1	3	4	ENERGIZE POWER	201	201	202	202	0
58	59	5	4	6	ERECT PRECAST STRUCT. OFFICE	202	202	207	207	0
59	60	5	4	6	ERECT PRECAST ROOF OFFICE	207	207	212	212	0
60	61	10	4	7	EXTERIOR MASONRY OFFICE	212	212	222	222	0
61	64	10	4	5	INSTALL PIPING OFFICE	222	222	232	232	0
61	65	4	4	4	INSTALL ELEC BACKING BOXES	222	222	226	226	0
64	67	4	4	5	TEST PIPING OFFICE	232	232	236	236	0
65	66	10	4	4	INSTALL CONDUIT OFFICE	226	226	236	236	0
66	67	0			DUMMY	236	236	236	236	0
67	68	5	4	7	LATH PARTITIONS OFFICE	236	236	241	241	0
68	69	5	4	7	PLASTER SCRATCH AND BROWN	241	241	246	246	0
69	70	10	4	7	PLASTER WHITE COATS	246	246	256	256	0
70	71	10	4	8	WOOD TRIM OFFICE	256	256	266	266	0
71	72	10	4	7	PAINT INTERIOR OFFICE	266	266	276	276	0
72	80	10	4	7	FLOOR TILE OFFICE	276	276	286	286	0
72	78	0			DUMMY	276	276	276	276	0
78	80	10	4	7	ACOUSTIC TILE OFFICE	276	276	286	286	0
3	6	4	1	3	WATER TANK FOUNDATIONS	7	8	11	12	1
6	7	10	1	6	ERECT WATER TOWER	11	12	21	22	1
7	8	10	1	5	TANK PIPING AND VALVES	21	22	31	32	1
31	33	3	3	6	ERECT MONORAIL TRACK P-W	103	105	106	108	2
3	9	10	1	1	EXCAVATE FOR SEWER	7	11	17	21	4
9	11	5	1	5	INSTALL SEWER AND BACKFILL	17	21	22	26	4

Figure 11-21 (continued).

I	J	DUR-ATION			DESCRIPTION	START EAR	START LAT	FINISH EAR	FINISH LAT	TOTAL FLOAT
11	12	3	1	4	ELECTRICAL DUCT BANK	22	26	25	29	4
12	13	5	1	4	PULL IN POWER FEEDER	25	29	30	34	4
35	37	5	3	7	BUILT UP ROOFING P-W	114	119	119	124	5
72	73	0			DUMMY	276	281	276	281	5
73	80	5	4	5	TOILET FIXTURES OFFICE	276	281	281	286	5
18	21	5	2	3	FORM+ POUR RR LOAD DOCK P-W	65	73	70	78	8
18	22	5	2	3	FORM+ POUR TK LOAD DOCK P-W	65	73	70	78	8
21	22	0			DUMMY	70	78	70	78	8
37	43	10	3	4	POWER PANEL BACKFILL BOXES P-	124	136	134	146	12
3	10	1	1	1	EXCAVATE ELECTRICAL MANHOLES	7	20	8	21	13
10	11	5	1	4	INSTALL ELECTRICAL MANHOLES	8	21	13	26	13
37	39	10	3	7	MASONRY PARTITIONS P-W	124	137	134	147	13
39	42	5	3	8	FRAME CEILINGS P-W	134	147	139	152	13
42	44	10	3	8	DRYWALL PARTITIONS P-W	139	152	149	162	13
44	46	0			DUMMY	149	162	149	162	13
46	52	25	3	7	INSTALL DUCTWORK P-W	149	162	174	187	13
52	58	15	3	7	INSULATE H+V SYSTEM P-W	174	187	189	202	13
61	62	5	4	8	EXTERIOR DOORS OFFICE	222	236	227	241	14
61	63	5	4	7	BUILT UP ROOFING OFFICE	222	236	227	241	14
61	68	5	4	7	GLAZE OFFICE	222	236	227	241	14
62	63	0			DUMMY	227	241	227	241	14
63	68	0			DUMMY	227	241	227	241	14
70	77	0			DUMMY	256	271	256	271	15
71	80	5	4	8	HANG DOORS OFFICE	266	281	271	286	15
77	78	5	4	8	INSTALL CEILING GRID OFFICE	256	271	261	276	15
3	12	6	1	4	OVERHEAD POLE LINE	7	23	13	29	16
44	48	10	3	7	CERAMIC TILE	149	167	159	177	18

Figure 11-21 (continued).

In Table 11-7, we compare these PERT T_E values with the CPM early event times (Figure 11-13).

Now the late event times are calculated in the same manner as CPM. Starting with the T_E for the last event (event 13), t_e values are subtracted. The longest path back to an event determines the latest time at which that event can start and still not delay the completion of the project. The late event times for Figure 11-25 are shown in Table 11-8.

CPM and PERT are compared in Table 11-9.

PRECEDENCE NETWORKS

The form for precedence networks was originally termed "activity" on "node." The activity description is shown in a box or oval, with the sequence or flow still shown by interconnecting lines. In some cases, arrowheads are not used, although this leaves more opportunity for ambiguous network situations.

Figure 11-26 shows the John Doe network in precedence form. Seventeen precedence activities are shown, the same number as the regular activity-oriented CPM network. However, simplicity of form is one of the great advantages of precedence networks. In situations where activities have to be subdivided to show phased progress, the precedence network results in a substantially lower number of notations on it. In some cases, the reduction can be more than 50 percent, so that the precedence network has the advantage of a simple appearance. To those utilizing precedence networks continually, interpretation is straightforward and easy. However, this interpretation is not as easily acquired by someone

I	J	DUR-ATION			DESCRIPTION	START		FINISH		TOTAL FLOAT
						EAR	LAT	EAR	LAT	
13	14	1	2	2	BUILDING LAYOUT	34	34	35	35	0
3	6	4	1	3	WATER TANK FOUNDATIONS	7	8	11	12	1
16	17	5	2	3	POUR PILE CAPS PLANT-WAREHSE	50	50	55	55	0
17	18	10	2	3	FORM+POUR GRADE BEAMS P-W	55	55	65	65	0
18	21	5	2	3	FORM+POUR RR LOAD DOCK P-W	65	73	70	78	8
18	22	5	2	3	FORM+POUR TK LOAD DOCK P-W	65	73	70	78	8
22	29	10	2	3	FORM+POUR SLABS P-W	78	78	88	88	0
23	24	4	2	3	SPREAD FOOTINGS OFFICE	38	68	42	72	30
24	25	6	2	3	FORM+POUR GRADE BEAMS OFF	42	72	48	78	30
28	29	3	2	3	FORM+POUR OFFICE SLAB	55	·85	58	88	30
3	12	6	1	4	OVERHEAD POLE LINE	7	23	13	29	16
10	11	5	1	4	INSTALL ELECTRICAL MANHOLES	8	21	13	26	13
11	12	3	1	4	ELECTRICAL DUCT BANK	22	26	25	29	4
12	13	5	1	4	PULL IN POWER FEEDER	25	29	30	34	4
20	22	5	2	4	UNDERSLAB CONDUIT P-W	73	73	78	78	0
27	28	3	2	4	UNDERSLAB CONDUIT OFFICE	52	82	55	85	30
37	38	2	3	4	SET ELECTRICAL LOAD CENTER PW	124	124	126	126	0
37	43	10	3	4	POWER PANEL BACKFILL BOXES P-	124	136	134	146	12
37	93	20	5	4	AREA LIGHTING	124	266	144	286	142
38	43	20	3	4	INSTALL POWER CONDUIT P-W	126	126	146	146	0
43	49	15	3	4	INSTALL BRANCH CONDUIT P-W	146	146	161	161	0
45	51	5	3	4	ROOM OUTLETS P-W	161	186	166	191	25
49	50	15	3	4	PULL WIRE P-W	161	161	176	176	0
50	54	5	3	4	INSTALL PANEL INTERNALS P-W	176	176	181	181	0
51	56	10	3	4	INSTALL ELECTRICAL FIXTURES	166	191	176	201	25
54	55	10	3	4	TERMINATE WIRES P-W	181	181	191	191	0
55	56	10	3	4	RINGOUT P-W	191	191	201	201	0

Figure 11-22. John Doe output by work category (partial).

TABLE 11-5

Event number	Milestone
0	Project starts
3	Site rough grading complete
13	Site utilities complete
18	Plant and warehouse foundations complete
25	Office foundations complete
29	Ready for steel erection
37	Warehouse and plant closed in
56	Ready to energize power
58	Plant and warehouse complete
68	Office closed in
80	Office complete

used to either PERT or CPM. That is, it is easier for a PERT-oriented planner to use CPM networks, or for CPM planners to use PERT. The transition is mainly one of acclimation.

Professor John Fondahl of Stanford University, who was established in the early 1960s as an expert on noncomputerized solutions to CPM and PERT networks, was one of the early supporters of the precedence method terming it the "circle and connecting arrow technique." Professor Fondahl's study for the Navy's Bureau of Yards and Docks included

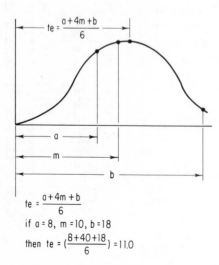

$$te = \frac{a+4m+b}{6}$$

if $a = 8$, $m = 10$, $b = 18$

then $te = (\frac{8+40+18}{6}) = 11.0$

Figure 11-23. Beta distribution curve.

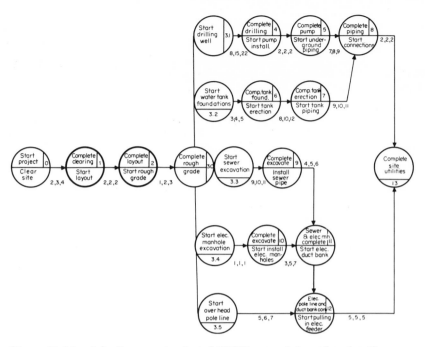

Figure 11-24. John Doe, event-oriented PERT network (complete detail).

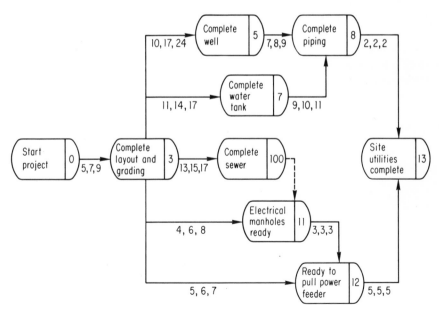

Figure 11-25. John Doe PERT network (event oriented); site preparation and utilities (summarized).

TABLE 11-6

Connection	a	m	b	t_e
0–3	5	7	9	7
3–5	10	17	24	17
3–7	11	14	17	14
3–100	13	15	17	15
3–11	4	6	8	6
3–12	5	6	7	6
5–8	7	8	9	8
7–8	9	10	11	10
8–13	2	2	2	2
11–12	3	3	3	3
12–13	5	5	5	5
100–11	0	0	0	0

descriptive material and gave the technique early impetus, particularly on Navy projects.

An IBM brochure credits the H. B. Zachry Company of San Antonio with the development of the precedent form of CPM. In cooperation with IBM, Zachry developed computer programs which can handle precedent network computations on the IBM 1130 and IBM 360. This is particularly significant since in 1964 Phillips and Moder indicated the availability of only one computerized approach to precedence networks versus 60 for CPM and PERT.

TABLE 11-7

Event	PERT	CPM
0	0	0
3	7	7
5	24	24
7	21	21
8	32	32
100	22	
11	22	22
12	25	25
13	34	34

TABLE 11-8

Event	PERT	CPM
13	34	34
12	29	29
11	26	26
100	26	
8	32	32
7	22	22
5	24	24
3	7	7
0	0	0

TABLE 11-9

Consideration	PERT	CPM	Different	Similar
Based on logic network	yes	yes		x
Emphasis	event and activity	activity		x
Time estimate, project time	yes	yes		x
Method of estimating time	one or three	one		x
Probability	yes	no	x	
Scheduled event times	yes	yes		x
Total float (slack)	yes	yes		x
Free float	no	no		x
Negative float (slack)	yes	yes		x
Used for planning new work	yes	yes		x
Used to monitor existing work	yes	Yes		x
			1	10

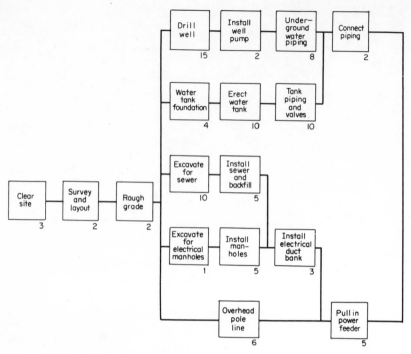

Figure 11-26. John Doe precedence network.

Precedence Logic

One reason for the greater simplicity of precedence networks is that a work item can be connected from either its start or its finish. This allows a start-finish logic presentation without breaking the work item down.

Figure 11-27 illustrates the three basic relations: start to start, end to end, and start to end. Although the networks are simpler in appearance, greater thought must be given to the reading and interpretation of the network.

One problem in converting precedence diagrams into computer input format is the lack of event numbers. The computer must have numerical identification, so that the work items are identified. In the IBM programs, any code up to 10 characters long (alphabetic or numeric) can be used to identify a work item. The only restrictions are that all items have to be uniquely numbered, work item 1 must be used only for the scaling work item, and the last work item has to be identified with the highest number assigned in the network.

The computational portions of the networks are quite similar to CPM calculations and use the same calendar dating routines.

Work-Package Calculations

The work-package calculations are quite similar to the CPM event calculations. The first stage is the establishment of a work-item-and-duration chart. A table of relations is then constructed based upon the typical relations shown in Figure 11-27. The early start time for the first work item is 0, although a calendar start date can be inserted later. The early start time at the beginning of each of the other work items is the greatest of the paths entering the beginning of the work item. The value of these paths is computed by the following methods:

1. *Start to start:* The early start time for the preceding work item is the early start time for the work item.

2. *End to start:* The early finish time for the preceding work item is the early start time for the work item.

3. *End to end:* The early finish time for the preceding work item less the duration of the work item itself is the early start time for the item.

The longest path to the beginning of the work item determines the

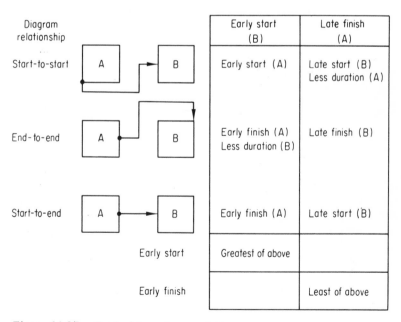

Figure 11-27. Typical precedence relations.

early start time. The early finish time for a work item is the early start time plus the duration.

By definition, the late finish time for the last work item is set equal to the early finish time for that item, which establishes a critical path. The late finish time for other work items is determined by subtraction or a backward pass from the late, or the finish, time for the terminal event. The late finish time for other work items is the least of the paths leading into completion of the work item, as follows:

1. *End to start:* The late finish time is the latest start time for the following work items.

2. *End to end:* The late finish time for the work item is equal to the late finish time for the following work item.

3. *Start to start:* The late start time for the following work item plus the duration of the work item itself determines the late finish time for the work item.

Late start time equals late finish time less duration. Float for a work item can be calculated by the same formulas as were utilized in the CPM approach. Similarly, the critical path can be identified by using the standard rules.

Project Example

Figure 11-28 is a sample project network consisting of 34 work items. The work-item identification numbers identify work items by function. For instance, concrete items are grouped in the 300 series, and the electrical items are in the 700 series.

The networks indicate interrelations between work items and also options having to do with lag-time factors. Three of the four lag-time options have been included in the network illustrated. Durations for work items are shown in the small boxes under the work items.

The network indicates that the drilling of piers (work item 110) may begin after 50 cubic yards of excavation have been completed in work item 100, and this is represented by the line leading from 100 to 110. This shows that part of the duration of work item 110 may be concurrent with work item 100. The estimated quantity of work in work item 100 is 150 cubic yards, so that work item 100 may start after approximately 33 percent of the excavation operation has been done, or in direct proportion, after one-half day has elapsed. The top line leading from work item 100 to work item 110 indicates that the second work item cannot be completed until at least half a day after the completion of the first work item 100.

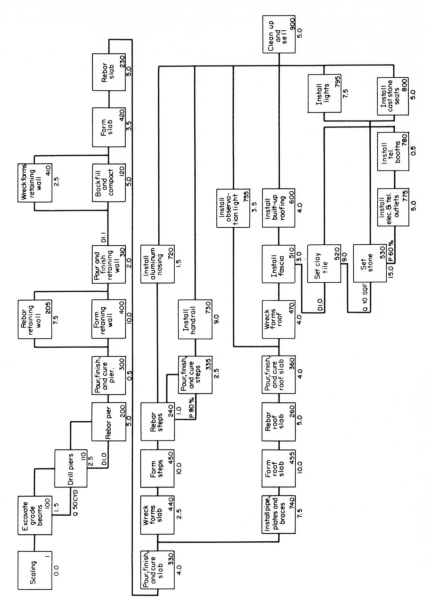

Figure 11-28. Precedence example (From: IBM).

309

The rebar of pier 200 is shown to begin at least one day following the start of drilling the piers. This is shown by a lag time of one day on the connecting line. The relation of work items 205 and 400 to item 300 and following work item 310 is very similar to other diagraming relations showing concurrent activity.

Between work items 310 and 410, a delay of one day is shown. This lag permits one day of curing before the form stripping is started, and it could have been included by adding one more day to work item 310 or by introducing a work item 311 called *initial cure*.

The various delay and lag options shown in the precedence network can be duplicated by a CPM network, but additional arrows or activities are required.

The work-item report is a listing printed in early-start sequence (Figure 11-29). In addition to the obvious descriptive material, the "PC" column contains the amount of the operation completed in percentage, while the column "CAL FC HR S D" contains the hours per shift, shifts per day, and days per week or the calendar factor.

Some precedence programs will accept schedule dates and therefore will produce negative slack. Certain CPM programs also will do the same.

Figure 11-30 is a precedence field report which summarizes the information according to functional numbers or series. This report includes all the 100 and 200 series and part of the 300 series. Items marked with an asterisk are on the critical path.

NETWORKS IN THE DESIGN PHASE

Construction is the time when the bottom of the iceberg emerges, and the entire project can be viewed and understood by many. However, in most projects today, construction is equaled or exceeded in terms of time by the preconstruction design period. If disciplined project control techniques are applied early, substantial time savings—and therefore cost savings—can be achieved at relatively low unit cost. The preconstruction phase of a project is the one which can produce the best expediting and acceleration results at the lowest cost. The input of additional funding during this preconstruction phase can result in tremendous time reduction.

Figure 11-31 illustrates the typical cash flow on a project of 31 months duration from budgeting through design, construction, and opening of an elementary school. Note that in the first 50 percent of the project, less than 20 percent of the overall budget is expended.

Design professionals are often quite reluctant to be the subject of a network. Ironically, these same design professionals have been instrumental in the broad acceptance of networking during the design phase. The argument against networking the design phase lodges in the intangible

WORK ITEM	DESCRIPTION	REMAIN DURATN	DURATN	CAL PC HR / FC S D	EARLY START	LATE START	EARLY FINISH	LATE FINISH	TOTAL SLACK	FREE SLACK
100	EXCAVATE GRADE BEAMS	1.5	1.5	8 1 5	4MAY	4MAY	5MAY	5MAY	.0	.0
1	WORK ITEM FOR SCALING CALENDAR	.0	.0	8 1 5	4MAY	4MAY	4MAY	4MAY	.0	.0
110	DRILL PIERS	2.5	2.5	8 1 5	4MAY	4MAY	6MAY	6MAY	.0	LAG
200	REBAR PIER	5.0	5.0	8 1 5	5MAY	5MAY	12MAY	12MAY	.0	LAG
300	POUR, FINISH AND CURE PIER	.5	.6	8 1 7	12MAY	12MAY	12MAY	12MAY	.0	.0
400	FORM RETAINING WALL	10.0	10.0	8 1 5	12MAY	12MAY	26MAY	26MAY	.0	.0
205	REBAR RETAINING WALL	7.5	7.5	8 1 5	12MAY	15MAY	22MAY	26MAY	2.5	2.5
310	POUR AND FINISH RETAINING WALL	2.0	2.0	8 1 5	26MAY	26MAY	28MAY	28MAY	.0	.0
120	BACKFILL AND COMPACT	5.0	5.0	8 1 5	1JUN	1JUN	8JUN	8JUN	.0	LAG
410	WRECK FORMS RETAINING WALL	2.5	2.5	8 1 5	1JUN	4JUN	4JUN	8JUN	2.5	LAG
420	FORM SLAB	3.5	3.5	8 1 5	8JUN	8JUN	12JUN	12JUN	.0	.0
230	REBAR SLAB	5.0	5.0	8 1 5	12JUN	12JUN	19JUN	19JUN	.0	.0
330	POUR, FINISH AND CURE SLAB	4.0	4.1	.714	19JUN	19JUN	24JUN	24JUN	.0	.0
740	INSTALL PIPE, PLATES AND BRACES	7.5	7.5	8 1 5	24JUN	11AUG	26JUN	14AUG	33.3	.0
440	WRECK FORMS SLAB	2.5	2.5	8 1 5	24JUN	24JUN	26JUN	26JUN	.0	.0
450	FORM STEPS	10.0	10.0	8 1 5	26JUN	14AUG	13JUL	28AUG	33.3	.0
455	FORM ROOF SLAB	10.0	10.0	8 1 5	6JUL	6JUL	20JUL	20JUL	.0	.0
240	REBAR STEPS	1.0	1.0	8 1 5	13JUL	28AUG	14JUL	31AUG	33.3	.0
335	POUR, FINISH AND CURE STEPS	2.5	2.5	.714	14JUL	28AUG	16JUL	1SEP	33.3	LAG
720	INSTALL ALUMINUM NOSING	1.5	1.5	8 1 5	14JUL	14SEP	16JUL	15SEP	42.4	42.4
730	INSTALL HAND RAIL	9.0	9.0	8 1 5	16JUL	1SEP	29JUL	15SEP	33.3	33.3
260	REBAR ROOF SLAB	5.0	5.0	8 1 5	20JUL	20JUL	27JUL	27JUL	.0	.0
360	POUR, FINISH AND CURE ROOF SLAB	4.0	4.1	.714	27JUL	27JUL	30JUL	30JUL	.0	.0
470	WRECK FORMS ROOF	4.0	4.0	8 1 5	30JUL	30JUL	5AUG	5AUG	.0	.0
755	INSTALL OBSERVATION LIGHT	3.5	3.5	8 1 5	30JUL	10SEP	5AUG	15SEP	28.5	28.5
510	INSTALL FASCIA	3.0	3.0	8 1 5	5AUG	5AUG	10AUG	10AUG	.0	.0
520	SET CLAY TILE	9.0	9.0	8 1 5	6AUG	6AUG	19AUG	19AUG	.0	LAG

Figure 11-29. Precedence output, early-start sort (partial) (From: IBM).

JOB NO. 1440 *** FIELD REPORT *** PAGE 1
15 MAY

	WORK ITEM	DESCRIPTION		DURATION TOTAL	DURATION REM	PERCENT T-D	PERCENT PER	ESTIMATE QTY	ESTIMATE UNIT	TO DATE QTY	CAL HR	FC S D	START DATE	FINISH DATE	TOTAL SLACK
•	1	WORK ITEM FOR SCALING CALENDAR		.0	9.0						8	1 5	4MAY	14MAY	0
							PWI								
•	100	EXCAVATE GRADE BEAMS		1.5	.0	100		150	CYD	175	8	1 5 A	5MAY	A 6MAY	0
							PWI	1							
•	110	DRILL PIERS		2.5	.0	100					8	1 5 A	5MAY	A 7MAY	0
			LAG FACTOR		50	Q Z	PWI	100							
•	120	BACKFILL AND COMPACT		5.0	5.0						8	1 5	1JUN	5JUN	0
			LAG FACTOR		1.0	D C	PWI	310							
•	200	REBAR PIER		5.0	.0	100					8	1 5 A	7MAY	A 14MAY	0
			LAG FACTOR		1.0	D Z	PWI	110							
	205	REBAR RETAINING WALL		7.5	6.8	10					8	1 5 A	15MAY	25MAY	0
							PWI	300							
•	230	REBAR SLAB		5.0	5.0						8	1 5	11JUN	18JUN	0
							PWI	420							
	240	REBAR STEPS		1.0	1.0						8	1 5	10JUL	28AUG	33
							PWI	450							
•	260	REBAR ROOF SLAB		5.0	5.0						8	1 5	17JUL	24JUL	0
							PWI	455							
•	300	POUR, FINISH AND CURE PIER		.5	.0	100					8	1 7 A	14MAY	A 14MAY	0
							PWI	200							
•	310	POUR AND FINISH RETAINING WALL		2.0	2.0						8	1 5	26MAY	27MAY	0
							PWI	400		205					

Figure 11-30. Precedence field report (From: IBM).

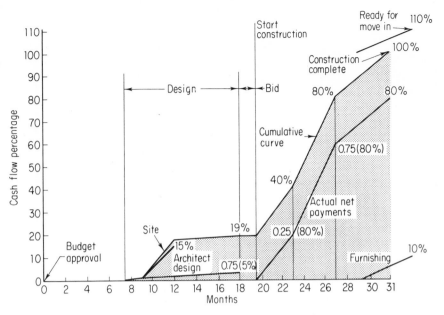

Cash flow, typical elementary school

Figure 11-31. *Time-cost curve Elementary School (From:* **CPM in Construction Management,** *McGraw-Hill, 1971.)*

nature of many of the design phases. Architects, in particular, are reluctant to have their creativity scheduled.

However, most of design involves fairly routine stages, which do follow a definite sequence through schematic, design development and contract document or working drawing phases. Many of the activities can be clearly evaluated. Most tend to take longer in the more routine stages, such as generation of the actual specification, than the design professionals like to admit. The effect of networking the design phase can be to pinpoint the large amount of time required for routine well-identified activities, thereby identifying the time remaining for creative design.

Networking of the design stage can also be a useful tool for the construction manager in achieving decisions and reviews by the using agency or owner, as well as freezing design comments too late into the period—or at least pointing out to an owner or using agency the time impact of the late decisions. Figure 11-32 illustrates the funnel nature of permissible decisions without time impact during the design phase.

Experience indicates that the network for the design phase probably should not be computerized. The network provides a framework for design activity. If each and every activity is put in, it would be almost

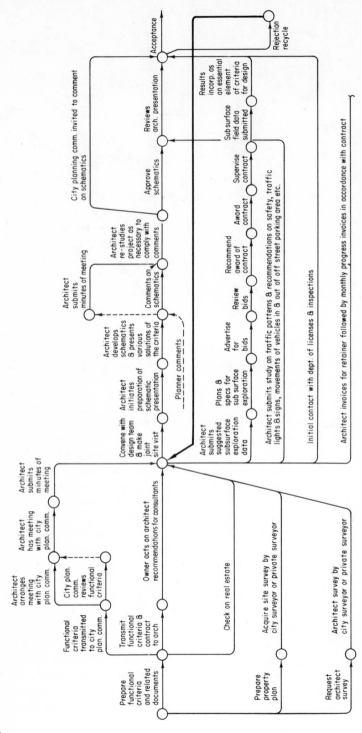

Figure 11-32. Standard design network—Philadelphia School System (From: CPM in Construction Management).

314

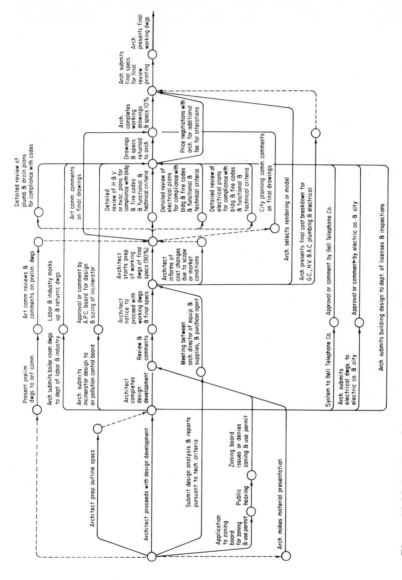

Figure 11-32 (continued).

315

impossible to correlate the continuing liaison required between the various design disciplines. A network of 100 to 200 activities can usually adequately demonstrate the flow of work to be accomplished. A network of this size lends itself to hand computation and to time scaling also. The time-scaled version permits regular monitoring of progress in a form which is readily understood by an owner as well as the design teams.

An exception to the noncomputerized evaluation during the design phase would be in the case of an overall project plan in which both the design and construction are computerized, particularly in the case of fast-track or phased construction. In this situation, computer computation would be an option—but for specific reason.

The design-phase network often lends itself to a stereotype or standard approach. For instance, in a capital expansion phase, the Philadelphia school system had several hundred major projects in the revitalization of its capital plant. For a new facility, there were specific steps and stages, many of them involving city agencies. The steps were laid out using the information and experience of the school district facilities department. The result was the flow chart shown in Figure 11-32. The upper portion is a flow chart for the activities from the start of design to the acceptance of the schematic phase. At this point in time, if accepted, the lower portion of the network has to be followed. If the schematic design was rejected, then the rejection cycle required a reevaluation of certain areas as indicated.

Using this standard plan, a sepia copy was made up for each project. Any special project requirements were imposed on the reproducible sepia, and that document became the method of monitoring the progress through the design phase. All monitoring was manual. However, the design progress was regularly transposed to a summary system.

CONSTRUCTION PHASE

Unfortunately, CPM for the construction phase—however prepared—is usually working against a stacked deck. By the time construction starts, many of the time options and alternatives have been obviated, and the typical construction phase is a race against time. The scheduled period itself usually is based on the owner's needs rather than the practicalities of the time specified.

Properly applied, CPM is only a realistic mirror and cannot be expected to achieve the impossible. (In a discussion regarding CPM, one engineer observed, "After all, what you are really telling us is that CPM just gives us the bad news sooner.")

Development of the CPM working plan is usually done principally by the CPM scheduler whether he is a member of the owner's staff, part of the construction manager's staff, a consultant, or a member of a contractor's staff. Usually, the scheduler can draw enough information in two or three hours of discussions with others working on the project to proceed for several days in the preparation of his schedules, if he is knowledgeable in construction technique.

This initial CPM activity requires principal input from the general contractor. It emphasizes the effect of the building foundations and structure, since these set the original pace. After the building is closed in, the emphasis shifts to the mechanical and electrical trades. In the preparation of the CPM, the electrical, HVAC, and plumbing contractors often feel neglected—and with good reason. It is possible for the scheduler to prepare the CPM without their input, blocking out times he assumes are reasonable.

Often this is accepted without comment because at least it indicates the intent of the general contractor in establishing the initial pace. But the mechanical, electrical, and plumbing contractors actually have an opportunity during this initial CPM preparation to add a sequence reflecting their intentions.

This information can set the pace in the interior once the structure has been completed. Almost without exception, the CPM scheduler will be very receptive to this type of sequencing. Further, if the sequencing patterns are in conflict, it can be determined at this early stage and the trade sequences coordinated.

For example, some general contractors prefer to work a high-rise building's finishing sequence from the top down, bringing all their debris with them. But on one 20-story building, the space between the tenth and eleventh floors was a full mechanical floor; in this instance the HVAC contractor preferred to work in both directions with his risers. The general contractor was willing to sequence his finishing trades accordingly.

In some cases, however, the owner's preference in terms of initial occupancy determines the working sequence rather than contractor preferences.

Even though the mechanical/electrical (m/e) system designers and contractors are not in the lead role initially in CPM scheduling, their role is crucial in terms of the ultimate success of the scheduling process—and a comprehensive CPM application should recognize their inputs as well as their special problems.

On occasion, usually in frustration, the electrical or mechanical contractors have discussed the possibility of preparing an independent CPM. In building projects, this is not feasible. In fact, *any* plan projected by the general contractor is better than no plan. In at least one project with multiple prime contractors, the HVAC and electrical contractors took the lead in preparing the CPM through the construction manager because the general contractor was performing poorly. In essence, the CPM was used to coordinate the work of all the other prime contractors around the reluctant general contractor. Though the project finished somewhat late, the combined effort—which was coordinated with the CPM—saved at least six months time.

Fast Tracking with CPM

The construction manager concept, particularly when applied immediately after budget approval of a project, offers the best single opportunity for the application of CPM when it is most needed—at the start of the project. From this vantage point, opportunities for overlapping activities—i.e., phased construction, or fast tracking—can be evaluated. And the CPM network can be the model for evaluation.

Much has been written about phased construction and its utilization by construction managers. CPM also has served to evaluate certain special problems that develop as a result of breaking the job down into its many pieces. The most significant problem is the requirement for additional mobilization time, because each set of contractors has to gear up, particularly in ordering materials.

For example, in the major national Postal Service program, fast tracking was used quite effectively. In phase 1, a group of contractors provided site grading and foundations. In phase 2, steel was provided and erected. In phase 3, the building was closed in and mechanical equipment installed. (The Postal Service program was major: for bulk-mail handling, typical facilities cost about $30 million each; more than 20 were built across the country.)

The Corps of Engineers, formerly construction manager for the Postal Service, awarded the various phases in overlapping fashion so that each new phase had time for mobilization and materials ordering while the preceding phase was still in field construction.

This scheduling avoided startup delays and saved the time gained by fast tracking.

Each phase was performed under a CPM prepared by the contractor and updated on a monthly basis. The Corps of Engineers, long a CPM user, carefully monitored progress on the basis of both field observations and the CPMs.

In other applications, CPM is able to evaluate the advantage of the owner's prepurchasing materials in order to maintain the advantage of time gained by fast tracking. For industrial clients, CPM can identify advantages of the owner's purchasing department buying all materials of substantial quantity, particularly when the owner is a multiproject builder.

Materials

Materials coordination and expediting should be strong points of the construction manager. The effect of these activities is particularly acute in fast tracking or phased construction.

Materials are involved throughout a construction project. Usually early delivery of materials cannot speed up an activity because the progress of other activities controls the early-start time. However, failure to deliver the material for an activity can delay it indefinitely. Thus, unfortunately, the project purchasing agent or materials coordinator has a difficult problem. If he delivers late, he delays the project; if he delivers early, the field group complains about extra handling and storage of materials. The problem reaches its most acute stage in urban areas where project supervision would like to lift materials from truck or rail car right to final location.

Just as subcontractors complain that the general contractor neglects the situation, most purchasing agents complain that their own company fails to keep them informed about material needs. Obviously, this is a need which can be satisfied with CPM information. One method is to locate those activities which require key materials. Since almost every activity requires materials, you would have to review every activity if you try to control all materials. A practical method is to separate materials into two classes. Those materials which can be ordered out of stock for delivery in a week or less can be classified as *commodities*. The schedule for the first shipment of any type of commodity is useful. *Key materials* are those with long delivery times, or those which are custom orders. Review of the network computer run can furnish all the necessary material information, particularly the order in which key material orders should be placed. However, by adding an arrow to the diagram for each key delivery, the material information is generated as part of the computer run. Figure 11-33 is the site-preparation network for the John Doe project with the delivery arrows shown in Table 11-10 added.

Of these, well pump and water tank would definitely be key deliveries. The others could be commodities or custom items depending upon the specification to be met. If it is assumed that all materials are on hand (for instance, if the owner is furnishing them), the time duration for these activities would be zero. The computed information for the deliveries is shown in Table 11-11. Since materials would not usually be available at the start of the project, reasonable delivery time estimates are assigned to these delivery activities as shown in Table 11-12.

The introduction of delivery times has increased this portion of the project from 34 days to 52 days as shown in Figure 11-34. The critical path has shifted and is now through events 0-6-7-8-13. The old and new event times are given in Table 11-13.

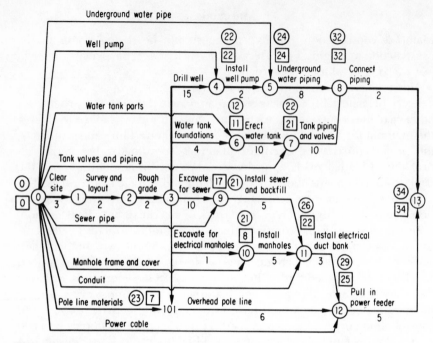

Figure 11-33. *Deliveries for John Doe site preparation, zero delivery times.*

TABLE 11-10

Activity	Delivery
0–4	Well pump
0–5	Underground water pipe
0–6	Water tank parts
0–7	Tank valves and piping
0–9	Sewer pipe
0–10	Manhole frame and cover
0–11	Conduit
0–12	Power cable
0–101	Poles, crossbars, guys, insulators

TABLE 11-11

I-J	Duration	Description	ES	EF	LS	LF	Float
0–4	0	Well pump	0	0	22	22	22
0–5	0	Underground pipe	0	0	24	24	24
0–6	0	Water tank	0	0	12	12	12
0–7	0	Tank valves	0	0	22	22	22
0–9	0	Sewer pipe	0	0	21	21	21
0–10	0	Manhole frame and cover	0	0	21	21	21
0–11	0	Conduit	0	0	26	26	26
0–12	0	Power feeder	0	0	29	29	29
0–101	0	Pole line materials	0	0	23	23	23

TABLE 11-12

Activity	Assume	Duration
0–4 Well pump	Stock delivery, 4 weeks	20
0–5 Underground water pipe	Mechanical joint, 6 weeks	30
0–6 Water tank parts	Standard size, 6 weeks	30
0–7 Tank valves	Standard gate valves, 4 weeks	20
0–9 Sewer pipe	Terra cotta, 1 week	5
0–10 Manhole cover	Stock, 1 week	5
0–11 Conduit	Stock, 1 week	5
0–12 Power feeder	Special order, 8 weeks	40
0–101 Pole material	Stock order, 2 weeks	10

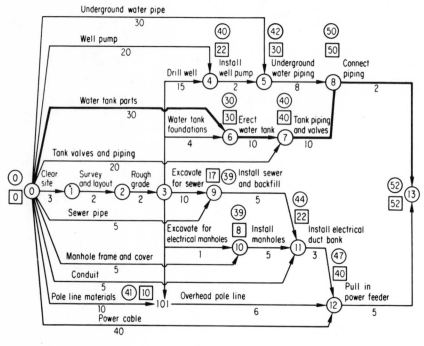

Figure 11-34.   Delivery times for John Doe site preparation with delivery times.

TABLE 11-13

Early event times		Event	Late event times	
Old	New		Old	New
3	3	1	3	21
5	5	2	5	23
7	7	3	7	25
22	22	4	22	40
24	30	5	24	42
11	30	6	12	30
21	40	7	22	40
32	50	8	32	50
17	17	9	21	39
8	8	10	21	39
22	22	11	26	44
25	40	12	29	47
34	52	13	34	52
—	10	101	—	41
Changes	7			14

Twenty-one event times of a possible twenty-eight have changed. Using the new late-start information, the purchasing department would deliver the materials in the order presented in Table 11-14.

Although this list gives the order to which materials should be ordered, it has two distinct weaknesses. First, although the late-start dates for ordering are important, they are extremes. If the order is placed this late, all activities following the delivery will be critical. Second, the early-start times have very little value. In this example, the purchasing department could initiate nine orders the first day of the project. What, for instance, if an enthusiastic buyer orders the sewer pipe and conduit on the first project day? The conduit would arrive on site about eight weeks before it was needed; the sewer pipe would be seven weeks early. The field group would have a storage problem—and a poor opinion of the office group.

These problems have often discouraged the use of CPM for the coordination of material procurement. What is the real defect in the system thus far? The early-start time is unrelated to the field work. Leaving delivery arrows to represent delivery time, just as they were, add another set of arrows to represent the actual movement of the material from storage to

TABLE 11-14

Activity	Description	Late start
0–6	Water tank	0
0–12	Power feeder	7
0–5	Underground water pipe	12
0–4	Well pump	20
0–7	Tank valves	20
0–101	Pole material	31
0–9	Sewer pipe	34
0–10	Manhole cover	34
0–11	Conduit	39

the job site. These "on-site material" arrows have zero time duration and the same late-finish times as the delivery arrows. Figure 11-35 has these nine new arrows. Since they have a zero time duration, the early start equals early finish, the late finish equals late start. The *ES, LS,* and float times are shown in Table 11-15.

Note that the late-finish times for these activities are the same as the late-finish times for the delivery arrows. However, the early times and float times are now related to the field progress.

On this basis, priority of ordering would be as presented in Table 11-16. Note that all but two of the items are in a different position of priority on this second list.

In addition to time required for delivery of materials and the determination of the delivery time which should be specified on the order, there are a number of other steps in material procurement which are time-consuming and must not be neglected. These can include shop-drawing approval, architect's review of shop drawings, resubmittal time for shop-drawing corrections, and review by cognizant agencies (HHFA, HFA, HRB, etc.). These steps can sometimes be accelerated for critical activities (when they are, in fact, identified as critical). However, there is a tendency to minimize the impact of these routine steps. Take care to reflect them properly on your diagram. Figure 11-36 shows the interrelation between two material orders (hardware and door bucks) before either reaches the job site. Note that in this example the door buck delivery has five days' float because of the additional time required to prepare hardware templates. Larger equipment may require additional time for the submission of formal bids.

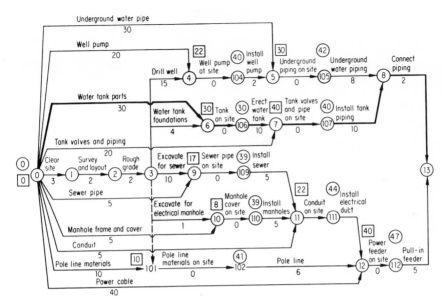

Figure 11-35. On-site delivery times.

PROJECT SCHEDULE

CPM separates planning and scheduling. With the collected project information and time estimates, activity times can be computed. Where does planning cease and scheduling start? The first computation marks the end of the planning phase. Once there is a project duration to compare with

TABLE 11-15

Activity	Description	ES	LS	Float
4–104	Well pump at site	22	40	18
5–105	Underground pipe at site	30	42	12
6–106	Water tank at site	30	30	0
7–107	Tank valves at site	40	40	0
9–109	Sewer pipe at site	17	39	22
10–110	Manhole cover at site	8	39	31
11–111	Conduit at site	22	44	22
12–112	Power feeder at site	40	47	7
101–102	Pole material at site	10	41	31

TABLE 11-16

Priority	Position on first order list	Delivery as early as	Delivery no later than	Float
1. Water tank	1	30	30	0
2. Tank valves	5	40	40	0
3. Power feeder	2	40	47	7
4. Underground pipe	3	30	42	12
5. Well pump	4	22	40	18
6. Sewer pipe	7	17	39	22
7. Conduit	9	22	44	22
8. Manhole cover at site	8	8	39	31
9. Pole material	6	10	41	31

the desired schedule, the scheduling effort starts. The first comparison is for end date.

If the end date exceeds the desired date, the first area to be examined is the critical path. There are two distinct methods for shortening the critical path. First, examine the path for series sequences which could be in parallel. For instance, in the John Doe project, it would shorten the critical path by 74 days if the company were able to revise their ground rule about doing the office building after the plant/warehouse. However, if this is not possible, other possible areas of overlap should be studied, such as:

1. In the foundation contract, do the pile caps (16–17) and grade beams (17–18) in parallel rather than in series. Time savings: 5 days.

2. In the foundation contract, do the underslab plumbing (19–20) and conduit (20–22) in parallel rather than in series. Time savings: 5 days.

3. Parallel the floor slabs (22–29) with the structural steel and craneway erection (29 through 33). This would be possible by working from opposite ends of the building. Time savings: 10 days.

4. Start siding erection earlier, at event 33 instead of 35. Time savings: 5 days.

This is a time savings of 25 days. The plant/warehouse area does not offer much opportunity for time savings because several paths would have to be shortened.

If this time reduction is not sufficient, the next possibility would be to reexamine the critical activities with longer durations. Perhaps by adding equipment and manpower, some of these could be shortened. For instance:

15–16   Shorten "excavation" from 5 to 3 days.

16–17   Shorten "pour pile caps" from 5 to 3 days.

17–18   Shorten "grade beams" from 10 to 5 days.

Take care not to shorten durations arbitrarily. There is an unfortunate tendency to be optimistic when estimating the project time required for an activity. Few people fall into the trap of using the best time they have ever experienced. However, it is easy to overlook the time inevitably lost in coordinating many activities. Experienced estimators must include this factor in their estimates.

CONTINGENCY

Projection of the end date desired is unfortunately not an acceptable schedule. This is not surprising since CPM has not furnished us with a crystal ball. Since the activities and time estimates used in the network are based upon experience, the project rarely finishes ahead of the computed end date. Since such factors as bad weather, difficult site conditions, and labor disputes are not only unavoidable but rather unpredictable, the actual completion date tends to exceed the first CPM end date. It is, then,

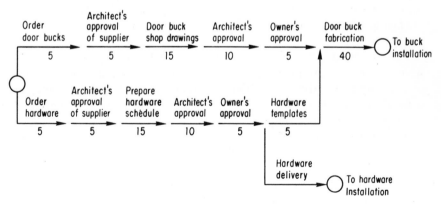

Figure 11-36.   Typical material procurement cycle.

reasonable to allow for some contingency between the CPM end date and the actual desired completion date. How much of a contingency? There is no definite answer for this; it will vary with the specific circumstances of the project. However, if you need a 12-month completion, set your CPM goal at about 11 months, and so forth. Some people have been reluctant to set a flat contingency at the end of the schedule. Contingency can be buried in the activity estimates, but if it is, you will not be able to separate true estimates from contingency.

Look at the dates computed and compare the activity with the weather you might expect at that time of the year. This is an area where you are much better equipped than the computer. What if you find that concrete work or earthwork are going to have to be done during an unfavorable time of year? First, facing up to the fact that a winter job will cost more, try a delay of the project until spring. If your end date is acceptable, set your schedule on this basis. If you cannot afford the delay, consider applying overtime or extra crews at the *start* of the project to complete as much as possible before the onset of bad weather.

MONITORING AND UPDATING

Figure 11-37 is the John Doe network with progress shown by dark lines. The event times are shown for the activities in progress. The first path to check is, of course, the critical path. This status is as of project day 150; a check along the critical path shows that the activity "install branch conduit" (43–49) has 10 days to go and is one day ahead of schedule. The activities in progress with float have the status given in Table 11-17.

All the float times are within the allowable CPM range. The dry wall and heating and ventilating units should be pushed so that ductwork installation can start. Figure 11-38 is another representation of the same status. This format could be used to submit a quick weekly status report.

Having located status by the logic plan, you can forecast the expected project completion.

Experience has shown that the CPM logic will hold up very well. If so, what was wrong with the original idea of leaving the CPM schedule "on its own"? The fact is that only about 5 percent of the logical sequence will shift or change. However, the shift or addition of even one activity can delay or improve the completion date.

The periodic review of the CPM plan both to determine and to review the logic is termed "updating." The object in updating the network (either with the computer or manually) is to introduce the project status as well as any logical revisions into a new computation of the completion date. To do this, all completed activities are given a duration of zero. Activities in progress are assigned the time duration required to complete them.

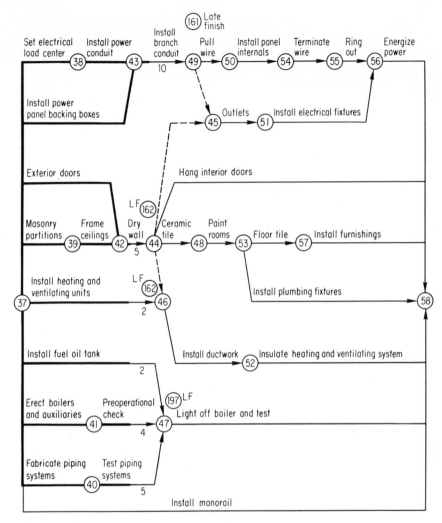

Figure 11-37. Plot of progress, project day 150.

Activities are removed, added, or assigned new event numbers to recognize any logical revisions. The first few updatings may have extensive revisions as plans are influenced by job conditions. However, after the project gets into full swing, there will be perhaps only five or ten arrow revisions per updating. The exact extent of logical revisions to be expected is of course unpredictable.

When the updating information has been entered in the network, a new computation is made from the present date (calendar or project day). This

TABLE 11-17

I-J	Description	Time remaining	New float	Original float
42–44	Dry wall	5	7	13
37–46	Heating and ventilating units	2	10	23
37–47	Fuel tank	2	45	70
41–47	Boiler check	4	43	43
40–47	Test piping	5	42	33

new run must be checked, just as the first ones were; an updating is not immune from error. After the run has been established as a valid one, the results are analyzed. The critical path may shift, and often does. Float activities may become near critical and must be monitored regularly. It is possible for the project to be late because of a "turtle-and-hare" situation. In the project race, the critical path is the hare and the float jobs are the turtle.

Another advantage of updating is that it gives management an objective look at the project at regular intervals. The preparation of a weekly non-CPM report is useful to the field as well as management because it ensures that the field office will review the project regularly. However, the non-CPM report can be as indefinite as a bar graph and is, in fact, often submitted in bar-graph form. The CPM report is objective because it is based upon actual activity completions. The report is most effective when it avoids personalities, excuses, or rationalizations.

The project progress should be plotted on the field office network daily. A weekly CPM progress report should be prepared by the field office and forwarded to all interested groups. At regular intervals, an updating should be conducted by an outside party. This can be a consultant, or someone from the contractor's or owner's office. This will add objectivity to the report and should be a cooperative effort with the field office. The updating by an "outsider" can help the field office view the forest instead of the trees. Surprisingly, people somehow seem to avoid adding up facts which they already know. This is not usually deliberate, but people seem to build up their own blind spots.

REPORTS AND EVALUATION

It is unfortunately very easy for computerized project management tools to become paper mills. Once set up, the computer can generate pounds of paper at a staggering rate. In the early networking days, project planners felt they had reached their objective when the computer spit out, not the answer, but reams of paper.

Management depends upon the planner using project management tools to evaluate the output.

While it is important to monitor and update on a regular basis, it is easily as important to carefully evaluate the output. If the frequency of updating is so rapid that there is no time to evaluate results, to project

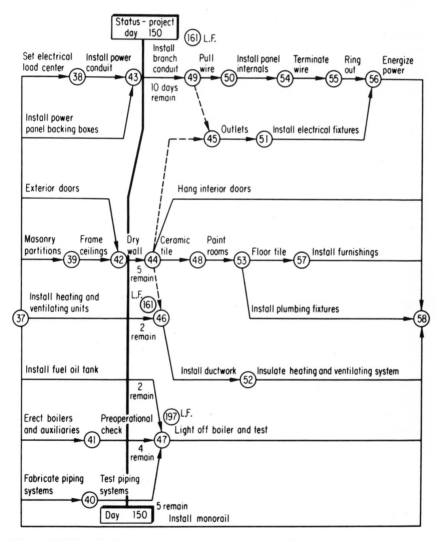

Figure 11-38. Quick status report, sample for day 150.

solutions, or allow some time for those solutions to function, then the management tool is liable to be counterproductive. Network information can be correlated for presentation to management in various ways. The much-criticized bar graph is excellent for presentation of information—if the information has been developed on a rational and carefully considered basis. Thus, while most network specialists argue against the bar graph for basic planning, it remains the single, most effective visual tool for communication purposes.

Many of the systems, including MSCS and Project 2 can generate bar graph output. However, the planner must input his own judgment to produce a selective bar graph. Bar graphing of the total output is overwhelming and becomes ineffectual.

SUMMARY NETWORK

A useful supplement to the written report is the summary network. This is a simplified network used to discuss the results. In the summary network, one arrow represents a group of arrows. For instance, on the John Doe network, the seven arrows concerned with the well (3–4, 4–5), water tank (3–6, 6–7, 7–8) and water piping (7–8 and 8–13) could be represented with one arrow "install water system" (3–13). This summary arrow would have a duration of 27 days. These summarized arrows are then used to draw a summary network. Since this diagram is for presentation purposes only, restraint arrows need not be shown. Figure 11-39 is the summary diagram for the John Doe project. One advantage of the CPM network is that it is not drawn to scale. However, the summary diagram can initially be drawn to scale because the critical path is identified and can form the backbone of the diagram. As the project progresses, the scale will become approximate rather than exact since neither the critical path nor the time durations will remain static.

There are several graphic methods for portraying a CPM network, using magnetic arrows and nodes, tracks to take activity descriptions, or even homemade devices. These are not practical for large working CPM diagrams but can be handy for a summary diagram. They take longer to prepare but may have a nice appearance. Colors can be used and these models can be photographed if copies are to be distributed.

RESOURCE CONTROL

Resource requirements can be assigned by activity and programmed in a fashion quite similar to the cost requirements for a project. On a manual basis, this involves plotting activities to a time scale, then plotting resource requirements on the same scale. Much in the nature of a cash-flow projection, resources can be plotted on an early- or late-start basis.

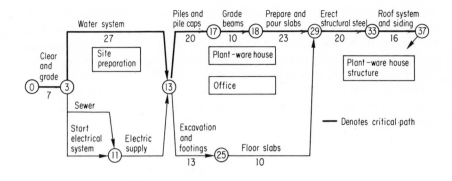

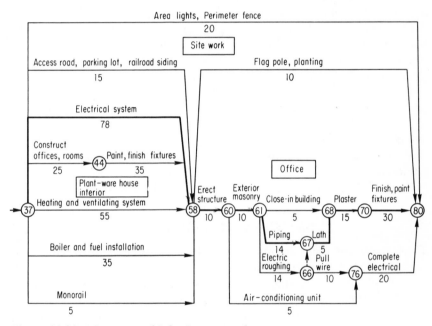

Figure 11-39. Summary of John Doe network.

Obviously, within the project framework, resources can be scheduled between their early and late dates (where there is scheduling float available), thus leveling the resource requirements. Experience indicates that plotting resources to the late start is more realistic because of the inevitable inertial build-up problems on a project. Further, with a detailed network, there really is a limited area of scheduling flexibility in the typical project, so that the late resource curve can be used as a guideline.

Computer programs for plotting resource requirements are sophisticated and somewhat limited in their availability. Most of the available programs go to the next major step which is resource leveling. In this step, using the network as a base, the limitations on resources, including money, can be imposed and a stretch-out projection made. The computer involvement is an order-of-magnitude more involved than the basic projection of resources according to the plan.

Resource planning by computer has been used particularly effectively in the petrochemical industry. Here, during turn-around operations and other labor-intensive operations, the controlling factor is manpower and equipment—not usually a single or even several critical paths.

In the broader construction utilization, resource planning and leveling has been acknowledged but used only to a limited extent. The computer cost is easily several times more expensive. Also, the inputting and evaluation of resources requires at least twice the human effort.

The MSCS by McDonnell Automation and Project 2 software systems both have resource planning and leveling options. Earlier resource programs were related to pre-IBM 360 machines, and have generally been phased out. These included the RPSM program and RAMPS program.

The IBM PMS program, which requires a large memory capability, promised resource planning in version III and apparently has achieved it in version IV. For budgeting purposes, the computer cost for each resource run would be on the order of 50 cents per activity. This figure can vary substantially with the network, number of resources to be planned, complexity of the operation, number of activities, and the program used—as well as the contractual relationship with the data center.

NETWORK SPECIFICATIONS

There have been many attempts to specify CPM scope. Unfortunately, it is easy to specify the letter but not the spirit of the application. Exhibit A is an example of a comprehensive CPM specification by the Army Corps of Engineers for a small housing project. The GSA specifies their own CMCS (Construction Management Control System) for larger projects. The key to CMCS success is that it is implemented by the construction manager or by a CMCS supervisor provided by GSA.

The U.S. Postal Service, the Veterans' Administration, and others specify network requirements in a manner similar to Exhibit A. The basic failure has been the ability of contractors to subcontract for these services at too low a level of scope and quality. There are two means of combatting this problem. The best is the implementation of the networks by the CM/PM who has been selected on the basis of the scope and expertise of his management skills, including networking.

Another approach is the establishment of networking as an allowance item, so that the owner directly controls the scope in dollars as well as the selection of a consultant.

EXHIBIT A
Network Analysis System

31. *Contractor-Prepared Network Analysis System:* (Apr. 1968) (ASPR 7-604.5). The progress chart to be prepared by the contractor pursuant to the General Provision entitled "Progress Charts and Requirements for Overtime Work" shall consist of a network analysis system as described below. In preparing this system the scheduling of construction is the responsibility of the contractor. The requirement for the system is included to assure adequate planning and execution of the work and to assist the Contracting Officer in appraising the reasonableness of the proposed schedule and evaluating progress of the work.

A. An example of one of the numerous acceptable types of network analysis systems is shown in Appendix I of Corps of Engineers Regulation ER 1-1-11 entitled "Network Analysis System": single copies of which are available to bona fide bidders on request. Other systems which are designed to serve the same purpose and employ the same basic principles as are illustrated in Appendix I will be accepted subject to the approval of the Contracting Officer.

B. The system shall consist of diagrams and accompanying mathematical analysis. The diagrams shall show elements of the project in detail and the entire project in summary.

C. Diagrams shall show the order and interdependence of activities and the sequence in which the work is to be accomplished as planned by the contractor. The basic concept of a network analysis diagram will be followed to show how the start of a given activity is dependent on the completion of preceding activities and its completion restricts the start of following activities.

D. Detailed network activities shall include, in addition to construction activities, the submittal and approval of samples of materials and shop drawings, the procurement of critical materials and equipment, fabrication of special material and equipment and their installation and testing. All activities of the Government that affect progress, and contract required dates for completion of all or parts of the work will be shown. The activities which comprise the various separate buildings and features shall be separately identifiable by coding or use of subnetworks or both. Since the project will be comprised of several buildings, groups of which will be essentially identical, the following supplemental guidance is given for preparation and updating of the Network Analysis.

    (1) A separate typical detail network diagram shall be prepared for each type of building proposed, i.e., duplex, fourplex, etc. A minimum of 35 activities, exclusive of dummies, shall be included for each building.

    (2) A time-scaled summary diagram for the entire project shall be prepared showing the order in which the individual buildings are planned to be constructed, their proposed start and completion dates, and any interdependencies (manpower, equipment, or other restraints) between the various buildings. Each individual building shall be shown on the summary diagram, summarized to a minimum level of 9 milestones to include, but not limited, to start foundations, complete foundations, structure, close-in, plumbing rough-in, HVAC rough-in, electrical rough-in, dry wall, complete unit. All site work, procurement activities, and Government-Furnished Equipment shall

be shown on the summary diagram, with appropriate restraints. If procurement is to be phased, this should be indicated.

(3) The summary network events shall be numbered so that the summary network and detailed networks can be calculated simultaneously by computer. Each detailed activity shall be assigned a monetary value. The value assigned to any activity shall be subject to the approval of the Contracting Officer. This cost per activity breakdown shall be the basis of progress payments. No activity cost, once approved, may be changed without the approval of the Contracting Officer.

(4) The selection and number of activities shall be subject to the Contracting Officer's approval. Detailed networks need not be time scaled but shall be drafted to show a continuous flow from left to right with no arrows from right to left. The following information shall be shown on the diagrams for each activity: preceding and following event numbers, description of the activity, cost, and activity duration, in calendar days.

(5) Sheet size of diagrams shall be 30 by 42 inches. Each updated copy shall show a date of the latest revision, and the date of the latest updating.

(6) Initial submittal and complete revisions shall be submitted in 3 copies. (original tracing and two prints).

E. Submission and approval of the system shall be as follows:

(1) A preliminary network defining the contractor's planned operations during the first sixty (60) calendar days after notice to proceed will be submitted within fifteen (15) days. The contractor's general approach for the balance of the project shall be indicated. Cost of activities expected to be completed or partially completed before submission and approval of the whole schedule should be included.

(2) The complete network analysis system consisting of the detailed networks and network diagrams shall be submitted within 30 calendar days after receipt of notice to proceed.

(3) The mathematical analysis of the networks (detailed and summary) will be provided by the government. This will be on a service center basis and the contractor shall be responsible for adjustments to the logic and/or durations to meet contract time limits.

(4) Schedule of anticipated earnings as of the last day of the month shall be submitted 10 days after contractor has mathematical analysis.

F. The contractor shall participate in a review and evaluation of the proposed network diagrams and analysis by the Contracting Officer. Any revisions necessary as a result of this review shall be resubmitted for approval of the Contracting Officer within ten (10) calendar days after the conference. The approved schedule shall then be used by the contractor for planning, organizing and directing the work, reporting progress, and requesting payment for work accomplished. If the contractor thereafter desires to make changes in his method of operating and scheduling, he shall notify the Contracting Officer in writing stating the reasons for the change. If the Contracting Officer considers these changes to be of a major nature he may require the contractor to revise and submit for approval, without additional cost to the Government, all or the affected portion of the detailed diagrams and mathematical analysis to show the effect on the entire project. A change may be considered of a major nature if the time estimated to be required or actually used for an activity or the logic of sequence of activities is varied from the original plan to a degree that there is a reasonable doubt as to the effect on the contract completion date or dates. Changes which affect activities with adequate slack time shall be considered as minor changes, except that an accumulation of minor changes may be considered a major change when their cumulative effect might affect the contract completion date.

G. *Updating:* The contractor shall accomplish monthly updatings and submit for progress and payment in accordance with the following:

(1) Utilizing a mathematical analysis listing all detail activities for each building, show status of each activity in progress as a basis for computing progress and earnings. Update the summary diagram to reflect the status of each building as determined from updating the detail networks, and to reflect the status of site work, procurement, and GFM.

(2) Entering of updating information into the mathematical analysis will be subject to the approval of the Contracting Officer.

(3) The update shall show the activities or portions of activities completed during the reporting period and their total value as basis for the contractor's periodic request for payment. Payment made pursuant to the General Provision entitled "Payments to Contractor" will be based on the total value of such activities completed or partially completed after verification by the Contracting Officer and this updated network analysis shall be used as a basis of partial payment.

(4) Computer analysis of the network will be performed by the Government.

H. The contractor shall be prepared to effect schedule revisions in the networks in response to changes to the contract under the terms thereof, at the direction of the Contracting Officer. In the event that change orders are experienced, they shall be reflected as new activities in the network, or as changes in logic and/or time framing of existing activities. They shall be introduced at the next updating after receipt of a change order, and shall be subject to the approval of the Contracting Officer. Change order logic shall affect only those intermediate activities and performance dates directly concerned. Adjustments required in completion dates for those intermediate dates, or for the contract as a whole, will be considered only to the extent that there is not sufficient remaining float to absorb the additional time which may be authorized for completion of individual activities.

I. In those cases where the time of contract performance is delayed due to causes arising from the GENERAL PROVISIONS: "CHANGES," "CHANGED CONDITIONS," "TERMINATION FOR DEFAULT-DAMAGES FOR DELAY-TIME EXTENSIONS," "SUSPENSION OF WORK" or other clauses, as a condition precedent to a time allowance in the form of tentative NAS revisions the contractor shall first submit a preliminary time proposal in such form as to identify the specific subnet diagram and activities affected. Further, the proposal shall reflect the changed work or delays involved, and demonstrate their effect on the completion date.

J. Based on the information contained in the mathematical analysis, the contractor shall prepare three earnings—time curves ("S" curves), as follows, indicating the schedule of anticipated earnings as of the last day of each month:

(1) A curve based on all activities completed by the earliest finish time (EFT), as determined by the mathematical computations.

(2) A curve based on all activities completed by the latest finish time (LFT), as determined by the mathematical computations.

(3) A curve based on finish times scheduled by the contractor within the limits of available float.

Earnings shall be expressed in dollar and percentage terms, the percentages being determined by dividing the cumulative earnings by the total contract amount. The graph shall be updated monthly to reflect actual progress, and revised as necessary to reflect time extensions of modifications of substantial amounts of money which have a material effect on the schedule.

K. Float or slack is defined as the amount of time between the early start date and the late start date, or the early finish date and the late finish date, of any of the activities in the NAS schedule. Float or slack is not time for the exclusive use or benefit of either the Government or the contractor. Extensions of time for performance required under the contract General Provisions entitled "CHANGES," "DIFFERING SITE CONDITIONS," "TERMINATION FOR DEFAULT-DAMAGES FOR DELAYING TIME EXTENSIONS" OR "SUSPENSION OF WORK" will be granted only to the extent that equitable time adjustments for the activity or activities affected exceed the total float or slack along the channels involved.

L. If the contractor fails to submit the networks, updatings and reports as required by this Special Provision, the Contracting Officer may withhold approval of partial payment estimates, until such submittals are made.

12
Cost Control

Cost control by the construction manager has two very distinct stages. During the preconstruction phase (budget, programming, and design), the CM furnishes cost estimating information and participates in value analysis/management. During construction, the CM controls progress payments and change-order negotiations.

PRECONSTRUCTION

Cost is the principal dimension in value analysis. Without cost for comparison, the analysis of value must necessarily be subjective—and consequently fall short of the full potential.

When used in value analysis, cost estimating is problematic in that the area to be estimated is not fully defined at the time of greatest potential for value analysis. After the design has been completed, the preparation of cost estimates is a relatively straightforward matter, but at this stage of development many of the value alternatives have been precluded and therefore many opportunities for value improvement are lost.

Whatever cost figures are used for the comparison between values must be comparable and compatible.

The most common figure used to describe the cost of a project is the construction cost or contractor's cost. Where there is one general contract, this would be a single figure. Where there are separate prime contractors, the contractor's cost would be the aggregate of all contract prices including: site work; general construction; structural costs; mechanical, electrical, and plumbing costs; elevator contract; HVAC; and special contracts.

Many important considerations hinge upon the contract cost. One of the most important is the designer's fee, which is often an agreed-upon percentage of the expected contract cost or the actual cost—whichever is lower. Project costs must also be considered. Table 12-1 represents a range of reasonable project costs relative to construction costs (CC).

Thus, it is clear that the cost of this project is at least 50 percent more than the basic construction costs. In a private venture, additional costs would include taxes during construction, insurance during construction, finder's fee and permanent loan fees, legal and closing costs, title insurance, appraisals, and various leasing commissions.

It is most important to look at the total cost picture in early stages such as budgeting and programming when performing value analysis.

Life-Cycle Cost

In buildings, the initial investment is approximately matched over 20 to 30 years by cost of maintaining and servicing the building, including electric power and other forms of energy. In buildings such as schools and hospitals, the cost of changes and alterations is substantial, often equaling 50 to 100 percent of the original cost.

Study by the General Services Administration indicates that the salary cost of the personnel utilizing the facility over its life span will be about 18 times the original cost. Accordingly, any investment in the original cost which improves the productivity of the people utilizing the building will be paid many times over. (However, it becomes problematical in regard to who is the recipient of this production improvement.)

If a developer is going to operate the building after completing it, value to him would include efficient means of energy utilization. If, on the other hand, the developer intends to sell the building at completion, he or she

TABLE 12-1

Project	Relative cost, percentage CC
Budgeting and programming	2
Site acquisition	10
Design	7
Project management	4
Construction cost	100
Changes in scope	5
Interest during construction	12
Furnishings and move-in	10
	150

will be much less interested in operating costs. If the developer is the owner and will operate the building, he or she is particularly interested in the environmental situation insofar as it directly affects the productivity of the people utilizing the building. In cases where the owner is not designing, building, or developing his own facility, he or she should carefully specify all requirements so that the final result will incorporate the proper level of value without increasing the cost.

Cost Estimating Stages

The method of cost estimating varies with the stage of development of the project. Major project cost decisions must be made in the early budgeting and programming phases. Unfortunately, this is the time when the least is known about the building configuration, dimensions, and scope. Accordingly, the costs which support value analysis at these stages must be similarly limited. Since the cost information available is limited, the estimating techniques utilized are those appropriate to more limited scope information.

As the project becomes better defined, better cost information and estimating techniques are used, and value analysis can be utilized to counter the natural tendency for costs to inflate without increase in value.

Distribution of Cost

The key to the selection of areas of value analysis is the distribution of cost over the various categories making up the building. Figure 12-1 is an example of one format which can be used to list the cost for a building. The distribution or breakdown can be increased if the level of information available is in more depth. The initial figures entered are estimates. As actual bids are received, these can be entered and coded by circling or other indication to show that they are actual rather than estimate.

Taking average building-systems costs per gross square foot for a private-office high-rise building and spreading them according to the format in Figure 12-1 gives the equivalent breakdown shown in Figure 12-2. According to the Pareto distribution, 20 percent of the items should represent 80 percent of the cost. Of the 17 items listed, the 4 most expensive are:

Superstructures	$5.90
HVAC	5.80
Exterior walls	4.60
Electrical	4.00
Subtotal	$20.30

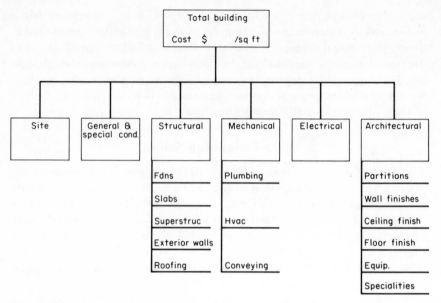

Figure 12-1. Cost distribution format (Source: **Value Analysis in Design and Construction, McGraw-Hill, 1976).**

This indicates that 24 percent of the items equal only 55 percent of the cost. Actually, the rule of thumb is even less effective, since the electrical work can be broken down into power source, distribution system, and fixtures. The HVAC system would break down into heating, ventilating, air-conditioning equipment, and distribution systems. The value analyst should still select the high-price categories for review, but the categories should be true functional components, not just a broad disciplinary category. In the model shown in Figure 12-2 obvious areas for review would be the superstructure at $5.90 and the exterior walls at $4.60.

Computerized Estimating

The experienced CM faces a problem in developing useful cost estimates during the design phase. A/E-type estimates, and some CM estimates, are generally of the quantity survey type—taking off units and then extending their unit cost from a company data bank, a published source, or a combination of both. Early in the design, the units are not available. Estimates are typically done by parameter (square foot of floor space or cubage). These parametric estimates do not provide a good cost distribution which is the necessary prerequisite to value analysis.

The contractor-oriented CM usually uses contractor-type estimating which is principally pricing by subcontractors, within a framework of quantity surveying. Early design does not provide the data needed for this approach.

One solution is offered by the use of a computerized cost model, such as the CODE system, developed by AMIS Systems of New York.

The AMIS system is a computer model which accepts basic parameters ranging in square foot per student to dimensions and numbers of stories, percentage occupancy of site, perimeter configurations, glass percentage, and other specific desires of the owner or designer. Given this input, the system generates a design based on the information furnished. Where information has not been furnished, the program has prestored selected features which are reasonable for the type of facility. Page 1 of the output relates this input information or assumption.

The result of the estimate is a raw construction cost which can be factored for area, overhead, location, and type of contract. These factors can be preloaded into the program.

A model can be iterated to generate quantities in cost for various design factors, such as change in the exterior configuration in terms of glass percentage or length-to-width ratios.

The AMIS system provides a means of rapid comparison of alternatives at a time when the owner or designer has the least specific information

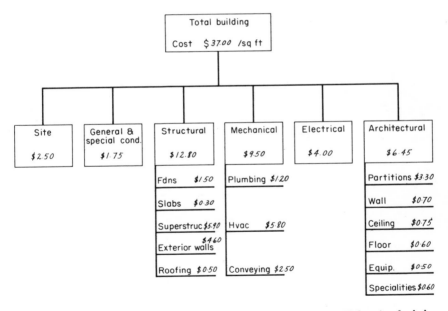

Figure 12-2.   Breakdown of average building systems cost (Source: **Value Analysis in Design and Construction,** *McGraw-Hill, 1976).*

available. This provides specifics for value analysis, since the model breaks the building down into its components and identifies the areas most suitable for value analysis.

The example shown in Figure 12-3 was prepared for a proposed office building in central Florida. There were no drawings available, since this estimate was prepared during the feasibility study for the project. Nevertheless, a full and detailed unit breakdown was generated in less than 15 minutes.

The AMIS model is generated without a design prerequisite. It can be maintained and continued during the design phase, with definite specific information introduced into the system as it is available.

The figure generated in this particular estimate is raw and represents the subcontract cost of these items. For an overall single general contract, the total figure of $11,283,504 should be increased to at least $12,186,000.

This cost estimate was generated concurrently with the cost feasibility study for this project. That particular study assumed that this particular office building would have almost 500,000 square feet and 383,000 net square feet. Actually, the building estimated had only 280,000 net square feet, resulting in a lower rentable area. Also, on the basis of 316,200 gross square feet, the square-foot cost of this building would be $33.74. This

FEDERAL S&L OFFICE BUILDING

BASIC INPUT DATA

SECTOR DATA

(0. VALUE MEANS - DATA NOT AVAILABLE.)

SEC NO.	SECTION NAME	NO OF BLDGS IN SECTION	NET AREA OF SECT.	NO. OF OCCUPNTS	SITE AREA	GROSS/ NET RATIO
1		1	280000.	0.	130680.	1.29

SECTOR NO. 1

BLDG NO.	BLDG NAME	NO OF STORIES	NET AREA	GROSS/ NET RATIO	FLOOR PERIM.	GLASS PCT	BSMNT PCT
1	SINGLE TOWER	25.	280000.	1.29	520.	50.	100.
BLDG NO.	BLDG NAME	COLUMN SPACING	NO. OF COLS.	SLAB LOAD	ROOF LOAD	SOIL/PILE CAPACITY	HVAC SYST.
1	SINGLE TOWER	25.0X20.0	40.	125.	100.	100.	

ASSUMED INPUT DATA

SECTOR DATA

(0. VALUE MEANS - DATA NOT AVAILABLE.)

SEC NO.	SECTION NAME	NO OF BLDGS IN SECTION	NET AREA OF SECT.	NO. OF OCCUPNTS	SITE AREA	GROSS/ NET RATIO
1		1	280000.	0.	130680.	1.29

SECTOR NO. 1

BLDG. NO.	BLDG NAME	NO OF STORIES	NET AREA	GROSS/ NET RATIO	FLOOR PERIM.	GLASS PCT	BSMNT PCT
1	SINGLE TOWER	25.	280000.	1.29	520.	50.	100.
BLDG NO.	BLDG NAME	COLUMN SPACING	NO. OF COLS.	SLAB LOAD	ROOF LOAD	SOIL/PILE CAPACITY	HVAC SYST.
1	SINGLE TOWER	25.0X20.0	40.	125.	100.	100.	FAN COIL

Figure 12-3. *Federal S & L Office Building* (*Source:* Value Analysis in Design and Construction, *McGraw-Hill, 1976*).

FEDERAL S&L OFFICE BUILDING

SUMMARY

ITEM	UNIT	QUANTITY	UNIT PRICE	TOTAL	GRAND TOTAL
EXCAVATION				30036.	
FOUNDATION CONCRETE				324574.	
STRUCTURAL STEEL				1026502.	
METAL DECK				252839.	
CONCRETE				729631.	
EXTERIOR WALLS				1243554.	
WINDOWS&GLAZING				555100.	
ENTRANCES				45000.	
DAMPPROOF'G & WATERPROOF				34187.	
ROOFING & SHEETMETAL				27558.	
MISC. IRON				251650.	
INTERIOR PARTITIONS				710223.	
SPRAY ON F.P				63629.	
HOLLOW METAL				118450.	
CARPENTRY & MILLWORK				176019.	
HARDWARE				64770.	
FURR&LATH				98885.	
CERAMIC & QUARRY TILES				95572.	
RESILIENT FLOOR				120186.	
ACOUSTIC TILE				372963.	
PAINTING & DECORATING				161060.	
ELEVATORS				584000.	
SITE WORK				196020.	
GENERAL CONDITIONS				436944.	
PLUMBING				595200.	
SPRINKLERS				25300.	
H.V. & A.C.				1900270.	
ELECTRIC				1030320.	
SITE LIGHTING				13068.	
TOTAL COST BID					11283504.

Figure 12-3 (continued).

figure is in excess of the high range used in the feasibility study. It would be imperative that these figures be reintroduced into the feasibility study to determine whether or not to proceed with the project.

Review of the summary sheet indicates that value and analysis would be best performed in the areas of structural steel, exterior walls, HVAC, or electrical systems. However, review of the detailed breakdown provides more specific identification of the areas with the highest incremental cost. This list would again include structural steel and exterior walls. These items approach $1 million in cost.

Items in the half-million-dollar range would include windows, acoustical tile, plumbing fixtures, fan coil units, and electric light fixtures. The refrigeration equipment is the third most expensive item.

COST CONTROL—CONSTRUCTION PHASE

A basic concept in cost control is the assignment of cost to the individual activities in the network. One of the reasons that this has not expanded in

FEDERAL S&L OFFICE BUILDING

PROGRAM BUDGET ESTIMATE

ITEM	UNIT	QUANTITY	UNIT PRICE	TOTAL	GRAND TOTAL
EXCAVATION					
SITE GRADING	S.F.	19492.3	0.10	1949.	
MASS EXCAV. & BACKFILL	C.Y.	6174.3	2.00	12348.	
FOOTING & PIT EXCAVATION	C.Y.	2859.1	3.00	8577.	
BACKFILL	C.Y.	1460.9	3.00	4382.	
POROUS FILL	S.F.	13892.3	0.20	2778.	30036.
FOUNDATION CONCRETE					
CONCRETE IN FOOTGS/CAPS	C.Y.	940.5	80.00	75244.	
CONCRETE IN PIERS	C.Y.	18.6	120.00	2240.	
FOUND. WALLS	S.F.	7354.8	5.25	38612.	
PIT WALLS	S.F.	321.1	5.50	1766.	
PIT SLABS	S.F.	136.0	1.00	136.	
REINFORCING STEEL	TON	64.0	400.00	25613.	
MISC. PADS ETC.	L.S.			14361.	
PILES	L.F.	23800.0	7.00	166600.	324574.
STRUCTURAL STEEL					
STEEL	TON	2211.0	425.00	939675.	
STUDS	S.F.	347307.6	0.25	86826.	1026502.
METAL DECK					
DECK	S.F.	361199.9	0.70	252839.	252839.
CONCRETE					
S.O.G	S.F.	13892.3	1.05	14586.	
FILL ON METAL DECK	S.F.	361199.9	1.05	379259.	
CONC. SPANDRELS	L.F.	13520.0	12.00	162240.	
REBARS	TON	347.0	400.00	138800.	
MISC.	L.S.			34744.	729631.
EXTERIOR WALLS					
EXTERIOR WALLS	S.F.	158600.0	6.00	951600.	
COPING	L.F.	520.0	15.00	7800.	
PERIPHERAL ENCLOSURE	L.F.	13520.0	15.00	202800.	
MISC. WORK	L.S.			81354.	1243554.
WINDOWS&GLAZING					
WINDOWS	S.F.	79300.0	7.00	555100.	555100.

Figure 12-3 (continued).

popularity is the basic difference in the way in which a project is analyzed from the scheduling viewpoint and broken down by cost. Cost estimating by activity would impose a much more severe accounting problem to the estimator. Most estimating is done by system or category times area.

In breaking down cost by activity, a rough estimating approximation is generally utilized. The effect in the construction phase is a much more logical cost breakdown than the typical percentage breakdown. Another salutory effect is the generation of much greater interest in the CPM output on the part of the contractor, since payment requisitions must be tied to network activities.

Using the John Doe project (see Chapter 11), if the cost for the category "foundation concrete" is $36,800, list all the activities having foundation concrete by sorting the CPM activities under that code (Table 12-2).

The yardage breakdown by activity can be approximate. However, the total should equal the exact figure taken from the original detailed estimate. If the actual yardage for the office grade beams (24–25) was 96.5 cubic yards and for the plant slab (22–29) 153.3 cubic yards, the effect on each cost would be insignificant.

Figure 12-4 is an example of a monthly progress invoice keyed directly to the CPM for the John Doe project.

FEDERAL S&L OFFICE BUILDING

PROGRAM BUDGET ESTIMATE

ITEM	UNIT	QUANTITY	UNIT PRICE	TOTAL	GRAND TOTAL
ENTRANCES					
ENTRANCES	S.F.	1500.0	30.00	45000.	45000.
DAMPPROOF'G & WATERPROOF					
DAMPPROOFING	S.F.	7354.8	0.30	2206.	
FABRIC FLASHING	L.F.	13520.0	1.00	13520.	
INSULATION	S.F.	39095.2	0.40	15638.	
MISC. WORK	L.S.			2822.	34187.
ROOFING & SHEETMETAL					
FILL	S.F.	13892.3	0.60	8335.	
BUILTUP ROOF	S.F.	13892.3	1.00	13892.	
FLASHING	L.F.	520.0	5.00	2600.	
MISC. WORK	L.S.			2731.	27558.
MISC. IRON					
STAIRS	EA.	75.0	1250.00	93750.	
LINTELS	L.F.	13520.0	5.00	67600.	
MISC. FRAMING & GRATING	S.F.	361200.0	0.25	90300.	251650.
INTERIOR PARTITIONS					
MASONRY PARTITIONS	S.F.	54179.9	1.90	102941.	
STUDS & DRYWALL	S.F.	307019.8	1.10	337721.	
FURR & DRYWALL	S.F.	187659.9	1.00	187659.	
COLUMNS F.P	S.F.	63000.0	1.30	81900.	710223.
SPRAY ON F.P					
SPRAY ON F.P	S.F.	424199.9	0.15	63629.	63629.
HOLLOW METAL					
EXTERIOR DOORS & BUCKS	EA.	7.0	100.00	700.	
INTERIOR DOORS & BUCKS	EA.	1570.0	75.00	117750.	118450.
CARPENTRY & MILLWORK					
HANG DOORS	EA.	1577.0	20.00	31540.	
PROTECTION & MISC. WORK	S.F.	361200.0	0.40	144479.	176019.
HARDWARE					
EXTERIOR DOORS	EA.	7.0	100.00	700.	
INTERIOR DOORS	EA.	1570.0	40.00	62800.	
MISC. DOORS	L.S.			1270.	64770.

FEDERAL S&L OFFICE BUILDING

PROGRAM BUDGET ESTIMATE

ITEM	UNIT	QUANTITY	UNIT PRICE	TOTAL	GRAND TOTAL
FURR&LATH					
BLACK IRON	S.F.	329619.9	0.30	98885.	98885.
CERAMIC & QUARRY TILES					
C.T. FLOORS	S.F.	17337.5	1.75	30340.	
C.T. WALLS	S.F.	32615.6	2.00	65231.	95572.
RESILIENT FLOOR					
V.A.T FLOORS	S.F.	286276.0	0.30	85882.	
BASE	L.F.	85759.9	0.40	34303.	120186.
ACOUSTIC TILE					
ACOUSTICAL TILE	S.F.	286276.0	1.00	286276.	
METAL PAN	S.F.	43343.9	2.00	86687.	**372963.**
PAINTING & DECORATING					
WALLS	S.F.	801699.6	0.12	96203.	
EPOXY	S.F.	40084.9	0.50	20042.	
DOORS & FRAMES	EA.	1577.0	10.00	15770.	
MISC PAINTING	L.S.			29043.	161010.
ELEVATORS					
ELEVATORS	EA.	8.0	73000.01	584000.	584000.
CLEANING		361200.0	0.00	0.	0.
MISC CONTR.		361200.0	0.00	0.	0.
CABINETS & CASEWORK				0.	0.
SITE WORK					
SITE WORK	L.S.			196020.	196020.

Figure 12-3 (continued).

FEDERAL S&L OFFICE BUILDING

PROGRAM BUDGET ESTIMATE

ITEM	UNIT	QUANTITY	UNIT PRICE	TOTAL	GRAND TOTAL
GENERAL CONDITIONS					476944.
SUBTOTAL					
BOND					7719350.
					0.
OVERHEAD & PROFIT					
					0.
SUBTOTAL GEN CONSTR.					
					7719350.
PLUMBING					
FIXTURES & CONNECTIONS	EA.	493.0	1200.00	591600.	
ROOF DRAINS	EA.	6.0	600.00	3600.	
SPRINKLERS					595200.
SPRINKLERS	HDS.	253.0	100.00	25300.	25300.
PLUMBING SITE CONNET.		0.0	0.00	0.	
H.V & A.C					0.
REFRIGERATION EQUIP.	TON	1338.0	600.00	802800.	
FANS	CFM	397399.9	0.30	119219.	
DUCTS	LBS	198699.9	1.50	298049.	
PUMPS	EA.	7.0	2000.00	14000.	
FAN COILS	EA.	676.0	900.00	608400.	
CONTROLS	EA.	289.0	200.00	57800.	1900270.
H.V & A.C UTILITY CONN.		0.0	0.00	0.	0.
ELECTRIC					
MAIN POWER CONN.	KVA.	3612.0	15.00	54180.	
LIGHT&POWER PANELS	EA.	181.0	1000.00	181000.	
LIGHT FIXTURES	EA.	5160.0	80.00	412800.	
SWITCHES	EA.	1290.0	50.00	64500.	
RECEPTACLES	EA.	3612.0	50.00	180600.	
TEL. OUTLETS	EA.	722.0	40.00	28880.	
EQUIPMENT CONNECTIONS	L.S.			108359.	1030320.
SITE LIGHTING					
SITE LIGHTING	L.S.			13068.	13068.
					11283504.
TOTAL					11283504.

Figure 12-3 (continued).

In Figure 12-5, one sheet of a multisheet network output listed by I–J order is shown. This sheet is the standard CPM, except for the additional line under each activity. This line includes the total cost of the activity, percentage complete, and cost to date. In Figure 12-6, the information on cost is assembled without the time information. This cost report can be sorted by area or trade.

TABLE 12-2

I–J	Description	Approximate cubic yards	Cost
3–6	Water tank foundation	20	$ 800
11–12	Electrical duct bank	100	4,000*
16–17	Pour pile caps	200	8,000
17–18	Grade beams, plant-warehouse	200	8,000
23–24	Spread footings, office	100	4,000
24–25	Grade beams, office	100	4,000
22–29	Slab, plant-warehouse	150	6,000
28–29	Slab office	50	2,000
	Totals	920	$36,800

*This is cost for concrete only. The conduit cost must be added.

Invoice No. 10

PERIOD MARCH 1 THROUGH MARCH 31

	Value	*Invoiced previously*	*This period*
15–16 Excavate plant-warehouse	$3,000	$2,000	$1,000
14–23 Excavate office building	$1,500	$ 500	$1,000

Activities started and completed this period:

	Value
16–17 Pour pile caps, plant	$6,000
17–18 Grade beams, plant	$4,000
18–19 Backfill, plant	$ 500
23–24 Spread footings, office	$1,000
24–25 Grade beams, office	$1,500
25–26 Backfill	$ 500

Activities started this period:

	Value		This period
19–20 Underslab plumbing, plant	$ 900		$ 500
			$16,000
		This invoice	$16,000
		Retainage 10%	1,600
			$14,400

Invoiced to date $46,000
Total contract $500,000
Percent invoiced to date 10.6%

Figure 12-4. CPM-based invoice.

Cost Forecasting

Time-and-cost dimensions can be combined to forecast the rate of spending on a project. If the project is on schedule, the contractor will earn the cost of an activity somewhere between the early finish and the late finish. To plot the cumulative cost of activities completed against project time: cost against early completions will give the maximum amount of money required on any project day; cost against late finish will give the minimum amount of money required on any project day. On any project day x, the

| NETWORK REPORT | | BULK MAIL CENTER, WASH., D.C. FOR U.S. POSTAL SERVICE — UPDATE #25 | | | | | | | | PAGE | 9 |

| SORT KEYS ARE | IJ | | CONST.: NORFOLK DIST CORPS OF ENGS. | | | | | | CPM: J.J.O'BRIEN | DATA DATE 01/25/75 |

I	J	ACTIVITY DESCRIPTION	ORG DUR	REM DUR	CODES		EARLY START	EARLY FINISH	LATE START	LATE FINISH	TOTAL FLOAT
1352	1376	TRY STBLZRS SSM1&2 SO END	15.0	0.0	/	/	A 16SEP74	A 27JAN75	ACTIVITY	COMPLETE	
TC/PC/CTO		$4,000/100/ $4,000									
1354	1374	COMP CHN & CRRGS PSM 1&2	10.0	0.0	/	/	A 18NOV74	A 27JAN75	ACTIVITY	COMPLETE	
TC/PC/CTO		$24,000/100/ $24,000									
1356	1380	COMP RNCUT CHUTES PSM 1&2	15.0	1.0	/	/	A 08NOV74	29JAN75	13NOV74	14NOV74	49.0—
TC/PC/CTO		$11,000/ 95/ $10,450									
1357	1381	PACKAGE CATCHER AREAS 10	10.0	9.0	/	/	A 24JAN75	17MAR75	01NOV74	14NOV74	82.0—
TC/PC/CTO		$20,000/ 15/ $3,000									
1358	1384	COMPL BLTNG B CNVYRS	10.0	0.0	/	/	A 13SEP74	A 25OCT74	ACTIVITY	COMPLETE	
TC/PC/CTO		$2,000/100/ $2,000									
1364	1390	COMP WKWYS ETC AREAS 7&8	15.0	1.0	/	/	A 12AUG74	30JAN75	26NOV74	27NOV74	41.0—
TC/PC/CTO		$9,000/ 95/ $8,550									
1366	1378	COMP PAINT CONVYORSCEG	10.0	0.0	/	/	A 14AUG74	A 26DEC74	ACTIVITY	COMPLETE	
TC/PC/CTO		$14,000/100/ $14,000									
1368	1386	TOUCH UP PAINT & PUNCHOUT	20.0	14.0	/	/	A 19NOV74	19FEB75	22NOV74	16DEC74	44.0—
TC/PC/CTO		$12,000/ 30/ $3,600									
1374	1398	ST PAINTING PSM SSM CNVYRS	20.0	0.0	/	/	A 06AUG74	A 25SEP74	ACTIVITY	COMPLETE	
TC/PC/CTO		$26,000/100/ $26,000									
1376	1394	PAINT PSM SSM R CON INDTN	20.0	1.0	/	/	A 14AUG74	30JAN75	10DEC74	11DEC74	33.0—
TC/PC/CTO		$41,000/ 95/ $38,950									
1378	1396	ST BELTING CONVYORSCEG	20.0	0.0	/	/	A 06AUG74	A 25OCT74	ACTIVITY	COMPLETE	
TC/PC/CTO		$19,000/100/ $19,000									
1380	1410	PAINTING RUNGUT CHUTES	20.0	1.0	/	/	A 16AUG74	30JAN75	10DEC74	11DEC74	33.0—
TC/PC/CTO		$21,000/ 95/ $19,950									
1381	1420	PAINT CATCHER	20.0	20.0	/	/		17MAR75	15APR75	14NOV74	16DEC74	82.0—
TC/PC/CTO		$12,000/ 0/ $0									
1382	1412	PAINTING	15.0	0.0	/	/	A 13AUG74	A 25NOV74	ACTIVITY	COMPLETE	
TC/PC/CTO		$11,000/100/ $11,000									
1384	1400	TOUCH UP PAINT & PUNCHCUT	15.0	2.0	/	/	A 07NOV74	31JAN75	12DEC74	16DEC74	31.0—
TC/PC/CTO		$4,000/ 90/ $3,600									
1390	1402	WALKWAYS AREA 9&10	20.0	1.0	/	/	A 20AUG74	31JAN75	27NOV74	02DEC74	41.0—
TC/PC/CTO		$12,000/ 95/ $11,400									

Figure 12-5. CPM Output, including cost information by activity.

| COST REPORT | | BULK MAIL CENTER, WASH., D.C. FOR U.S. POSTAL SERVICE — UPDATE #25 | | | | PAGE | 20 |

| SORT KEYS ARE | IJ | | CONST.: NORFOLK DIST CORPS OF ENGS. | | CPM: J.J.O'BRIEN | DATA DATE 01/25/75 |

I	J	ACTIVITY DESCRIPTION	REM DUR	CODES		TOTAL COST	PERCENT COMPLETE	TO DATE COST
1344	1366	ST PAINTING CONVYORSCEG	0.0	/	/	$21,000	100	$21,000
1346	1364	ST WKWYS ETC AREAS 7&8	0.0	/	/	$9,000	100	$9,000
1348	1368	COMP BLTNG A&AA CNVYRS	0.0	/	/	$15,000	100	$15,000
1350	1388	PUNCHOUT	1.0	/	/	$12,000	95	$11,400
1352	1376	TRY STBLZRS SSM1&2 SO END	0.0	/	/	$4,000	100	$4,000
1354	1374	COMP CHN & CRRGS PSM 1&2	0.0	/	/	$24,000	100	$24,000
1356	1380	COMP RNOUT CHUTES PSM 1&2	1.0	/	/	$11,000	95	$10,450
1357	1381	PACKAGE CATCHER AREAS 10	9.0	/	/	$20,000	15	$3,000
1358	1384	COMPL BLTNG B CNVYRS	0.0	/	/	$2,000	100	$2,000
1362	1389	ST CHAIN & CRRGES PSM 3&4	0.0	/	/	$18,000	100	$18,000
1364	1390	COMP WKWYS ETC AREAS 7&8	1.0	/	/	$9,000	95	$8,550
1366	1378	COMP PAINT CONVYORSCEG	0.0	/	/	$14,000	100	$14,000
1368	1386	TOUCH UP PAINT & PUNCHOUT	14.0	/	/	$12,000	30	$3,600
1374	1398	ST PAINTING PSM SSM CNVYRS	0.0	/	/	$26,000	100	$26,000
1376	1394	PAINT PSM SSM R CON INDTN	1.0	/	/	$41,000	95	$38,950
1378	1396	ST BELTING CONVYORSCEG	0.0	/	/	$19,000	100	$19,000

Figure 12-6. Project Cost Report by activity.

plot determines a maximum-minimum range of funds required. The actual cost will be somewhere between the two. For the contractor, this will be a forecast of his earning rate on the project. Working back from this, he can borrow just that money which he needs to finance the project until sufficient cash is derived from invoices to make the project financially independent. The savings to the contractor will depend upon his mode of financing. If he is borrowing the sum outright, he will achieve a specific saving in interest by borrowing less. If he is working against a credit commitment, this approach will define the number of projects which he can handle within that amount.

The owner's savings from the cash forecast are even more definite. If the owner is financing the project from securities, he can liquidate at the latest time practical, and thus earn interest for the maximum length of

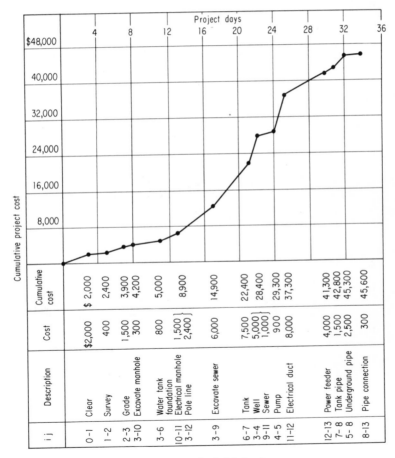

Figure 12-7.   Cost versus time, early finish basis.

time and maintain the principal at its largest practical value. If the owner receives the total construction fund, as in a bond issue, he can schedule a greater portion for higher-interest long-term investments, holding only what he must in lower-interest short-term investments.

Figure 12-7 is a plot of the John Doe site-preparation costs based on early-finish times. Figure 12-8 is a similar plot of money versus time, but in this case late-finish times. Figure 12-9 shows both curves on the same plot. Look at day 21. The most money which could be spent by that date would be $25,800, and the least would be $11,300. The expected expenditure would be about $18,500. This is an unusually wide spread for these curves. The reason is the lack of detail in the sample network. In an actual network, the early and late cost curves tend to parallel each other. Also,

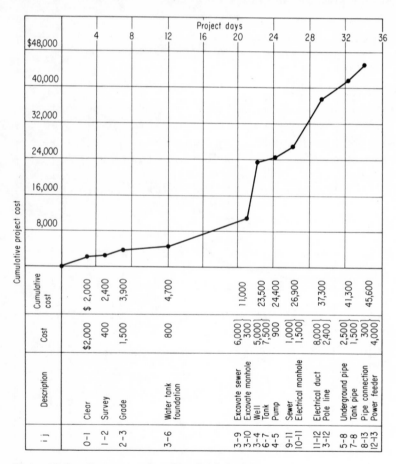

Figure 12-8.   Cost versus time, late-finish basis.

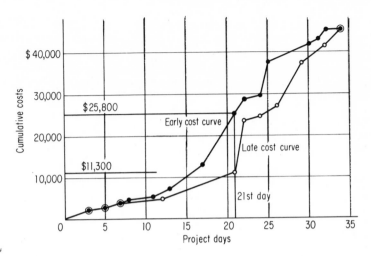

Figure 12-9. Comparison of early and late cost versus time curves.

the curves are usually smooth, with very few inflection points. The time scale is usually in weeks or months since these are of more concern in broad financial control.

The cost forecast is meaningful because it is plotted to a true time scale. While the example plot was done manually, computer-generated curves are very economical for large networks. As the project moves slightly ahead or behind schedule, current curves can easily be generated. The recommended updating frequency for the cost curves is about quarterly.

In Figure 12-10 an actual cost curve for a small dormitory renovation job costing approximately $350,000 per unit had its cost projected over the 21-week time duration. The asterisks are the earliest rate at which money could be spent according to the schedule, while the blocks are the latest time. Note that neither curve exactly fits the traditional construction S curve. The late curve is smoother, but the early curve has a flat spot for two weeks in weeks 10 and 11. At first glance, it was thought that a mistake had been introduced. However, investigation into the network showed that door buck deliveries could not be made until week 12, and that no matter how rapidly the early work progressed, there would be a delay while waiting for material. On the basis of the cost information, a change was made in the time planning. Here was a secondary benefit of the cost projection, in that it provided an additional dimension for evaluation. In Figure 12-11, projects ranging over 6 years were combined. The value of the work totaled approximately $40 million. The purpose of the combined early and late cost flow curves was to provide the sponsoring agency

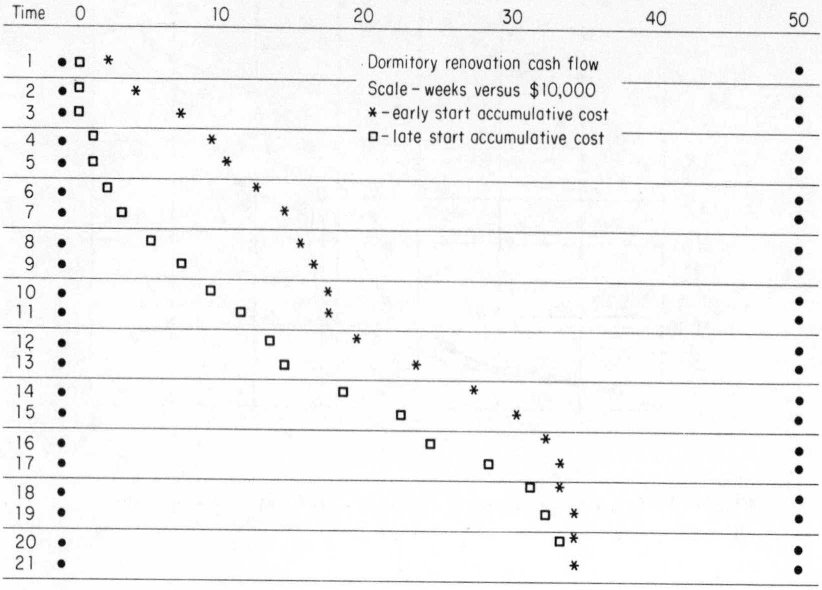

Time 0 10 20 30 40 50
Dormitory renovation cash flow
Scale – weeks versus $10,000
*-early start accumulative cost
□-late start accumulative cost
1 2 3 4 5 6 7 8 9 10 11 12 13 14 15 16 17 18 19 20 21

Total expenditures to date 13550.

Period	ES cost	A cost	LS cost	Acost
1	21128.	21128.	7120.	7120.
2	21116.	42244.	1600.	8720.
3	30697.	72940.	720.	9440.
4	23897.	96837.	8400.	17840.
5	12843.	109679.		17840.
6	17616.	127295.	2320.	20160.
7	14531.	141826.	10225.	30384.
8	10941.	152767.	23825.	54209.
9	11943.	164709.	16145.	70354.
10	7400.	172109.	23489.	93843.
11	5300.	177409.	19865.	113708.
12	21950.	199359.	17365.	131073.
13	35360.	234719.	9842.	140915.
14	41986.	276705.	43731.	184645.
15	31170.	307874.	39675.	224320.
16	14904.	322778.	23035.	247354.
17	7756.	330534.	41253.	288607.
18	5873.	336407.	23567.	312173.
19	3963.	340369.	9703.	321876.
20	1730.	342099.	13303.	335178.
21	400.	342499.	7321.	342499.

***Figure 12-10. Computer-generated cash flow for dormitory (Source:* Scheduling Handbook, *McGraw-Hill, 1969*).**

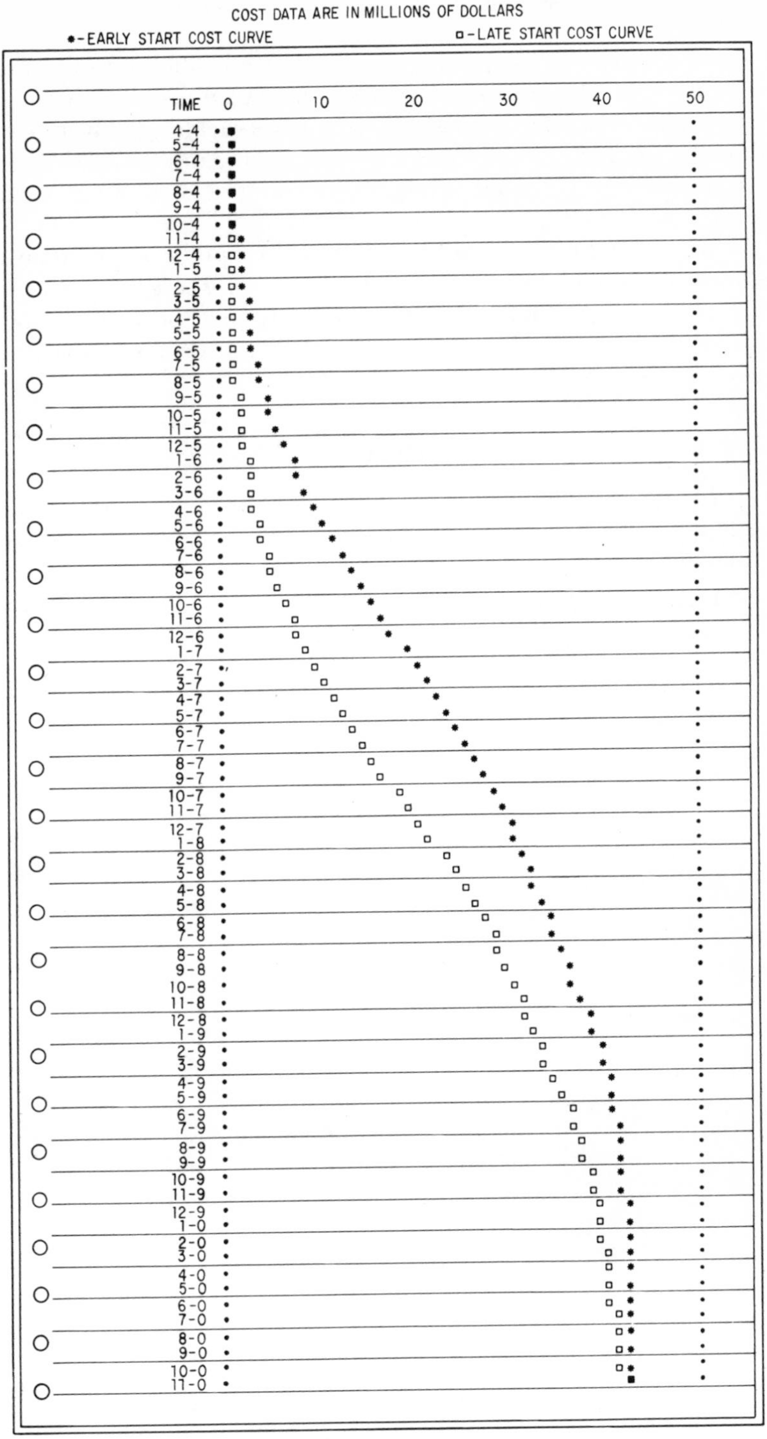

COST DATA ARE IN MILLIONS OF DOLLARS
●–EARLY START COST CURVE   □–LATE START COST CURVE

Figure 12-11.   Cash forecast based on combined networks (Source: CPM in Construction Management*).*

with a cash requirement. Experience indicates that in almost no situations will the early curve be improved upon, so that a plan for switching high-yield long-term securities into short-term lower-yielding securities was predicated upon the early curve. This permitted the institution to optimize its investment program while maintaining a substantial capital program.

If the cost breakdown is normally part of the computer output, then the generation of this type of information by computer is much lower in cost per report. However, if it is to be generated only once, or seldom, during the life of the project—then a manual system can be very competitive costwise.

SUMMARY

The construction manager must include control of project cost as one of his most important tasks. Since CM involves earlier utilization of construction expertise, new methods of cost control must be used by the construction manager because traditional methods are keyed to the slow evolution of the project cycle rather than the dynamic CM fast track.

13
Quality Control

The control of quality on a construction project is concerned with those aspects of inspection of field or manufacturing plant operations which guarantee that the workmanship, physical properties, equipment, and materials supplied by the contractor conform to the plans and specifications prepared by the architect/engineer (A/E). Responsibility for quality control (also quality assurance) is normally assigned to the construction manager (CM), although it may in special instances be designated to the architect/engineer.

In the earlier evolution of professional services for construction, the design A/E was often assigned field responsibility for quality control or inspection. In the federal establishment, these were often referred to as Title II services. Typically, the full-time field inspection role is beyond the scope of the AIA and NSPE recommended design services. A usual method of performance was the assignment of clerk-of-the-works-type personnel on a full-time resident basis to augment the usual construction follow-up activities of the designer. The results were often as costly in the aggregate as CM services—and usually at a lower level of performance.

The CM normally performs the inspection functions of quality control with a staff of competent field and/or off-site inspectors, which may include the contracted services of commercial testing laboratories—the latter particularly in connection with inspections associated with verification of quality by ASTM standards for such construction materials as steel, concrete, timber, or manufactured elements.

In general, the construction project plans and specifications (prepared by the architect/engineer) will spell out the detailed ASTM standard specifications to be met by all materials and workmanship as well as the complete details and procedures for securing approvals of all components of the construction project (such as the submission of sample materials and even panels of brick, masonry, and similar major selections). These specifications also spell out in detail the extent to which inspection is necessary, as governed by the tolerable variation in quality of the materials without danger to life and property. There must be also a reasonable cost of inspection with respect to the value of the materials involved, which will cover such tests as are essential to proper quality assurance. The CM can also secure further effective use of inspection as a means of translating field observations into future specification provisions to eliminate costly elements which do not contribute to quality, such as tolerances which are specified too closely. For some construction materials, extensive inspection manuals have been prepared and are available through industry organizations such as the Portland Cement Association (PCA), Prestressed Concrete Institute (PCI), American Concrete Institute (ACI), Concrete Reinforcing Steel Institute (CRSI), American Institute of Steel Construction (AISC), and others.

Categories of Inspection

Inspection operations can be classified as to the location at which the inspection is performed. Since construction is basically an on-site manufacturing operation, the focus of inspection is primarily on the workmanship and materials entering into the operations on the site. However, many of the products entering into site operations (such as machinery, structural steel castings, concrete, etc.) may be produced elsewhere; quality control of these elements may be a necessity.

A second classification of inspection operations is concerned with the nature of the specific inspections and their details, and these vary with the wide variety of material components entering into the construction process; they may also be distinguished as regards raw or crude materials (such as sand and gravel) versus semifinished or finished manufactured or processed products (such as doors, door frames, or windows).

Inspections made by the CM inspection staff may not only be to ensure good workmanship, but may also include a measurement of quantities, costs, and other data needed to verify payment claims. Inspectors should be provided with appropriate credentials, especially on off-site inspection work, to establish their authority and identity.

The Inspector

The inspection team is subject to an unfortunate attitude—that of adversary. With the seller (contractor) placed diametrically opposite to the buyer (owner, designer, agency), sides are clearly taken at the beginning of a construction project. The less-intuitive inspector assumes that anything he can do to slow down, impede, or control the contractor is to the advantage of the owner. Nothing could be further from the truth. Without exception, jobs which go smoothly cost the owner less, and those which are dogged with problems cost everybody more. It is vital that the inspector control quality, but if in doing so he impedes progress, he inevitably costs the owner money. This is not always obvious to the owner.

The following description, from a manual on *Construction Inspection Procedures* (Ref. 1) discusses the role of the inspector:

The primary function of the field personnel of the construction division is inspection, and the persons assigned to this task are designated as inspectors. There are three classifications of field inspectors: general, mechanical, and electrical. . . . The Inspector must be able to look upon and view critically the particular phase of the construction project to which he is assigned. This requires some degree of experience in the construction field. In addition to experience, the Inspector must also have the ability to evaluate and analyze what he is inspecting. Therefore, a most important and necessary requirement is that the Inspector be able to fully read, comprehend, and interpret the contract plans and specifications. It is also very important that the Inspector have the ability to maintain records that will fully reflect the inspections performed. The Inspector must closely follow the progression of each stage of construction. He must be alert to existing conditions and be able to foresee future problems. When the Inspector notices through his daily inspections that certain phases of the work are not being done in accordance with the plans and specifications, or when other problems occur, he is to immediately report these errors, violations, or problems to "management" for further action.

In effect, the Inspector is not authorized to revoke, alter, substitute, enlarge, relax, or release any requirements of any specifications, plans, drawings or any other architectural addenda. In addition, the Inspector must not approve or accept any segment of the work which is contrary to the drawings and specifications. At no time is the individual Inspector allowed to stop the construction work or interfere with the contractor's employees.

It must be recognized that the title "Inspector" creates a barrier between him and the contractors on the job. How effective he can be in his role depends mainly on how he handles himself in this relationship. He must display knowledge, experience, integrity, ability and the use of good judgment.

The Corps of Engineers has the following suggestions to the inspector on his role:

An Inspector should at all times be thoroughly familiar with all the provisions of the contract which he is administering. This includes familiarity with the plans and specifications including all revisions, changes, and amendments. In addition, the Inspector must be thoroughly familiar with pertinent Corps of Engineers, individual District, and supervisor's administration policies.

An inspector has different responsibilities and authorities, dependent upon the organizational setup under which he is working. Each inspector should know his part in the organization and should be aware of the importance of high-quality construction. He should understand his own level of technical knowledge and accept his responsibilities without overstepping his authority.

In order to do this, the inspector must be aware of the extent of his authority. To that end, he always has the authority to require work to be accomplished in accordance with the contract plans and specifications. Procedures and policies on stopping work for safety violation or construction deficiencies should be reviewed with appropriate supervision before being employed.

In dealing with contractors, the inspector should be impersonal but friendly, fair, and firm. He should be businesslike, cooperative with the contractors, and should attempt to have a clear, accurate, and appreciative understanding of the contractor's problems. Within this viewpoint, the inspector's decisions and instructions should provide the greatest latitude possible to the contractor without prejudice and without waiving contract requirements in choice of equipment, material, or methods.

The Inspection Team

The role of the inspector in construction management is important. The construction management team does not replace inspection, but incorporates it. Further, the inspector is management's contact with the job. Through the inspection process, he develops not only knowledge of specific problems, but a general awareness of the attitudes of the contractors in the various trades. He can identify friction and problem areas and single out situations which may require management attention.

The inspection team becomes the five senses of the construction manager on the job site. Further, the inspection team provides a natural training ground for new construction management staff. Construction management should work in the long range to reduce the adversarial role between contractor and owner, by closing the communications gap.

The responsibilities of the resident inspection team include the following:

1. Ensuring compliance by the contractor with the plans, specifications, and contractual provisions for the project.

2. Monitoring, and where appropriate, ensuring that the project progresses according to schedule; where it cannot, management must be kept aware of problems.

3. Coordination and monitoring of reviews, approvals, and tests as required by the specifications and contract.

4. Stopping work and progress when safety concerns override basic contractual commitments or when continuation will result in the inclusion of substandard work.

5. Approval, or revision so that they can be approved, of the contractor's estimates of progress—which result in progress payments, perhaps one of the strongest areas of the inspector's authority, since the name of the contractor game is money, and delay in payment costs money itself.

Inspection Environment

The work of the inspection team is necessarily influenced by the environment within which the team must function. For instance, any of the following factors may call for different attitudes and vigilance on the levels of response by the inspection team.

1. Contractor attitude, either where a contractor has a habit of working as close to the letter of the contract as he can or, more usually, where a contractor believes that he has submitted too low a bid and is constantly attempting to make up the difference through his liberal interpretations of the plans and specifications. The inspection team must provide a careful balance—not overreacting, but not being complacent either.

2. Contractor capabilities cause different reactions from the inspection team. The contractor's attitude may be excellent, but he may have reached too far in bidding a project or may have assigned project supervision that is "way over their heads." Either situation may cause problems.

3. The general trade atmosphere varies from place to place, and the inspection team can be prepared for more problems in certain areas than others.

4. The ability of the field team itself is important to the individual inspector and affects his ability to perform. It also sets the

scene for the way in which he will perform. If the balance of the team is skilled, highly motivated, and well organized, an inspector can emphasize his own areas of expertise.

5. The practicality and completeness of the project plans and specifications will have an impact upon the inspection effort. In some cases, the plans and specifications will result in an excellent structure; but buildability was not one of the considerations, and many construction problems will occur. When the plans and specifications include errors and omissions, the result is many negotiations with the contractor(s) in order to complete.

6. Field conditions can be such, particularly when unanticipated, that they greatly influence the attitude of all parties at the job site. A designer working in an air-conditioned office may recognize field problems, but may still have failed to appreciate the inhibiting attitudes resulting from extremes in temperature, either very wet or very dry working conditions, very hot or very cold working conditions, high noise levels, and other environmental facts.

Inherent Authority

It is not in the best interests of the owner to have the inspection team become nitpickers. When a contractor has to rework a low-value item at high cost when that item has no significant functional or dollar impact upon the building, the inspector has wasted some of his inherent authority. Later, when an item with functional value or a high-cost item requires work which might conceivably be the responsibility of either the owner or the contractor, we can assume that the owner will have to pay the bill. Unfortunately, the traditional definitions of the role of inspection appear to give the inspection team little or no latitude. There is latitude inherent in the role, and it can be applied positively.

The inspector must take care to conduct himself carefully and without any potential conflict of interest. He can take no favors, gifts, or other rewards from the contractor for doing his job in a cooperative fashion. The inspector's reward has to be the successful progress of the job at no real cost in quality to the owner. In doing this, the inspector must constantly keep in mind that any delays while he determines a fair evaluation of what is acceptable are more than delays to the contractor: they are costs, for time is money to the contractor. Accordingly, an inspector who makes judicious and proper decisions, but does not make them in a timely fashion, can indeed be the cause of a poor attitude or resentment on the part of the contractors. The inspector who fails to inspect, or who allows the widest range of latitude to the contractor, in turn, does favor to neither the contractor nor the owner. Thus a balance must be achieved.

The inspection team should be willing to call on its own management and/or consultants when in doubt. The designer offers a pool of available information, although the inspection team should be aware of the contractual agreement between the designer and the owner. In most cases, the design team is required to furnish at least an interpretation of intent and almost inevitably will be willing to cooperate by phone call, if not site visits. In those cases in which the design team is not available, the inspector must not be reluctant to call upon appropriate supplemental professional help such as surveyors, testing labs, manufacturer's representatives, and others who could add to his understanding of potential problems.

Inspection Team Mobilization

In the early portion of the job, it is important for the contractor to organize carefully. Just as the contractor is actually pulling together his key field staff, so the construction manager is calling upon his resources to staff the job. There tends to be a mutuality of willingness to delay, combined with the optimism that much time remains in order to get the project completed.

It is often expeditious to place a specialist in site preparation on the initial clearing, foundations, and heavy-construction phase. Key activities are surveying and checking excavations, soil backfilling, and foundations.

The measurement of quantities in terms of angles and lengths on the job site falls within the province of the surveyor. Surveys, to have legal meaning, must be accomplished by either professional engineers or licensed surveyors, who must be licensed in the state in which the job is located. However, a substantial amount of the surveying accomplished on the job site is done by unlicensed surveyors, and it is quite common for the inspection team to become part of the surveying party, or conversely, to have the surveying party double as inspectors.

Temporary Construction

During construction, a wide range of structures are designed and built by the contractor—often without the guidance of the structural engineer. It is in the interest of the inspection team to ensure the safety of these structures which include, but are not limited to, scaffolding and shoring.

Scaffolding is used for many purposes during construction. It may be used to support working platforms, stairways, hoists, trash chutes, and more recently has been used to support shoring. The Scaffolding and Shoring Institute has defined safety rules for scaffolding.

Scaffolds are no better than the base upon which they are erected. The recommended procedure is to provide adequate sills and base plate, use adjusting screws instead of blocking to adjust to uneven grade, and plumb and level all scaffolds as the erection proceeds. Scaffolding depends very much upon the ability of tubular columns to carry load, and this ability in turn is dependent upon vertical structures. Cross bracing is important, so fasten all braces securely. Freestanding scaffold towers must be restrained from tipping by guying or other lateral restraint.

When planning scaffolds, make them to a sufficient height. Do not attempt to stack ladders or crates on top scaffolding to increase the height.

Calculate the safe load for scaffolds, preferably through the scaffolding contractor. Do not overload. (OSHA safety factor is now 4 to 1, minimum.)

The recommendations of the Scaffolding and Shoring Institute apply to shoring for various purposes, principally for the support of concrete formwork.

Shoring installations must be properly designed by qualified people. The shoring layout must include details which take into account unusual conditions such as ramp, cantilevered slabs, and heavy beams, showing both plan and elevation views. The inspection team should be certain that the plan has been approved by appropriate structural engineers.

The minimum design load for any formwork and shoring must be not less than 100 lb/ft^2 for the combined live and dead load regardless of slab thickness, and the minimum allowance for live load must be at least 20 lb/ft^2. When motorized carts are to be used to place the concrete, design loads must be increased 25 lb/ft^2. Allowable loads must be based on a safety factor, consistent with the type of shoring used.

Shoring must not be removed prematurely, and when removed, should be replaced by partial reshoring. In high-rise slabs, it is usual to replace partial shoring for seven floors below the floor in progress. Usually, slabs can be stripped on the following day, but support must be maintained for at least three days, and preferably seven. Some shoring is needed up to 28 days when the concrete develops its full strength. The stripping of forms is subject, also, to the live load on the new structure.

Shoring may also be used to carry anticipated overloads during construction.

Testing

Some materials, particularly those mixed on the job site, require special testing. The contract may require the contractor to conduct the test with observation by the inspection team, or the inspection team may take samples and conduct tests.

To accomplish job-site testing, appropriate reference documents must be available, since the specifications usually refer to testing procedure by reference to standards such as the ASTM, ACI, ASME, ANSI, or others. The inspection team should review specifications and be certain that referenced standards are available and have been reviewed before testing is called for. It is often appropriate to conduct a trial or rehearsal test before actual job materials are mixed.

In accordance with test requirements, required testing equipment must be available and checked out at the job site.

Often it is appropriate for testing to be done under the auspices of the materials manufacturer, although the obvious vested interest involved must be considered. Architect/engineers often recommend the use of special testing laboratories or groups as an adjunct to the inspection team. This can be both effective and economical, since it limits the amount of specialized testing equipment which must be purchased and does not require the inspection team to develop special skills which are used only on a limited basis on a project. Conversely, where large amounts of material are used on the job, it may be appropriate for the inspection team to learn the skills for specific tests. For instance, on large excavation or backfill projects, certain special moisture-content tests are run so frequently that it is appropriate for the field team to conduct them.

In other cases where materials were mixed off the job site, such as ready-mix concrete, it may be appropriate to have a special test team assigned to the assembly or batching area. Typically, certified laboratory services are retained to perform the tests at the batch plant. This is particularly appropriate for premixed concrete and asphalt.

Special measuring devices are used for setting of equipment. Basically, these are precision millwright tools using dial indicators and similar machine shop equipment to accurately check clearances. Feeler gauges and other manual devices are incorporated in this type of measuring. For measuring speed of rotation, stroboscopic equipment can be used.

For checking welds and piping, x-ray or ultrasonic equipment can be used for nondestructive testing of the soundness of connections.

For measurements such as ambient noise levels, noise meters can be used on a spot basis, or can be set up to be self-recording.

The General State Authority of Pennsylvania has specific testing procedures for the inspection team, directing as follows:

1. All materials, equipment, concrete batch plants and their products, fabricators and their products, and erectors and their services must be approved in writing prior to the performance of any tests.

2. If the Contract Documents, laws, ordinances, rules, regulations, or orders of any public authority having jurisdiction require any work to be inspected, tested, or approved, the Contractor must give the Authority timely notice of its readiness and of the date arranged so the inspection team can observe such inspection, testing or approval.

The Contractor shall bear all costs of such inspections, tests, and approvals unless otherwise provided.

3. The inspectors are authorized to reject work which does not conform to the Contract Documents and to direct any or all Construction Contractors to stop work or any portion thereof, or to require special inspection or testing of the Work as provided in the General Conditions.

4. If such special inspection or testing reveals a failure of the Work to comply (1) with the requirements of the Contract Documents or (2) with respect to the performance of the Work, with laws, ordinances, rules, regulations, or orders of any public authority having jurisdiction, the Contractor shall bear all costs thereof, including additional design services made necessary by such failure. (If the Work is satisfactory, the Authority bears the cost of testing.)

The Specifications

The contract specifications are the base for most inspection activity, since they define the quality required. Today, most technical specifications are organized according to the 16 divisions defined by the Construction Specifications Institute.

The division breakdown is as follows:

Division 1   General requirements

Division 2   Site work

Division 3   Concrete

Division 4   Masonry

Division 5   Metals (structural and miscellaneous)

Division 6   Carpentry

Division 7   Moisture protection

Division 8   Doors, windows, and glazing

Division 9   Finishes

Division 10   Specialties

Division 11 Equipment

Division 12 Furnishings

Division 13 Special construction

Division 14 Conveying systems

Division 15 Mechanical

Division 16 Electrical

Within these divisions, the specifications can be further broken down into innumerable subdivisions and sub-subdivisions.

REFERENCES

1. *Construction Inspection Procedures*, General State Authority of Pennsylvania [now General Services Department of Pennsylvania], Harrisburg, Pennsylvania, 1975, 71 pp.
2. James J. O'Brien, *Construction Inspection Handbook*, Van Nostrand Reinhold, 1974.

14

Labor Relations

Introduction

Construction is a labor-intensive industry, as contrasted with manufacturing. Since 1960, the average yearly employment has represented approximately 5 percent of the working force, according to U.S. Bureau of the Census activities. Using the Bureau of Labor Statistics figures for 1976, the seasonally adjusted job statistics count for the construction industry totalled 3.43 million in January 1976, and fell below 3.4 million for each following month (preliminary figures for September show the lowest figure of 3.33 million). Average hourly earnings for construction workers (unionized and nonunionized) have always ranged substantially higher than wages for manufacturing workers, sometimes as much as 50 percent. (In July 1976 the construction rate was $7.68 as compared with the manufacturing rate of $5.20 per hour.) In 1973, average wage rates for unionized building-trades workers in the larger cities (over 100,000 population) rose to slightly more than $7.79 per hour. When fringe benefits are added, this amounts to a little over $9.09 per hour (this latter figure representing 1974 averages). In 1975 wage increases averaged 8.7 percent, although unemployment totals were rising because of the recession in the mid-1970s. The Bureau of Labor Statistics reported that the unemployment rate in the construction industry climbed to over 20 percent in 1975, nearly double the rate for the manufacturing industry. In 1976 the construction unemployment rates as seasonally adjusted were still over 15 percent while comparable rates in other industries and for the national average had fallen to under 8 percent.

In spite of this, the construction industry is shackled to an obsolete craft system, which even during the mid-1970s with high unemployment within the industry, seems to be the source of most of its problems. This craft system has dictated the source, size, quality, and productivity of the construction labor force, to an extent that the industry is in serious trouble. Employment of open-shop labor has made inroads in some parts of the country, and in others to the point where many contractors are going "double breasted," employing both union and nonunion labor. The industry also faces major issues in its apprenticeship and journeyman training programs which paradoxically are unable to meet the needs for skilled craftsmen, as exemplified by shortages of workers in critical trades (found in various geographic areas). Minority and racial issues abound in the industry. The result of all these influences is represented by the higher rate of unemployment in the construction industry than the nationwide average. (In September 1976 the construction rate was 15.8 percent while the national average was 7.8 percent.)

In consequence of the above, no single area will be found facing the construction manager in applying his schedule, cost, and quality controls as challenging and as transcending in potential impact as that of the area of labor relations. By the same token, the growing sophistication of private, industrial and commercial owners, and of governmental agency owner-builders, will lead them to place more stringent demands and expectations on the CM in handling labor-related issues arising on construction projects. These private and public sector owners will therefore seek advice and guidance from the construction manager on such diverse matters as improving productivity, collective bargaining agreements, manpower needs and availability, safety and OSHA requirements, open versus closed shops, hiring halls versus selectivity in employment, programs for manpower training (specialists, supervisors, management trainees), and the use of college cooperative programs, Equal Employment Opportunity (EEO) and Affirmative Action requirements, and absenteeism, termination, and labor turnover. These owners will also look to the CM to possess the qualities of fairness and firmness in his dealings with unions on grievances, in a display of a professional understanding of worker attitudes and worker motivation, and in his interest in personnel development. The latter quality was strongly emphasized above as among the most desirable of the personal attributes of a construction manager. Not the least among the CM's obligations will be the ability to make recommendations and render assistance as necessary for the development of an effective labor relations program for the project and the avoidance of labor disputes during construction.

Indeed, the CM process may itself enable the construction industry to attain a better balance at the bargaining table (Ref. 1). This could be achieved by an effective, coordinated bargaining entity to produce more responsible labor contract settlements and improved labor relations generally, through the mechanism of the Contractors Mutual Association (CMA) and a new organization known as the Construction Industry Management Board (CIMB). These two organizations, committed to the idea of industrywide bargaining, will help develop the leadership that can enable management and organized labor to serve the best interests of the industry, its clients, and the public. Together, management and labor can aid in preventing a recurrence of the irresponsible bargaining of the mid-1960s which tagged the industry as a ringleader of inflation and which at the same time set the stage for rapid open-shop growth. The CIMB will accomplish this through the medium of a nationwide databank on construction wages and working conditions as part of a broad-based effort to improve construction labor relations. It will utilize information previously collected by the Construction Industry Stabilization Committee (CISC). The new Construction Industry Management Board is composed of representatives of six of the industry's coordinated employer bargaining units that have affiliated with Contractors Manual Association (CMA), a national association of general and specialty contractors that operate under collective bargaining agreements. Other organizations are expected to join the CIMB. Additional areas of concern of CIMB include a restructuring and reformation of current industry employment practices including classifications, use of manpower, and journeyman-apprentice ratios; establishing communication links between employer groups prior to and during collective bargaining negotiations; and resolution of cost-of-living escalator clauses in labor contracts, and of jurisdictional disputes.

Organizational Relationships

The rise of the trade union movement in the United States, under the protection of the National Labor Relations Act of 1935, was a rational consequence of the limited bargaining power of workers which characterized the early adaptation of the factory system, particularly its abuse by the widespread use of piecework and hourly rates based on production. The trade unions succeeded in protecting workers against reduction in hourly rates and in equalizing pay between workers, as well as in outlawing certain unfair practices of employers. Much of the high standard of living achieved in the United States unquestionably is attributed to the success of the labor movement here.

For practical purposes, construction projects may be organized so as to be set up in four distinct categories:

1. *Labor Unions* (closed shop). Essentially, the construction industry in the United States is completely organized by some

17 construction trade crafts (such as the laborers, teamsters, carpenters, cement finishers, operating engineers, ironworkers, electricians, plumbers, fitters, sheet metal workers, painters) under the aegis of the Building & Construction Trades Union of the AFL-CIO; a contractor operating under union rules is said to operate under a "closed-shop" system. For the purposes of this section, a craft is here understood to be an assemblage of journeymen practicing a skilled trade.

The contractor may negotiate directly with the local unions involved, or with district councils in any craft; or he may operate under nationwide agreements, under international agreements (where Mexico and Canada are included), under regional agreements set up to cover several states, or under project agreements (such as that under which the Bay Area Rapid Transit System [BART] in San Francisco, California, was built in the 1960s). The contractor who operates on a union-shop basis may employ only union members. He is free to hire anyone, so long as that individual joins the union as a dues-paying member within a seven-day period after commencing work.

Unions normally develop work rules to protect members against exploitation by their employers. The general terms of these rules define hours of work, compensation, fringe benefits, method of payment, overtime pay, job security, employee-foreman ratio, shop stewards, working conditions, safety, a statement of craft jurisdiction, expiration date of agreement, procedures for selecting bargaining units, and means of settling disputes. Some union rules, such as that governing the famous *Philadelphia Door* case[1], have been unduly restrictive and expensive from both the contractor's and owner's viewpoint.

2. *Open-Shop (nonunion) Operation.* Contractors who do not operate under a union-shop agreement have the option of hiring nonunion labor and operating on an "open-shop" basis. In recent years, open-shop operation has claimed an increasing share of the construction labor market. The growth of

---

[1]*National Woodwork Manufacturers Association v. NLRB*, 1967—The decision in which a trade union at the construction site claimed and received payment for equivalent work saved by the doors being precut for the hardware. The labor saving, and resultant cost saving, therefore, was eliminated as a result of the interpretation of the prevailing labor agreement.

open-shop construction in the mid-1970s is the major by-product of the high labor cost and resulting low productivity. It has been reported that in 1975 approximately 40 percent of commercial and 25 percent of industrial construction was open shop.[2] When added to the majority of residential construction which traditionally has been open shop, a statistic of over 50 percent of the nation's construction being open shop ensues. This is a significant statistic when one considers that the majority of construction in urban areas and major heavy-construction projects, regardless of location, as the interstate highway program (starting in 1954, continuing through the 1970s) or Rapid Transit Developments with federal aid (e.g., BART, San Francisco; WMATA, Washington; MARTA, Atlanta), are accomplished by union-shop labor.

3. *Double-Breasted Operation.* This relates to the remaining alternative open to the contractor wherein a project may be constructed using a combination of open- or closed-shop as defined above. Increasing numbers of contractors have utilized this method of operation. Although a single contractor or common owner may establish such an operation, the actual operations are run separately including the management, labor force, and support staff. Because of increased competition from independent open-shop companies, union contractors have started to move into this area by spinning off a separate group utilizing existing resources to form the independent operation.

4. *Contractor Groups.* Numerous construction (employer) associations exist to achieve the benefits of a cooperative response to union pressures. Typical among these are the Building-Trades Employer's Association (BTEA), the Associated General Contractors of America (AGC), the National Constructors' Association, the National Electrical Contractors Association, the Mechanical Contractors Association of America (MCAA), the National Association of Homebuilders (NAHB), the Mason Contractors Association, the National Association of Minority Contractors (NAMC), the National Utility Contractors Association (NUCA), the American Road Builders Association (ARBA), the American Subcontractors Association (ASA), the Associated Builders & Contractors (ABC), the Associated Landscape Contractors of America (ALCA), and the Painting

---

[2]E.N.R., September 8, 1975.

& Decorating Contractors of America, many of which operate on both national and local levels.

CONSTRUCTION LABOR LEGISLATION

It behooves the construction manager to have an intimate understanding of federal, state and local legislation affecting the project, particularly as this relates to labor laws and labor relations, which can indeed be extremely complex and may differ substantially from the application of the same laws to other industries.

Federal Labor Legislation

Any restructuring and long-term change to existing labor practices and relations will only occur through a combination of many factors, and most significantly through the political process.

The CM process concerns itself primarily with technical and management practices. It must recognize the importance, however, of existing legislation such as minimum-wage laws (Fair Labor Standards [Wage & Hour] Act of 1938) and equal-employment laws, and all newly proposed legislation, originating from both sides of the political spectrum, such as the state's right-to-work laws and the legalization of common situs picketing. In evaluating the influence of labor legislation in both federal and state regulations of the construction industry, it is necessary and helpful to place the CM process into proper context to review the historical development of major labor legislation.

Considering the complexity of regulations that presently exist and that have been evolving during the past decade, one must not overlook the basic concepts of our democratic and political system that are found in the laws and in their interpretation by the courts. This is exemplified by the early evolution of labor laws and rights founded on the concepts of freedom of speech, freedom of enterprise, and protection of individual rights and leading to the present-day regulations and controls. A summary of significant dates and events follows:

Pre-1842.   Until 1842 any union activity in any field of endeavor was treated as a conspiracy. Then, as a result of a Massachusetts court decision in the case of *Commonwealth v. Hunt,* union activity was declared to be lawful, per se. The court ruled that in order to be convicted under the conspiracy doctrine it must be shown that there was an unlawful activity. Essentially, therefore, by this court decision the previously held premise that there was identity between union activity and the conspiracy doctrine was dissolved.

1895. In a Supreme Court decision, *in re Debbs petition,* the constitutionality of the labor injunction was upheld. The United States government sought an injunction to prevent a series of strikes that were taking place against the railroad. The United States government was able to prevent labor dislocation caused by the strike; the Court upholding the use of the injunction.

1931—Davis-Bacon Act. This act established the minimum-wage rates for laborers and mechanics on all public work projects over $2,000 in value. There have been numerous and continued proposals to repeal or modify this act. In existence since 1931, it was utilized within the industry to protect the basic rights of workers when employed on public works. At the present time, however, it has been criticized for escalating the costs of projects rather than protecting the rights of workers. Application of the Davis-Bacon Act is formulated by the publication of minimum-wage rates that must be met on specific projects for the various trades that may be utilized on any work, for which federal funds are utilized.

1932—Anti-Injunction (Norris-LaGuardia) Act. This act was the forerunner of present-day labor legislation. It was known as the Anti-Injunction Act because its purpose as a matter of public policy was to sanction collective bargaining and the effective operations of labor unions. Although it did not give unions new rights, it gave them more freedom of action to function and operate. This act prevented the issuance by courts of injunctions against union activity except for *specific* cause; this gave the workers the ability and right to organize. This legislation can be considered as the forerunner of the growth of the present-day labor movement.

1933. This year was the passage of the first *Buy America Act.* This legislation, still on the books, has been amended numerous times and is often utilized on various projects to protect the rights of American industry (e.g., purchase of American-made steel).

1934—National Labor Relations or Wagner Act. The act actually had its birth when the previously passed National Industrial Recovery Act of 1933 was declared unconstitutional by the Supreme Court in 1935. This act was intended as an economic stabilizer to promote greater self-determination for workers and also to improve the economy. Essentially this act was focused upon manufacturing and *non*construction types of industry, but later it formed the basis of the national labor relations laws which are very specifically applicable to the construction industry. This act was the forerunner of the National Labor Management Act of 1947 (Taft-Hartley) and the 1959 Amendment (Landrum-Griffin Act).

1936—The Walsh-Healy Act.   This act is very similar to the coverage of the Davis-Bacon Act and gives authority to the Secretary of Labor to establish minimum wages for specified federal projects. It does not have as broad an application as the Davis-Bacon Act. It is still applied in the 1970s although its impact is similar to the Davis-Bacon requirements.

1938—Fair Labor Standards or Wage & Hour Act.   This act established minimum-wage schedules for all employers. It is periodically revised and updated by legislative action. This act defines rates as well as services of employees covered by the act. As of January 1, 1976, the minimum hourly rate was established by law as $2.30 per hour. Its coverage applies to all nonsupervisory employees, including those employed by federal and state governments. It continues to have exemptions which include such categories as:

- Certain retail establishments

- Outside sales personnel

- Retail sales not in interstate commerce

- Baby sitters

The exemption categories over the years of amendment have been greatly reduced to place a greater proportion of the working population under the protection of this act.

1947—The National Labor-Management Relations Act or the Taft-Hartley Act. This act was an amendment to the Wagner Act of 1935, but broadened the scope of labor law. At time of passage, it was considered a *pro*management law; however, the intent of Congress was to balance the legal rights of management and labor under the law. It is a very detailed definition of the duties of the National Labor Relations Board which was previously established under the Wagner Act. It establishes and defines unfair labor practices, the rights of employees as individuals and the rights of employers. The act also established a cooling-off period during national emergency strikes.

1959—The Labor-Management Reporting Disclosure (the Landrum-Griffin) Act. As the name of this act implies, the purpose of the act was to establish more detailed and specific disclosure requirements for both management and unions. Essentially it covered requirements for proper disclosure and methods of financing union management; it established procedures for the control of union funds and financial audit requirements; it dealt with protection of individual union member's rights.

1964—The Equal Employment Opportunity (EEO) Laws.   These civil rights laws outlawed discrimination in hiring, dismissal, or conditions of work in respect to race, color, or national origin. In this year (1964) the EEO Commission (EEOC) was established to carry out policies through the Department of Justice. This law was a precursor of the detailed and complex regulations applying to equal employment at the present time. The law has both been amended and enforced by executive order with the development of affirmative action and related programs. Present regulations encompass minority groups including women as a minority, discrimination because of age, and require employers to take *affirmative action* to provide employment opportunities to minority groups.

1975—Occupational Safety and Health Act or Williams Steiger Act.   This act established specific requirements for compliance for all employers working under the purview of federal legislation. The act essentially covers every construction contractor, as it applies to all employers with two or more employees who are involved in interstate commerce. Offices of compliance, fining systems, and compliance and inspection requirements have been established. The requirements for safety compliance for construction projects are defined under this act.

State Labor Legislation

Most states have prevailing wage laws on public construction projects. Most states also have their own versions of equal-opportunity legislation and right-to-work laws, but details vary between wide limits. Most states have wage-payment laws establishing paydays, frequency and method of payment of wages, and payment of discharge wages, etc. Similarly, most have state laws mandating time off with pay for workers to exercise their right to vote in general, special, and primary elections.

PUBLIC INTEREST—PUBLIC POLICY

The question of public policy and what is in the public interest will continue to dominate the construction process as it does any aspect of our economic system and twentieth-century society. The intertwining and web of activity pertaining to the political process with the resulting lobbying activities of various interests groups can be exemplified by the (1975–1976) history pertaining to the Common-Situs picketing bill. This bill has been proposed in Congress in various forms ever since the Supreme Court decision in the Denver Building Trade Council case in 1951.[3] In

---

[3]*Denver Building Trade Council v. United States*, 1951.

this case the Supreme Court held it illegal for a union which had a labor dispute with one employer to picket a site, the common site, where another employee group, namely, a nonunion operator, was working. It was held that the picketing would be an action against a nondisputing employer and therefore would constitute an illegal secondary boycott. Because of this decision limiting the possibility of picketing construction sites, the construction labor unions have been proposing and initiating legislation to overturn this decision since 1951. Over the years this proposed bill, more often than not, if reported out of committee, has only been acted upon by one branch of Congress. In 1976, the Ninety-fourth Congress, however, passed a Common-Situs bill. This bill during the debate in Congress was supported by the Administration; however, after its passage it was vetoed by President Ford. Although not treated jointly, the passage of the Common-Situs bill was closely connected with another bill entitled The Construction Industry Collective Bargaining Act of 1975. This legislation would have established a tripartite (labor-management-government) committee to promote labor and wage stability within the construction industry. The policy had been vigorously promoted by the then Secretary of Labor John T. Dunlop to establish wage stability within the industry. Nobody has or will question this need. The mechanism utilized by the Secretary—an authority in the labor and construction field—was to promote the two pieces of legislation simultaneously because on the surface, the situs bill served the interests of labor, and the collective bargaining acts served the interests of management. Because it was in the public interest to promote wage stability within this highly fragmented industry, the administration was supporting this legislation.

However, in early 1976 the incumbent President had already become involved in the beginning stages of the Presidential reelection campaign. Although an incumbent, President Ford was faced with a primary challenge by former Governor Ronald Reagan, a challenge from the conservative right wing of his party. Facing this primary challenge, the President vetoed the proposed common-situs legislation. It can be argued that the President made his decision on viable political grounds because of this challenge and his approval of this piece of legislation in early 1976 would have clearly damaged his standing within his own party while seeking the primary nomination. It can be argued further that his consent in 1975 to the then proposed legislation was made considering a broader political base. If the President had already been nominated at the time the legislation came to his desk for action, it can be questioned whether he would have exercised his veto power.

Examples of public interest and public policy legislation, which represent not only existing legislation and have a broad impact on the construction industry and as a consequence directly relating to the CM's potential involvement, can be found in two major areas, Equal Opportunity and Affirmative Action and Safety legislation.

Equal Opportunity and Affirmative Action

A decade after the passage of the Civil Rights Act in 1964, equal opportunity and affirmative action are inherent parts of the labor structure of the construction industry. It is beyond the purpose of this volume to do more than define the parameters and give the history of the more pertinent legislation or administrative orders that regulate the industry. It is these orders that essentially define the requirement, establish broad objectives and influence the CM's activity both as an employer and as a manager of others' activity. Following the passage of the Civil Rights Act, Executive Order of the President, No. 112465, was promulgated in 1965 and later amended by Executive Order No. 11375.

In the mid-1970s, as a result of legislation, not only federally-funded but most public-funded construction projects are by law required to afford *specific* opportunities to minority groups. These groups have been viewed in the traditional sense as *ethnic* groups, such as black, Puerto Rican (Spanish surnamed), and Oriental, but now these minorities also include female and handicapped groups.

Tracing the major milestones and legislative history, the first significant date is 1957, the year in which the U.S. Commission on Civil Rights was established. This commission was given the following powers:

- Investigate complaints that citizens are being deprived their right to vote by reason of their race, color, religion, or national origin, or by reason of fraudulent practices.

- Study and collect information concerning legal developments constituting a denial of equal protection of the laws under the Constitution.

- Appraise federal laws and policies with respect to equal protection of the law.

- Serve as a national clearinghouse for information in respect to denials of equal protection of the laws.

- Submit reports, findings and recommendations to the President and Congress.

Despite the powers of this Commission, it was only because of the passage of the federal legislation, the Civil Rights Act of 1964 (Title VII), in 1964 that the equal opportunity and affirmative-action programs of the 1970s were able to be initiated.

Title VII of the Act prohibits discrimination because of race, color, religion, sex or national origin, in all employment practices, including hiring, firing, promotion, compensation and other terms, privileges and conditions of employment. The U.S. Equal Employment Opportunity Commission (EEOC) was created to administer Title VII and to ensure equal treatment for all in employment.

Pertinent provisions of this act are as follows:

- All private employers of 15 or more persons
- All educational institutions, public and private*
- State and local governments*
- Public and private employment agencies
- Labor unions with 15 or more members
- Joint labor-management committees for apprenticeship and training

The implementation of the 1964 legislation was by Executive Order No. 11246 issued on September 24, 1965.

This order required affirmative-action programs by all federal contractors and subcontractors and requires that firms with contracts over $50,000 and 50 or more employees develop and implement written programs, which are monitored by an assigned federal compliance agency.

The main parts of the order were as follows:

Part I—Statement of Policy of Nondiscrimination in Government Employment.   The responsibility for administration was vested in the heads of executive departments, with supervision by the Civil Service Commission.

Part II—The Policy of Nondiscrimination to Be Implemented in the Employment of Government Contractors and Subcontractors.   The Secretary of Labor was given authority to adopt necessary rules to achieve purposes of policy. Such rules required:

- Affirmative action by the contractor
- Solicitation and advertisement to show nondiscrimination
- Notice to labor unions of commitments to the Executive Order
- Reporting and audit requirements to enable Secretary of Labor to ascertain compliance

*New coverage added by 1972 Amendments

• Penalties, such as contract cancellation for noncompliance

• Compliance by subcontractors of same regulations

• Application of policy to training program

The Secretary of Labor was given power to:

• Investigate employment practices

• Investigate employee or prospective employee complaints

• Conduct hearings for compliance, enforcement, or educational purposes

• Enforce the rules in addition to contract cancellation by recommending appropriate proceedings to be taken against the contractor by the Department of Justice or EEOC.

Part III—The Same Policies as Applicable to Federal Contracts were to Be Applied to Federal-Assisted Construction Contracts. The same provisions of enforcement, audit, and control requiring affirmative action to be required of applicant for federal aid.

In 1967 by Executive Order No. 11375, issued on October 13, the prior Executive Order (No. 11246) was amended to provide the same regulation to discrimination on account of sex, as well as race, color, and national origin.

A typical example of the scope *and* range of an affirmative-action program for equal employment opportunity as applicable to the construction industry and as implemented by one state is the program issued by the Treasury Department of the State of New Jersey, applicable to its state building programs.

Construction Safety

The remarkable piece of legislation known as the Williams-Steiger Occupational Safety & Health Act (PL 91-596) commonly known as OSHA became law on December 28, 1970, in response (1) to a dramatic increase in accidents and deaths that took place in the American work place in the preceding decade and (2) to the overriding moral concern that people have a right to a work-place environment conducive to their health and safety. While safety immediately brings to mind the more mechanical accident-avoidance system to mitigate the effects of explosions, fire, or other situations which may cause injury, the act also focused on controlling the health environment by reducing inherent stresses, be they chemical (gases) or physical (heat) to tolerable levels. In other words, industrial hygiene was joined with the traditional concept of safety under the act.

Safety has always implied the creation of a safe working environment, including proper machinery guards, training in safe work procedures, proper work habits, and restricting access to potentially dangerous work areas. Industrial hygiene concerns itself with monitoring the worker's environment, coupling it with knowledge of toxicology, to ensure that the worker will not suffer impairment of health on the job. Thus, the limitations placed on sprayed-on asbestos as a fireproofing for structural steel represent an effort to control the worker's exposure to the occupational disease of asbestosis, mesothelioma, and cancers of the gastrointestinal tract.

Because of the high-risk nature of the construction industry, safety has always been of paramount concern to all involved. There are numerous job-site slogans, such as "A Clean Job is a Safe Job" and "Safety First"— and all for good reason. As differentiated from work in a plant, work on a construction site involves continuous changes in job conditions thus creating more difficulty and resultant costs for maintaining necessary safety functions, such as barricades, secured ladders, etc. Their installation and erection for use may require daily effort (high-rise building) and therefore the margin for error increases. Successful and competent contractors know that a safe job is a profitable one and therefore in principle have no argument with the objective of safety legislation.

OSHA (PL 91-596) set up three new groups:

1. An Occupational Safety & Health Administration (OSHA) within the Labor Department to administer the act, with a new post for an Assistant Secretary of Labor to head up the Administration.

2. An independent Occupational Safety & Health Review Commission (similar to FTC, FPC, ICC, and other existing federal commissions), solely adjudicative in nature.

3. A National Institute for Occupational Safety & Health (NIOSH), a research arm within the Department of Health, Education & Welfare, to develop data, criteria and standards for OSHA.

Typical OSHA inspections are conducted by compliance officers and industrial hygienists, who may arrive unannounced at the project site. After presenting their credentials, these officials inspect the work place, talk with management and employee representatives, and then hold a conference with employers to discuss alleged violations. Following their inspection, the compliance officers return to their area office and discuss with the area director the conditions that they observed. Between them they decide if there were any violations, whether these were serious or not, and then whether citations or proposed penalties should be issued or not. Their decisions are mailed by certified letter to the employer who then has 15 days to agree that what he has received is correct. There is a mandatory requirement of the employer to post the citation for at least three days, even if the violation is abetted immediately. He then either pays the penalty or contests the citation or proposed penalties (also within the 15-day period) before the Occupational Safety & Health Review Commission—the three-person quasi-judicial body separate from the Labor Department, which has a cadre of judges around the country to hear contested cases and make rulings. Should the employer still be dissatisfied by the ruling of the review commission, his next step is to appeal his case to the U.S. district court of appeals.

One of the major complaints against OSHA, by both large and small employers, is the lack of assistance from the federal government in attempting to comply with the law. The Labor Department has taken the position that it cannot provide on-site consultation to any employer without issuing citations for violations found. A number of bills in Congress are attempting to rectify such deficiencies.

Unfortunately, the OSHA regulations promulgated under PL 91-596 have had the effect of statutory law and have created serious conflict, overlap and duplication with existing, recognized building codes. These affect the architect/engineer design professions, and therefore indirectly the CM process. Areas of concern in design include (1) the retroactive provisions of OSHA standards (existing building laws are not retroactive except in certain state conditions of unusual hazard), (2) the language of the OSHA provisions (the standards that have been promulgated by OSHA in the area of building-design law are consensus standards which, when promulgated by the sponsoring organizations, were understood to be voluntary and not mandatory, as they become when adopted by OSHA), (3) the interpretation problems of OSHA standards (building design standards promulgated by OSHA frequently contain problems of interpretation due to their language and conflicts with building laws in existence for many decades), (4) conflicts with existing building-design laws (many examples might be cited: guardrails of different sizes than commonly required; ladders 7 inches instead of the common 6 inches out from a wall; exit-sign letters 6 inches instead of the commonly accepted 5 inches; etc.), and (5) the appeals procedures under OSHA—existing building laws acknowledge the principle of separation of powers by rendering the appeals process in the hands of local or state appeals boards (judicial) separate from the promulgating agency (legislative) and the administering agencies (executive).

As difficult as the interpretive effects of the new OSHA regulations are with respect to the design professions (architect/engineers), they have a far more direct and severe impact on contractors. After all, the contractor is the employer of the bulk of construction labor and tradesmen, and therefore is subject directly to the financial and other penalties set for violations of the regulations. These penalties are severe and can run as high as $1,000 for each violation, but may also run up to $10,000 "for willful or repeated violations." The construction manager, nonetheless, as the agent of the owner, has the responsibility to oversee and monitor the effectiveness of the safety program and housekeeping of the contractor(s) to avoid possible delays in the scheduled project completion. (This does not relieve the contractors of their responsibility for safety of persons and property, and compliance with all rules, regulations, and orders applicable to the conduct of the work.)

OSHA compliance may also affect costs. Some architect/engineers claim that accountability to OSHA standards increases the material costs by 5 percent and inflates labor costs by as much as 10 percent. The rationality of such increased costs due to the OSHA regulations is strengthened by a consideration of the potential savings in costs to the construction industry of from $3 to $5 billion per year due to elimination of injuries due to these accidents. Even contractors with top safety records, having had exemplary safety programs in operation for years and accustomed to spending large sums for safety, can expect to face some additional cost if they are to comply fully with the detailed provisions and requirements of OSHA. Of paramount importance in this respect is the obligation of the construction manager to see to it that project plans are not completed, bid upon, and executed with violations of OSHA regulations designed into the construction.

Most contractors, and their insurance companies, are concerned about the safety of their employees, and make an honest attempt to ensure safe job conditions for these employees. Compounding the contractor's difficulties, however, is the relatively massive network of regulations included by reference; for example, on the national level, those of the American National Standards Institute (ANSI), The National Electrical Code, the National Electrical Safety Code, the National Fire Protection Association Codes, the codes of the American Conference of Industrial Hygienists, of the Nuclear Regulatory Commission, the Society of Automotive Engineers, the American Society for Testing and Materials, CFR, the National Bureau of Standards, the Federal Aviation Agency, the American Society of Mechanical Engineers, the Power Crane & Shovel Association's Standard, the U.S. Army Corps of Engineers, the Bureau of Reclamation, and the American Society of Agricultural Engineers; and on the state level, states have been encouraged to adopt regulations of their own, with the federal government paying a large part of the costs of organizing and enforcing these regulations. These state-based regulations must be at least as stringent as the federal, but the resulting confusion certainly will make interstate operation by contractors more difficult.

PL 91-596 also recognized the nonexistence of standards for all eventualities and for all times, by including a "general duty clause" which requires every employer to furnish a place of employment which is "free from recognized hazards that are causing or likely to cause death or serious physical harm to his employees." An employer found to be in violation of the general duty clause is liable for penalties and fines up to $10,000 or, in certain occasions, imprisonment up to six months.

OSHA is an all-encompassing piece of legislation not only detailing specific requirements and incorporating existing standards such as the construction, general industry, and marine standards already found in the Code of Federal Regulations[4] but also introducing specific standards on site inspections and enforcement powers to the industry.

The construction manager should therefore keep abreast of developments in respect to the Occupational Safety & Health Act. The list of references included at the end of this chapter should assist in this. The CM should protect the owner's interest by seeing that the contractor(s) train and educate workers in safety and health; that written safety policies, procedures, rules, and practices are established in order to document "good-faith" intent to meet purpose and objective of the law; that supervisory personnel are indoctrinated to enforce safety and health controls with respect to employee actions; that plans are made in advance for OSHA inspection, which may come about without prior warning; and that safety and health clauses to the effect that OSHA standards are included in all purchases, construction, service, and labor contracts.

The Role of the CM in Labor Relations

Since the CM is more closely affiliated in his professional capacity as agent of the owner with the interests of the latter and of the contractor(s) in keeping the project on schedule in the face of potential labor troubles, it would be helpful for him to have a basic understanding of the strategies employed by unions to organize and control the crafts in a given location. This most often involves the use of the *strike* and *picketing* to deny the contractor the use of both a work force and a materials supply. It further may use the union hiring halls as an effective weapon against the contractor, but the Taft-Hartley Act restricted this somewhat by requiring the

[4]General Industry Standards, 29 CFR 1910; Construction Standards, 29 CFR 1926; Marine Standards, 29 CFR 1915, 1916, 1917.

hiring halls to supply both union and nonunion workers if the hall is the employer's sole source of workers.

Unions may also control the entrance of skilled workers as apprentices, although this is largely eliminated, in theory at least, by the Equal Employment Opportunity Act. Finally, unions may seek to restrict the entrance of open-shop contractors in the area in question.

Against the threat of a strike or of picketing, the employer at one time had the options of many alternative courses of action, including laying off and blacklisting union members, lockouts (stopping work on a project), strikebreaking (hiring of workers to replace those on strike), or the obtaining of an injunction or court order against the union for illegal actions. Many of these are, in fact, now illegal under the statutes previously described.

The strategy of the CM in labor relations must therefore be restricted to one of firmness and fairness in dealing with both labor and management arguments, seeking to balance the potential harm caused to union members if strikes are carried out, against the potential savings in time and costs to the owner and contractor should strikes be avoided.

The construction manager will also find it beneficial to seek the advice and assistance of the international representative of the labor unions in the work force planning of large projects. The CM will also find it advisable to schedule a prejob meeting at the site with the Building Trades Council representatives (business agents) of all local unions to review project conditions, work force requirements, time schedules, and unusual materials or methods. The CM, of course, has a standing contract obligation to moderate the settlement of labor problems on the project as they arise, by calling meetings of the involved parties, and can well serve as a model of even-handed fairness in dealing with all parties concerned.

Jurisdictional Disputes

One of the most troublesome areas in which the CM may render such assistance is the adjudication of jurisdictional disputes involving conflict in the boundaries of work of several different trades. Jurisdictional strikes are banned by the Taft-Hartley Act, which also spells out [in sections 10(k) and 10(l)] the procedures by which injunctive relief may be obtained from the National Labor Relations Board. Because such processes are complex and time-consuming, at best, private settlement of such disputes is usually resorted to. The National Joint Board for the Settlement of Jurisdictional Disputes, and the National Appeals Board, are frequently resorted to for voluntary resolution of these disputes. Local joint boards (such as in New York City) are often available.

The CM should urge the contractor, in making subcontracts, to include the requirement that parties are to be bound by the published decisions of the National Joint Board.

An invaluable reference for the CM in this matter is the so-called "Green Book," (Ref. 5) or *Plan for Settling Jurisdictional Disputes Nationally and Locally*, by the National Joint Board, and *Agreements and Decisions Rendered Affecting the Building Industry* (Ref. 6).

Productivity

The avoidance of jurisdictional disputes (which originated in an era when a large multiplicity of craft unions existed) is of utmost importance to the construction industry, which is presently in a state of flux and change due to the introduction of new developments in design and construction techniques. This is especially true if the benefits to be derived by the construction industry in improved productivity of construction labor are to be achieved, evidenced by current trends toward massive construction unemployment and open-shop operation throughout the country.

Productivity is measured generally by the output per hour of input. By virtue of the character of the construction industry, with its single-product, site-based manufacturing process, concentrated on heavy labor-intensive utilization, the annual increase in productivity in this industry is less than 1 percent, and far short of what is considered normal (3 to 4 percent in the United States) in other more conventional industries. Construction productivity has simply not kept pace with the rapid escalation in construction wages in recent years. Improvement in productivity comes about through two channels: improved technology and equipment, an improved rate of effort by workers. The second does not infer a "speed-up" or exploitation of the labor force in any way.

Donald G. Malcolm, a management specialist, has recently cited[5] the importance of the first channel in improving productivity, as follows:

> Mitchell Fein[6] has estimated that nearly all of the increase in productivity accomplished in U.S. industry each year has been achieved via *technological and equipment changes*. Thus, productivity resulting from greater individual effort expenditure has not been a factor in American industry

[5]Malcolm, Donald G., "Management and the Engineer—Harnessing Technology in Pursuit of Better Management," 7th *R. P. Davis Lecture*, April 1974, West Virginia University.

[6]Fein, Mitchell, "Rational Approaches to Raising Productivity," *AIIE Monograph*, 1974. New coverage added by 1972 Amendments

productivity growth. Fein indicates this is mostly due to an impasse between management and labor over a proper approach to incentive payments for individual performance. Fein argues the present policies of labor and management which contain "no ceilings" to earnings actually lead to the pegging of production at rates which labor feels are safe from management attempts to set higher norms at which incentives become operational. Labor feels that, with management having the prerogative to determine the method of work, it would soon move in on performances that were too high above some safe level. Hence, a "no ceiling" provision really inhibits productivity above some small gain. Fein proposes ceilings above which management would buy a higher standard of performance from labor by paying one full year of the increase rate. Fein feels this buy-back arrangement would benefit both labor and management and put incentives on a meaningful basis.

Only 26% of U.S. workers are now on incentives. If incentives were employed for the balance, this could increase productivity some 63.8% in rate of production, or 24.6% after sharing the gains with the worker(s). Thus there is a great opportunity to improve productivity in basic labor when one considers that over half of production workers are not under incentive arrangements.

Collective Bargaining

It was previously indicated that a contractor may follow several paths in attempting collective bargaining with a union: (1) he may proceed as an individual and bargain on his own; (2) he may join with other contractors in a formal association to bargain with the union; (3) he may sign one of the national agreements covering his requirements; and (4) he may use a combination of the preceding methods. In any case, the unions constitute a formidable opponent in the collective bargaining process; they are powerful, well organized, and have a long background of successful bargaining experience. The following preparation for the negotiating process has therefore been recommended by a nationally known construction labor attorney, Vincent J. Apruzzese of Apruzzese & McDermott, Springfield, New Jersey (Ref. 2):

1. Gather the following items before negotiations with any craft begin:

   - The collective bargaining agreement.

   - A copy of every trust agreement or agreements covering that craft (i.e. welfare, pension, vacation, supplementary unemployment etc.). (Do any of these funds have reciprocal agreements so that if a tradesman goes from one area to another he gets credit for hours in another jurisdiction?)

- Directory of trustees and all people who sit on every one of these funds—including names, addresses and companies and their affiliations by contractor association or whether they are independents.

- A list of all contractors who have contracts on file with that particular fund (including delinquent contractors).

- Name of legal counsel for each fund, both labor and management as well as accountants, administrators, actuaries, insurance companies (if any) used for benefits, bank or banks with whom each fund does business.

- Copy of IRS submission form used by funds when they apply for tax exempt status as well as copy of tax exempt funding.

- Where there is an industry advancement fund, find out who collects the money, what fees, if any, are paid to whom, on what basis you should have an audit and what the money is being spent for.

- A certified copy of the audit of every fund this particular union has.

- Copy of plans for eligibility (criteria that make a worker eligible for hospitalization or pension or vacation, etc.).

- Copy of reporting form for every craft. (The form that is used by contractors to report hours worked and contributions to be made.)

- Copy of D1 and D2 forms that are filed with Federal government (if possible).

- Copy of EEO2 and EEO3 forms that are filed with Federal government (if possible).

- A copy of any actuarial reports for the pension fund.

- A directory of business agents or officers of the particular union or craft in the entire jurisdiction or state.

- Names of the associations that are in collective bargaining relationship with this particular union, association or associations.

- A list of those who are in charge of these particular associations, who the staff people are, the accountants and legal counsels.

2. Choose your negotiating committee carefully.

3. Pick one spokesman for your group.

4. Empower your spokesman to act.

5. Let your committee be guided by a clear-cut policy.

6. Keep a word-by-word record, or history, of all clauses involved, the wording they started out with, how they were interpreted, used, arbitrated, changed, added to or subtracted from.

7. Do your homework on the history of past disputes, arbitrations and agreements under a clause and on similar contracts with other associations in your area.

8. Have a copy of the current cost-of-living index.

9. Put clauses in writing—and sign them.

10. Agree on "housekeeping" rules before bargaining begins.

11. Negotiate on neutral ground.

12. Negotiate during the day.

13. Split the tab for costs.

14. Don't be brainwashed by the business agent.

15. "Feel out your opponent" during the opening round.

16. If a mediator is brought in, find out as much as possible about him.

17. When nothing else helps, call a conference between the two top members of your team and the top two from the other side.

18. All through negotiations, keep assessing how well you can withstand a strike.

19. When you finally conclude a contract, get it down on paper and sign it.

Construction labor contract bargaining continues to occupy an important segment of each year's calendar as the bulk of union labor settlements are for one year. Even in the midst of high unemployment in 1974 and 1975 negotiated labor agreements in several states produced increases in wages and benefits of well over 10 percent. The unemployed worker realizes such increases are illusory. The industry, as evidenced in 1976 in various regional union agreements, has begun to modify work rules in efforts to control and reduce costs. Such efforts are possibly a start of a new era in labor-management relations within the industry. It is evidence of a recognition that without major revisions in the present price structure of the construction industry the efforts to revitalize the construction marketplace and create jobs within the industry will be severely hampered.

REFERENCES

1. "Bargaining Unity Is Attainable," (editorial), *English News Record,* Oct. 10, 1974, p. 76.

2. *Cockshaw's Construction Labor News & Opinion,* March 1973, vol. 3, no. 3. Also, *Construction Capsules,* March 1973, vol. 3, no. 3.

3. C. R. Schrader, "Motivation of Construction Draftsmen." *J. Constr. Div. ASCE,* September 1972, p. 257–273.

4. J. J. O'Brien, and R. G. Zilly, *"Contractors Management Handbook,"* McGraw-Hill, New York, 1971.

5. National Joint Board for Settlement of Jurisdictional Disputes, *"Green Book"* or *Plans for Settling of Jurisdictional Disputes Nationally and Locally.*

6. National Joint Board, *Agreements and Decisions Rendered Affecting the Building Industry,* 1970, 152 pages.

7. P. S. Hopf, *Designer's Guide to OSHA,* McGraw-Hill, New York, 1975.

8. *Construction Safety Manual,* Construction Methods & Equipment, New York.

9. S. W. Malasky, *System Safety: Planning/Engineering/Management,* Hayden, Rochelle Park, N.J., 1974.

10. C. R. Anderson, *"OSHA" & Accident Control through Training,* Industrial Press, New York, 1975.

11. Manual EM 385-1-1 *"General Safety Requirements"* U.S. Army, Corps of Engineers.

12. OSHA Regulations and Guides:

   a. Occupational Safety & Health Act of 1970—Law and Explanation. AIA, 1735 New York Ave., N.W. Washington, D.C. 20006 ($2.00 to members, $3.00 to nonmembers). A booklet containing the basic enabling legislation and pertinent legislative history; helpful for understanding how OSHA was established.

   b. Record Keeping Requirements under the Williams-Steiger Occupational Safety & Health Act of 1970. Occupational Safety & Health Administration, U.S. Dept. of Labor, 1726 M Street, N.W., Washington, D.C. 20210, Attn: Publications (free). Procuring this booklet is mandatory since it contains the "notice" to be posted in each place of employment and forms to be used for record keeping and reporting injuries and illnesses.

   c. What Every Employer Needs to Know about OSHA Recordkeeping, Report 412 (rev.) U.S. Department of Labor, Bureau of Labor Statistics, Washington, D.C. 20210 (free). A booklet written in question-and-answer format for a number of commonly discussed OSHA record-keeping and reporting requirements.

   d. Occupational Safety & Health Standards Par 1910, *Federal Register,* Wed. Oct. 18, 1972, vol. 37, no. 202, part II. U.S. Government Printing Office, Washington, D.C. 20402 (20¢). This is the most recent cumulative printing of the General Industry Standards. Other standards (construction safety) are also available.

e. *Subscription Service for OSHA Standards.* U.S. Dept. of Labor, Government Printing Office, Washington, D.C. 20402 (vol. I—General Industry Standards $21; vol. III—Construction Standards $8).

f. *Compliance Operations Manual,* January 1972, Dept. of Labor, OSHA 2006, Superintendent of Documents, GPO, Washington, D.C. 20402 ($2). A manual of guidelines for OSHA inspectors and others responsible for administering and implementing the act.

g *Occupational Safety & Health Reporter.* Bureau of National Affairs, 1231 25th Street N.W., Washington, D.C. 20037 (approximately $180 per year).

h. *A Guide to the Procedures of the Occupational Safety & Health Review Commission.* (OSHARC Form 2, 11-1-72 [free]). Occupational Safety & Health Review Commission, 1825 K Street N.W., Washington, D.C. 20006. A guide to understanding procedures for contesting a citation.

i. U.S. Dept. of Labor, *Construction Safety & Health Regulations,* Part 1926, June 1974, OSHA no. 2207 ($1.30), U.S. Government Printing Office, Washington, D.C.

Index